D1536187

Lean Six Sigma
DeMYSTiFieD®

DeMYSTiFieD® Series

Accounting Demystified
Advanced Calculus Demystified
Advanced Physics Demystified
Advanced Statistics Demystified
Algebra Demystified
Alternative Energy Demystified
Anatomy Demystified
asp.net 2.0 Demystified
Astronomy Demystified
Audio Demystified
Biology Demystified
Biophysics Demystified
Biotechnology Demystified
Business Calculus Demystified
Business Math Demystified
Business Statistics Demystified
C++ Demystified
Calculus Demystified
Chemistry Demystified
Circuit Analysis Demystified
College Algebra Demystified
Corporate Finance Demystified
Data Structures Demystified
Databases Demystified
Differential Equations Demystified
Digital Electronics Demystified
Earth Science Demystified
Electricity Demystified
Electronics Demystified
Engineering Statistics Demystified
Environmental Science Demystified
Everyday Math Demystified
Fertility Demystified
Financial Planning Demystified
Forensics Demystified
French Demystified
Genetics Demystified
Geometry Demystified
German Demystified
Home Networking Demystified
Investing Demystified
Italian Demystified
Java Demystified
JavaScript Demystified
Lean Six Sigma Demystified

Linear Algebra Demystified
Logic Demystified
Macroeconomics Demystified
Management Accounting Demystified
Math Proofs Demystified
Math Word Problems Demystified
MATLAB® Demystified
Medical Billing and Coding Demystified
Medical Terminology Demystified
Meteorology Demystified
Microbiology Demystified
Microeconomics Demystified
Nanotechnology Demystified
Nurse Management Demystified
OOP Demystified
Options Demystified
Organic Chemistry Demystified
Personal Computing Demystified
Pharmacology Demystified
Physics Demystified
Physiology Demystified
Pre-Algebra Demystified
Precalculus Demystified
Probability Demystified
Project Management Demystified
Psychology Demystified
Quality Management Demystified
Quantum Mechanics Demystified
Real Estate Math Demystified
Relativity Demystified
Robotics Demystified
Sales Management Demystified
Signals and Systems Demystified
Six Sigma Demystified
Spanish Demystified
SQL Demystified
Statics and Dynamics Demystified
Statistics Demystified
Technical Analysis Demystified
Technical Math Demystified
Trigonometry Demystified
UML Demystified
Visual Basic 2005 Demystified
Visual C# 2005 Demystified
XML Demystified

Lean Six Sigma
DeMYSTiFieD®

Jay Arthur

Second Edition

New York   Chicago   San Francisco   Lisbon   London   Madrid   Mexico City
Milan   New Delhi   San Juan   Seoul   Singapore   Sydney   Toronto

The McGraw·Hill Companies

Cataloging-in-Publication Data is on file with the Library of Congress

McGraw-Hill books are available at special quantity discounts to use as premiums and sales promotions, or for use in corporate training programs. To contact a representative, please e-mail us at bulksales@mcgraw-hill.com.

Lean Six Sigma DeMYSTiFieD®, Second Edition

ISBN 978-0-07-174909-1
MHID 0-07-174909-8

Sponsoring Editor Judy Bass	**Copy Editor** Carol Loomis
Editorial Supervisor Stephen M. Smith	**Proofreader** Monoleena Misra
Production Supervisor Richard C. Ruzycka	**Cover Illustration** Lance Lekander
Acquisitions Coordinator Michael Mulcahy	**Art Director, Cover** Jeff Weeks
Project Manager Manisha Singh, Glyph International	**Composition** Glyph International

Contents

About the Author

Jay Arthur, The KnowWare® Man, works with companies that want to plug the leaks in their cash flow using Lean Six Sigma. After graduating with a B.S. in systems engineering, Jay spent 21 years in the telephone company developing software in every environment from mainframes to minicomputers to microcomputers. He became a quality improvement evangelist in 1990 using Florida Power and Light's Deming Prize–winning methodology.

Since leaving the telephone company in 1996, he's helped companies save millions of dollars using the essential tools of Lean Six Sigma. He knows what it takes to succeed at Lean Six Sigma, and he also knows the tar pits that trap companies and prevent them from leveraging the tools of Lean Six Sigma.

Using the essential tools of Lean Six Sigma (not all of the tools in the Black Belt lexicon), you can learn how to start reducing defects, delay, deviation, and lost profits in 5 days or fewer. Not in months or years, but *right now.* In industry after industry, business after business, team after team, Jay has found that a handful of tools will solve most problems with speed and quality. He offers 1-day Lean Six Sigma trainings and 3-day boot camps to cover these tools and develop your initial improvement projects. He also consults with companies both in person and remotely to accelerate their results. He creates custom dashboards and scorecards for companies to standardize the measurement of their core measures.

Haven't you waited long enough to start squeezing more profit out of your business while increasing employee satisfaction and customer delight? Start using the simple methods and tools of *Lean Six Sigma Demystified* and the power of the QI Macros to find and fix the root causes of delay, defects, and deviation that are devouring your profit margins.

Preface

In the April 2009 *Inc.* magazine, Jim Collins said, "There has been a big shift away from seeing the essence of entrepreneurship as the creation of a better mousetrap to viewing it as the development of a *better process*." Instead of building a better mousetrap, he says, "isn't it much more important to create a better process that will produce many mousetraps over time?"

Build a Better Process

The essence of Lean Six Sigma is to build a better, faster, cheaper, more profitable process. Lean Six Sigma will help you

- *Simplify.* Use Lean to *simplify* the work area.
- *Streamline.* Use spaghetti diagrams and value stream maps to *streamline* the work flow.
- *Optimize.* Use Six Sigma to *focus, improve, sustain,* and *honor* your progress toward eliminating all defects and deviation.

If good is the enemy of great, why not become a process entrepreneur? Why not become obsessed with tweaking existing processes to delight customers and employees?

There are two basic ways to get great profit margins: charge higher prices or reduce costs. Lean Six Sigma can help you design products that are worth a higher premium and reduce costs without sacrificing quality, productivity, or profitability. Any employee who doubts that his or her business is producing a profit is sadly misguided.

Whenever I say *Lean Six Sigma*, people's eyes automatically glaze over as visions of complex statistical formulas dance in their heads. If you feel this way, you're not alone. I have found that many people have a phobia of anything resembling math or technology. Sometimes both. Let me set your fears to rest.

First, Lean Six Sigma is a *mindset* for solving specific business problems. Lean Six Sigma offers some essential methods and tools that you can learn and apply without ever having to do a single calculation. Lean Six Sigma involves simple insights about how to look at your business that will transform how you simplify and streamline it for maximum productivity and profitability. In other words, once you learn how to look at your business through these filters of Lean Six Sigma perception, you'll never be stumped for ways to become better, faster, cheaper, more productive, and more profitable.

Second, you can apply the methods and tools of Lean without any technology other than Post-it notes and a flip chart. And aggressive applications of the *3-57 rule* can take you a long way toward the kinds of speed and quality that your customers demand.

Third, once you learn how to use the *4-50 rule* of Six Sigma, you'll always be able to laser-focus your improvement efforts for maximum benefit *with minimum effort*. This book will cover the bare-bones, essential methods and tools you need to know to start making breakthrough improvements. Lean Six Sigma is first a mindset for problem solving and then a set of methods and tools to support that mindset.

Now for the bad news: Most businesses, while profitable, are barely three sigma in performance. This means that every step in your process has a 1% to 3% to 6% error rate. Add these up across any business and you get a 6% to 12% to 18% error rate that devours 25% to 40% of your total expenses and slashes profit margins; that's up to $4 million out of a $10 million business. Using Lean Six Sigma you can cut these costs of poor quality to 5% or less while doubling productivity and profitability and tripling growth.

To get to four or five sigma levels of performance, you're going to want to learn how to use the essential tools of Lean Six Sigma. You'll want to learn how to use a few key statistical and graphical tools to improve your business, and more importantly, to sustain the improvement. A handful of tools will take you from three to five sigma in as little as 24 months. To go from five to six sigma will require more advanced tools discussed in the latter part of this book— Design for Lean Six Sigma.

QI Macros Lean Six Sigma Software

Here's the good news about Six Sigma: Yes, there is some complex statistical stuff, but it's easily handled by simple software that you can download *for free* for 90 days. "Oh no!" you think, "software, computers, technology. Arrggh!" Again, let me put your mind at rest. The QI Macros Lean Six Sigma SPC software is an add-in for Microsoft Excel that is so easy to use that most people say they can learn it in about 5 minutes. Forget all the fancy formulas. The QI Macros will do that for you. Just focus on what the graphs are telling you about how to improve your business. Since most business data are already kept in Excel or are easily exported to Excel, you can get started using the tools right away. Without software, Six Sigma becomes too laborious for even the smartest employee, so the QI Macros will facilitate the process.

Download your 90-day trial from www.qimacros.com/demystified.html.

There's even free monthly webinars on Lean Six Sigma and the QI Macros at www.qimacros.com/webinars/webinar-dates.html. You will also find links to download the data for the exercises throughout the book.

Focus on Results

While most Lean Six Sigma books and training spend a lot of time trying to turn readers into statisticians, I think it's a waste of time. What's more important is learning how to use the methods and tools to reduce defects, delay, deviation, rework, waste, and lost profits. If you want to learn all of the statistical formulas, buy *Juran's Quality Handbook* (McGraw-Hill). Everything you ever wanted to know about statistics and quality is between the covers of the handbook, but beware: Too much information can be confusing, and you won't know where to begin. This is one of the principles of Lean—too much inventory is a bad thing, even knowledge about Lean Six Sigma.

Belts

Unfortunately, Six Sigma has fallen into the trap of counting the number of belts trained as a measure of success. It doesn't matter how many Green or Black Belts you have in an organization, if you can't find and fix the causes of long lead times, errors, mistakes, scrap, waste, and lost profit. I don't care if you ever become a Green or Black Belt. I want you to become a *Money Belt:* Someone who can find ways to make dramatic improvements in speed and quality that translate into cost savings or more sales because of improved performance.

Sadly, every employee wants to be certified as a Green or Black Belt because it looks good on his or her resumé, but that person just wants to go to class and get a certificate at the end. Training is just the beginning. Improvement projects are where the rubber hits the road. Can you find and fix the causes of delay, defects, and deviation? Can you become an indispensable Money Belt?

Unfortunately, people lose 90% of what they've learned in less than 3 days if they don't apply it. What does that mean? It means that if you spend 5 days in a Green Belt class, you've forgotten most of what you learned on Monday by Thursday. And after a weekend, you've lost most of what you learned during the whole week. Fortunately, I've found some ways to change the learning process to integrate learning with project experience that will enable you to learn and apply Lean Six Sigma more quickly and effectively. I'll discuss those methods in the implementation part of this book.

One of the real problems I see with the extensive education requirements of most Six Sigma *belt* programs is the volume of information. The American Society for Quality put together a body of knowledge for a Black Belt that you can download from www.asq.org/certification/docs/sixsigma_bok.pdf. Most of this information is overkill. I recently saw a debate between H. James Harrington and Peter Pande (two Six Sigma gurus) at the Quality Expo in Detroit. The one thing they could agree on was that most Black Belts would never use even a fraction of what is taught in these classes. Maybe you've noticed this in other situations—a handful of tools do most of the work. Go into any hardware store and you'll see hundreds of tools, but at home most of your needs will be met by a hammer, pliers, a saw, and a screwdriver. The same is true of Lean Six Sigma; a handful of tools will solve 90% of the problems. So, in this book, I'll focus on the key methods and tools first, and the less frequently used tools second.

Culture and Implementation

The mindset, methods, and tools of Lean Six Sigma are simple and easy to learn. Getting your corporate culture to adopt these methods, tools, and mindsets is the challenge. If your employees are like most employees, they've experienced too many panaceas and programs of the month. It's hard to keep Lean Six Sigma from ending up in the junkyard of failed culture changes.

Most Lean Six Sigma books and programs dive into the top-down, endless training required to make Lean Six Sigma fly. I call this *wall-to-wall, floor-to-ceiling*

Lean Six Sigma. Unfortunately, research has shown that at least half the time this method fails. But there are better ways to implement Lean Six Sigma.

So I'm going to encourage you to aim straight for results. No one can argue with success. Start small and get successful immediately, and the change will pick up momentum. If you struggle a little bit at the start, and this is normal, you won't trigger what I call the corporate immune system, which will attempt to kill Lean Six Sigma before it even gets started. We'll look at these implementation strategies later in the book.

Structure

From a high level, the book will cover

1. *Lean* for reducing delay and non-value-added activities. Lean thinking can be applied to any business process, service or manufacturing, without the need for any exotic tools. The 3-57 rule and liberal application of Post-it notes will simplify and streamline any process.

2. *Essential Six Sigma* for reducing defects and deviation. The application of the 4-50 rule and a handful of tools will solve 90% of problems with mistakes, errors, and defects that cause excessive rework, waste, and lost profit.

3. *Transactional Six Sigma* for reducing errors in information systems.

4. *Implementation*—the human factor.

5. *Robust Six Sigma* for designing Six Sigma into products and services.

Each chapter will cover the what, why, and how of each improvement strategy:

- *Lean Six Sigma jargon.* While Lean Six Sigma borrows from its predecessors like Total Quality Management (TQM), it has its own jargon. I'll illuminate and define the jargon as we go and link it back to its origins wherever possible.

- *Methods for solving problems.*

- *Tools* for defining, measuring, analyzing, improving, and sustaining the problem and its solution.

- *Case studies* to show the methods and tools in action.

- A *quiz* to review your knowledge.

- *Exercises* to apply the knowledge you've learned.

Lean Six Sigma Is a Journey

Lean Six Sigma is a journey, not a destination. The good news is that you can start today; the bad news is that you're never finished. There will always be better, faster, and cheaper ways to perform any process. There will always be customers demanding that next level of perfection.

The good news is that if you're the first one in your industry to embrace Lean Six Sigma, you get a decided first-mover advantage. The bad news is that if you're a slow follower like the U.S. automotive industry, you'll always be playing catch-up. Japanese cars still have fewer defects per car than U.S. cars and are produced in less time.

Customers expect ever-higher levels of quality. If you can't deliver, they'll find someone who can. The typical lifespan of any business is 30 years. Will your company still be around on its 30th or even 100th birthday? Or will it suffer from the rigidity of *the way we've always done things here*? It's up to you. Lean Six Sigma can help, but you've got to be willing to look at what's not working and focus on your weaknesses, not your strengths. It's sometimes painful, but always rewarding. It's the breakfast of champions. Are you ready to take the first step?

Jay Arthur

How to Use This Book

In order to learn Lean Six Sigma, *you don't need any math skills*. Math skills won't hurt you, but their lack won't hinder you. It does help if numbers don't scare you or turn you off. Six Sigma is a numbers game.

What you will need is the ability to detect patterns and follow a process. So, if you can notice that trees budding out is a sign of spring (a pattern) and you know enough to put your pants on before you put on your shoes or to follow a recipe (a process), you can learn Lean Six Sigma. It also helps if you like solving problems, saving money, and making life better for customers and employees.

To learn and use the tools of Lean, you won't need anything more exotic than a pad of Post-it notes, a flip chart, a marking pen, and a few coworkers who want to eliminate the bottlenecks in their work area. Six Sigma, however, requires more tools. You can't do Six Sigma without data (i.e., numbers about what's wrong) and some software to draw the charts. With the 90-day free trial of the QI Macros that you can download from www.qimacros.com/demystified.html, you'll be able to draw all the charts and diagrams easily in Microsoft Excel. Don't have a copy of Excel? Buy an older version on eBay.com. The QI Macros run in every version from 2000 to 2010.

Too many Six Sigma books spend a lot of time trying to teach you the formulas for every chart and how to draw them by hand. Let's face it—you don't have the time or inclination to learn all of these formulas or to draw *any chart* by hand. You're not a statistician; you're a businessperson who needs to make things better, faster, and cheaper. You don't have to know electromechanics to turn on a lightbulb. Why would you need to know everything there is to know about statistics and charting, when the QI Macros will do all the math and draw the graph for you?

And another confession: Most Six Sigma books spend a lot of time trying to cover every possible method and tool. I can't do it. Joseph Juran, the godfather of quality, spoke of the vital few versus the trivial many. After two decades in quality improvement, I have found that a handful of tools will solve most of the quality problems haunting companies. In this book, you'll spend most of your time on the vital few. I've concentrated these methods and tools toward the front of the book; the trivial many are toward the back.

Over the last couple of years, I've had Black Belts tell me that the First Edition of *Lean Six Sigma Demystified* brought unmistakable clarity and direction to the crazy quilt of methods and tools they learned in training. And I've had complete novices tell me that it made them comfortable with learning Lean Six Sigma. It will for you too.

One of the principles of Lean is to change things *immediately*. Here's what I do when I'm reading a book: If something strikes me as applying to me or my business, I test-drive it *immediately*. I'd recommend you do the same. If the thought of using a pad of Post-its to create a spaghetti diagram of your work area seems like an exciting idea, *put the book down and just do it*. If one of the Pareto chart examples makes you wonder what a Pareto chart of your production or service defects would look like, *put the book down and just do it!* This is how adults learn, by doing. Reading the book won't make you an expert; *doing* the book will.

Expect to struggle a bit. It's new and unfamiliar. You may have to *unlearn* something to let the Lean Six Sigma knowledge sink in. Seek to improve, not to be perfect right out of the gate.

I've been at this for two decades, and I'm still learning something new at least once a month. You can't learn *everything* there is to know about Lean Six Sigma in a day, a week, or a month, but you can learn the vital few methods and tools quickly. Then you have to apply them immediately to a situation *and learn something*. What worked? What didn't? What could you do better the next time?

You'll notice that this book contains quizzes, exercises, and a final exam. The questions are all multiple choice. You might consider reading the chapter-ending quiz *before* you read the chapter, because it highlights what I think is really important in the chapter. And it will help you retain the information more easily. It will create a mental indexing system for your mind. The quizzes are open-book. The answers are listed in the back of the book.

If your business is a service, you won't need to read every chapter. You'll never use measurement systems analysis and rarely use hypothesis testing or Design for Lean Six Sigma. Get good at Lean and problem solving; then expand into the other tools.

There's a final exam at the end. Take this exam when you have finished the book and appropriate chapter quizzes. The goal is to refresh the learning from the whole book, giving your mind a chance to store it in long-term memory.

Have fun learning Lean Six Sigma, a set of skills you can use at home and at work in any job.

chapter 1

What Is Lean Six Sigma?

Lean Six Sigma, simply, is a set of methods and tools that help companies create a competitive advantage by becoming faster, better, and cheaper than their competition. Lean helps companies cut the time it takes to meet to customer demands. Six Sigma helps find and fix the mistakes, errors, and defects involved in every aspect of delivering what the customer wants. Together, they are a powerful toolkit for maximizing productivity, profitability, and growth. Just as any other toolkit, Lean Six Sigma can't do everything. Lean Six Sigma won't make you more innovative, but it can help you deliver high-quality innovations faster. And you don't have to know every tool in the toolkit to start making dramatic improvements. A handful of tools help companies of all sizes slash turnaround times and defects by leaps and bounds.

CHAPTER OBJECTIVES

In this chapter, you will

- Get an overview of Lean Six Sigma
- Debunk the manufacturing versus service question
- Identify the three big leaks in cash flow
- Discover your hidden fix-it factory
- Learn the universal improvement process

1

I have spent 21 years working in various parts of the Bell System—one of the best cash cows of the last century. In the 1990s I led improvement teams that, in a matter of months, saved $20 million in postage expense and $16 million in adjustment costs. Other teams reduced computer downtime by 74% in just 6 months. Since then, I've helped other companies find ways to save $25,000 to $25 million per project or more. And you can too, using the power of Lean Six Sigma.

Has your business grown into a cash cow? Are you comfortable with your current level of productivity and profitability? Or do you still have a nagging feeling that they could be much higher? Well they can be, and here's why.

When someone mentions the Aborigines of Australia or the Bushmen of Africa, it's easy to think, how primitive! But businesses around the world aren't much more advanced than these cultures. Businesses often rely on headmen or rainmakers (the shamans of business) to deliver the profits.

When we think about these primitive cultures, we often think of Stone Age tools like flint knives and arrows. When I go to conferences and see the improvement stories offered by attendees, they all use primitive tools, sometimes just words, sometimes a line graph or a bar chart.

I'd like you to consider that most businesses are still in the Stone Age when it comes to using data to manage and improve processes. Few use control charts or histograms to measure performance and improvement. Few use Pareto charts to identify opportunities for improvement. None use Excel's pivot tables to find million dollar improvement projects. Most are content with their primitive methods, but they are in danger from the businesses willing to embrace the methods and tools of Lean Six Sigma. Once a competitor gains a lead in speed, quality, or cost, it's hard to catch up. The fast eat the slow.

At the other end of the spectrum, statisticians are building starships of advanced charts and tools that no one is ready to use. They endlessly debate the merits of one control chart over another. And all this statistical mumbo jumbo frightens potential users of Lean Six Sigma and SPC. They're afraid someone will challenge whatever chart or statistic they use and they won't know how to defend their choice.

So they don't do anything at all.

Stone Age and Space Age Tools

Gut feel, trial and error, and common sense are primitive tools of the Kalahari or Outback, not the tools of operational excellence. Similarly, futuristic tools invented by statisticians hoping to leave their mark on the world are inhibiting the spread of Lean Six Sigma.

There's a handful of methods and tools that will solve over 90% of the common business problems. Isn't it time to make it easy for these primitive business tribes to embrace these tools?

What do I think are the essential tools? The ones I use most of the time are

- XmR control chart to show performance over time
- Pareto chart to identify improvement opportunities
- Histogram to analyze deviation from target
- Ishikawa (fish bone) diagram to show cause and effects
- Value stream map to identify delays between process steps

Go to *www.qimacros.com/demystified.html* to download the QI Macros Lean Six Sigma SPC software for Excel that makes drawing these charts effortless.

The QI Macros provide easy, affordable access to tools (download your 90-day trial from www.qimacros.com/demystified.html). Everything else is overkill for these primitive corporate tribes. Get them comfortable and feeling safe in the use of these tools and then we can begin to add in the others.

To create successful businesses and an unstoppable economy, we need to make it easy for every business to adopt the methods and tools of Lean Six Sigma, not just the ones with deep pockets and lots of time on their hands.

Virtually all companies grow from wobbly start-ups into cash cows using trial and error and common sense. Current methods of conducting the business developed in an ad hoc fashion, reacting to problems without much forethought. The bad news about this ad hoc, trial-and-error method of adaptation is that most companies stop improving when they reach 1%, 2%, or 3% error levels in marketing, sales, ordering, and billing.

At least once a week I hear from some poor employee who's been told to investigate Lean Six Sigma. They lament that it's their job to find and fix problems in the business. The business is already successful. Earnings are already up for the year. Why would they need Six Sigma to do what they already think they're doing well?

I call this the foolishness of the five senses. Just because your five senses let you detect problems and patterns at one level, you think that they'll work at even more subtle levels of detection. They won't. As patterns and problems become less frequent and more subtle, they become less and less detectable.

For your five senses to detect all of the varying levels of problems in your business you would need

- The awareness of a world champion poker player to detect all of the opposing player's "tells"
- Eagle eyes
- Bat radar
- Dolphin sonar
- Dog ears
- Shark smell
- Surgical feel
- Gourmet taste

Here's my point. Your normal sensory apparatus isn't up to the task of finding and fixing the more subtle problems that affect your job, department, or business. Like a doctor using an EKG or MRI, you need the right kind of tools to help you detect patterns you cannot detect with the naked eye.

Sure, every once in a while a problem will happen frequently enough with sufficient unpleasantness to trigger some action. You'll feel good about that, but you'll have missed the huge opportunities that lie just below the surface of your detection capabilities.

That's why you need control charts, Pareto charts, histograms, and control charts: to help you detect hidden patterns and problems.

Control charts are like an EKG; they show the pulse of your business processes *over time*.

Pareto charts are like an MRI; they help you slice the problem into clearly observable patterns.

Control charts and histograms have the added benefit of showing expected variation that allows you to predict your performance.

Just because you can't see, hear, feel, smell, or taste a problem doesn't mean that there isn't one. It just means that your sensory system isn't precise enough to detect the problem.

Did you know that there are dogs that can *smell* cancer? They don't need any fancy equipment because they've got a nose that's 10,000 to 100,000 times better than ours.

Humans, however, have the ability to create tools to extend the five senses. The tools of quality can give you an eagle's eyes and a dog's ears, if you let them.

The primitive methods and tools that took you to sustainable profitability will take you no further. To turn your cash cow into a golden goose, you will need the *common science* in Lean Six Sigma to make breakthrough improvements. Here's what you can accomplish with Lean Six Sigma.

1. *Double your speed without working any harder*. Most companies have extensive delays *built into* their processes. Eliminate the delays, and you can run circles around your competition.

2. *Double your quality* by reducing defects and deviation by 50% or more. Lean alone has been shown to reduce defects by 50%. Add Six Sigma and you've got a recipe for world-class performance.

3. *Cut costs and boost profits* because every dollar you used to spend fixing problems can now be refocused on growing the business or passed right through to the bottom line. Instead of wasting 25% to 40% of every dollar you spend fixing things that shouldn't be broken, most of that money can fall through to the bottom line boosting margins through the roof.

Top 10 Ways You Know You Need Lean Six Sigma

10. Customers still complain about your products and services.

9. Employees complain about the roadblocks to serving customers.

8. Blaming customers.

7. Blaming employees.

6. Customers return products for refunds.

5. Warranty costs climb.

4. Customers switch to your competitors.

3. Sales flatline or fall.

2. Margins are thin.

1. Growth stagnates or shrinks.

Find Your Fix-It Factory

Every company, service or manufacturing, has two "factories:"

1. *A "good" factory* that creates and delivers your product or service. In a printing company, this might be the pressroom. In a hospital, this would be the emergency room, surgical rooms, and nursing units. In an automotive manufacturer, this would be the assembly line.

2. *A hidden fix-it factory* that cleans up all the mistakes and delays that occur in the main factory. Some printing companies recycle 250,000 lb of paper and ink every quarter **because of** errors. Hospital emergency rooms all experience repeat visits from the same patient in the **same** day. Doctors misdiagnose illnesses 15% of the time according to one *BusinessWeek* article. Every automotive manufacturer experiences recalls over safety and other issues. If your company is a typical company (and virtually all non–Lean Six Sigma companies are), then the fix-it factory is costing you $25 to $40 of every $100 you spend.

Your Expenses	Potential Savings
$1 million	$250,000–$400,000
$10 million	$2.5–$4 million
$100 million	$25–$40 million
$1 billion	$250–$400 million

Still Struggling

Ever purchased a product only to get home and find out it doesn't work, and then have to take it back? You were part of the retailer's fix-it factory.

Ever make a mistake at work and have to work overtime to correct it? You were part of your company's fix-it factory.

Double Your Profits

If you're like most businesses, reducing defects, delays, and costs by 20% would more than double your profits.

Calculate your benefits

Your Business	Reduce Costs	Example
1. Gross revenue	$_____	$10 million
2. Annual expenses	$_____	$9 million
3. Current net profit (1 – 2)	$_____	$1 million
4. Reduce costs by 10% (2 × 10%)	$_____	$900,000
5. New net profit (3 + 4)	$_____	$1,900,000

Just think what saving a fraction of that waste could do for your productivity and profitability!

The urgencies of any business can consume all of your time. Fortunately, given the right gauges on your operation's dashboard, it's easy to diagnose where to focus your improvement efforts even while you are still working in your business.

The End of Common Sense

When I worked in a telephone company, managers used to say that process improvement is "just common sense," but what I've learned is that common sense will only get you to a 1% to 3% error rate. Hospitals get to a 1% error rate on things like infection rates and medication errors, but that's where they reach the edges of human perception, *the end of common sense.*

When you reach the end of what you can do with one problem-solving technology (e.g., common sense), you need to look to the next level: systematic problem solving and the tools of Lean Six Sigma.

It's Not Your Fault!

You know there are still unsolved problems in your business, but it's not your fault. In *The Structure of Scientific Revolutions,* Thomas Kuhn found that humans are natural problem solvers. He discovered a pattern to our ongoing ability to solve problems: an S-shaped curve. When confronted with a new type of problem, new methods are tried and the most successful one is rapidly adopted. But over time, the method's ability to solve that class of problems levels off.

At this point, almost everyone is fully vested in the old paradigm and a fringe group is exploring ways to "jump the curve" to the next paradigm of solution. The success of the old method often blinds people to the value of a new method (e.g., digital versus mainspring watch, cell phone versus wired phone). I find the same thing holds true when working with managers and business owners. The instinctive methods of solving problems level off at about 3% error. You aren't going to want to abandon the strategies that have taken you this far and made you successful, but that's where the next level of performance can be achieved.

If you want to move to higher levels of quality and profitability, you will want to jump the curve by learning to apply the enhanced methods and tools of Lean Six Sigma.

Innovation, Customer Intimacy, and Operational Effectiveness

In *The Discipline of Market Leaders* (Wiersma, 1995), the authors created a compelling argument that to be recognized in your industry, you will want to be known for innovation (e.g., Intel), customer intimacy (e.g., Nordstrom), or operational efficiency (e.g., Walmart). These form the legs of a triangle (Fig. 1-1). They recommend that to create a recognizable *brand*, you will want to *maximize one of these three and optimize the other two.*

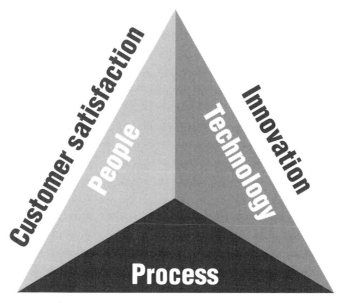

FIGURE 1-1 • Market leadership triangle.

Since Lean Six Sigma can clearly help you become more efficient operationally and Design for Lean Six Sigma can help you be more innovative, you're going to need the tools of Lean Six Sigma. It may not become your best-known feature, but it will be key to continued leadership and profitability.

Manufacturing versus Service

I can't tell you how many times I've heard people ask about Lean Six Sigma Isn't that just for manufacturing?

The short answer is No, Lean Six Sigma is good for *any* business process—IT, customer service, administrative, and so on. Why? Because every business suffers from the three profit demons: delay, defects, and deviation.

If you look closely at U.S. industry, more and more manufacturing jobs are moving offshore. Only one-third of the *Fortune* 100 make a physical product. Two-thirds thrive on services. In manufacturing companies, only 20 employees out of every 100 actually work on the assembly line; the rest work in support functions. More than half of the gross national product comes from information and service industries like Microsoft and McDonald's. But these industries are lagging behind manufacturing in the quest for quality.

That's why there's so much opportunity for the business that decides to use Lean Six Sigma to break through to new levels of productivity and profitability—because no one else is doing it.

When I first started working with improvement processes in the telephone company, many people said it wouldn't work because it only works for manufacturing, not services. Nothing could be further from the truth. This is just a convenient way for crafty employees to dodge learning these powerful improvement strategies.

What Is Manufacturing?

Manufacturing involves the development and production of tangible products. Other terms used to describe these are *plant floor, production, engineering,* and *product development*. Driven by the marketplace, most manufacturing functions have had to embrace improvement methodologies and statistical process control (SPC) just to survive. And, to lower overhead, most manufacturers have moved to Asia. The computer and laptop this book was written on were made in China, not the United States.

What Are Services?

Services include sales, finance, marketing, procurement, customer support, logistics, IT, and human resources (HR). A few of the other descriptions of these activities include transactional, commercial, nontechnical, support, and administration. These business functions have tried to hide from improvement methods and many have been successful, but the wisdom of Lean Six Sigma is shifting from blue-collar jobs to white-collar ones. There are huge opportunities for improvement in service industries and the service components of manufacturing.

The Death of Manufacturing

The PBS *Nightly Business Report* from Diane Eastabrook offered some startling statistics and insights.

The United States has lost roughly 3 million, or one out of every six, factory jobs in the past decade. About half of them disappeared over the last 3 years.

The Federal Reserve Bank of Chicago began a project to find out if manufacturing is dying in the United States. The Fed wants to know if factories shed jobs in recent years because of the recession or because of a structural change in the economy. It says one problem can be corrected with interest rate cuts, but the other problem can't.

The statistics aren't promising. At the end of World War II, one in every three Americans worked in a factory; today, one in eight does.

Economists fear that the apparel and textile industries face the greatest risk. But industries that require more skill, that involve R&D, capital, and high skill, are most likely to survive and prosper: instruments and controls, parts and transportation, and chemicals.

While job growth has been flat in manufacturing over the past 50 years, it has been rising steadily in the service industry.

Economists say that this could mean the United States is evolving into a service-based society, instead of a manufacturing one.

This means that we need to shift our attention from manufacturing quality to service quality. More and more, the United States is becoming the "brain" of the planet and other countries are the hands. I recently spoke to an executive who was retiring after 32 years from a manufacturing company. They had just completed offshoring their manufacturing business. Only a few dozen managers remained to oversee the business. And I've talked to small manufacturing shops that are doing well, meeting the needs of companies like Toyota and Honda who continue to manufacture in the United States.

Ninety-nine percent of manufacturing companies are small businesses. In these companies, only 20 percent of the employees are actually engaged in manufacturing; the other 80 percent work in backroom service functions like purchasing, payroll, accounts receivable, accounts payable, and so on. They will continue to need quality improvement and control to succeed in a global marketplace. But hardly a week goes by that some service company manager doesn't call to ask whether Six Sigma applies to service businesses. The answer is Of course! *Every business, regardless of size, suffers from three profit-eating problems that can be solved with Six Sigma methods and tools: delay, defects, and deviation.*

Although manufacturing businesses had to embrace quality to survive, *service businesses have yet to realize that they will need to embrace quality.* The same is true of information technology professionals (which is where I see our economy headed over the long term).

We're facing the end of manufacturing, and the explosion of services and information technologies (IT) will be the core of our economy. We can fight the change or lead it. It's up to us.

Manufacturing and Service

At an abstract level there's no real difference between a service process and a manufacturing one. They both encounter unnecessary delays, defects, deviation, and costs. One may produce purchase orders instead of computers, bills instead of brake liners, but they all take time, cost money, create defects, cause rework, and create waste.

In an IT department, we might focus on downtime or transaction delays. We might focus on manual rework of order errors or the costs of fixing billing errors. Even a great manufacturing company can suffer tremendously from IT problems.

In a hospital, we might focus on medication errors. We might focus on variation in admission, diagnosis, treatment, or discharge delays. We might focus on the costs of medical errors that result in longer hospital stays.

In a hospital, the clinical side is only one element. Defects and delays in issuing bills and insurance claims can cost millions of dollars. This is true in any company, from a family-owned restaurant to a *Fortune* 500 company. Incorrect bills, missing charges, incorrect purchase orders, overpayment, underpayment, and so on can cost a fortune. Fielding the phone calls and fixing the financial transactions can cost more than some invoices are worth.

Purchasing is another area for investigation. What does it cost to get quotes from three different vendors for the same product? What does it cost when you delay a purchase to squeeze a couple of extra pennies off the order? What does it cost when you order the wrong part and it stops your production line?

Call centers are another area for exploration. What does it cost to take a call from a customer? The average is around $9. Are your systems and literature set up to force your customer to call you for every little thing? Or are your systems set up to let customers serve themselves when they need it?

So, if you're a good manufacturing company, use Lean Six Sigma to simplify and streamline your *service* components. If you're a good service company, use Lean Six Sigma to make breakthrough improvements that will differentiate you from all of your competitors.

Small versus Large Businesses

Many small business owners don't think they can afford the time and effort to learn and apply Lean Six Sigma. Nothing could be farther from the truth. Are you a small business guerrilla? Are you willing to ignore the conventional, but incorrect, "wisdom" about how to implement Lean Six Sigma? Are you willing to start making immediate improvements in productivity and profitability using only a small fraction of your employees, time, and money? Or would you rather follow the *Fortune* 500 path to Lean Six Sigma and spend a lot of time and money, and then have to wait up to a year for bottom-line, profit-enhancing results?

Still Struggling

Small or large, service or manufacturing, your company follows some sort of procedure or process to deliver products and services. Those processes can be dramatically simplified, streamlined, and optimized using Lean Six Sigma.

Tricks of the Trade

After a meal at a local Chinese restaurant, my fortune cookie said "If you keep too busy learning the tricks of the trade, you may never learn the trade." When I think about how this applies to Lean Six Sigma, it seems obvious that far too much Lean Six Sigma training is dedicated to the tricks of the trade and not enough to the actual trade.

The Long Tail of Six Sigma Tools

To fill the long weeks of Six Sigma training, most trainers cover every tool in the toolbox as if they are equally important. One trainer admitted that their Black Belt training for health care included 3 days of design of experiments (which health care never needs).

A 2003 study by *Quality Digest* magazine confirmed what I've known for years: *a handful of tools and methods are delivering most of the benefit from Lean Six Sigma*. Focused application of these tools will carry you from average to excellent in as little as 24 months, *while delivering staggering improvements in productivity and profits*.

In any profession, there are a handful of tools that are used all the time and a slew that are used once in a very long while. This is true of Six Sigma. There is a "long tail" of tools (Fig. 1-2).

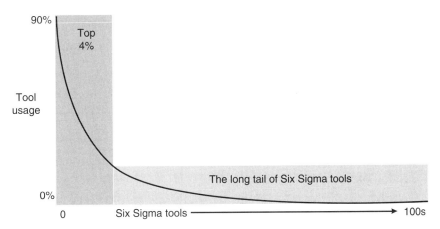

FIGURE 1-2 • The long tail of Lean Six Sigma tools.

Master the Top 4%

One of the principles of adult learning is that participants must use what they've learned in 72 hours or they lose 90% of what they've learned. Most Six Sigma training is done in a week-long format. This means that by Thursday, participants have forgotten Monday; by Friday they've forgotten Tuesday; and by Monday of the following week they've forgotten most of the previous week.

I know a lot of trainers are thinking "But we have case studies they do in class." I have found that unless people apply Six Sigma methods and tools to their own work environment, it just doesn't stick. Classroom case studies are nice, but they won't add money to the bottom line.

This should be unacceptable.

A handful of tools (the top 4%) like control charts, Pareto charts, and fish bone diagrams will solve 90% of common problems with defects. If there's a lot of variation (I call it *deviation* because *variation* sounds too nonthreatening), throw in a histogram or two.

Master these tools first. Then add the long tail of tools as needed. (Admit it; that's how your home toolkit grew: from a hammer, a screwdriver, and a pair of pliers into a toolbox of gadgets.)

Use company data, not case study data, to tailor the learning to the participants. Using the company's data, these tools can be learned and applied in a day, not a week.

Learn the Trade, Not the Tricks!

In school, we learned reading, writing, and arithmetic, but we didn't learn calculus right out of kindergarten. We shouldn't expect employees to skip grade school and start college, but that's what we've done with Six Sigma by covering the long tail of tools—tools they will rarely use.

Let's start teaching people how to solve common problems in their business. Let's make them successful with the top 4% of tools and then add the long tail as needed. I run into people I trained 15 years ago who are still using these tools in whatever job they've taken. When they pull their improvement stories out of their desk to show me, I feel good knowing that the 1-day training stuck in their skull, took root and flourished.

Let's teach them the trade, then the tricks. It's hard to make money in a training business that way, but it's a powerful way to deliver bottom-line savings and boost profits.

The Lean Six Sigma Toolkit

Lean Six Sigma is the best toolkit for helping you *think outside the business*. The tools are designed to help employees see the business more clearly than ever before.

Lean Six Sigma is a result-oriented, project-focused approach to quality, productivity, and profitability. These reductions translate into cost savings, profit growth, and competitive advantage. And the process is simple.

1. *Focus* on key problem areas by counting and categorizing your delays, defects, misses, mistakes, errors, and deviation.

2. *Improve* by eliminating delays, defects, and deviation.

3. *Sustain* the improvement by monitoring key measures and responding if they become unstable.

4. *Honor* your progress.

If we applied Lean Six Sigma to

- *Tax returns*, there would only be 340 defects in the 100 million returns filed each year.

- *Baggage handling*, airlines would only lose temporarily 10,000 bags a year instead of 30 million (1% of the 3 billion bags processed). Airlines permanently lose 200,000 bags a year. The bags go missing temporarily for 31 hours on average. It costs carriers $2.5 billion a year to correct the mishandled luggage. The biggest root cause is the mishandling during transfer from one flight to the next. (Is this why so many airlines have added a baggage fee, to pay for their mistakes?)

- *Teen pregnancy*, there would only be 34 pregnancies a year instead of 1 million.

- *Driving*, there would only be 3.4 accidents per million miles driven.

- *Hospital intake*, there would only be 3.4 deaths per million hospital admissions instead of 1 per 100 as reported by the National Academy Press (1999).

Why Lean Six Sigma?

Why now? *Fortune* 500 companies like GE are using these tools to save big bucks. In 1998, GE invested $450 million to achieve $2 billion in savings. Make no mistake about it, when Jack Welch, the CEO of GE, got behind Six Sigma, it took a big leap forward. Unfortunately, the *Fortune* 500 version of Lean Six

Sigma comes with an exorbitant price tag and lengthy implementation process that most companies can't afford. That's why I distilled the essence into *Lean Six Sigma Demystified*.

Plug the Leaks in Your Cash Flow

Have you been overlooking the biggest profit-making opportunity in your business? Are you so busy trying to recruit new customers by selling and marketing harder to a relatively stable market segment that you've failed to uncover the hidden profits in your business? Are you so busy trying to create innovative products that you've overlooked opportunities to increase your bottom line by creating innovative processes? I'm willing to bet that your business can be a lot more profitable than it is now. Lean Six Sigma gives you the methods and tools to plug the leaks in your cash flow.

I've worked with businesses ranging in size from a muffler shop to a Baby Bell. I've worked in hospitals and bulk-mail shops. I've helped businesses save millions that could be added to the bottom line in less than 6 months. The processes and tools are simple, but almost every business overlooks this opportunity to bank more cash and boost the bottom line.

In business, *it doesn't matter how much money you make; all that matters is how much you keep*. Lean Six Sigma can help you hang on to a lot more cash, and using this book, you can do it without spending a fortune.

Every Business Has Two Sources of Cash Flow

Cash is the lifeblood of your business. To boost profits, you will want to earn more or lose less. Every business has two sources of cash flow.

1. *External customers* give you money for your products and services.

2. *Internal processes* that leak cash like a rusty bucket. Why are internal processes a source of cash? Because when you plug the leaks in your cash flow you get to keep all that money! And it's a lot of money—25% to 40% of your expenses.

I'd like you to consider that businesses spend most of their time and money focused on trying to fill the cash bucket with new customers and virtually no time or money plugging the leaks caused by internal processes. Almost every company will spend a small fortune trying to gain a slight edge in sales and marketing that will allow them to get or keep a customer. The only problem is that this elusive edge is constantly in peril from competitors and the fickle perceptions of customers. You can never fully control this aspect of your cash flow.

You do, however, have complete control of the processes and technology inside the walls of your facility. Every process leaks cash. Even if you only make one mistake in every 100 transactions—orders, bills, purchase orders, payments, products, or services—that 1% error rate can add up to 6% to 12% or up to 18% across the facility or business.

The Juran Institute has found that the cumulative cost of delays, mistakes, rework, and scrap will add up to 25% to 40% of your total expenses (Fig. 1-3). Don't believe it's that much? Spend a day tracking every mistake, glitch, and customer complaint in your facility or department. Then calculate the cost of finding and fixing each one. How much time, energy, and money does that take away from doing your *real* business? What does it cost? If you weren't fixing the mistakes, what could you be doing instead? Multiply this by the number of days in the week, month, or year. Ouch!

These errors aren't your fault, and they're not the fault of your people. It's your systems and processes that are at fault; they let people make mistakes that could be prevented.

HINT *Blame your processes, not your people.*

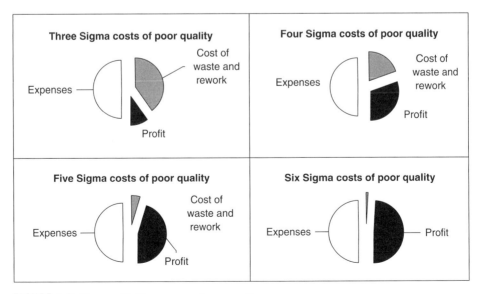

FIGURE 1-3 • Three to Six Sigma costs of poor quality.

Every Business Process Has Three Big Leaks

It doesn't matter if you're in manufacturing or services, health care or groceries, injection molding or consulting; every business is leaking cash. Most three sigma businesses try to blame these problems on their employees, but the problem isn't the people.

Big Leak 1—Delays. The delays between the steps in your process cost you time and money that dampen your productivity and profitability.

Big Leak 2—Defects. The defects, mistakes, and errors that have to be fixed or scrapped. Fixing mistakes that shouldn't have been made in the first place consumes time and money that could be better spent serving customers and boosting the bottom line.

HINT *Watch your process, not your people!*

Big Leak 3—Deviation. The small to large differences from piece to piece, day to day, month to month of your products and services.

HINT *Forget specification limits; focus on target values. Tiny deviations from your customer's target value cost time and money.*

Even a small reduction in delay, defects, and deviation in your mission-critical processes can give you a sustainable competitive advantage. Customers aren't stupid. They can tell a finely tuned supplier from a clumsy one. Once you have a head start, your competitors will always be playing catch up.

Every Business Has Two Improvement Focuses

Every business consists of (1) the core business activity and (2) the supporting operational processes.

1. *The core business.* In a hospital, its the diagnosis and treatment of patients that involves doctors, nurses, lab work, and so on. A printer focuses on getting an image on some kind of media. A manufacturer focuses on getting products manufactured to specifications. An hotelier focuses on a customer's stay. With all the data I've looked at, even caring for patients in a hospital, no business is better than 0.6% error (6,000 mistakes per million). The 1999 study, *To Err Is Human,* found about a 1% mortality rate

in all aspects of hospital care making it the eighth leading cause of death in the United States. An article in 2009 indicated that this hasn't improved. Your business may not involve life-or-death services or products, so your mistake rate is unlikely to be any better. Even if you are 99% good, fixing the 1% bad can cost a fortune.

2. *Operations.* Operations include every aspect other than the core business: marketing, sales, orders, purchasing, billing, payments, and so on. I've seen data that shows a 3% error rate on patient armbands, 17% order errors, and $100 million dollars in rejected insurance claims. These are all operational problems.

Most businesses spend too much time working on their strengths (making the core business process more effective and efficient) and too little time working on their weaknesses (marketing, sales, invoicing, billing, shipping, purchasing, and payments). Although the customer-affecting improvements to the core business are important, the profit-affecting ones on the operations side are critical to reducing costs and boosting profit. To make breakthrough improvements in speed and quality possible, you have to take some time out of your busy schedule and shift your focus.

Secret 1: Work on Your Department or Business, Not in It

I recently went into Sears to order a dishwasher and a TV. I got the part numbers and went to one of the checkouts in Appliances. They said that they could order the dishwasher, but not the TV. I'd have to go to the TV department to order the TV. The TV department wanted to charge me double to have it delivered on the same day as the dishwasher. Doesn't this sound stupid to you? Shouldn't I have been able to order and pay for them both at the same time?

Have you ever walked into someone else's business and almost immediately noticed some way that they could improve their operation to be better, faster, or cheaper? Why haven't they noticed what you find obvious?

The answer isn't obvious: they're busy working *in* their business, but they rarely ever step out and work *on* their business.

We all get trapped mentally inside of our companies and our orientations because we spend so much time working *in* them. It takes some mental gymnastics to learn how to step outside of the business, to get some distance from it, so that you can work *on* the business and its processes. If you want a reliable, dependable business that produces predictable, consistent results, you will need proven methods and tools to make it happen.

Still Struggling

While dealing with getting things done and day-to-day crisis management, It's hard to rise above chaos and study what's causing all of the firefighting and rework. To prevent this daily firefighting, you have to get outside of the business so that you can work on it.

Secret 2: Watch Your Process, Not Your People

Startup businesses succeed because smart people figure out how to turn a profit. Customer-serving processes grow up in an ad hoc fashion. Business owners come to rely on their people, not their processes, to deliver a consistent return on investment.

Because companies often start from humble beginnings and grow rapidly beyond their grassroots capabilities, it's easy to get hooked on the excitement of crisis management and firefighting. It becomes a way of life in most businesses. When daily heroics are required to avoid missing commitments and preventing mistakes, companies come to rely on heroes. The clinical side of health care is especially prone to this process. There's even a place dedicated to heroics: the emergency room.

This is another mistake. This often comes from your business orientation.

People-oriented companies focus their attention on *who* is doing the job. People-oriented businesses believe that quality and productivity are a function of their people, not their processes. They think "If I could only get the right person in this job, everything would be peachy." Unfortunately, great people come at a premium price, and when they leave, they take their wisdom and process with them.

Process-oriented businesses, on the other hand, rely on mistake-proof processes to ensure that care is delivered on time and error-free. Process-oriented companies focus on developing and following the right process. They depend on good processes to produce superior results. Here's some good news: with a great process, you can hire and train the lowest-skill-level people available. They have procedures for everything from cleaning restrooms (e.g., McDonald's) to maintaining Navy jet fighters. If the Air Force can teach 18-year-olds to maintain $30 million jets, you can develop processes that anyone can follow.

Hospitals all over the nation, for example, have to deal with codes when a patient's vital signs crash. Less than 5% of the patients can be revived. On the basis of research done in Australia, most hospitals are implementing rapid response teams (RRTs) to prevent codes. There are a few key vital signs that indicate a patient is heading for a code; nurses are being trained to identify these trends and call in an RRT. The hospitals that have implemented RRTs have cut their codes (and mortality rates) by half or more. Similarly, hospitals have identified a few key procedures and therapies that can prevent problems for heart attacks, heart failure, ventilator-acquired pneumonia, and infection. Some of these are as simple as an aspirin at arrival and discharge. The Institute for Healthcare Improvement (IHI) estimates that these therapies saved 122,346 lives over an 18-month period from 2004 to 2006. This is the power of good processes. They not only save time and money; they can save lives.

When you have good processes, there's less need for overtime and you can hire the lowest skill level necessary for the job. Labor costs are cheaper because you are not bidding for a small group of the best people; you can hire anyone and train them for the job.

Still Struggling

Too many business owners think that if they could only get better people, they could deliver a better product or service. The only way to deliver a better product or service consistently is to tune up the sluggish, error-prone processes that let people make mistakes.

Success Secret 3: Watch Your Customers, Not Your People

If you watch the employees in your business, they're usually busy. Watch customers work their way through your facility, and you'll most likely find that they're only being cared for about 5% of the total time. The rest of the time they're waiting for something to happen.

If you want to learn how to make your product or service more useful, don't bother watching your coworkers use or prepare the product or service. Watch your customers. What are they doing? Maybe they've invented an even better way to use it. Maybe you can easily see ways to make your product more beneficial, easier to use, less likely to fail, and so on.

Success Secret 4: Watch Your Product, Not Your People

Trying to make employees more efficient is usually a waste of time; a 50% improvement in employee efficiency will barely make a dent in your overall cycle time. Making your product or service more efficient is a great use of time. How long does it take to gather all the information to issue an invoice or bill? Why isn't it all up to date and available immediately? Why does a purchase order take so many approvals? Why does it sit in so many in baskets waiting for a signature? Face it, your product or service is lazy. It's sitting and waiting for someone to work on it over 90% of the time. Watch your product, not your people.

When you take these secrets to heart and start making improvements, you'll see a rapid improvement in the bottom line.

Still Struggling

Too many business owners try to make their employees work harder, but this only leads to more mistakes and rework. If, instead, you focus on making the product faster and the customer's experience faster, you will automatically delight customers, grow the business, and reduce mistakes and errors.

Secret 5: Implement a Proven Improvement System

Because of this people orientation, most managers and employees think they should be able to find and fix problems in their business using their instincts, and they can, up to a point where they hit a wall. This isn't their fault. Research into the science of change has found that one set of problem-solving methods (e.g., common sense and trial and error) will work for a certain class of problems, but not for another. Then you will want to discover a new set of methods and tools to solve the next class of problem. Consider antibiotics: they fight bacterial infections, but not viruses like the common cold. The same is true in business.

Since most processes are created by accident in an ad hoc way, problems with the processes are fixed using *common sense* and *trial and error* as the business grows. But at some point, the ability of these two methods to solve the more mysterious and complex problems begins to fall off. Eventually, they stop working all together. This early-success and later-failure syndrome affects all problem-solving methods.

Throughout time, people have routinely found ways to solve seemingly unsolvable problems. Edison invented the light bulb. The Wright brothers figured out how to fly. But to do this, they invariably had to invent new ways to solve problems that exceeded the grasp of the old methods.

Fortunately, the methods and tools for creating and improving your processes and systems have already been developed and proven in every industry. Lean Six Sigma has a seemingly bottomless pit of tools and techniques to make improvements, but I have found that a few key tools used in the right sequence are all you need to start making immediate breakthrough improvements in speed, quality, productivity, and profitability.

Every business has to improve the key aspects of performance every year just to keep even with the competition. The only question is whether you're going to rely on the declining effectiveness of common sense and trial and error or are you going to upgrade your ability to solve the stubborn, seemingly unsolvable problems in your business? If you aren't going to employ the proven strategies of Lean Six Sigma Simplified, what are you going to do instead?

Turn your business into an asset that produces predictable results. Don't let your business run you. Aren't you tired of dealing with the seemingly unrelated problems that occur every day in your business? Haven't you waited long enough to find a new and improved way to plug the leaks in your cash flow?

The Universal Improvement Method

Give a man a fish and you feed him for a day; teach a man to fish and you feed him for a lifetime.

—Asian proverb

Regardless of the acronym used for describing business process improvement— TQM, PDCA, DMAIC, DFSS, and so on—the overarching method is always the same. My acronym for this method is FISH—Focus, Improve, Sustain, and Honor. Few companies achieve success overnight. Companies that achieve lasting success do so by getting better *over time*. They've learned the secrets of knowing how to FISH.

Life and business involve a series of incremental, sustaining improvements punctuated by periodic, dramatic, and disruptive improvements.

These breakthrough improvements or process innovations can rarely be planned, but come about as a result of focused improvement. Invariably, this process of personal and professional evolution involves four key steps.

1. *Focus* on one key problem, skill, or area of your business life at a time.

2. *Improve* significantly in that area.

3. *Sustain* the improvement through repetition and practice until it becomes an unconscious habit. Measure and monitor to ensure that you sustain the new, higher level of performance.

4. *Honor* your progress through simple rewards. Then review what you've learned and refocus on another area for improvement.

This simple process is the secret of mastering every aspect of your business. You won't do it overnight, but you will over time!

Focus

One arrow does not bring down two birds.

—Turkish proverb

Who begins too much accomplishes little.

—German proverb

Most people are unclear about what they actually want from their business. This lack of clarity translates into confusion about what to do and when to do it.

The secret of success is to avoid trying to do everything and instead focus on the most important, highest-leverage things to improve. Far too many people "major in minor things" as Zig Ziglar would say.

The 4-50 Rule

Pareto's 80/20 rule states that 20% of what you do will produce over 80% of the results. In working with people and businesses, I have discovered a refinement of this rule that I call the 4/50 rule: 4% of what you do will create over 50% of your results. This is where you should spend your time. You don't have to improve everything in your business, just a few key things that really matter.

To narrow your focus from an enterprise perspective, you will want to use two key tools.

1. *Voice of the customer analysis* to understand the links between what customers want and what you do.

2. *Balanced scorecard* to establish key measures and targets for improvement in four key areas: financial, customer satisfaction, quality, and growth.

Still Struggling

You don't have to fix everything to make progress; you only have to fix a few key problems to make 50 percent improvements in speed, quality, and cost.

Improve

He who would learn to fly one day must first learn to stand and walk and run and climb and dance; one cannot fly into flying.
—Friedrich Nietzsche

Action will remove the doubt that theory cannot solve.
—Tehyi Hsieh

The only sustainable advantage may be the ability to learn faster than your competition.
—Peter Senge, author of *The Fifth Discipline*

Step 1. Get started, but start simply, inexpensively. Focus in one of the two broad areas: (1) eliminating delays using Lean or (2) reducing defects or deviation using Six Sigma.

Step 2. Identify one mission-critical problem to solve. It must be something you can affect directly. You can't, for example, fix loss of market share directly, but you can reduce the product defects and delivery delays that are causing customer defections.

Step 3. Make the invisible visible. If you want to reduce delay, defects, and deviation,

1. *Reduce delay*

   - Flowchart or value stream map your process.

   - Analyze where most of the delay occurs and eliminate it.

2. *Reduce defects*

   - Count your misses, mistakes, and errors and plot them on a control chart.

   - Categorize your misses and display them using a Pareto chart.

   - Analyze the root causes of these mistakes and how to prevent them using a fish bone diagram and countermeasures matrix.

3. *Reduce deviation*

All processes produce varying results. A hospital admission process may take a little more or a little less time. Housekeeping staff may take a little more or a little less time to clean a room. A manager may take a varying amount of time to make a decision. Getting bids for purchases will take varying amounts of time. Getting approvals for purchases takes a widely varying period of time.

A bottling factory may fill each bottle a little more or a little less. An injection-molding factory may make bottles that are a little bigger or a little smaller, or the neck or caps may be a little bigger or a little smaller. Variations in temperature, pressure, and time of day, shift workers, or whatever may cause these variations.

To reduce variation, you will want to

- Measure your performance in cycle time, length, width, weight, volume, or money

- Use histograms and control charts to understand the variation

- Analyze the root causes of variation and reduce it

Sustain

Perhaps the most difficult part of any change is sustaining the new way of thinking, being, doing, or acting. It's easy to fall back into the old rut.

Step 1. Make the invisible visible. Start using special graphs called *control charts* and histograms to monitor the behavior of your processes. To use them; you just have to know how to read them. Control charts will tell you when something abnormal happens to your process. There are rules built into the QI Macros software that will alert you to each potentially unstable condition so that you can take action.

Step 2. Monitor and sustain the improvement. In the beginning, be patient and open to learning about how these charts will reveal the inner mysteries of how your business works. As they alert you to changes, take action to restore the new, higher level of performance.

Go to *www.qimacros.com/demystified.html* to download the QI Macros Lean Six Sigma SPC software for Excel that makes drawing these charts effortless.

Honor

In every work, a reward added, makes the pleasure twice as great.

—Euripides

Most businesses are constantly improving, but sometimes we forget to take time to honor our progress. There will always be more to learn and more to do. If you only focus on what you don't yet know, what you haven't yet done, you'll eventually burn out. So it makes sense, periodically, to look back over the last week, month, and year.

- What worked? What have you learned?
- What have you accomplished?
- How have you grown?
- What's next?

Life is often lived in fits and starts, moving ahead and falling back, but in general, with the right set of starting beliefs and values, the quality of life improves. Where were you 5 or 10 years ago? What has improved? What have you let go of that you no longer need? Without rewards, anyone will eventually give up their quest for improvement. And since the outside world is busy and sometimes thoughtless, you'll usually need to figure out how to reward and recognize the improvement teams and process.

Develop a system of rewards and recognition. Once your mind connects pleasure with improvement, you'll be surprised by the quality and quantity of ideas you'll find to achieve and experience more pleasure in life.

Once you've identified, improved, and sustained a new level of performance in one area of your business, something else will become more vital to your personal and professional evolution.

How will you know what to focus on next? Return to your measurements. What's next?

- Delay?
- Defects?
- Deviation?

Lean Six Sigma Demystified

Lean Six Sigma will focus your improvement efforts to drive dramatic improvements in speed, quality, and profitability. The methods and tools of Lean will help drive dramatic improvements in speed and productivity. The methods and tools of Six Sigma will help drive radical reductions in defects and deviation that will improve productivity and profitability. Regardless of the acronyms used or the number of steps, Lean Six Sigma follows a universal improvement process: Focus, Improve, Sustain, and Honor (FISH). There are a handful of tools that you will need for each of these steps to move from three to five sigma. To rise to Six Sigma, you will need some more robust tools, but you won't be ready for their rigor until you've embraced and mastered the basic tools.

There are some additional methods and tools that you can use to design innovative products and processes from scratch. These are called *Design for Lean Six Sigma* (*DfLSS* or *DFSS*).

Although most books start you on the path toward total domination of the corporate culture and business processes, I'd like you to start by piloting some focused improvement projects involving Lean and Six Sigma. As you begin to master the improvement processes, then, and only then, would I like you to consider expanding the scope to include more people and projects to the point that Lean Six Sigma becomes a way of doing business, not just a program of the month or the pet project of a CEO.

The methods and tools are the easy part; *changing culture is hard.* When you start by creating successful projects and let the corporate grapevine sell Lean Six Sigma for you, it will be easy to change the culture, because the culture will adopt and adapt Lean Six Sigma on its own. When you start by trying to force

Lean Six Sigma down everybody's throat with endless training, changing the culture can get hard, if not impossible.

Lean Six Sigma will not fix everything about your business. It won't fix suppliers. It won't fix customers. It won't fix morale. It won't fix boring products. It won't fix poor leadership. But it is a management system that can improve morale, leadership, and products indirectly. Learning Lean Six Sigma will help you choose and improve your suppliers. It will help you understand and better serve your existing and undiscovered customers.

Take some time to test drive each of the improvement methods and tools. Apply them to your business and your processes. Use the QI Macros tools to Focus, Improve, Sustain, and Honor your progress. You'll be surprised how easy it can be to find and make dramatic improvements. Best of all, these methods and tools have stood the test of time. You'll be able to use them in any business and any job you ever have. And you will be recognized because you're the employee who can find the hidden gold mine in the business.

The May 3, 2004, *Business Week* reported Xerox's savings from using Lean Six Sigma.

- Reducing the loss of toner during production saved $240,000.
- Improving software for translating user manuals into foreign languages saved $1 million.
- Xerox helped Bank of America save $800,000 by consolidating document centers.

In 1999, the story was a little different. Customers started receiving incorrect bills that had incorrect prices and extra equipment they'd never ordered. As customers started to defect, Xerox turned to GE Capital to handle its billing. Using Lean Six Sigma, GE showed Xerox how to find and fix problems as well as eliminate steps from their processes to save time and boost profits.

In 2003, Xerox boasts a $6 million return on their investment with more expected for 2004. And, while sales are down 20% from 1998 peaks, profits are up. 2003 net income was $366 million, up 50% from the previous year.

Starwood Hotels introduced Six Sigma in 2001 to great employee skepticism. In 2007, Six Sigma delivered over $100 million in profit to the bottom line and a net margin of 15%, six points higher than the 9% industry average. Starwood uses green belt (GB) and black belt (BB) change agents and SWAT teams to help hotels meet their objectives. Starwood rolls out new projects to its hotels every 2 weeks. One safety-related project cut accident rates from 6 per 100,000 work hours to only 1. In 2010, *iSixSigma* magazine rated Starwood Hotels as the number one place to work for Six Sigma professionals.

Bank of America documented over $2 billion in savings from Lean Six Sigma.

Apogee Enterprises Inc., a glass company, saves $5 to $12 million a year using Lean Six Sigma.

Boeing's C-17 tail cone team improved safety and reduced time per aircraft by 66 hours saving over $900,000.

The Naval Surface Warfare Center in Indian Head, Maryland, used Six Sigma to save over $4 million in 2005 and $3.6 million in 2006.

Chevron used Six Sigma to save $200 million worldwide in 2007. The average Six Sigma project saves Chevron a million dollars.

What could you accomplish with Lean Six Sigma?

QUIZ

1. **Lean Six Sigma can help you solve problems with**
   A. delays and waiting.
   B. overproduction.
   C. movement.
   D. defects, mistakes, and errors.
   E. deviation and variation.
   F. inventory.
   G. all of the above

2. **Companies have two "factories"**
   A. The _____ factory.
   B. The _____ factory.

3. **Lean Six Sigma can be used in**
   A. administration.
   B. health care.
   C. information systems.
   D. manufacturing.
   E. services.
   F. food and drug.
   G. small business.
   H. all of the above

4. **The universal improvement steps are**
   A. Focus, Improve, Sustain, Honor.
   B. Plan, Do, Check, Act.
   C. Define, Measure, Analyze, Improve, Control.
   D. any of the above.

5. **Every business has two sources of cash flow.**
   A. External _____
   B. Internal _____

6. **The goal of Lean Six Sigma is to**
   A. reduce costs.
   B. boost profits.
   C. increase productivity.
   D. grow market share.
   E. all of the above

7. **When it comes to data-driven improvement, most businesses are still in the**
   A. Ice Age.
   B. Stone Age.
   C. Space Age.

8. **Use control charts to show**
   A. approximation.
   B. undulation.
   C. variation.

9. **Lean Six Sigma will help any business**
   A. double its speed.
   B. double quality.
   C. double profits.
   D. all of the above

10. **To embrace the Lean Six Sigma mindset, turn your attention from**
    A. people to process.
    B. people to product.
    C. employees to customers.
    D. all of the above

chapter **2**

Lean Demystified

Ask what the greatest point of need for improvement is and start from there.
—Taiichi Ohno

Perhaps the easiest way to get started in Lean Six Sigma is with the methods and tools of Lean. You don't have to know any math or statistics. You won't need any exotic computer software. If you've ever cooked a meal at home or eaten at Subway, you already understand the essence of Lean. You can figure out how to "lean" a process or work area with a pad of Post-it notes, a flipchart, and some focused attention. First, let's take a look at one familiar example of the power of Lean.

CHAPTER OBJECTIVES

In this chapter, you will

- Discover the power Laws of Speed
- Learn about the Toyota production system
- Learn the lean process
- Discover the seven speed bumps of Lean
- Learn how to map a value stream
- Learn how to use spaghetti diagramming

33

Seems like everywhere you look you see Dell computers or laptops—on airplanes, in retail stores, or in business offices. Most users don't think about how Dell became so successful, but the essence of Michael Dell's strategy is Lean. Rather than build big batches of standard PCs to be sold in retail stores as HP or Compaq do, Dell aims at customers who order their customized computer online or on the phone. Then, using *one-piece flow*, Dell builds a custom, made-to-order PC for that customer. This gives Dell a "first-mover advantage" in the marketplace. Since the First Edition of this book, competitors have stepped up their capabilities, but it's still useful to analyze Dell's strategy.

> *Mass production . . . naturally generates an abundance of waste.*
>
> —Taiichi Ohno

Traditional batch production manufacturing pushes products to consumers by purchasing parts and assembling products based on forecasted demand. This results in large inventories of finished goods, in this case, computers. Dell, on the other hand, assembles a customer's computer *after* the order is placed. This means that they can maintain little or no inventory. Dell turns over its inventory 80 times a year compared to 10 to 20 times for its competitors.

Dell's suppliers also build to order. Dell orders parts, suppliers deliver them, and Dell immediately places them in production. Shippers pick up the finished computers within hours of their completion and deliver them directly to the customer. This strategy minimizes inventory, reduces lead time, and accelerates the introduction of new technology. Since Dell doesn't buy any more chips, memory, or disk drives than they need for a few days of production, they can immediately incorporate faster chips or better drives into their products. Moore's law says that computers double in power every 18 months and halve in cost, so you don't want to have too much unsold inventory when technology advances. With Dell, you don't have to wait 3 to 6 months for the latest technology from a batch manufacturer; Dell can deliver it almost immediately.

With less inventory and lower costs driven by this Lean approach to computer manufacturing, Dell can deliver better profit margins than most players in their industry and pass the savings along to customers.

Dell had 3 to 14 days of inventory from 1996 to 2008. Apple Computer, which once had over 50 days of inventory, has reduced their inventory to 10 days.

> *Inventory is fundamentally evil. It declines in value by 1% to 2% a week in normal times, faster in tough times.*
>
> — Tim Cook, chief operations guru for Apple Computers

How Stale is Your Inventory? Apple's *days of total inventory* has been as low as 0.4 day and now stands at 10. Dell computer has been as low as 3, now at 7. HP, however, is at 33 days.

What Kind of Inventory? There are three main kinds of tangible inventory:

1. Raw materials
2. Work in process
3. Finished goods

If you warehouse or store any of these types of inventory, then there are costs associated with managing, moving, rearranging, and tracking them. It takes space, time, and people. None of it adds value to the product or service. It just eats profit.

I've worked with companies that have hundreds of millions of dollars of raw and finished goods inventory, far more than they need to meet the needs of their customers.

Intangible Inventory? The same kind of thinking can be applied to back office functions. Have you invoiced what you've produced? What is your inventory of unbilled goods or services? What is your inventory of accounts receivable? How stale are they? What about purchasing and payments?

I've worked with health care companies that have hundreds of millions of dollars in insurance claims being negotiated with insurance companies. These claims can be over 300 days old.

The carrying cost of tangible and intangible inventory can devour the profits of a company. *Inventory is fundamentally evil!* Set a big hairy audacious goal for days of total inventory and aggressively improve the process to achieve your goals.

"You kind of want to manage [inventory] like you are in the dairy business," Cook says. "If it gets past its fresh date, you have a problem."

Dell and Apple use the power of Lean to cut costs and boost profits. You can too.

Mind the Gap

If you've ever been to London and ridden on the famous Underground, you've probably seen signs that say Mind the Gap (Fig. 2-1). While the signs are designed to keep travelers from wrenching an ankle, I believe the idea also applies to Lean Thinking.

FIGURE 2-1 · Mind the Gap.

Here's what I mean: Hold up your hand and spread your fingers wide apart. What do you see? Most likely, you're first drawn to look at your fingers, not the gaps in between. This is how most people look at process improvement, by looking at the people working, not at the *gaps between people*.

When you take your eye off the people working and put your eye on the product or service going through the process, you quickly discover there are huge gaps between one step in the process and the next. You'll discover work products piling up between steps which only creates more delay—a bigger gap.

Your lead time problems are in the gaps, not the fingers. You can make the people work faster, but you'll find that this often makes you slower, not faster, because more work piles up between steps widening the gap, not narrowing it.

Still Struggling

Become your product or service. Follow a patient around an emergency room; follow a customer around a restaurant from the time they arrive until they leave. Follow a car repair around an automotive dealership. You'll be stunned by how much time the customer or product spends waiting for the next step in their journey. Mind the Gap—Eliminate the delays.

Value Stream Mapping

The other sign you often see in the London Underground is a tube map (Fig. 2-2). Although much more interconnected than a typical value stream map, you'll notice that the stations are quite small and the lines between them quite long.

This is true of most processes; the time between stations is much greater than the time spent in the station. As this map suggests, 95% of the time is *between* stations, not in them. If you want to reduce the time it takes to serve a customer, you have to mind the gaps.

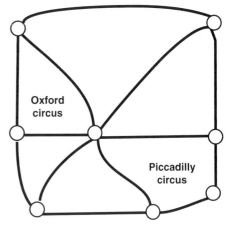

FIGURE 2-2 • Tube map.

You Already Understand Lean

To think that mass produced items are cheaper per unit is understandable—but wrong.

—Taiichi Ohno

I'd like to suggest that you already have been exposed to and understand the concepts behind Lean. Kitchens, for example, have long been designed as "Lean cells" for food preparation. The refrigerator, sink, and stove should form a V-shaped work cell. The tighter the V, the less movement is required of the cook. My kitchen looks like the diagram in Fig. 2-3: Food comes out of the refrigerator, gets washed in the sink, cut up on the counter, cooked on the stove, and delivered to the table. Unlike mass production where different silos would be put in charge of frozen and refrigerated food, washing, cutting, and cooking, there's usually only one cook that handles each of these steps. Each meal is a small *batch* or *lot*. You never cook in batches big enough for the entire week. A trip to the supermarket each week replenishes the limited inventories of raw materials required. Ever noticed how most kitchens are right off the garage? That way each week's groceries come straight out of the garage right

FIGURE 2-3 • Lean kitchen layout.

into the kitchen with a minimum of movement. Your kitchen is the essence of a Lean production cell.

How can you set up your workplace to use the insights gleaned from your kitchen?

The Fast Food Experience

If you walk into a Subway, your sandwich is created right in front of you in a Lean production cell and it's ready when you pay. The right-sized bread ovens are directly behind the ordering station. The first worker cuts the bread and puts on the cheese and meat, the second worker adds the vegetables and sauces, and the final worker rings up the meal. In contrast, have you ever been to an upscale, but poorly designed fast-food restaurant where you place your order, pay, and then stand in a crowd of other people waiting for their sandwich? A crowd forms right in front of the soda machine or the door to the bathroom creating bottlenecks. How can you set up your workplace to use the insights gleaned from Subway?

Lean Administration

In *The Organized Executive*, Stephanie Winston, suggests that the best way to handle anything that crosses your desk is to TRAF it: Toss it, Refer it, Act on it, or File it. This is the essence of Lean production and one-touch, one-piece flow for paperwork.

To understand how Lean can affect your business, you'll want to understand and use what I call the power laws of speed.

The Power Laws of Speed

It's not the big that eat the small, it's the fast that eat the slow.
—Jason Jennings and Laurence Haughton

If you can't quickly take throughput times down by half in product development, 75 percent in order processing, and 90 percent in physical production, you are doing something wrong.
—James P. Womack and Daniel T. Jones

In a global economy, everyone is competing against the clock. Customers today demand speed and customized solutions. So, speed is critical to your success.

In *Competing Against Time* (Free Press, 1990), authors Stauk and Hout present compelling evidence for the power laws of speed. I don't know about you, but I grew up on the wisdom of Henry Ford: *mass production and the economies of scale*. But while I was learning about Ford in the '50s, Toyota was developing and mastering what is now known as the Toyota Production System (TPS) and the *economies of speed*. Stauk and Hout distilled the essence of Lean down to a few key rules and I've tweaked them a little.

The 3-57 Rule. The amount of time it takes to deliver a product or service is far greater than the time spent adding value to the product or service. Most products and services are worked on for only 3 minutes out of every 60 minutes of total elapsed time. Those 3 minutes are considered value added, the rest (57 minutes), non-value added. This is why it makes no sense whatsoever to try to make employees work faster; *cutting employee time by half will only save 1.5 minutes per hour*. Why does it take so long? Delay. What's happening during the other 57 minutes? The product or service is sitting idle waiting for the next step in its journey. This 57-minute gap is unnecessarily wasteful.

Examples. A manufacturer of heavy vehicles only spends 2 days assembling a vehicle, but 45 days preparing the order. A claims processing group only spends 7 hours processing a claim, but it takes 140 days for each claim. A human resources group takes 82 days to fill an entry level job vacancy, but there's only 8 *hours* of actual work.

The 15-2-20 Rule. Every time you reduce the time required to provide a product or service by 15 minutes per hour, you double productivity and cut costs by 20%. It has been my experience that most of the time you can reduce cycle and lead times by 30 to 50 minutes per hour, so productivity increases, costs fall, and profit margins improves by 20% to 60% or more.

The 3 × 2 Rule. When you slash your cycle time for your mission-critical processes, you enjoy growth rates three times the industry average and twice the profit margins. This is a good thing, because most companies find that they only need about two-thirds of the people to run the business after applying Lean, but if you're going to grow three times faster than the industry, you're going to need all of those displaced employees to meet the demand.

HINT   *The fear of job losses is the single biggest barrier to implementing Lean.*

Economies of Speed

There is always a best way of doing anything.

—Emerson

One of the best ways to improve your process is to find and eliminate as much of the delay as possible. Although the people are busy, the customer's order is idle up to 95% of the time—sitting in queue waiting for the next worker. Delays occur in three main ways.

1. Delays between steps in a process
2. Delays caused by waste and rework
3. Delays caused by large batch sizes (The last item in the batch has to finish before the first item can go on to the next step.)

So the obvious answer is to eliminate delays by

- Eliminating delays between steps
- Working steps in parallel instead of sequentially
- Using Six Sigma to reduce or eliminate the defects and variation that cause waste and rework
- Reducing batch size (to one if possible) Toyota, for example, can produce up to nine different models of car on the same production line simultaneously and customize each one produced.

Toyota Production System

Toyota invented Lean production according to Jeffrey Liker, author of *The Toyota Way*. It's also known as the *Toyota Production System* or TPS for short. And it seems to work well.

Toyota's annual profit in 2003 was larger than the earnings of GM, Chrysler, and Ford combined. Toyota has a 2006 market capitalization of $181.3 billion versus GM's $15.7 billion and Ford's $12.2 Billion. Toyota's new cars take 12 months or less to design versus 2 to 3 years elsewhere. Toyota and Lexus lead in defects per vehicle (25 per 100 cars versus 50+ per 100 in other companies) (*The Toyota Way*, Jeffrey Liker).

In 2010, Toyota suffered from safety recalls. The chairperson even apologized in public. I didn't hear AIG or any of the big banks apologize for creating the financial crisis of 2008–2009. This shows, however, how easy it is for a leadership team focused on growth and profits to cut corners on quality and injure the company's reputation. Toyota, long renowned for quality, will quickly solve its safety problems and return to preeminence.

At its heart, Lean is about speed and the relationship between steps in a process. It's about eliminating non-value-added elements from the process. It's about shrinking batch sizes down to create a one-piece flow.

Lean thinking originated at Toyota with the TPS. Sakichi Toyoda formulated the original ideas in the 1920s and 1930s. Taiichi Ohno began to implement these ideas in the 1940s but only made the leap to full implementation in the 1950s.

The two pillars of the Toyota Production System are

1. *Just in time (JIT)*. The right parts reach the assembly line when needed in the amount needed. Taiichi Ohno admits that, in the beginning, JIT "seemed to contain an element of fantasy."

2. *Autonomation. Automation with the human touch*, meaning that a machine will stop on its own if it detects an error allowing a single worker to handle multiple machines. Toyoda's automated weaving looms would stop automatically if the thread broke. The same is true of their automotive production lines.

I tried thinking about the transfer of materials in the reverse direction: a later process goes to an earlier process to pick up only the right part in the quantity needed at the exact time needed.

—Taiichi Ohno

Some of the principles of Lean (e.g., pull and Kanban) came from a surprising source: U.S. supermarkets where small quantities of inventory are replenished as customers pull them off the shelves. Shelves are restocked as they become depleted. In a pull system, the preceding process must always do what the subsequent process tells it. The visual ability to see low stock and replenish it became known as the kanban (aka *card*) system. Supermarkets are the essence of a *kanban* inventory and *pull* system. (How can you create a supermarket-style inventory system?)

A kanban is a piece of paper in a clear envelope attached to materials or products. It contains information about production quantity, source, destination, and transfer. Kanban lets products carry their own information.

Here's Toyota's critical discovery: When you make lead times short and focus on keeping production lines flexible, you actually get better quality, responsiveness, productivity, and utilization of equipment and space. Some core beliefs include

- The right process will produce the right results.
- Developing your people and partners adds value.
- Continuously solving root problems drives organizational learning.
- One-piece flow increases productivity, profitability, and quality.
- Products don't like to wait in line. Material, parts, and products are impatient.
- The only thing that adds value is the physical or informational transformation of raw material into something the customer wants.
- Errors are opportunities for learning.
- Problem solving is 20% tools and 80% thinking.

The hardest part of learning to think Lean is abandoning old ideas about economies of scale and mass production. These are basically push systems based on projected customer demand. Quality is inspected into the product. These *batch-and-queue* ideas must be the first casualties of the Lean transformation.

In Lean, quality, productivity, and low cost come from producing small batches of a given product, start to finish without any piles of partially finished goods, also known as work in process (WIP).

Still Struggling

In a manufacturing plant, look between the machines to see where interim products stack up. In a restaurant, look at where orders and food stack up waiting for processing or delivery. In a hotel, look at where guests stack up. Airlines, for example, have switched to online check-in to reduce lines at the airport. How can you eliminate stacking of products or customers?

The Lean Process

The first step toward breakthrough improvements with Lean starts with reducing the time required to perform your mission critical processes. Analyzing processes to eliminate delay and making them faster follows the FISH process.

Focus. To focus the improvement effort on mission-critical business processes and delays

Improve. To reduce non-value-added (NVA) delay, waste, and rework

Sustain. To stabilize and monitor the improvements

Honor. To recognize, reward, and refocus efforts

Core Ideas of Lean

The principles of Lean are pretty simple, whether you apply it to manufacturing, service, or administration.

1. *Determine value.* What does the customer want (voice of the customer)? Determining value, from the customer's point of view, can be a challenge for a number of reasons.

   - Value is an effect of doing things right. The effects of improving speed, quality, and cost leads to higher customer satisfaction, retention, and referrals. All of which lead to growth and profitability.

   - What has value in one situation may not have value in another. If I want a product or service delivered on a Friday, it doesn't matter to me if you can deliver it on any of the weekdays before Friday. (Voice of the customer: I want it when I want it, not when you can deliver it.)

2. *Use pull systems.* To avoid overproduction. Big inventories of raw materials or finished goods hide problems and inefficiencies. Ohno says "Efficiency is never a function of quantity and speed."

3. *Institute one-piece flow.* Make the work flow, so that there are no interruptions, wasted time, or materials using small lot sizes and quick changeover.

4. *Level out the workload.* (Hejunka) To the rate of customer demand or pull.

5. *Stop and fix problems.* Immediately to get quality right the first time.

6. *Standardize.* To support improvement.

7. *Use visual controls.* So that no problems remain hidden.

8. *Use only reliable technology.* That supports the people and the process.

9. *Compete against perfection.* Not against competitors.

Toyota worked with one supplier to reduce lead time by 46%, work-in-process (WIP) inventory by 83%, finished goods inventory by 91%, and overtime by 50% and to increase productivity by 83% (*The ToyotaWay*, Jeffrey Liker).

Matsushita produces cell phones, fax machines, and security cameras. In 2002, they had a loss of $3.7 billion; by March 2007 they're expecting a profit of $1.7 billion—an annual increase in profit of 23% on a 1% increase in sales. In 2002, it was taking 60 hours for a production run to deliver its first finished product (big batch sizes cause these delays). Using Lean, Matsushita reduced the lead time to 40 minutes (99% of the time was delay; 1% was production). It used to take 3 days and multiple shifts to make 1500 phones; they now make 500 per shift. This has reduced inventory costs because components spend one-third less time in the factory. An early Lean change involved switching from production lines (big batches) to work "cells" (small batches). They also right-sized their machines to produce smaller batches. Faster robots on the assembly line were sitting idle waiting on slower robots. Matsushita doubled up on slower robots to feed more quickly the faster ones and increase flow. Despite the faster pace, defects are at an all time low.

Matsushita serves 75 different markets, and phones alone have over 1500 design variations. With over 77 parts for each circuit board, changeover from one cell phone to another was taking too long. Matsushita designed a circuit board that needed far fewer changes per model. As you can imagine, probably 80% of the parts were the same and 20% different. If you can keep 80% of the board the same, it would reduce changeover time and costs.

Matsushita has seven plants worldwide producing 35 million products a year; so they test new production concepts in the mother plant in Japan and replicate the changes in all of their other plants. Since no two plants are of the same size or shape, it can take up to three months to adapt the changes to fit each plant.

The Lean Mindset

Here's the mindset shift that you will want to embrace to understand Lean.

From. If you build it, they will come (mass production).

To. When they come, build it fast (Lean production).

What's weird about this kind of thinking?

1. The top priority is to produce products at the rate of customer demand, not to keep workers busy.

2. Sometimes the best thing you can do is to stop making stuff. Finished but unsold inventory is wasteful (e.g., Compaq versus Dell).

3. Create only a small inventory of finished goods to level out the production schedule.

4. The more inventory you maintain, the less likely you will have what you need! Too much inventory creates clutter and hides shortages.

5. It's usually best to work out a process manually first before adding technology.

Lean versus Mass Production

The old models of business required stability, not the unpredictable nature of today's markets. In the good old days, you could make and sell products using some sort of strategic planning. In the volatile, ever-changing marketplace of today, however, you must be able to rapidly sense what customers want and respond to their needs quickly.

Lean Production	Mass Production
Build to order	Make and sell
Economies of speed	Economies of scale
Effective	Efficient
Pull (from customer)	Push (to customer)
Small lots	Large batches
Quick changeover	Changeover unimportant
Production cells that do everything	Functional silos and production lines
Right–sized machines	Big, fast machines
Fast to respond	Slow to change
Adaptive	Rigid, inflexible
General knowledge	Specialized knowledge

Lean prizes flexibility and speed. Mass production focused on the economies of building lots of things at a lower unit price. When you get good at Lean, you can often produce a product for the same price as a mass-produced item and charge more for it because it's ready immediately, not whenever the batch is finished and shipped from some faraway place. Although a lot of people are worried that U.S. manufacturing is moving overseas, a Lean shop may find it easy to compete with low-cost, mass producers who incur shipping costs. If your industry is worried that China will take over your markets, get Lean!

The Seven Speed Bumps of Lean

There is no waste in business more terrible than overproduction.

—Taiichi Ohno

The seven speed bumps of Lean focus on non-value-added waste, which includes any activity that absorbs money, time, and people but creates no value. Toyota describes these as

1. *Overproduction.* (The most common type of waste) It creates inventories that take up space and capital.

2. *Excess inventory.* Excess inventory caused by overproduction is waste.

3. *Waiting.* Don't you hate standing in line? So do your products or services. Are they always waiting for the next value-adding process to start? Don't you hate waiting on your computer to boot up? So do employees. Are they waiting for missing parts or late meeting attendees? Waiting is waste.

4. *Unnecessary movement of work products (i.e., transportation).* When you break down the silos into cells, the work products don't have to travel so far between processes. My mind, however, seems to respond with more energy to the phrase "Inventory is fundamentally evil."

5. *Unnecessary movement of employees.* Are parts and tools too far from where they're needed? Are employees walking too far to get supplies or deliver a work product? Taiichi Ohno says "Moving is not necessarily working. Find ways to turn moving into working."

6. *Unnecessary or incorrect processing.* Why have people to watch a machine that can be taught to monitor itself? Why do things that add no value? Is one group doing something that the next group has to correct? Stop doing the unnecessary, and start doing everything right the first time.

7. *Defects.* They lead to repair, rework, or scrap.

Lean will help you reduce or eliminate numbers 1 to 6. Six Sigma will help you reduce number 7. When you rearrange your production floor into production cells with right-sized machines and quick changeover, you can quickly reduce most of these common kinds of non-value-added waste by 50% to 90%.

Still Struggling

Simply eliminating delays between steps will dramatically improve productivity and profitability. Then focus on reducing the batch size produced or the amount of inventory maintained. When you get fast, you won't need as much inventory. When you can produce products on demand, you won't need big batches.

The Five S's

In 1982, an article appeared in the *Atlantic Monthly* suggesting that merely fixing broken windows and cleaning the streets would reduce crime. A building with broken windows would invite further vandalism that would lead to squatters and drugs and crime. Litter on the streets would give even regular citizens permission to toss their used bottles and bags on the ground, not in the trash. Graffiti on subway cars would lead to escalating violence on the trains.

Preventing petty crimes of vandalism and littering encourages solid citizens to stay in the neighborhood, and this prevents the escalation to more serious crimes.

In my neighborhood, I take my dog for a walk every day. I invariably find bottles, cans, and fast food restaurant bags along the streets, creek, and canal where I walk. I've taken to carrying plastic bag not just for the dog's waste, but for people's as well.

Although there are many factors that affect crime, the data suggests that rapid repair of vandalism and cleaning up the trash does reduce petty crime and ultimately major crime.

Sounds a lot like Lean's 5S strategy. The 5S concepts are a great way to understand what's going on in your process. The 5S principles of reorganizing work so that it's simpler, more straightforward, and visually manageable are

1. *Sort*. Keep only what is needed. Pitch everything else.

2. *Straighten*. A place for everything and everything in its place.

3. *Shine.* Clean machines and work area to expose problems.

4. *Standardize.* Develop systems and procedures to monitor conformance to the first three rules.

5. *Sustain.* Maintain the standard processes for sorting, straightening, and shining.

I've worked in many hospital laboratories. If the lab has been around for more than a few years, there's usually a lot of inventory to 5S. It takes about 4 hours to 5S a 2000-sq-ft lab. Lab workers usually find one to two dumpsters worth of stuff to throw away. It's amazing how many chemicals are left over from prior equipment. There can be three places for the same pipette at one workstation instead of just one place. There were stashes of gloves all over the lab, not in one place; this causes over ordering.

Using 5S, corporate offices discover tons of out of date forms, supplies, and machinery. Any workspace can benefit from 5S.

Once you've thrown away all of the clutter and organized what remains, you can more easily see the products flowing through your workspace.

Red Tagging

Of course, you might be afraid of throwing away something important. Just put a red tag on it showing the date discarded and put it in a place designated as the red tag room. That way, other shifts can find and retrieve needed items. (This rarely happens.) At the end of 30 days, throw it away or donate it to some cause.

Value Stream

Having just done the 5S's on your factory, you'll be in great shape to understand the overall value stream. A key starting point for implementing Lean is the concept of *value* and the *value stream*. Value is defined by the customer, not the company, business unit, manager, or employee. When I worked in information technologies, for example, programmers often focused on cool, new technology, not on what was fast, proven, and effective for the customer. Craftsmen bear allegiance to their craft, not to their customer.

Since most businesses have grouped work together into functional silos, each silo often skews the definition of value. Although each silo attempts to optimize its own operation, the company fails to optimize the overall flow of products and services, which creates tremendous waste.

Purchasing departments, for example, try to minimize the cost of goods purchased. They ask for three bids and wait for the best price, never considering the high cost of this process. Purchasing is often rewarded for saving money, but not penalized for delayed or defective production.

Become the Product or Service

Most people find this hard to believe, but when you take the perspective of the product or service and notice how long you sit around waiting for something to happen, how many things go wrong and have to be reworked, you get some idea of the waste in the process. All of this delay and rework can be eliminated using Lean Six Sigma.

Whenever I go in to work with a group on Lean, I start wherever the product starts and follow it around. I ask dumb questions about why things are done this way. The usual answer is that it's always been done this way. Then I'll ask, what if we move this machine over there so that the product or employee doesn't have to travel so far? Often the team will say it can be done. Then I ask Can we do it now?

This is the essence of Lean. The moment you notice one of the seven speed bumps, ask yourself Can I change this now? If so, just move the machine, tool, or material. Most people are surprised when Japanese counselors come into a plant and they just start moving machines into production cells. Don't study it to death; get on with making things better.

Double Your Speed!

How long does it take to build a three-bedroom, two-bath, two-car garage house with all of the plumbing, fixtures, paint, carpet, and landscaped yard? If you're like most people, you'd guess a few days to a few weeks.

There is an annual contest to build a house as fast as possible. Last year's record was 2 hours and 48 minutes. They do it by taking all of the idle time out of the process, combining steps, and getting all of the construction steps in the right order.

When it comes to Lean, there are a few main principles for innovative solution development.

- *Pull versus push.* Let the customer *pull* the product or service; don't push.
- *No delay versus delay.* Eliminate delays.

- *Parallel versus sequential.* Do more things in parallel.
- *No action versus action.* Eliminate unnecessary processing.
- *No movement versus movement.* Eliminate unnecessary movement.

Pull versus Push

The Toyota Production System is a pull method.

—Murumatsu Runtaro

Once you understand what the customer wants, then you can redesign the process to produce it in a way that minimizes time, defects, and cost. The secret is to only produce the product or deliver the service when the customer asks for it. This is the essence of a pull system.

When I was 14, my father taught me how to shoot trap. In trap or skeet shooting, you stand at a position, load your shotgun, and shout pull! Then a clay target flies from the trap, left, right, or straight away. Then you do your best to break the target with a single shot. Notice that nothing happens until you (the customer) "pull" the clay target from the trap. Compare this with mass production that produces large batches of finished inventory in anticipation of future demand. Instead of producing inventory for projected demand, pull thinking forces you to produce parts and products when the customer actually orders them. If a customer orders a car, for example, it should kick off a series of requests for a frame, doors, tires, engines, etc. which should kick off a series of requests for raw materials, and so on.

In Tokyo, for example, you can place a custom order for a Toyota and have it delivered within 5 days. Pull means that no one produces anything until a customer downstream asks for it, but when they do, you make it very quickly. Optimally, you would want to build one piece or service one customer at a time.

Still Struggling

If you go into Starbucks (a pull system), they make one of a thousand possible custom coffee drinks for you when you arrive. The barista often asks for your order before the cashier takes your money. Speed is one of the secrets to Starbucks success. Another is their one-drink-at-a-time (one-piece flow) strategy.

Redesign for One-Piece Flow

One of the goals of Lean is to reduce the size of a batch or lot to one. While this may not always be possible, small lots and quick changeover approach it. In the beginning, changeover took an hour or more. Now, it's 3 minutes or less. What are the benefits of one-piece flow?

1. Builds in quality

2. Creates flexibility

3. Increases productivity

4. Frees flow and space

5. Improves safety

6. Improves moral

7. Reduces inventory

Here's the mindset shift for one-piece flow.

From. Big batches

To. Single pieces or small batches

The trick is eliminating all of the delay between value-adding steps and lining up all of the machines and processes so that the product or service flows through the value channel without interruption. Mass production and large batches ensure that the product will have to sit patiently waiting for the next step in the process. The mental shift required to move from mass production to Lean thinking is to focus on continuous flow of small lots.

Common Measures of Flow

- *Lead (or cycle) time.* Time product stays in the system
- *Value-added ratio.* (Value-added time)/(lead time)
- *Travel distance.* Of the product or people doing the work
- *Productivity.* People hours per unit; number of handoffs
- *Quality rate.* Or first-pass yield

Tesco, a grocery store chain in the United Kingdom, reduced *stock outs* dramatically while slashing in-store inventories by more than 50%. In-store inventories are one-eighth of the U.S. average (*Lean Thinking*, Womack & Jones).

The Redesign Process

1. The first step is to focus on the part, product, or service itself. Follow the product through its entire production cycle. In a hospital, you would follow a patient through from admission to discharge. In a printing company, you'd follow a job from start to delivery. In a manufacturing plant, you'd follow the product from order to delivery. You can use a spaghetti diagram to show the movement of parts, products, and people through the current production maze.

2. The second step is to ignore traditional boundaries, layouts, and so forth. In other words, forget what you know about how to assemble the product or deliver the service.

3. The third step is to realign the workflow into production cells to eliminate delay, rework, and scrap.

4. The fourth step is to right-size the machines and technology to support smaller lots, quick changeover, and one-piece flow. This often means using simpler, slower, and less automated machines that may actually be more accurate and reliable.

The goal of flow is to eliminate all delays, interruptions, and stoppages and not to rest until you succeed.

Work Cell Design

A cell is a group of workstations, machines, or equipment arranged such that a product can be worked progressively from one workstation to another without having to sit and wait for a batch to be completed and without additional handling between operations. Cells may be dedicated to a process, a subcomponent, or an entire product. Cells can be designed for administrative as well as manufacturing operations.

Cell design helps build products with as little waste as possible. Arrange equipment and workstations in a sequence that supports a smooth flow of materials and components through the process, with minimal transport or delay. Cells can help make your company more competitive by

- cutting costly transportation and delay
- shortening lead times
- saving floor space

- reducing inventory

- encouraging continuous improvement.

A work cell contains three to nine people and workstations in a compact U-shaped arrangement (Fig. 2-4). A cell ideally manufactures a range of highly similar products. It should be self-contained with all necessary equipment and resources. The U-shape makes communication easy because operators stay close to each other. This improves quality and speed.

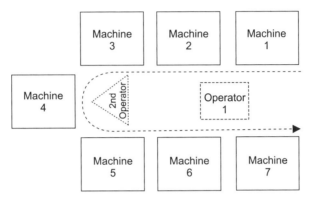

FIGURE 2-4 · Lean cell layout.

Most factory floors and even office floors are organized into functional cells. Functional cells consist of similar equipment and activities. In a factory, a functional cell might include a bank of lathes or presses or welders. In the offices of old, there were groups of typists transcribing handwritten documents. In information systems, there might be groups of system testers. In check processing, there might be huge banks of check-sorting machines and clusters of people balancing the amounts in each batch of checks. In medical imaging, X-rays, CT scans, and MRIs form machine-based cells.

These functional cells do not serve to create a Lean environment. Some of the problems include

- WIP often accumulates in front of these functional cells due to large batch sizes.

- Transportation from one functional cell to another can be extensive.

- Functional cells use large, expensive equipment to gain economies of scale.

- Defects occur because operators are generally focused on their function and not aware of the overall process, so quality suffers when work is organized in functional cells. Defects created in one cell aren't detected until much later in the process.

U-shaped, work cells create the product through a series of operations that are all done within the cell. Remember Matsushita? The only way to produce the first phone in 40 minutes versus 3 days is to organize into cells that do everything.

Many hospital emergency departments (EDs) have their own portable X-ray machines; the patient doesn't have to move at all to be X-rayed. Some also have CT scans and even MRIs to reduce patient's travel and accelerate diagnosis. Some emergency rooms are using point-of-care lab testing. If you can get lab test results in 10 minutes in the ED versus 40 minutes in the lab, it shaves 30 minutes off your patient's wait time and accelerates flow through the ED. While the cost per test is currently higher, it also costs an estimated $6000 or more to turn away an ambulance when the ED is full.

Work Space

C. Northcote Parkinson coined the law *Work expands to fill the time allotted to it.* Every student has had that experience, cramming for a test on the last night before a final. The same holds true for home projects and work projects, unless you're really Lean about how you get work done.

Arthur's Axiom to Parkinson's Law

Having done many Lean projects with various companies, I have found a similar pattern.

Work expands to fill the available space.

If you've got lots of room on the floor, production machines will spread out over the space. It's designed to give people more room which causes more walking which causes delays which cause longer turnaround times.

When I designed our kitchen remodel, I put the triangle of stove, sink, and refrigerator close to each other. I barely have to move when I cook. In contrast, I look at some of the mansions they're building, and the kitchen is immense. You need a golf cart to commute from the refrigerator to the sink to the stove. It's no wonder people in big houses rarely cook; it's faster to go out to eat.

If you want to know how far people travel, have them wear a pedometer for a few days. In hospital labs, we found technicians were walking 2 to 5 miles a day in a 2400-sq-ft space—the distance from Denver to Pittsburgh—every year. When we redesigned the space, they traveled less than half that distance and I think there was still room for improvement.

INSIGHT *Never use a fixed workbench, desk, or other work area. Everything should be mobile so that you can reconfigure on a moment's notice any time you discover a better way to handle the product or service.*

Have you let the work in your office or factory expand to fill the available space? Couldn't you tighten it up to reduce unnecessary travel of people and products? How might this reduce your turnaround times and minimize errors?

It's not unusual to reduce your space requirements by 20% and double productivity. Don't let work expand to fill the available space. Shrink the space to match the work and optimize throughput. Your customers will love you for it.

Lean Tools

Having said all that, there are two key tools used to help visualize problems with speed: value stream mapping and spaghetti diagrams.

- *Value stream mapping* (Fig. 2-5). To visualize the flow of the process (http://www.youtube.com/watch?v=3mcMwlgUFjU). Go to our website: *http://www.qimacros.com/demystified.html* and fill in your email address to download the QI Macros which contain a template for value stream mapping.

- *Spaghetti diagrams* (Fig. 2-6). To visualize the flow of work through the production area (http://www.youtube.com/watch?v=UmLrDjT5g8o).

With these two tools you can identify most of the problems associated with delays and non-value-added waste.

A simple way to begin is to map the value stream and analyze each element for non-value-added waste. Then redesign the flow to remove as much of the non-value-added waste as possible and standardize the ongoing process.

Value stream mapping assumes that an idle resource or product is a wasted resource. An activity or step that doesn't in some way directly benefit a customer is also wasteful. Some examples include

- Rework—fixing stuff that's broken—is one of the more insidious forms of non-value-added work: The customer wants you to fix it, but she or he really didn't want it to break in the first place.

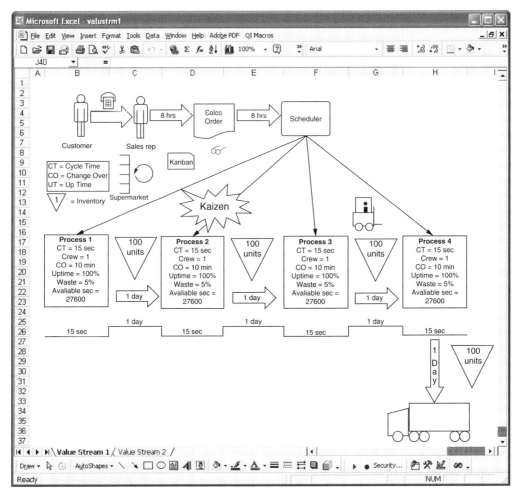

FIGURE 2-5 · QI Macros value stream map.

• Requests for change may spend months in a prioritization cue before being worked (non-value-added.)
• An order may sit idle waiting for an approval or material.

On a process flowchart or value stream map, most of the non-value-added time will be found in one of three places.

• *Arrows.* Delay between process steps
• *Rework loops.* Fixing errors that should have been prevented
• *Scrap processes.* Discarding or recycling defective products

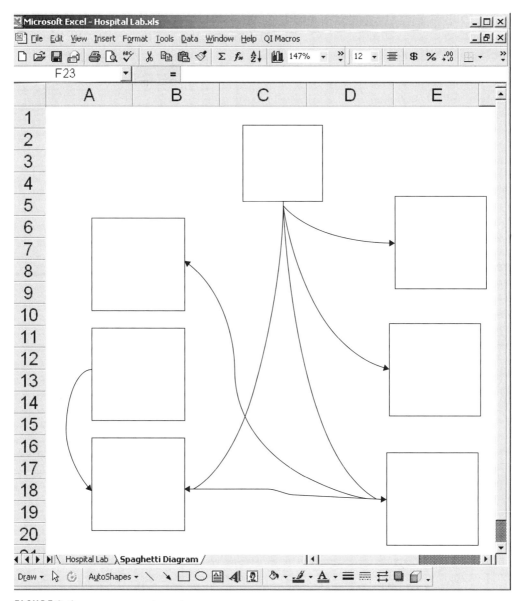

FIGURE 2-6 · QI Macros spaghetti diagram.

To eliminate these non-value-added activities, ask yourself how you can

- Eliminate or reduce delay between steps
- Combine job steps to prevent wasteful delay
- Initiate root cause teams to remove the source of the rework

Value stream mapping, flowcharting, and value-added flow analysis will help you find ways to eliminate the delays between each step of the process. Employees won't have to work any harder; you just eliminate the delay. The value stream includes every activity required to deliver a product or service. Remember, only 5% of any slow-speed process adds value; 95% is non-value-added effort and delay, what Toyota calls *muda* ("waste").

The goal is to group all of the essential steps into work cells that encourage a continuous flow with no excess inventory, wasted motions, interruptions, batches, or queues. When you do this, the amount of people, time, technology, space, and inventories required can be cut in half. To do this, start by listening to the voice of the customer and evaluating how all of your activities support their needs.

Map the Value Stream

Purpose: Evaluate the existing or improved process as a starting point for improvement.

1. Start by identifying customer needs and end with satisfying them.
2. Use square Post-it notes to lay out processes.
3. Use arrow Post-it notes to show delays.
4. Place activities in the correct order.
5. Identify inventory levels carried between each step.

I worked with one government organization that took 140 days to process a request, but there were only 8 hours of actual work in the 140 days. Although I thought it could be done in a couple of days, they reduced it to 30.

Spaghetti Diagrams

Spaghetti diagrams help detect crazy patterns of behavior in the production workspace. *Purpose:* To examine the existing flow before redesigning it.

1. Use square Post-it notes to lay out a floor plan of machines or processing stations.
2. Draw arrows to show movement of the product or service through the floor plan.
3. Assess how many times each processing station is used. Is the highest volume closest to incoming materials or products?
4. Identify ways to redesign the flow to reduce unnecessary movement of people and materials.

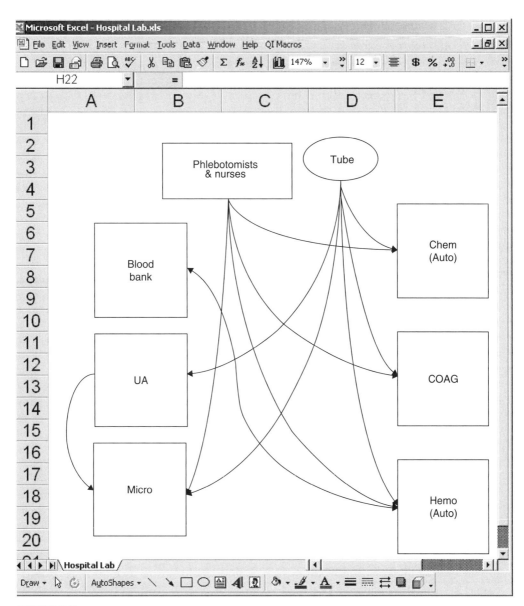

FIGURE 2-7 · Hospital lab spaghetti diagram.

Here's an example from a hospital laboratory (Fig. 2-7). There are five main processing areas: hematology (HEMO), chemistry (CHEM), coagualtion rate (COAG), urinary analysis (UA), and microbiology. Many of these areas have both automated analyzers and manual processes.

Notice that although hematology has 300 orders a day, it's farther from the pneumatic tube than UA, which only has 48 orders a day. Moving automated hematology and chemistry analysis closer to the tube and UA farther from the tube could reduce unnecessary travel for hundreds of samples.

Once redesigned, the hospital lab saved

- 17% of floor space (400 sq ft).
- 54% of travel time for technicians, phlebotomists, and samples (10–12 mi a day).
- 7 hours of delay per day, which reduced turnaround time, accelerated diagnosis and treatment in the ED.

Still Struggling

Sometimes the only way to understand these concepts is to use them. Pull out a pad of sticky notes and use them to create a diagram of work flow in your job. If it's a process, pay special attention to the delays between steps. If it's a factory layout, notice where the high volume processing is done. Is this flow or layout optimal or causing delays, defects, and deviation?

Value-Added Flow Analysis

Another method I've used that's similar to value stream mapping is what I call value-added flow analysis. First you flowchart the process and then you examine every action, decision, and arrow in the flowchart for non-value-added activities.

First step? Define the existing process as a starting point to begin improvement. A flowchart uses a few simple symbols to show the flow of a process (Fig. 2-8 QI Macros Flowchart template).

The symbols are Process flowcharts use a swim lanes format to separate activities by group or organization. Instead of writing directly on the flipchart, use square Post-it notes for both the decisions and activities. This way the process will remain easy to change until you have it clearly and totally defined. Limit the number of decisions and activities per page. Move detailed subprocesses onto additional pages.

Across the top of the flowchart list every person or department that helps deliver the product or service. Along the left-hand side, list the major steps in

FIGURE 2-8 · QI Macros flowchart.

your process. In general, most processes have four main steps: planning, doing, checking, and acting to improve. Even going to the grocery store involves creating a list (plan), getting the groceries (do), checking the list, and acting to get any forgotten item. Virtually all effective business processes include these four steps.

What we must decide is perhaps how we are valuable rather than how valuable we are.
Everything is worth what its purchaser will pay for it.
— Publilius Syrus

What may be false in the science of facts may be true in the science of values.
— George Santayana

Purpose: Identify the waste, rework, and delay that can be eliminated from the process.

Over time, processes become cumbersome, inefficient, and ineffective. This complexity consumes more time and accomplishes less. Each activity, decision, and arrow on the flowchart represents time and effort. From the customer's point of view, little of this time and effort adds value; most of it is non-value added. From the customer's point of view, delay and rework do not add value. We can increase productivity and quality by simplifying the overall process—eliminating delay and the need for rework.

Step Activity

1. For each arrow, box, and diamond, lists its function and the time spent (in minutes, hours, days) on the value-added checklist (Fig. 2-9).

2. Now become the customer. Step into the customer's shoes. As the customer, ask the following questions:

   • Is the order idle or delayed?

   • Is this inspection, testing, or checking necessary?

   • Does it change the product or service in a valuable way, or is this just fix-it error correction work or waste?

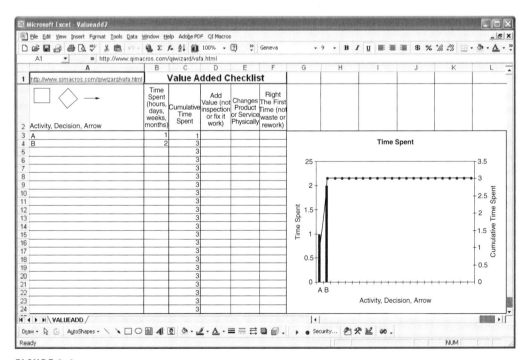

FIGURE 2-9 • QI Macros value-added flow analysis.

3. If the answer to any of these questions is yes, the step may be non-value-added. If so, can we remove it from the process? Much of the idle, non-value-adding time in a process lies in the arrows: Orders sit in in-boxes or computers waiting to be processed; calls wait in queue for a representative to answer. How can we eliminate delay? Can we do multiple steps in parallel?

4. How can activities and delays be eliminated, simplified, combined, or reorganized to provide a faster, higher-quality flow through the process? Investigate handoff points: How can you eliminate delays and prevent lost, changed, or misinterpreted information or work products at these points? If there are simple, elegant, or obvious ways to improve the process now, revise the flowchart to reflect those changes.

Stop the Line

To better serve customers, employees often work around problems when they occur. Work-arounds may be expedient, but they are inefficient. They are a form of rework: The system isn't working properly, so people learn to cope with it. And coping takes longer and costs more than fixing the system.

One of the principles of Lean thinking is to stop the line when there's a problem. At Toyota, any employee can stop the line when a problem is detected so that you don't continue to make bad products or deliver bad service. Then everyone rushes in to solve the problem before restarting the line.

When you fail to stop the line, the pressure to serve the customer is like the flow of water, it finds another path. If you don't come back to the problem soon, the work-around becomes the new non-value-added channel for handling customer needs.

This is another S in Lean thinking: Stop! What if every person on the line had the right to stop production when an error was detected? Stopping production is far cheaper than producing defective parts that simply have to be fixed later. When the line stops, there are visual signals that show exactly where the process stopped so that problem solving can begin immediately.

What have you been working around? Isn't it time to stop the madness? What processes do you need to simplify and streamline? What information system changes do you need to make to redirect the flow of work into a smoother channel?

Most problems do not call for complex statistical analysis. Instead, they need detailed problem solving.

Still Struggling

It's easier to understand "Stop the Line" in a manufacturing plant, but what about a service like healthcare? Virginia Mason hospital encourages every doctor, nurse, patient or family member to call a "patient safety alert" (PSA) which brings managers, clinicians and families together to solve a potential problem that could harm a patient. What kind of alert system could you implement?

Production Floor Problem Solving

Once you've redesigned the value stream or work flow, you will want to continuously improve the process. Toyota does not have a Six Sigma program, but they have one of the highest levels of quality in the industry. Toyota says "Most problems do not call for complex statistical analysis, but instead require painstaking, detailed problem solving. We have a very sophisticated technique for solving problems: We ask 'Why?' five times."

Your goal is to compete against perfection, not competitors. Here's where Lean Six Sigma comes into play. The idea of perfection through endless improvements is key to Lean thinking. You can't start at perfection, but you can arrive at perfection by iteration.

> *Seeing and hearing things with your own eyes and ears is a critical first step in improving or creating a breakthrough. Once you start observing carefully, all kinds of insights and opportunities can open up.*
> —Tom Kelly CEO of IDEO

1. Go and see where production was stopped.
2. Analyze the situation.
3. Use one-piece flow to surface problems.
4. Ask "Why?" five times.

Lean Six Sigma can help drill down into more complex problems using data collected from daily operation.

Get the Right-Size Machines

Lean thinking has some counterintuitive ideas about machinery. Slower machines may be faster. Smaller machines may be faster than big ones.

Pratt and Whitney right-sized their turbine blade machines; this increased actual processing time from 3 to 12 minutes, but reduced total cycle time from 10 days to 75 minutes. WIP fell from 1640 to 15. Space was reduced by 60%. Total costs were cut by 50% (*Lean Thinking*, Womack & Jones).

In hospital labs, they have big bucket centrifuges that spin samples for 10 minutes. They also have smaller STAT centrifuges that can spin a sample in 3 minutes. Labs that want to accelerate patient results can benefit from buying smaller, faster STAT centrifuges.

What machines can you right-size to accelerate production and flow?

Mistake-Proofing with Color

One of the principles of Lean is to make the workplace *visually intuitive*. Why are so many work environments a dull gray or tan when the Earth is vibrant with color? We sometimes forget that humans can see in color. Stoplights use red, yellow, and green. Why can't we use more color to help mistake-proof processes? (For some ideas about how to use color in factories, offices, and health care go to www.visualworkplaceinc.com/gallery.html.)

Color for Processing

I just mailed in my taxes and I realized that the IRS uses colors to sort their incoming mail into ones with money and ones without. The white address label is for taxpayers who owe money. The yellow label is for refunds. One goes to Charlotte, North Carolina, and the other goes to Fresno, California. The processing and handling of checks on the one hand and writing checks on the other probably help simplify and mistake-proof their processing.

Hospital labs use different colored tubes to identify whether blood samples are going to hematology, coag, or chemistry. If you see a green tube (chemistry) in hematology (purple), you know it's misplaced.

In our office, we use a red folder for payment processing and plain manila folders for order processing. This way, checks don't get lost in the wrong folder.

The Mind Learns in Color

The human eye can readily detect color. Once your mind gets used to seeing a certain color associated with a certain tool, product, or process, the two become linked in your mind. So, when you see the right product (e.g., tube) with the wrong color or the right color in the wrong place, it sets off an alarm in your mind that will help prevent a mistake.

Work in technicolor! Still trapped in black-and-white thinking or just shades of gray? How can you start using color to mistake-proof your processes?

Get Started Immediately

Reorganize your company by product family and value stream. Topple the silos and implement the flow. Move the machines and people into product cells immediately. Reduce the number of suppliers. Help your remaining suppliers implement Lean. Downsize the laggards. Two steps forward and one step back, is okay. Devise a growth strategy. Kaizen (i.e., improve) each value stream multiple times. Teach Lean thinking and Lean Six Sigma skills to each pilot project team as you go. Right-size your machines and tools.

You should be able to create a positive cash flow from applying Lean in less than 90 days and become best in class in just 24 months. It doesn't take that long to get results with Lean. It does take a series of iterations to squeeze out all of the non-value-added delay, waste, and rework and to align your business to the principles of Lean.

How Do I Get Started?

First, you will need to create a crisis. This is easy during a recession; everyone needs to simplify, streamline, and optimize operations to maintain a positive cash flow. The most difficult step is the first one. You will need a change agent, a crisis in a mission critical process (externally or internally generated), and a determination to get results quickly. Then you'll need the determination to keep going. Leaders and employees who thrive on change and continuous improvement are often in short supply.

Demand immediate results. Pick a pilot area that's open to change and jump right in. Line up the machines and work steps. Eliminate delays. Slash the inventories. Dramatic reductions in lead times, inventories, space, and defects should be possible in weeks not months.

Stay the course. It may take 5 years to fully integrate Lean into your business. Experts estimate that it will take 3 years to get a Lean system fully in place and 2 years to make it self-sustaining.

Develop a scorecard or dashboard of key measures.

- Sales per employee (productivity)
- Products delivered on time (customer service)
- Inventory turns
- Defects per million (quality)

Set big, hairy audacious goals (BHAG).

- 20% increase in sales per employee
- 50% reduction in defects every year
- 100% on-time delivery
- Reduce order-to-ship time to less than a day
- 20 inventory turns per year
- Reduce time-to-market by 75%
- Reduce costs (hours/widget)

What Can You Do with All Those People?

Lean will free up 30% of your staff. The traditional response of downsizing will only make everyone resistant to Lean and Six Sigma. So let me ask you this: If you could add 30% more people at no cost, what projects do you have waiting in the wings or what new lines of business would you pursue that you can't now because you don't have the resources? And remember that Lean companies grow at *three times the rate of their competitors*. In a very short time, you will need all of those employees to handle the growth.

Piloting Lean

To get started with Lean, do the following:

1. Who is your customer (i.e., next process in the flow)? What does the customer want? (Use QI Macros Voice of the Customer matrix.)
2. Analyze the current state of your process (non-value-added, movement, etc.) Use Post-it notes and QI Macros value stream maps to capture the flow.

3. Develop a future state that

   a. Creates a one-piece flow (no big batches).

   b. Group work "cells" are a by product, not a process.

   c. Avoid handoffs.

   d. Level the load.

   e. Standardize the tasks.

   f. Eliminate redundancy.

   g. Include visual controls to make management easy.

   h. Reduce unnecessary movement of people and products.

   i. Reduce unnecessary delays.

4. Implement the change.

5. Measure performance.

   a. Lead or turnaround time (days).

   b. Percentage on-time deliveries.

   c. Defects in PPM.

   d. Productivity (widgets/hour).

6. Monitor and sustain the improvement.

7. Do it again.

Six Sigma and Lean

There is an obvious case for the harmonious marriage between Six Sigma, which fixes individual processes, and Lean, which fixes the connections among processes.

Use technology to support, not replace people. Focus on process and people first, then add information technology to support them. Use low-cost reliable alternatives to expensive new technology.

Make decisions slowly, implement decisions rapidly.

Learn by doing first and training second. "You cannot PowerPoint your way to Lean." The Toyota way is about learning by doing (LBD). In the early stages of Lean there should be at least 80% doing and 20% training. The best training is training followed by immediate doing, or doing followed by immediate training.

Use experts for getting quick results. The word *sensei* is used in Japan with some reverence to refer to a teacher who has mastered the subject. A sensei can quick-start the process by educating through action.

Six Sigma can help you improve the value-added steps, and Lean can help you eliminate the non-value-added delays and activities. Both Six Sigma and Lean are about achieving long life and long-term profitability for your company. As Toyota's leaders would say "You can't get anywhere by jumping willy-nilly from fad to fad."

Lean Decision Making

One of the principles of Lean thinking is to eliminate delays, which consume up to 95% of the total cycle time. Decision making is one such process. I've noticed several cases of decision-making delay involving Lean Six Sigma.

One health care organization contacted me over a year ago about initiating some improvement projects around insurance claims. They have *$150 million a year in rejected claims* and *$1 million a month in denied claims*. They are actually talking about getting started *next year.*

A steel company contacted me about doing some training and consulting back in March of 2004. They asked for references twice: once in March and again in August. In September, they had a quality problem that caused them to *melt a $100 million dollar furnace.*

If you're losing $1 million a month and encountering slowed cash flow of $150 million each year or risking the loss of a $100 million facility, wouldn't it seem as though you'd want to jump on those problems? Why does it take a year to decide to take action?

Urgent Beats Important

When you have problems caused by defects, delay, and deviation, the day-to-day firefighting and crisis management can eat up all of your time. You forget to spend time on important things like fire and crisis prevention.

Under Jack Welch, GE created a quick and dirty approach to solving small problems. It's called *Work Out.* Jack had noticed that his management team was having trouble making timely decisions. In Work Out, teams meet to brainstorm problems and solutions. Then in a town hall meeting, problems and solutions are presented and leaders have to give a thumbs up or a thumbs down to each proposal right then, no deliberation just decision.

Indecision Isn't Safe

Managers rarely get hammered for not making a decision, but they can often get pummeled for making the wrong decision. Indecision can kill your business just as easily as liberate it. A bad decision that you can learn from and reverse direction is better than no decision. In the movie *In Harm's Way*, with John Wayne and Henry Fonda, Fonda's character says "Indecision is a virus that can destroy an army's will to win." It can kill your company's will as well.

The Economies of Decision Speed

Speed doesn't just matter on the front line or the factory floor; it matters in the boardroom as well. Start measuring the cycle time for decisions. Reward people who make fast decisions. Reward people who have the flexibility to revise their decisions as they learn. Don't punish the slow to decide; just don't reward them. Put time in your schedule to work on important things, not just the urgent. Remember, it's not the big that eat the small; it's the fast that eat the slow. Accelerate your decision making—at work, at home, or in a restaurant. Learn to make faster, smarter decisions. Are decision-making delays hampering your business progress?

I do a lot of Lean Six Sigma process consulting. Sadly, I can tell by how long it takes a company to decide to hire me just how long it will take to make any of the changes. Slow decision-making begets slow implementation begets slow results. Delayed decisions keep companies from making rapid progress toward performance and profitability goals.

Decision-Making Mindset

Rapid decision-making requires the right mindset. Here's a test. Are your ultimate outcomes in life determined by external events and environments or ultimately are up to you and within your control? Do you believe that you need *all* of the information before making a decision or that 70% is enough to make a decision? Do you believe that decisions are based on facts or that gut feel and intuition play a big part in decision making?

Internal versus External

Jim Collins says that the best decision makers believe that *how life turns out is ultimately up to them.* If you think that everything is outside of your control, you won't even look for answers or solutions. Your own thinking becomes a trap.

Lately, I've been working with hospitals to accelerate the patient's experience. The biggest roadblock to this is the limiting belief that nurses can't influence the doctor's behavior or the family's behavior. (Discharging patients and getting them picked up by the family often determines the hospital's ability to accept more patients.) Once we asked "If you could influence doctor or family behavior, what would you do differently?" creative suggestions began to surface.

The biggest barriers aren't out *there*, they are *inside* your mind.

The 70-70-70 Rule

The Marine Corps teaches that "if you have 70% of the information, have done 70% of the analysis, and feel 70% confident, then move. A less than ideal action, swiftly executed, stands a chance of success."

In my own office, if I can try something easily with minimal risk; I just do it. It sometimes shocks my staff because it's so fast. I put one of my staff in charge of improving the standing of our Web pages in the search engines. She was worried about making a mistake, so I made a backup copy of the entire site that would allow us to put back any pieces we screwed up. No risk; get going.

The worst decision is to make no decision at all.

Fear of Making Mistakes

Most people are afraid of making a mistake. It's "caveman brain." the sort of fight or flight feeling that is designed to stop you from being eaten by a saber tooth tiger. In the modern world, maybe this comes from our educational system where every mistake means that you are less likely to get an A. But life and business aren't multiple-choice tests. Sometimes you have to guess and test.

Make some mistakes. Learn from them.

The obsession with perfection stops too many people from making decisions.

Break the Loop

Every once in a while, I find myself grinding on a decision. In software we used to put loop counters into the code so that if we got stuck in an infinite loop, the code counter would cause a break. I've learned that grinding on a decision means that I'm stuck in a loop. So I've learned at that point to give myself three more loops before I decide one way or another.

I call this the three-strikes rule: If someone in the office brings up the same subject three times without action, I require them (including me) to take action immediately. It's surprising how quickly things get done when one stops deliberating over them.

Faster decision making means that you'll make greater progress more quickly. How will you change your decision-making strategy right now?

Lean Pharmaceuticals

Merck used Lean to shave 0 months off the normal 4 to 5 years required to bring a drug to market. The bottom line benefits of a 9-month lead could be $1.5 billion! To do so, Merck had to involve physicians, patients and payors earlier in the process. The number of new products in their pipeline tripled since they began in 2002.

What was one of the biggest delays? Data entry of the trial data. It didn't start until the trials were over (big batch). Merck switched to just-in-time data entry (smaller batches) saving 5 months.

Lean Software

The August 15, 2005, issue of *Information Week* magazine had a short article about *agile programming*, which is the latest in a long line of attempts to accelerate the software development life cycle. First came RAD (Rapid Application Development), spiral, and then XP (eXtreme Programming). All of these have been attempts to apply the principles of Lean (manufacturing) to software. The good news is "Software developers are converging on a Lean methodology for software." The bad news is "Why did it take them so long?"

When I first got into computer programming, we used the waterfall method of development. It involved several big steps: requirements, design, code, and test. It could take years to get a product ready for demonstration; it seemed more like a glacier than a waterfall. I once saw the father of the Waterfall method speak at a conference. Dr. Winston Royce said that he had a much more iterative method in his mind, but the waterfall metaphor stuck and trapped software developers until someone coined the term *spiral* to restore the iterative concept.

Agile Programming

This is the latest iteration on an iterative development methodology. It involves breaking projects into small, manageable modules and using highly iterative development.

How do we map the principles of Lean onto software? Simple. The core concepts are

- Determine and create value. Waterfall delivers the final system; agile delivers immediately usable functionality.
- Use pull instead of push systems to avoid overproduction. Waterfall pushed solutions on users; Agile pulls the functionality out of the user bit by bit.
- Use one-piece flow. Make the work flow, one piece at a time; minimize interruptions. Waterfall needed all of the modules to work; Agile creates one usable module at a time.
- Eliminate the seven speed bumps using the five S's: sort, straighten, shine, standardize, and sustain.
- Use the five "whys?" of root cause problem solving to eliminate defects.

The seven speed bumps that Lean addresses are:

Over production. Most often caused by producing large batches (i.e., programs). In the Waterfall method, you had to produce the entire system. And, since we couldn't demonstrate it to the customer, we often produced things the customer didn't want and missed the functionality that he or she required.

In Agile, the entire project is divided into small modules that can be developed into fully functional, tested, and potentially usable releases in a short amount of time, often in less than a week or a day. Each Agile release can then be evaluated by the user and tuned before the next step is taken. This is the essence of one-piece flow using small batches.

Excess inventory. Caused by overproduction. Waterfall produced a lot of code that was later determined to be of no value because we took the wrong path. Agile only lets you produce the code that is immediately valuable.

Waiting. In Waterfall, modules and programs are created and unit tested and put on the shelf to await system testing. In Agile, they are immediately tested and integrated into a deliverable work product.

Unnecessary or incorrect processing. Waterfall delivered a lot of unnecessary code. Agile helps prevent this.

Defects. Lead to repair, rework, or scrap. Waterfall could let bugs sit in code for a long time before they were discovered through testing. "Instead of tacking testing onto the end, where the temptation to truncate the testing to meet deadlines is high, it's built into the coding cycle."

The only requirement for Agile is that you know the overall architecture: protocols, interfaces, and so on before starting on the project. Otherwise, the modules won't fit together.

After many decades of wrestling with trying to apply the old economies-of-scale manufacturing techniques to software, the software world is stumbling its way to the economies of speed and the techniques of Lean.

What about your business? Can it wait decades to evolve into a more productive system through trial and error, or do you need to apply the simple rules of Lean thinking to your business now?

Lean Call Centers

Have you ever noticed how some things seem to take forever and with others, time flies by? Have you ever gotten so involved in a task that hours pass without notice? Have you ever gotten in the slowest line at the supermarket or bank? This is the essence of time distortion. Perception overrides reality.

I've had the opportunity to work with some call centers lately. Although most want to handle calls more quickly, they're overlooking two key opportunities.

1. Reduce the number of callbacks within 48 hours (They didn't answer the call correctly in the first place.)
2. Reduce the number of non-profit generating calls.

Dell's Wake-Up Call

The September 18, 2006, *Fortune* magazine focused on Dell Computer's Call Center. Here's what Michael Dell had to say about the call center.

> *Last year we would say: "Hey, let's handle the calls faster." The problem is that if you handle the call faster, you solve 90% of the problems instead of 100%. So the guy calls back. And you've just pissed him off more and you haven't accomplished a damn thing.*

This year we said we're not going to measure how long we're on the phone; we're going to measure how well we did solving the problem. In the second quarter we had two million fewer calls than we had planned.

The team was managing cost instead of managing service and quality. Stop managing [solely] for cost. Manage for a great experience.

Get the idea? If you can answer the customer's question fully and completely the first time, they won't call back and they'll be more satisfied. One of the problems, of course, is diagnosing their problem correctly to begin with. To do that, see my KnowWare ezine on the metamodel questions.

Use Call Center Insights

Because call centers are the front line for customer complaints and problems, they are often ground zero for mistakes, errors, defects, and delays that affect customers. As such, call centers are an ideal source point for improvement data. Call centers can't fix the problems, but they can create the improvement stories to drive improvement in the rest of the company.

I worked with one wireless phone company. They had 300,000 calls a month from 600,000 customers. That's one call for every two customers. You can't make money if you're spending $6 to $9 on your call center for every two customers.

What were they calling about? Billing. No bills. Incorrect bills. Improperly posted payments. At the time the company had a 17% error rate on service orders to install or remove cell phone service. These errors translated into delayed bills, overbilling, late payment charges that had to be adjusted.

Using transactional Six Sigma, we were able to drop the error rate from 17% to 3%, saving $250,000 a month in the order correction process and a substantial drop in call center volume. This wasn't the only issue driving traffic to the call center, but it was a big piece. And the carnage and costs associated with an incorrect order far exceeded the $250,000 a month in corrections, but it was difficult to measure the full impact of customer churn, adjustments, calls, and so on.

Here's My Point

Your call center can have have two big impacts on customer satisfaction.

1. Correctly diagnose and answer the customer's question right the first time (measured by call backs within 48 hours).

2. Track and measure the type and cost of customer complaints, requests, and so on as input to the improvement process for the rest of the company. The call center is also a great place to get fresh ideas for product enhancements and innovations.

Isn't it time to start leveraging the value of your call center?

Perception Is Reality

AT&T did a call center study to analyze customer perceptions of hold time. They found that customer's perceptions of hold time were almost twice as long as reality. A 1-minute wait seemed like 2 minutes. I can tell you that customers begin to abandon calls after 60 seconds. They hate to wait.

I've been working in hospitals lately. If you've ever been a patient in an emergency room, you know that time passes slowly. If a study could be done, I'd bet that a patient's perception of time distorts 1 minute into 5 or even 10 minutes. *To your customer, any delay seems longer than it really is.*

Employee Perception

Employees, on the other hand, experience something quite different. A nurse in an emergency room (ER) is often handling two or more patients simultaneously. They are multitasking. It's not unusual for 5 or 10 minutes to flash by in the blink of an eye.

ER nurses are often required to collect blood samples from patients. Any delay in collection delays lab work, and this delays diagnosis and treatment. If the collection isn't done immediately after the doctor orders it, the collection can be delayed by up to 30 minutes because the nurse simply loses track of time.

To the patient, eons have passed by; to the nurse, only a few seconds or minutes. Which one is right? Neither. Who matters most? The patient. What does wait time feel like to your customer?

From your employee's point of view, time flies. From your customer's point of view, time drags whenever they have to wait for anything. Change your processes to eliminate delay whenever and wherever possible. Customers will take notice.

The Religion of Reuse

I've been reading Michael George's book on *Fast Innovation*. Chapter 6 reminded me about something I do all of the time: *the religion of reuse*. Although Lean Six Sigma can speed up and mistake-proof your existing processes, the religion of reuse can accelerate everything about your speed to market and response to customers.

What Is Reuse?

When I worked for Bell Labs in the late 1970s, I was introduced to the *Unix* operating system and the *Shell* programming language. It was a bunch of tiny applets that could be put together easily to make remarkably complex systems. This is where I learned the religion of reuse.

Our software development team was tasked with delivering a new information system on an incredibly short timetable. We looked at the functionality and the time available, and we all agreed that we couldn't do it unless we created reusable modules for almost everything.

In a 6-month window we built 40,000 lines of code that were the equivalent of 250,000 lines of custom code. We made our deadline, and the code was much more reliable because it was used in so many places. Reuse gave us speed *and* quality.

One of my heros in software development, Fred Brooks, said "The most radical solution for constructing software is *not to construct it at all*. The reuse of software n times multiplies the productivity of developers by n." Although this thought is over 30 years old, it's still true, but most software developers feel the need to redevelop rather than reuse existing code; this is why so many software projects are late and short on functionality.

Reuse at Toyota

George reports that between 60% and 80% of Toyota's designs reuse existing materials, components, and assemblies; this radically reduces their time to market. That means that only 20% to 40% of the new functionality needs to be designed and developed. Is it any wonder Toyota can bring a new car to market in half the time of the big three?

The Law of Lead Time (Little's Law)

> Lead time = (number of things in process)/(average completion rate)

If you can double the completion rate, you can cut lead times by 50%. Reuse can help you do this by reducing the number of custom parts required to produce a final product.

The 80-80-80 Rule

George says "With reuse, the probability of meeting specs without a significant overrun is very high because you already know it has worked before." *If an innovation consists of 80% reuse, then lead time can be cut by 80% at 80% average utilization* [of existing resources].

The Advantages of Reuse

George reminds me that with reuse you

1. Avoid long lead times.

2. Reduce the challenge faced by your teams because they can focus on the vital few, not the reusable many.

3. Reduce time to develop a new product or service by 50% or more.

4. Use smaller teams which will be more agile and productive. In *Fast Innovation*, I especially like Buca's Law of Gilligan's Island: *Try not to have more people on a team than were on Gilligian's Island.*

QI Macros Software Reuse

I reuse the QI Macros SPC templates all the time to create measurement dashboards for companies. I just create an input sheet and link the input data to the p chart or XmR template. It makes it easy to create dashboards and scorecards.

Writing Reuse

Many people ask me how I write so much. Truth be told, I write a little and reuse a lot. Small ideas go into the blog. Bigger ideas go into the ezine. The blogs and ezines provide the basis for articles and books. I try never to write anything that I can't eventually use somewhere else. I even used them to create XmR c, np, p, and u dashboards for multiple measures. Reuse is a powerful tool.

It's very expensive to sell once, do once. It's manual labor. But if you can do once and sell many times, then you start to get tremendous benefits from reuse.

Invest in Reuse

It takes a little more thought and a little more time to create things that can be reused, but the instant you can reuse it, the payoff is huge. And each time you reuse it, the ROI increases.

Ask yourself

- What's common?
- What could I reuse?
- How can I take what seems unique and make it reusable?
- What is truly unique and requires customization?

You'll be surprised by the reusable assets you can develop and the speed and quality with which you can serve your market.

Get the religion of reuse. It will help you grow your business, boost your bottom line, and delight customers. And isn't that what it's all about?

Still Struggling

Most new products (e.g., a car) are 80 percent standard parts and 20 percent new ones. How can you maximize reuse of existing designs and parts so you can maximize the attention paid to the new ones?

Conclusions

In the U.S., becoming Lean appears to have gone down a path of implementing tools such as "one piece flow," "value stream mapping," "standardized work," or "kaizen events," but results have not always followed. Toyota, by way of contrast, has stayed focused on its principles and a disciplined emphasis on process improvement to obtain results such as "making a profit." "reducing lead time." "improving productivity," "achieving built-in quality," as well as "respecting human dignity of employees," etc.
—Art Smalley

If the problem is quality, then figure out where the majority of the defects are occurring and why they are occurring, fix them, and prevent recurrence immediately.

If the problem is low productivity, then analyze jobs for non-value-added versus value-added time, figure out the points of the greatest amount of waste, and eliminate it.

If the problem is on-time delivery, then figure out what products are late and why they are late and fix the root cause.

If there is too much inventory and poor flow in the plant, then by all means, draw a value stream map and get about fixing the associated points in the process!

Do More with Less

For more than a decade, managers have been urged to do more with less. The endless downsizing and rightsizing and layoffs have wounded so many employees and their families that most businesses look like the *night of the living dead*. I'd like to argue that in many businesses (e.g., health care) we've hit the end of do more with less. It's time to refocus on do more with what you've got. Offshoring, rising costs, and thinning margins are going to force everyone to figure out how to increase productivity and profitability everyday on an ongoing basis.

Lean thinking will enable you to do more with what you've got. Double your productivity and triple your profitability without changing staff.

Focus on your product or service, not your people. Do more with less is about reducing headcount more often than not. But reducing headcount when your processes are clunky only exacerbates your problem.

I was observing an emergency room at a hospital. Their motto is: "treat 'em and street 'em." A teenager comes in with a broken nose. The doctor checks him out and orders an X-ray. The patient waits while the clerk enters the order for the X-ray into a system. The medical imaging department comes over to correct the order because it wasn't right. After 20 minutes, the teen is finally wheeled over to imaging for his X-ray. Then he's wheeled back to await the reading of the image by a radiologist. And 30 to 60 minutes later the doctor gets the reading and makes a diagnosis and determines what treatment is required.

Doing more with what you've got is about simplifying, streamlining, and mistake-proofing your processes so that the product or service *flies* through your business. How do you do that?

Never set the product or service down. This is the essence of one-piece flow. If you don't set it down, you don't have to pick it back up again. Don't leave the patient to enter the order. Start moving them through the next step in their diagnosis or treatment.

Eliminate delay. Let the ER doctor do a quick read of the X-ray before the radiologist does the formal reading.

Do things in parallel. While the X-ray order is being entered into the system, start moving the patient to the imaging department or start bringing the portable X-ray equipment to the patient.

Eliminate rework and mistake-proof the system. Fix the ordering system so that the X-ray order can be entered correctly every time. Or, wheel the patient with the doctor's orders to medical imaging, and let *them* enter the order so that it's right the first time.

It's time to shift your focus from your people to your product or service. Simplify, streamline, and mistake-proof every aspect of the process so that the product or service (in this case a patient) *flies* through the process. Accelerate your *product's experience*. Blazing speed and mistake-proof processes will deliver more with what you've already got. Customers will notice and you'll get more business, and you'll need your people to handle the load.

Lean for Doctor's Office

When I was 21, a pickup truck backed into me, knocking me down so hard that my glasses fell off and a class ring I was wearing flew off. I didn't think much about it, but later in life I started having some back problems. A friend referred me to a chiropractor.

I've been going to him for 15 years about twice a year when I get jammed up. He straightens me out.

Recently I called for an appointment but he was out of town. His voice mail referred me to a nearby chiropractor. I called and made an appointment. Although the treatment to straighten me out was pretty much the same, the experience was magically different. The new chiropractor runs a Lean practice; my existing chiropractor runs a mass production one.

Current Chiropractor's Process

My existing chiropractor has you sign in and fill out a sheet describing the symptoms. His assistant then leads you into one of three examination rooms, *where you wait*. After the treatment, the doctor spends a few minutes filling out paperwork to be added to your file.

In essence, he has a batch size of 3. After the treatment, the doctor spends a few minutes filling out paperwork to be added to your file.

A typical visit takes about an hour. I didn't realize how dissatisfactory this was until I visited the new chiropractor.

New Chiropractor's Process

I arrived a few minutes before my appointment expecting to have to fill out some paperwork. Instead, the doctor was ready and I was immediately led into her *single* exam room. She asked me a few questions and then started the exam. When she finished the treatment, she immediately turned to a computer terminal and using a touch screen, entered her notes about my treatment (in essence an electronic medical record which means little filing). She asked me to fill out some basic paperwork on my way out. She suggested I do a follow-up with my chiropractor in about a week.

I was in and out in 15 minutes. *I couldn't believe it*. And she was $12 cheaper! Then I realized that she has a much smaller office (fewer exam rooms), so her fixed costs are lower. She uses electronic medical records, so her filing room is much smaller. I knew I had to get another glimpse into this operation. So, since my chiropractor was still going to be out of town, I scheduled a follow-up visit.

The following week, I walked in as the new chiropractor was finishing with her current patient. I was immediately led into the exam room. We talked briefly about my progress, she adjusted my back, I paid and I was out in 15 minutes. *Wow!* Now that's my kind of patient care.

With my existing chiropractor, I knew that if I arrived a little late, I'd still have plenty of time to do the paperwork and get in some reading. With the new chiropractor, I know that I'd better be on time. Her speed demands my timeliness without ever having to say anything, post any signs or say anything.

Time Is Money!

My current chiropractor created an assembly line with three patients in the queue at any time. This means we have to wait 20 to 30 minutes in the exam room reading out-of-date magazines to fill the time while our back continues to spasm or be in pain.

I realized that my medical doctor also has a waiting room and numerous exam rooms to create a batch of three to five patients. It takes an hour to see her as well, even if you go first thing in the morning.

This new chiropractor understands the secrets of one-piece flow. One patient at a time, one exam room, and *no "work" in process*. Notes are entered immediately before you leave the room, not written on a piece of paper that needs to be filed.

So am I going to switch chiropractors on the basis of my experience? Let's examine the data I've collected so far.

Current Doctor	New Doctor
60 minutes	15 minutes
1	$12 cheaper!

I figure my time is worth a lot. I can do a lot in 45 minutes that I can't do if I'm sitting idle in an exam room. What would you do?

If you study any typical mass-production doctor's office, you'll find that the doctor is always busy, *but the patient is idle 90% of the time*. To accelerate patient flow, you have to *focus on the patient, not the doctor*. You have to optimize the patient's time, not the doctor's. And when you do, you'll find that you get greater productivity and patient satisfaction, but you have to unlearn the mass-production techniques of Henry Ford and embrace the simple principles of the Toyota Production System and Lean. The future belongs to those who embrace the principles of Lean and Six Sigma. Will your business be one of them?

The Biggest Barrier to Lean Six Sigma

I recently reread the 1990 book *The Machine that Changed the World* by James Womack, et al. It's about a 5-year MIT study of the future of the automobile. The essence of the message: U.S. and other manufacturers need to embrace Lean and the Toyota Production System (TPS) if they want to survive.

It's been 16 years since that book was published, but last year GM closed plants, laid of tens of thousands of workers, and offered all kinds of incentives to get customers to buy their excess inventory. So did Ford.

Overproduction Is Waste

In the 1990 book, the authors report that 8 million more cars were produced than the 50 million demanded by customers. They said "The world has an acute shortage of competitive Lean-production capacity and a vast glut of uncompetitive mass-production capacity. In the absence of a crisis threatening the very survival of the company, only limited progress seems to be possible. GM is the most striking example."

Haste Makes Waste, But Speed Makes Profit

Here's the comparison between GM and Toyota.

	GM	Toyota
Gross assembly hours	40.7	18.0
Assembly defects per car	1.3	0.45
Assembly space per car	8.1	4.8
Inventories of parts	2 weeks	2 hours
Engineering hours per new car	3 million	1.7 million
Lead time for new car	60 months	46 months

Less space, less time, less inventory, fewer defects. Is it any wonder Toyota makes more profit than the big three automakers combined?

Lean Organization

The truly Lean plant has two key organizational features.

1. It transfers the maximum number of tasks and responsibilities to the workers actually adding value to the product.

2. It has in place a system for detecting defects that quickly traces every problem once discovered, to its ultimate cause.

The authors state "Lean production is a superior way for humans to make things. It provides better products in wider variety at lower cost. Equally important, it provides more challenging and fulfilling work for employees at every level, from the factory to headquarters. *The whole world should adopt Lean production, and as quickly as possible.*"

GM and the other mass-production automobile manufacturers in the world have had decades to pick up this ball and run with it. Unfortunately, when you fall behind in the Lean Six Sigma game, it's hard to catch up. A recent issue of the AIAG (Automotive Industry Action Group) newsletter, *Actionline*, has an article that argues that *Embracing Heavy-Truck "Boutique" model could lure buyers back to showrooms*. Has this guy checked out the rising cost of gasoline?

The main barrier to Lean Six Sigma, as far as I can tell, isn't the methods or tools, but the thickness of the human skull. As one prospect told me at a recent trade show, "We won't do it [Lean Six Sigma] until they force us to do it." Jobs continue to migrate offshore and downsized employees continue to whine, but they don't seem to realize that this culture of incompetence is a huge part of the problem.

It Won't Work for Me

In the beginning, everyone resisted kanban [Lean], because it seemed to contradict conventional wisdom. It took 10 years to establish kanban at Toyota.
—Taiichi Ohno

Eighty percent of U.S. workers are employed in services, 19% in manufacturing, and 1% in agriculture. Maybe this is why so many people tell me that Lean Six Sigma is just for manufacturing. It doesn't work for services. Hospital workers tell me it works for inpatients, but not outpatients. No matter who I talk to, they are all trying to convince themselves that it works for someone else, but it can't work for me because *I'm different.*

Everybody wants to feel special, different, and unique. Get over it! From a purely process perspective, every process has suppliers, inputs, processes, outputs, and customers (SIPOC).

If your internal or external customers experience any kind of defects, mistakes, errors, delays, or slowness of service, then *you can use Lean Six Sigma make your business better, faster, and cheaper before someone else beats you to the punch.*

Or you can just hope for the best and pray that your company survives long enough for you to get a pension and benefits. But, according to Shell's study of corporate longevity, few companies live longer than 40 years. And why not? Hardening of the attitudes, inflexibility, and failure to adapt to an ever-changing world.

You can either lead the pack or struggle to catch up. Stop pretending that Lean Six Sigma won't work for you. Stop pretending it won't work because you're special; you're not. Figure out how to adapt it to your business. Reduce delay, eliminate defects, reduce costs, increase productivity, and enhance profitability before your global competitors get ahead of you.

In the early 1900s, most people were engaged in agriculture. But farming has been simplified, automated, and streamlined so that only 1% of the people are required to do the work. Then people moved into factories which have also been simplified, streamlined, optimized, and automated and now offshored to less-costly workers. And now people are migrating into services which will be simplified, streamlined, optimized, and automated, and offshored (e.g., call centers in Bangalore).

If Toyota can build cars in the United States using Lean Six Sigma principles as well as they can do it in Japan, then *the problem isn't geography, the problem isn't process. It isn't Lean Six Sigma methods or tools; it's mindset.* Change yours before a crisis changes you.

QUIZ

1. **The two pillars of Lean are**
   A. _____
   B. _____

2. **Lean principles can be used in**
   A. government.
   B. health care.
   C. manufacturing.
   D. service.
   E. all of the above

3. **The primary goal of Lean is to**
   A. reduce costs.
   B. eliminate the seven speed bumps.
   C. eliminate the 5S's.
   D. stop the line.
   E. achieve economies of scale.

4. **The seven speed bumps of Lean are**
   • _____
   • _____
   • _____
   • _____
   • _____
   • _____
   • _____

5. **The five S's are**
   • _____
   • _____
   • _____
   • _____
   • _____

6. **Lean reduces**
   A. delay.
   B. scrap.
   C. waste.
   D. *muda.*
   E. cost.
   F. all of the above

7. **Lean helps reduce or eliminate**
   A. value added (VA).
   B. non-value added (NVA).

8. **To identify unnecessary delays, use a**
   A. value stream map.
   B. spaghetti diagram.

9. **To identify unnecessary movement, use a**
   A. value stream map.
   B. spaghetti diagram.

10. **You already understand Lean work cell design because you**
    A. use a computer.
    B. drive a car.
    C. live in a house with a kitchen.

11. **Lean achieves cost reduction by**
    A. small lot sizes.
    B. quick changeover.
    C. production leveling.
    D. all of the above

EXERCISES

1. Use the 5S principles on one of your most messy production or service delivery processes.

2. Hang pedometers on your workers to get a sense of how far they travel in a given day.

3. Diagram the spaghetti-like travel in one work area that seems to require too much movement of people or materials. How would you start moving machines and workstations around right now to create a smoother flow with less travel?

4. Map the value stream in one mission-critical process using the QI Macros Value Stream template. Figure out the cycle time, changeover time, wait time, work in progress, and so on, so that you fully understand how the process works. Identify the value-added and non-value-added activities in this process.

5. Redesign the work flow into cells using one-piece flow, pull, and kanban.
   A. How can you create U-shaped work cells?
   B. How can you reduce the movement of people or materials?
   C. What machines can you right-size?

6. Develop a value-added analysis. Using a process flowchart, have participants do a value-added flow analysis of the macro process using the QI Macros value-added flow analysis template. Where in their existing process is most of the wasted (idle) time and rework? What improvements could they initiate to eliminate the waste?

chapter 3

A Faster Hospital in Five Days

Too many people think that Lean and Six Sigma only apply to manufacturing. Nothing could be farther from the truth. Leading hospitals are using Lean principles to accelerate patient flow. Health care is clearly a service business. If hospitals can do it, you can too.

CHAPTER OBJECTIVES

In this chapter, you will

- Learn how to use Lean to accelerate patient flow in hospitals
- Learn how to use Lean to get a faster emergency department
- Learn how to use Lean to get faster operating rooms
- Learn how to use Lean to get faster lab results
- Learn how to use Lean to get faster radiology

With all of the hoopla about health care reform, there's one huge missing piece; health care is going to have to get dramatically faster, better, and cheaper to help pay for the changes. Each of the nation's 5700+ hospitals must find ways to cut millions of dollars in unnecessary costs over the next decade. This may sound difficult considering that half of all hospitals lose money. Most hospitals exist on a 4% to 5% margin. But Lean can help hospitals start getting faster, better, and cheaper in just a few days.

One of the key principles of Lean thinking is to eliminate delays that consume up to 95% of the total cycle time (57 minutes per hour). If you've ever been a patient in a hospital emergency room or nursing unit bed, you know there are lots of delays. Over the years, health care has made tremendous strides in reducing cycle time in various aspects of care. Outpatient surgeries are one example: Arrive in the morning and leave in the afternoon. No bed required. But there is still room for improvement.

Goal: Accelerate the Patient's Experience of Health Care

Over the last decade I've consulted with many hospitals on all kinds of projects. Perhaps the most powerful tool that can be applied immediately to start slashing cycle times, medical mistakes, and cost is Lean. And it doesn't have to take forever. With the right focus and the right people in the room, it only takes a few days to find ways to speed up any health care process in a way that will reduce errors and boost profits.

Every hospital seems to have the same problem: patient flow. This shows up in many ways.

- Patient dissatisfaction
- In the ED (emergency department)
  - Divert (no ambulances due to overcrowding)
  - Patient boarding (holding patients until a bed is available)
  - LWOBS (Leaving without being seen)
  - Turnaround times of 4 hours or more
- In the OR (Operating Room) delays, turnaround times
- Imaging (i.e., X-ray) delays, turnaround times
- Lab (blood, chemistry, urine, microbiology analysis) delays, turnaround times

- Bed management delays (assigning beds to admitted patients)
- Late discharges (getting patients out of beds when they are discharged)
- Long patient length of stay (LOS) due to mistakes, errors, falls, and so on
- Lost revenue (all of these problems guzzle cash)

What one element is critical to both patient flow and satisfaction? Time—wait time and turnaround time.

A Faster Emergency Department (ED) in Five Days

Between 1996 and 2006, ED visits increased from 90 million to 119 million, but the number of EDs decreased from 4019 to 3833. The increase in patients and decrease in providers has resulted in overcrowding, boarding, wait times, and LWOBS (leaving without being seen), all of which lead to poorer outcomes and patient dissatisfaction.

In 2009, Press Ganey found that ED turnaround times still average *over 4 hours*, basically unchanged over the last decade. In stark contrast, Robert Wood Johnson Hospital, winner of the 2005 Baldridge Award, has ED turnaround times of

- *38 minutes for discharged patients* (three-quarters of all ED patients)
- *90 minutes for admitted patients*, **not 4 hours**

How is this possible? How did they do it? *They systematically eliminated the delays between registration, triage, exam, lab, imaging, and discharge or admission/ transport.* Because of reduced turnaround times, they offer a 15-minute door-to-nurse and a 30-minute door-to-doctor guarantees. Faster turnaround times enabled the hospital to grow by over 10% per year requiring the addition of a new nursing wing.

HINT *Faster patient flow means greater patient satisfaction, better outcomes and more money!*

Patient Satisfaction in the ED. Studies have shown that patient satisfaction begins to decrease when ED LOS exceeds 2 hours. There are two populations of patients who visit the ED, so let's first look at patients who get discharged.

If it only takes a couple of minutes to see the triage nurse, get registered, be examined by a doctor, then the total time spent on any one patient is perhaps

9 minutes. So why does it take most EDs over 2 hours to handle each patient? Sure, some patients need lab work (11 minutes) and others need radiology, but most of those tests take less than an hour. We're still looking at 35 to 60 minutes, not 2 hours or more.

If we look at admitted patients, they are taken (by ambulance or waiting room) into the ED immediately without having to wait. They see the doctor immediately. Tests are done STAT. Registrations are done at the bedside. Nursing floor bed assignments take only a few minutes. Nursing reports are fast. Transport to the ICU, cardiac care, or medical/surgical floors take only 15 to 20 minutes. These patients should fly through the ED, but they take longer than the discharged patients, two to three times longer. Sure they have to be stabilized, but why does it take hours to get them into an assigned bed?

The answer, across the board, is delay. There is too much time *between* clinical activities. The admission staff is busy, so patients have to wait. The triage nurse is busy, so patients have to wait. For those readers familiar with the Theory of Constraints (TOC), the triage nurse is a bottleneck. The ED boards patients who should be in a nursing unit, so patients have to wait. The ED nurse can't reach the floor nurse to give a report and vice versa. Neither nurse can leave to transport the patient. Beds are available but not staffed. And so on.

Lean thinking focuses on a key metric called *takt time*. *Takt* means "rhythm." For the sake of simple analysis, let's say that the ER handles 120 patients per day. That would equate to five per hour or one every 12 minutes.

Unfortunately, patients don't arrive in a rhythmic fashion; they arrive in waves. The biggest wave is between 3 PM and 9 PM due to rush hour traffic accidents, parents picking up sick kids from daycare, and so on. The smallest wave is usually 3 AM to 9 AM. So let's say patients arrive two to three per hour at off-peak times and ten per hour at peak times.

That's one every 6 minutes at peak times.

Still Struggling

Follow a patient or two through the ED from the time they arrive until they are discharged or admitted. You'll quickly discover that the patient sits and waits for most of the time they are in the ED. They wait in waiting rooms. They wait in exam rooms. These delays are unnecessary. Eliminate them.

Staffing for Speed

Most ERs of this size, at peak demand, have

- One triage nurse to evaluate walk-in patients by level of acuity with an average of 6 minutes per patient.
- One or two registrars to handle insurance and hospital paperwork: 6 to 12 minutes per patient.
- Two MDs (one off peak): 12 minutes per patient (some less, some more on the basis of acuity). One trauma patient can completely consume one or both MDs.
- One lab technician to collect blood samples (60% of patients require lab work: 10 minutes per patient).
- One nurse for every two patients (sometimes with 1:1 nursing for traumas): 12 minutes per patient alternating.

Lab work often takes 45 to 60 minutes start to finish (but only 11 minutes of value-added time, the rest is travel and delay). A third of all patients will also need some sort of medical imaging (X-ray, CT scan, MRI, and so forth) which also takes 45 to 60 minutes (most of it travel and wait time).

Transfer Time

Estimate that 25% of ER patients will be converted to inpatients. That means 30 per day or 5 per unit. Traumas go to ICU. Chest pain patients go to telemetry. The rest go to medical or surgical beds.

How long does it take to move an admitted patient to an inpatient bed? It shouldn't take any longer than 30 minutes although most hospitals run longer than this. Why? Trying to sync up the ER and floor nurse to give a report on the patient's condition and diagnosis.

Solution: Fax or voice mail the report and transport the patient to the floor as soon as a bed is ready.

Faster Door-to-Balloon (D2B) Time in Five Days

In 2004, The ED at UMass Memorial Health Care reduced D2B from 180 minutes to less than 60 minutes. To optimize D2B times, they measured and optimized the four key steps: (1) door-to-EKG completion, (2) data to diagnosis, (3) diagnosis to decision, and (4) decision to balloon. Door-to-EKG time fell to

1 to 2 minutes; this enabled the ED physician to stay in the room to diagnose, decide, and call in the surgical team. On-call teams were scheduled with at least one team member within 20 minutes of the hospital. Valet parking of team cars cut 5 minutes off the time. Electronic EKG transmission from ambulances to the ED removed additional delays allowing patients to go directly to the cardiac catheterization lab bypassing the ED and reducing D2B times to less than 50 minutes. These changes reduced AMI mortality to 11.7 percent, significantly below the 16.6 percent national average.

Lessons learned from D2B times were applied to door-to-incision time for vascular surgery and door-to-diuretic times for congestive heart failure patients.

Imagine a Faster ED

Imagine an emergency room where patients walk in and something surprising happens.

1. They use the magnetic strip on the driver's license, insurance card, or credit card to check in and register using a kiosk. The kiosk automatically takes pictures of all of these IDs and uses the data to find the patient's medical history, validate insurance, and so on.

2. Completing registration this way triggers a pull signal that brings the next nurse in the rotation to collect the patient from the entry area and move the patient to an exam room.

3. Entering the exam room and gathering the patient's vital signs triggers a pull signal for the next ED doctor in the rotation.

4. The doctor examines the patient with the nurse available and requests any tests or X-rays using a handheld device that kicks off the orders.

   a. The nurse draws any blood or other samples required and either sends them to the lab for processing or uses point-of-care testing to get results in 11 minutes or less.

   b. The nurse transports the patient to imaging if needed.

5. Completion of the tests triggers a pull signal to the ED doctor to collect the results, diagnose, and recommend treatment.

6. The doctor then initiates treatment. Any teaching material or paperwork is prepackaged and ready for the nurse to prepare the patient for discharge or admission.

7. Initiating admission kicks off a pull signal for a bed in the appropriate unit. If there isn't enough staff in that unit to handle the admission, a pull signal may request an on-call nurse to come to work.

8. Instead of all work being done manually, as most of this is now, it's all carefully orchestrated and technically linked to minimize all delay. Many of these activities can happen in parallel, not sequentially as they do today.

A discharged patient is in and out in 30 minutes. An admitted patient is in a nursing unit bed in 60 minutes. Of course there will be exceptions, a rush hour accident may tie up one of the doctors, but most patients are discharged. Finding ways to handle them in one-piece flow will dramatically improve ED performance.

Using Lean, Providence Health and Services reduced turnaround times in five hospitals ED; this has cut the ambulance diversion rates from 26% to 3%. Every ambulance is worth $7000 or more to a hospital's bottom line. Slashing diversion rates will boost the bottom line and improve outcomes because if your hospital's ED is closer, the patient has a better chance of survival than if he or she has to commute to a distant hospital for care.

Using Lean, St. Vincent Indianapolis Hospital cut the number of steps ED nurses take to get the supplies by 78%.

How could Lean help your ED provide faster, better care to more patients?

A Faster Operating Room (OR) in Five Days

Hospital operating rooms don't operate with anywhere near the efficiency of *Gray's Anatomy* on television. Surgeries run long. Some are cancelled. Some surgeons are faster than others. Elective surgeries sometimes block emergency surgeries. Every hospital wrestles with these problems.

Copenhagen University Hospital wanted to reduce the time between surgical operations. The improvement team found that too much time (60+ minutes) was spent

- Investigating if the patient got required information from the surgeon (10 minutes)
- Unpacking individual sterile disposables (30 minutes)
- Waiting for missing devices (5 trips per surgery)

- Waiting for the patient to regain consciousness to be transferred to recovery (20 minutes)
- Waiting for transport to recovery (10 minutes)

Using the tools of Lean, the team analyzed the process and implemented countermeasures to save 60 minutes.

- Surgeon draws an X on patient's wristband when the patient has been informed about the operation allowing anesthesia to begin. (No more checking!)
- Prepackaged sterile disposables replace individual disposables saving two theater nurses and 30 minutes. (This was the longest delay.)
- Standard checklists ensure that all materials are gathered before the operation starts. (Mistake proofing.)
- Anesthetic depth was adjusted so that the patient wakes up when operation is finished.
- Hospital orderlies move patients to recovery immediately.

Obviously, saving an hour per surgery will dramatically affect productivity and profitability without affecting patient safety or outcomes.

Apply the tools of Lean to a hospital OR and watch it accelerate patient flow.

Faster Medical Imaging in Five Days

Another roadblock to patient flow in most hospitals is medical imaging (i.e., X-ray). It's not like on *House*, were the doctors can do their own MRIs and the MRI is always available. Not only does it take a while to get the patient scheduled into the queue and imaged; it takes time to get the image read. And as many as 15 out of 100 have to be redone!

North Shore University Hospital wanted to improve patient throughput on its CT scanners to decrease length of stay and increase patient satisfaction. Average turnaround time (TAT) was 20.7 hours and varied from 8 to 34 hours. Target for improvement? 16 hours. Identified problem areas included

- Manual scheduling leading to calls from nursing units
- Time-consuming prep and delivery of contrast media

- CT tech travel to requisition printer (6480 ft per day; even walking fast, that's probably 30 minutes a day)
- Transporter availability and travel (432 ft per day)

After analysis of these various issues, the improvement team implemented several countermeasures.

- Relocated requisition printer in between the two CTs, saving over 6000 ft per day of unnecessary travel. (*Hint:* Move machines closer to the user.)
- Dedicated patient transporter.
- Excel-based schedule maintained in imaging and viewable by all nursing units. This reduced phone calls and cancellations due to improper patient prep or availability.
- Instead of a rigid schedule with no room for stat orders, a pull system adjusted the patient transport and scan to accommodate just-in-time stat scans.
- Contrast preparation was reassigned to the evening shift, refrigerated and delivered during the transporter's morning run for inpatients.
- One CT was dedicated to complex procedures, and the second was dedicated to routine high-volume procedures to maximize patient flow.
- Staffing was adjusted to demand.

The average TAT fell from 20.7 to 6.45 hours, resulting in

- 200 additional inpatient scans per month
- 60 additional outpatient scans per month
- $375,000 in additional revenue
- cancellations due to improper prep dropping from 30.6% to 22.7%

Similarly, St. Joseph Mercy Oakland Hospital in Pontiac, Michigan, used Lean to redesign the lab, radiology, and supply processes, reducing turnaround time by 50% in radiology.

In 2004, Newton-Wellesley Hospital had radiology wait times of 45 minutes or more. Before buying another X-ray machine, they did a little Lean analysis: Technicians were walking around too much, "collecting paperwork, ferrying patients to changing rooms, calling doctors to double-check orders." A few simple changes cut turnaround times to 25 minutes.

Mass General's Proton Beam facility was fully booked. Simple analysis found that patients requiring anesthesia had to wait for an anesthesiologist when they arrived for an appointment. By simply booking anesthesia patients as a group and scheduling an anesthesiologist for that time period, patient volume went from 29 to 39 a day (a 33% increase in throughput) without adding any hours of operation.

Want a faster imaging department? Use the tools of Lean to reduce delay and accelerate patient flow.

A Faster Lab in Five Days

Every hospital ED depends on lab work for 70 patients out of every 100 (most urban EDs handle around 100 patients a day). While the actual test may take only 6 to 12 minutes, the elapsed time from doctor's order to finished report can be an hour or more. Some of the samples get misplaced and are further delayed.

One 2400-sq-ft hospital lab decided to reduce turnaround times; this would reduce ED turnaround times and the length of stay in the nursing units. Using pedometers, they tracked their travel time for a week. They conducted what's known as a 5S (sort, straighten, shine, standardize, and sustain) to clean the area of 10 years' worth of clutter (4 hours), then mapped the value stream (4 hours) and redesigned the work flow (4 hours).

Using the advanced tools of Lean—Post-it notes and a flip chart—the lab team was able to redesign the lab to reduce

- Staff movement   54% (goal 30%)
- Floor space   17% (goal 10%)
- Phlebotomist travel   55% (21,096 ft ~ 4 mi ~ 1.5 FTE)
- Tech travel   40% (2304 ft; 0.15 FTE over three shifts)
- Sample travel   55% 23,400 ft and 7 hours of delay per 24 hours

Some changes could be implemented immediately, others required coordination to move machinery and recalibrate. The lab got a lot faster with less than 2 days of effort.

Want a faster lab? Use the tools of Lean to slash turnaround times.

A Faster Hospital Design in Five Days

The vast majority of health care organizations…are not really "designed" at all. The elements of most general hospital buildings, technologies, clinical services—have accreted over time.

—Richard M. J. Bohmer

I recently worked with an architectural firm to come up with a Lean design for two rural hospitals. Although the health care company asking for the design had been a longtime customer, the new designs were up for grabs.

Most rural hospitals are designed long and flat (which to me meant lots of walking for employees and patients and no sunlight for many patients). The architecture firm told me that the lab could be anywhere, to which I said "Nonsense, it should be next to the ED!" Everyone in health care, including architecture firms, have limiting beliefs about how health care should be conducted. "The lab can be anywhere" is one such belief.

Patients want easy access to the ED, lab, and radiology, rooms with sunlight and minimal travel (I'm sick; don't make me walk a mile!). Clinicians want many of the same things. The ED needs to be close to ICU to minimize transport. Transport between the ED and nursing units needs to be short and fast. Due to variability in patient census, hospital operations might want smaller nursing units (smaller batch sizes) so that some could be shut down during slow seasons.

The architecture firm had brought in other Lean experts who baffled them with takt time and value-streams and SIPOCs and so on. I pulled out several sizes of Post-it notes and started configuring various designs. I started from the patient's point of view (patient-centric, not physician-centric). In a few hours we'd come up with a couple of designs that minimized movement of ED patients, inpatients, outpatients, visiting families, clinicians, food service, and supplies while optimizing the number of patient rooms with sunlight. When you abandon what you know about how to deliver health care and focus on the patient, it's easy to come up with fresh ways of doing business that are better for everyone involved.

At the end of my 1 day with the architecture firm, I suggested they use the Post-it note approach to pitching the designs to their client. Get the client involved in configuring the overall design! What a radical idea! And guess what? They won the contract for both hospitals.

Similarly, in 2008 Seattle Children's Hospital scaled back a planned expansion from 110,000 to 75,000 feet using Lean to maintain the planned functionality. By building a scale model of the new facility and walking through the mockup, teams quickly spotted and corrected design flaws; this cut design time from months to weeks.

Efficiencies and inefficiencies are designed into most hospitals. It's hard to undo a building design. Individual units can be redesigned for greater efficiency however.

A Faster Nursing Unit in Five Days

Want faster nursing units? Nurses have to walk too far to get what they need. One redesigned nursing unit cut travel by 67% resulting in improved patient satisfaction, nursing satisfaction, and clinical outcomes. The unit got faster in a matter of days.

Delnor Hospital designated a nurse to handle maternity discharges; this cut the length of stay by 10 hours, making an $80 million expansion of the maternity ward *unnecessary*.

Additionally, nurses hesitate to take patients before shift changes, doctors make rounds at different times, orders are issued but not executed for a period of time, patients are discharged but no family member can collect them, and on it goes. Delay, delay, delay.

The solution to this problem? Eliminate the delay.

Hospital Beds

Most hospitals have at least

One intensive care unit (6 to 12 beds)

One telemetry unit for monitoring heart patients (12 to 20 beds)

Two medical or surgical units (15 to 30 beds)

Length of stay (e.g., takt time) in most of these units is 2 to 3 days.

Patients also arrive from the operating room (3 to 5 per day) and direct admissions from local physician offices (3 to 5 per day). Elective surgeries can place a strain on the hospital bed supply which forces the ED to board patients waiting for a bed.

On a peak day, any unit can admit 10 to 12 patients and discharge 10 to 12. The sum of these two is called the *bed turn rate* (20 to 24).

Faster Discharge

How long does it take to discharge a patient once the order is written? 2 to 6 hours. (Delays for lab, radiology, oxygen, medical equipment, family or other transportation.) Target: 60 minutes.

Solutions: Get physicians to discharge pending improved results 24 hours in advance. This allows nurses to do the paperwork and teaching required to prepare the patient for ongoing recovery at home.

Prioritize discharge lab or radiology work ahead of other inpatients and after ED/OR.

Set up home health requirements (e.g., oxygen, walker, etc.) in advance.

Get at least two phone numbers of family members who can pick up the patient during the time when they are most likely to be discharged (when the doctors do their rounds).

Faster Housekeeping

How long does it take to clean a bed after a patient leaves? 20 to 30 minutes (delay in starting 15 to 90 minutes).

Solution: Eliminate the delay. Are you staffed for peak bed turnover times? Probably not. Could the housekeeping team operate like a SWAT team, swarming a newly vacated room to cut cleaning time in half? Ask the housekeeping staff; they have ideas.

Take the pulse of your hospital. What's your rhythm? What's your wait time?

The Problem Isn't Where You Think It Is

Every department—ED, ICU, med/surgical nursing floors, radiology, lab, housekeeping, bed management, and so on—think they are doing the best job they can. Everyone is working hard, everyone wants to do a good job, everyone wants to serve the patient, but . . .

INSIGHT 1 *The patient is idle most of the time.*

Rule 1. Stop watching your clinical staff. Start watching the patient, because patient idle 57 minutes out of every hour of the total turnaround time.

Patient's length of stay doesn't increase all at once. It increases in 10- to 30-minute intervals.

- Why? Because the patient is idle, waiting on the next step in his or her diagnosis or treatment.
- Why is the patient waiting? Because the steps in his or her care haven't been linked up to eliminate delays.
- Why haven't the patient been linked up? Because no one is measuring and monitoring the time it takes for each step to get started.

Everybody seems to know how long it takes to do their job. It takes bed management 5 to 10 minutes to assign a bed, assuming one is available. It takes 15 to 20 minutes to transport a patient to a bed. It takes housekeeping 22 minutes to clean an ICU or medical/surgical bed. The ED triage nurse takes only a few minutes to evaluate a patient. The ED doctor only takes a few minutes to examine the patient.

But nobody knows how long the delays are between each of these steps.

Rule 2. Start measuring the delays *between* steps in the patient's care, because this is how LOS increases and patient satisfaction *decreases*.

INSIGHT 2   *Walking is waste!*

Any amount of time that a doctor or nurse or technician spends walking is waste. Reduce the distance he or she travels, and it will improve patient satisfaction and outcomes.

INSIGHT 3   *Speed is critical to patient satisfaction!*

Unfortunately, current hospital management practices discourage accelerating patient flow. The staff worries that if you move patients too quickly, they might have to send nurses home because of empty beds. Nurses depend on their income just like the rest of us, so they think they are actually being punished if they reduce patient delays.

As Robert Wood Johnson Hospital discovered, however, **faster patient flow leads to more jobs, not fewer.** Patients are smart; they can tell a faster hospital from a slower one.

Some of the clinical staff thinks that accelerating patient flow means making the clinicians work faster or harder. But accelerating patient flow has little to do with clinicians; it has to do with reorganizing the work to get faster *patients*.

The clinical staff also worries that haste makes waste, that faster turnaround times will lead to poorer outcomes, but that's only true if the clinician hurries. Accelerating patient flow isn't about making clinicians faster; it focuses on speeding up the patient. **Reducing delays between steps in patient treatment will actually give the clinician *more time with the patient,* not less.**

When the patient is handled in one, seamless interaction, there is less time spent learning what happened in the previous step (e.g., reading the chart) and more time spent with the patient. **Result: improved patient satisfaction.**

Handling a patient seamlessly also prevents the opportunity to miss a step or do a step twice. Simply reducing delays will cut errors by 50%. **Result: Fewer medical errors.**

Take the Dominos Challenge

Dominos made the guarantee that they could cook a pizza and deliver it to your home in 30 minutes or it was free. It began a revolutionary shift in customer expectations.

Google taught everyone that they could find anything they want immediately and often for *free*.

Customers used to want better, faster, and cheaper products and services; now they want everything free, perfect, and *now*, including health care.

That shift in customer expectations is hitting hospitals. Robert Wood Johnson Hospital offers a *guarantee* of 30 minutes from door to doctor in their ED. You might consider setting the same kinds of objectives.

- 30 minutes from door to doctor in the ED
- 30 minutes from bed requested to patient in bed
- 30 minutes from lab/radiology order to execution
- 30 minutes from discharge order to patient discharged
- 30 minutes from dirty room to clean room, dirty OR to clean OR

HINT *A faster patient means better health care. Take the Dominos challenge.*

Still Struggling

In 1999, Robert Wood Johnson Hospital instituted a 15-30 program: see a nurse in 15 minutes and a doctor in 30 minutes or your ED visit is free. They did it without losing money, you can too.

Less Inventory Means Better Care

Another important aspect of Lean is the concept that *inventory is fundamentally evil.*

New York City Health and Hospitals Corp (HHC) found its 11 hospital storage rooms stocked with over 10 million dollars in out-of-date supplies. By switching to just-in-time inventory, fresh supplies arrive as needed 5 days a week; this cut inventory in half and saved $5 million.

Denver Health used Lean to save $27 million in supplies and increased productivity.

How to Get a Faster Hospital in Five Days

> *The only realistic hope for substantially improving care delivery is for the old guard to launch a revolution from within. Existing players must redesign themselves.*
> —Richard M. J. Bohmer

Although the case studies in this chapter offer some constructive ideas, most clinical staffs will not implement an improvement *unless they have a hand in its design.*

Improvements Are Possible If It Helps the Patient or the Provider

Health care professionals want to help create improvements that

- Increase patient safety and satisfaction
- Improve quality of care
- Reduce lead or turnaround times
- Improve productivity without compromising patient outcomes
- Reduce medical errors

How Is It Possible to Get a Faster Hospital in 5 Days or Less? It Takes a Change in Focus

> *In the traditional world, medicine is organized around what doctors do rather than what patients need.*
> — Thomas H. Lee

Delos M. Cosgrove, CEO of Cleveland Clinic, was one of the first to make a serious commitment to putting patients first and measuring that commitment. "At first," says Thomas H. Lee, "the new data were available only to insiders; now they are published, warts and all, on the clinic's website."

Seattle's Virginia Mason Medical Center took the patients first idea to heart and added a corollary: Physicians and everyone else come second. Instead of making cancer patients commute all over for care, clinicians come to patient care rooms filled with natural light.

"These organizations understand that medical knowledge is now too voluminous to be stored in the heads of individual physicians," says Richard M. J. Bohmer of Harvard, "and must instead be embedded in protocols and routines."

Intermountain Healthcare in Utah found that about 70 conditions make up 90% of its caseload. Having protocols for these vital few conditions helps improve care, outcomes, and turnaround times.

How Is It Possible to Get a Faster Hospital in 5 Days or Less? It Takes a Team

Health care organizations around the world are guided by the question "What care can we provide with the resources we have? The question should be reversed: "What resources are required and how should they be configured for the care we need to provide."
— Richard M. J. Bohmer

1. Gather a team that believes it's *possible* to improve patient flow (e.g., ED doctor, ED nurses, ED clerk, and ED admissions). Some people just don't believe it's possible; if so, they won't be useful on the team. Don't load the team with skeptics.

2. *Prework.* Use pedometers to gather travel data about the clinicians. Identify and collect wait times for patients between steps in treatment.

3. Have a trained facilitator assist the team in identifying the major delays and unnecessary movement of people or supplies using tools like value stream mapping and spaghetti diagramming. Have the team identify possible countermeasures to these problems.

4. Implement the countermeasures and measure results.

   • Implement process-oriented improvements immediately

   • Move machines or supplies to more convenient locations immediately

   • Schedule and manage more complicated changes (e.g., IT systems changes, hardware changes, etc.)

5. Verify that the countermeasures actually reduce turnaround times. (Some times they don't.)

6. Standardize the improved methods and procedures as a permanent way of doing things.

7. Measure and monitor turnaround times to ensure peak performance.

Need Guidance?

Most health care organizations hesitate to take the first step toward faster, better, cheaper health care because they think it will take too long or cost too much. Some are afraid of learning Lean. Some are afraid of the consequences of using Lean. I think you will find that it's easier than you think and applying the principles with some guidance will make it easy to learn.

The first project may seem scary, but we can facilitate your improvement teams to achieve breakthroughs in patient flow. Once you've learned how, you'll find it easy to continue. Haven't you waited long enough to get a faster, better, cheaper hospital in five days or less?

QUIZ

1. **Lean can help hospitals reduce**
   A. patient wait times.
   B. medical mistakes and errors.
   C. adverse events.
   D. all of the above

2. **In a service business like health care, the Lean mindset shift is from**
   A. optimizing physician's time to optimizing patient's experience.
   B. better clinicians to better systems.
   C. functional silos to service.
   D. all of the above.

3. **To achieve better care, hospitals (and any service business) need**
   A. more workers (e.g., nurses).
   B. less walking.
   C. more time.

4. **To make a service business like a hospital faster, make**
   A. employees work harder and faster.
   B. managers help when there's a heavy load.
   C. the customer (e.g., patient) experience faster.

chapter 4

Excel Power Tools for Lean Six Sigma

While Lean doesn't require many tools other than a pad of Post-it notes, Six Sigma thrives on charts, graphs, and diagrams of performance data. To succeed at Six Sigma, you'll need a set of power tools.

CHAPTER OBJECTIVES

In this chapter, you will learn

- How to use Excel for Lean Six Sigma
- How to install and use QI Macros for Excel to draw Lean Six Sigma charts
- How to use control charts and Pareto charts to tell an improvement story

Microsoft Excel is a tremendously powerful tool for Lean Six Sigma, but most people don't even know how to use the basic capabilities of Excel. If you think you're a hotshot Excel user, read on because we'll look at how to use the QI Macros Lean Six Sigma SPC software for Excel. If you're not that familiar with Excel and how to set up your data to make it easy to analyze, chart, and graph, then you will get a lot from this discussion. If you don't own a copy of Excel or Office, you can usually pick up inexpensive copies of older versions at eBay.com. The QI Macros work in all versions of Excel.

REMEMBER *You can download your free 90-day trial of the QI Macros from www.qimacros.com/demystified.html.*

Setting Up Your Data in Excel

Using an Excel *worksheet*, you can create the labels and data points for any chart—line, bar, pie, Pareto, histogram, scatter, or control chart. This gives you a worksheet that looks like Fig. 4-1.

	A	B	C	D
1		Plant 1	Plant 2	Plant 3
2	Jan	15	77	44
3	Feb	23	56	33
4	Mar	56	33	55
5	Apr	33	33	22
6	May	77	23	66
7	Jun	33	15	11
8	Jul	14	14	77

FIGURE 4-1 · Spreadsheet of plant defects.

Step 1: Prepare Your Data

Data format. Other Lean Six Sigma software packages make you transfer your Excel data into special tables, but not the QI Macros. Just put your data in a standard Excel worksheet. The simplest format for your data is usually one column of labels, and one or more columns of data, but it can also be in rows. (Once you've installed the QI Macros, look in My Documents/QI Macros Test Data for sample data for each chart.)

Once you have your data in a spreadsheet, you will want to select it to be able to create a chart. Using your mouse, just highlight (i.e., select by clicking the mouse button and dragging it up or down) the data to be graphed, run the appropriate macro, and Excel with the QI Macros will do all the scary math and draw the graph.

Tips for Selecting Your Data

- *Click and drag with the mouse to select the data.*
- *To highlight cells from different columns* (Fig. 4-2), click on the top left cell and drag the mouse down to include the cells in the first row or column. Then, hold down the Control key, while clicking and highlighting the additional rows or columns.

	A	B	C
1		Plant 1	Plant 2
2	Jan	15	77
3	Feb	23	56
4	Mar	56	33
5	Apr	33	33
6	May	77	23
7	Jun	33	15
8	Jul	14	14

FIGURE 4-2 • How to select separate columns.

- *The QI Macros and the statistical tools work best when data is organized in columns, not rows.* So, for an XbarR chart, you might have Sample1, Sample2, . . ., Sample5 across the top, and then lot of numbers or dates down the left-hand side. The macros will work if your data is laid out horizontally in rows instead of columns, but vertical columns are the preferred method.

- *You may also use data in horizontal rows* (Fig. 4-3), but it's not a good format for data in Excel. Although most people tend to put their data in horizontal columns to mimic the format of a calendar, this makes

	A	B	C	D	E	F	G	H
11		Jan	Feb	Mar	Apr	May	Jun	Jul
12	Plant 1	15	23	56	33	77	33	14

FIGURE 4-3 • Selecting horizontal data.

it difficult to use all of Excel's analysis tools. Whenever possible, put your data in columns, not rows.

- *Numeric data and decimal precision.* Excel formats most numbers as General not Number. If you do not specify the format for your data, Excel will choose one for you. To get desired precision, select your data with the mouse, choose Format–Cells–Number and specify the number of decimals.

- Don't select the entire column (65,000+ data points) or row (255 data points), just the cells that contain the data and associated labels you want to graph.

- When you select the data you want to graph, you can select the associated labels as well (e.g., Jan, Feb, Mar). The QI Macros will use the labels to create part of your chart (e.g., title, axis name, legend). Make sure you follow these rules when inputting your data. Make sure you only select one row and one column of labels. Otherwise the QI Macros will try to treat each additional row as numbers.

People often put headings for a single column into multiple cells. If you put the heading in a single cell, right click on that cell, choose Format—Cells, click on Alignment, and click the Wrap Text button; Excel will word wrap the text for you.

- *Labels should be formatted as text.* If your labels are numbers (e.g., 1, 2, 3) you need to make them text so that Excel doesn't treat them as part of your data. To do this, you will need to put text in front of them. Some examples are Sample1, S1, Lot1, and L1. If you just want the 1 to show, then you will need to put an apostrophe in front of each number to change it from data to text (e.g., '1, '2, '3, etc.)

- *Data should be formatted as numbers.* Your data must be numeric AND formatted as a number for the macros to perform the necessary calculations. If you have data that are left justified or look like 001, 002, 003, then it is formatted as text and the QI Macros will attempt to convert it to numbers before graphing it.

TIP *Data exported from Microsoft Access is often in text format. To change it to numeric, (1) import the data to Excel, (2) put the number 1 in a blank cell, (3) Edit-Copy the cell with the 1 in it, (4) select the imported text data, and (5) choose Edit-Paste Special/Multiply to multiply every imported cell by 1 which will convert them to numeric data.*

- *Select the right number of columns.* Each chart requires a certain number of columns of data to run properly. They are

  One column: Pareto, pie, c chart, np chart, XmR chart

  One or more columns: line, run, bar, histogram

  Two columns: scatter chart, u chart, p chart

  Two or more columns: nox & whisker chart, dot plot, multivari, histogram, XbarR and XbarS

- *Beware of hidden rows or columns.* If you select columns A:F, but B and C are hidden, the QI Macros will use all five columns including the hidden ones. To select nonadjacent columns, use the control key.

Data Collection and Measurement for Six Sigma

Six Sigma's DMAIC has an early step for measurement. Although most companies have too much data, people can always identify something they aren't tracking that they should be tracking. Then they think that, they have to set up a whole system to collect the measurement. This is a mistake. You don't know if the measurement is useful until you have collected some. Rather than wait for a measurement system, start today using a few simple tools: a check sheet or a log of errors.

I've used these kinds of check sheets when I'm working with a team on the Dirty Thiry process for Six Sigma (Chap. 6). They find causes; I write them down and tally the number of times each occur. By the 30th data point, a Pareto pattern appears that points us at the most common (i.e., root) cause of the problem.

Check Sheet Data Collection

Nothing could be simpler than data collection with a check sheet. The QI Macros have a template in the improvement tools to get you started (Fig. 4-4). Simply print it out and start writing on it.

In column A, write the first instance of any defect, problem or symptom you detect. For example, if someone is calling us for support and has a problem with

	A	B	C	D	E	F	G	H
1					Week			
2	Defect/ Problem/ Symptom	M	Tu	W	Th	F	Sa	Total
3	Delay							0
4	Missed Commitments							0
5								0
6	Defects							0
7	Errors							0
8								0
9	Repeat Fixes							0
10								0
11	Total	0	0	0	0	0	0	0

FIGURE 4-4 • Check sheet.

	A	B	C	D	E	F	G	H
1				Week				
2	Defect/ Problem/ Symptom	M	Tu	W	Th	F	Sa	Total
3	Gage R&R							2
4	Excel disabled macros							15
5	SPC Question							3

FIGURE 4-5 · Check sheet of support calls.

understanding Gage R&R, then we'd write "Gage R&R" in A3 and put a stroke tally in the day of the week (e.g., Monday). Then continue adding to the check sheet as the week goes on, adding defects, problems, or symptoms. By the end of the week, you'll have an interesting picture of support calls (Fig. 4-5).

Just add up the number of calls and one bucket or another will jump out as the majority of the calls.

HINT: *Use a Pareto chart (Fig. 4-6) to show most common support calls.*

FIGURE 4-6 · Pareto chart of support calls.

But now the questions arise: Why is Excel disabling the macros? Request for quotes? Deliveries?

Spending a lot of time and money setting up a measurement system to track just these items, it wouldn't do much good. Instead, tune up the check sheet to provide better data (Figs. 4-7 and 4-8).

	A	B	C	D	E	F	G	H	I	J
1		Excel Version and Chart Type								
2		Excel					Control Charts			
3	Defect/ Problem/ Symptom	XL 2000	XL XP	XL 2003	XL 2007	Histograms	XmR, XbarR	c, np, p, u	Gage R&R	Total
4	Measurement Systems Analysis								||	2
5	Excel disabled macros				||| ⫴⫴					13
6	SPC Question					⫴	|||			8
7										0
8	Total			3	10	5	3		2	23

FIGURE 4-7 • Revised check sheet.

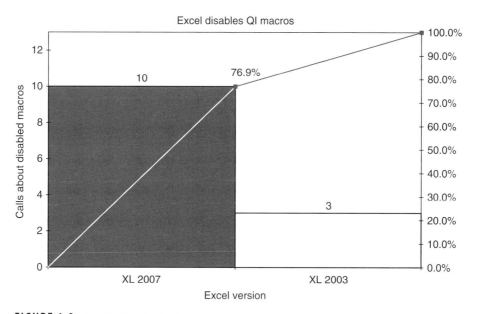

FIGURE 4-8 • Detailed Pareto chart.

Aha! Excel 2007 seems to disable the macros more than other versions. Did Microsoft change something? Is it something we can mistake-proof? And we get more histogram questions than control chart questions. Can we improve our online documentation about the histograms?

Get the idea? Use a check sheet to prototype your data collection efforts. Iterate until you start to understand what you really need to know to make improvements. A series of check sheets may be all you need to solve a pressing problem. If necessary, you can implement a measurement system to collect the data over time.

So please, don't wait for a magical, all-encompassing measurement system to deliver data. It's not going to happen. And I often find it's just an excuse to avoid making improvements. ("I can't because I don't have the measurements I need.")

Haven't you waited long enough to start making measurable improvements (even if your data collection tool is just a simple check sheet)? Or are you going to keep letting loads of cash slip through your fingers. All it takes is a check sheet and a pencil. Get on with it.

Error Log Data Collection

Another way to collect data uses an error log. In Excel, simply open a new workbook and enter headings for each data category (Fig. 4-9). In this case, it's denied charges in a hospital system. Then add a new line for each denied charge. It won't take long for a pattern to emerge (payment denied due to duplicate day of service [DOS]). An improvement team should be able to solve this problem easily.

Sometimes, these error logs get a bit more complex. To get useful data, you will want to mistake-proof the data collection.

	A	B	C	D	E	F
1	Region	ENT	ADM DATE	DENIED CHARGES	DESC	CATEGORY
2	North	Hosp1	2/13/03	543.07	REJECT - DUP DOS (MULTIPLE VISITS SAME DAY	BILLING ISSUES
3	South	Hosp2	7/13/02	215.4	REJECT - DUP DOS (MULTIPLE VISITS SAME DAY	BILLING ISSUES
4	South	Hosp2	12/6/02	157.92	REJECT - DUP DOS (MULTIPLE VISITS SAME DAY	BILLING ISSUES
5	South	Hosp3	10/20/02	90.73	REJECT - DUP DOS (MULTIPLE VISITS SAME DAY	BILLING ISSUES
6	North	Hosp1	5/7/03	4103.78	REJECT - DUP DOS (MULTIPLE VISITS SAME DAY	BILLING ISSUES
7	North	Hosp4	8/6/01	3224.83	REJECT - DUP DOS (MULTIPLE VISITS SAME DAY	BILLING ISSUES
8	North	Hosp5	4/15/02	3291.76	REJECT - DUP DOS (MULTIPLE VISITS SAME DAY	BILLING ISSUES
9	North	Hosp1	5/13/02	13845.9	REJECT - DUP DOS (MULTIPLE VISITS SAME DAY	BILLING ISSUES
10	North	Hosp4	9/16/02	1151	REJECT - DUP DOS (MULTIPLE VISITS SAME DAY	BILLING ISSUES
11	North	Hosp6	9/24/02	797	REJECT - DUP DOS (MULTIPLE VISITS SAME DAY	BILLING ISSUES
12	North	Hosp7	4/15/03	215	REJECT - DUP DOS (MULTIPLE VISITS SAME DAY	BILLING ISSUES
13	North	Hosp5	7/26/01	2124.86	REJECT - DUP DOS (MULTIPLE VISITS SAME DAY	BILLING ISSUES
14	North	Hosp4	6/2/03	12	REJECT - DUP DOS (MULTIPLE VISITS SAME DAY	BILLING ISSUES
15	North	Hosp6	8/8/03	304	REJECT - DUP DOS (MULTIPLE VISITS SAME DAY	BILLING ISSUES
16	North	Hosp6	8/8/03	89	REJECT - DUP DOS (MULTIPLE VISITS SAME DAY	BILLING ISSUES
17	North	Hosp6	8/8/03	89	REJECT - DUP DOS (MULTIPLE VISITS SAME DAY	BILLING ISSUES
18	North	Hosp6	2/4/03	3728	REJECT - DUP DOS (MULTIPLE VISITS SAME DAY	BILLING ISSUES
19	South	Hosp2	7/24/01	311.16	REJECT - OVERLAPPING DOS.	PAYER ISSUES
20	South	Hosp2	12/21/01	643.81	REJECT - OVERLAPPING DOS.	PAYER ISSUES

FIGURE 4-9 · Excel error log.

Still Struggling

Download and install the QI Macros from www.qimacros.com/demystified.html. In My Documents, you will find QI Macros Test data loaded with examples from manufacturing, healthcare, services, etc. Look for test data that is similar to your own company's data and use it as a template for your data.

Mistake-Proof Data Collection

People use Excel to create forms for all kinds of data collection: time sheets, scorecards, even mini-databases. Unfortunately, when they try to analyze it with pivot tables, they soon discover that humans are very creative spellers. One hospital system abbreviated *Medicare* with various acronyms: MDCR, Medcr, Medicr, and so on. This makes it difficult to do any data analysis or mining without a lot of cleanup. Excel's Data Validation function can eliminate the confusion.

Data Validation with Excel

The travel department of a major company asked its travel agents to track flights using dates, route codes (e.g., DEN-LAX-DEN), and destination cities. Travel agents found creative ways to make the analysis difficult: incorrect dates, swapping routes with destinations, misspelling destinations, leaving the hyphen out of the route (Fig. 4-10), and so on.

	A	B	C
1	Date	Route	Destination
2	2/20/2010	DEN-LAX-DEN	Los Angeles
3	Thursday	DEN_LAX-DEN	LA
4	21-Feb	Denver-LA	DEN LAX DEN

FIGURE 4-10 · Excel air travel log.

How can the travel group ensure that travel agents enter the data correctly? Data validation. Simply select the cells in the column and then specify a format and content for those cells.

In Excel 2000–2003, click on Data Validation (Fig. 4-11). In Excel 2007–2010, click on the Data tab and choose Data Validation.

Excel will pop up a menu with various choices: integers, decimals, dates, times, text, list, or custom (Fig. 4-12).

FIGURE 4-11 · Excel data validation.

FIGURE 4-12 • Data validation menu.

In the case of the travel group, it was time to mistake-proof the data entry form.

To clean up the dates, Excel's Data Validation can require specific formats, in this case a date after January 1, 2010. Just select column A, Data Validation, and specify the criteria (Fig. 4-13).

FIGURE 4-13 • Validate using Format.

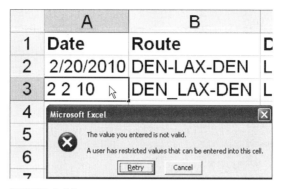

FIGURE 4-14 • Invalid format error.

If a travel agent tries to put in an incorrect date, Excel will tell the agent it's invalid (Fig. 4-14).

Select column B (the route), choose Custom, and insert a formula to check for a hyphen in character 4 (Fig. 4-15). Excel's MID function can check the cell for a hyphen. In this case, MID looks in the cell, at character 4, for a length of one: MID (B1, 4, 1). Since I selected the entire column, I used the first cell, B1, as the starting point, and it will apply to all of the cells. If an agent tries to put in anything that doesn't have a hyphen at character four (e.g., DENVER to LAX), Excel will display an error.

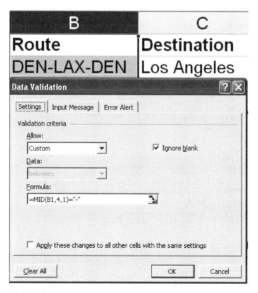

FIGURE 4-15 • Validate using Formula.

	A	B	C
1	Date	Route	Destination
2		DEN-LAX-DEN	Los Angeles
3		DEN-SFO-DEN	San Francisco
4		DEN-SEA-DEN	Seattle
5		DEN-ORD-DEN	Chicago
6		DEN-ATL-DEN	Atlanta
7		DEN-HOU-DEN	Houston
8		DEN-DFW-DEN	Dallas
9		DEN-JFK-DEN	New York
10		DEN-IAD-DEN	Washington DC
11		DEN-BOS-DEN	Boston
12		DEN-SFO-DEN	San Francisco
13			San Francisco

FIGURE 4-16 • Simplify data entry using autofill.

The destination column is a bit more challenging. Data Validation will let you specify a list of values, but travel destinations might be too varied. Excel, however, will autocomplete a cell after a few characters, so we could enter the ten most common destinations in C2:C11 (Fig. 4-16). Then, when an agent starts to type in that column, the destination will appear (e.g., San Francisco). If all trips originate from a common destination (e.g., Denver), we could enter routes as well.

Then, use Format-Row-Hide to hide rows 2–11 (Fig. 4-17). With rows 2–11 hidden, agents will be prompted with destinations and routes when they begin to type. Now let's look at another way to do this using a list.

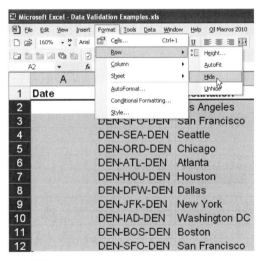

FIGURE 4-17 • Hiding rows.

Time Sheet Example

Imagine an HR staffer trying to get valid time sheets using Excel. The hours are rounded to the nearest half hour. But employees keep putting in values like 4:30 instead of 4.5. Here's how easy it can be to solve that problem with data validation.

First, in an empty column, enter 0 in the first cell (I2) and then a formula (=I3+0.5) in the next cell and copy/paste the formula down to get 24 hours (Fig. 4-18)

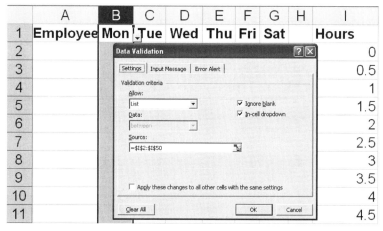

FIGURE 4-18 · Creating a validation list.

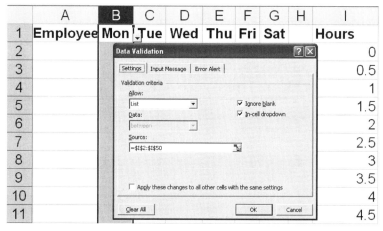

FIGURE 4-19 · Selecting list for validation.

Then select columns B:G and Data Validation-List to specify the source list (=$I$2:$I$50). See Fig. 4-19.

This will add a dropdown list to every cell so that employees can type a valid time (e.g., 2.5) or select a valid time (Fig. 4-20). Then just hide column I and save the workbook.

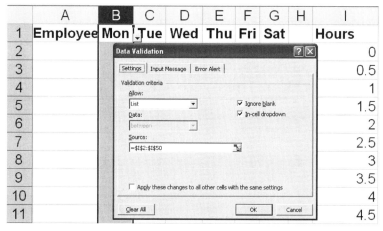

FIGURE 4-20 · Validation using menu of list items.

Custom Prompts

There are two other tabs on the Data Validation Menu: Input Message and Error Alert.

Input Messages

If you want to prompt people every time they enter data into a cell, Input Message can help them format it correctly (Fig. 4-21). This can be a little intrusive after people learn how to use the data sheet.

FIGURE 4-21 · Creating input messages.

Error Messages

Or specify an error message that only appears when users enter an invalid value (Fig. 4-22). If a user tries to enter 4 hours and 30 minutes as 4:30, the user will get the error message shown in Fig. 4-23.

Successful Six Sigma Project Needs Good Data

Gathering consistent, error-free data is one of the keys to process improvement. To create powerful Excel-based tools and improvement stories without a lot of data cleanup, you will need data entered in a consistent way.

FIGURE 4-22 · Creating custom error messages.

FIGURE 4-23 · Error message example.

Excel's Data Validation functions will train users to enter data correctly. Users can spend days in training, or Excel can just force them to learn the right way to enter data. Using Excel is faster and more effective.

Mistake-proof your data collection. It's just this easy.

QI Macros Introduction

There are many graphs, forms, and tools used in Lean Six Sigma and SPC. There are four key elements of the QI Macros: macros, templates, statistics, and data manipulation.

Ninety percent of common problems can be diagnosed with control charts, histograms, Pareto charts, and Ishikawa diagrams. Control charts will

1. Macros	2. Templates	3. Statistics	4. Data Transformation
Control charts	Control charts	ANOVA	Pivot Table Wizard
Histograms	Flowcharts	Regression	Word Count
Line, run, scatter	Fish bones	Sample size	Stacking
Pareto, bar, pie	Gage R&R	t-test, F-test	Restacking
Box & whisker	DOE & QFD	Chi-square	Box-Cox
Multivari	FMEA & PPAP	Correlation	Paste Link

help you sustain the improvements. Microsoft Excel can be used to create all of these charts, graphs, forms, and tools.

Installing the QI Macros

To install the QI Macros, simply

1. Go to our website *http://www.qimacros.com/demystified.html* and fill in your email address to download the QI Macros and the other free Lean Six Sigma quick reference cards. This will also sign you up for the free QI Macros and Lean Six Sigma lessons online course.

2. Download the QI Macros 90-day trial copy by clicking on the CD icon.

3. Double-click on QIDemo90Day.exe to install the QI Macros.

4. When you start Excel, the QI Macros menu will appear on Excel's toolbar in Excel 2000–2003 or the ribbon menu in Excel 2007–2010.

5. If you have any problems, check our website *http://www.qimacros.com/techsupport.html.*

6. Sign up and attend a free QI Macros Webinar at *www.qimacros.com/webinars/webinar-dates.html.*

Sample Test Data

The QI Macros for Excel installs test data on your PC in My Documents/QI Macros Test Data. Use this data to practice with the charts and to determine the best way to format the data before you run a macro.

Creating a Chart Using the QI Macros Menu

There are two different ways to create charts in the QI Macros. One is by selecting your data and running a macro from the menu. The second is by using the Fill-in-the-Blanks chart templates. To create a chart using a macro from the menu, just select the data to graph. Then, using the QI Macros menu (Fig. 4.24) select the chart you want to create. The QI Macros will do the math and draw the graph for you.

FIGURE 4-24 • QI Macros menu.

Creating a Control Chart

1. *Open a workbook (e.g., healthcare SPC.xls).*

2. *Select the labels and data to be graphed.* Click on the top left cell and drag the mouse across and down to include the cells on the right.

3. *From the QI Macro Menu, select Control Chart Wizard.* Excel will start drawing the graph. Fill in the graph title, and the *X*- and *Y*-axis titles as appropriate.

4. *To add text to any part of the graph, just click anywhere on the white space and type.* Then use the mouse to click and drag the text to the desired location. *To change titles or labels, just click and change them.* Change other text in the worksheet in the same way.

5. *To change the scale on any axis, double-click on the axis.* Select Scale and enter the new minimum, maximum, and tickmark increments.

6. *To change the color on any part of the graph, double-click on the item to be changed.* A patterns window will appear (Fig. 4-25). Select Font to change text colors, Line to change line colors and patterns, or Marker to change foreground and background colors. Control charts showing defects or delay are the key first step of any problem solution.

FIGURE 4-25 • Excel chart patterns window.

7. *To change the style of any line on the graph, double-click on the line.* The window (Fig. 4-26) is displayed. Changing the line style, color, and weight are all performed in this

FIGURE 4-26 • Excel format line window.

window. When you're done, click OK. The changed graph is now easier to read.

8. *To change the style of graph, right-click on the chart and choose Chart Type.* Click on the desired Graph format and then OK.

Still Struggling

Go to www.qimacros.com/qimacros-video-tour.htm to see examples of how to run any of these charts.

Fill-in-the-Blanks Templates

In addition to the charts listed on the menu, the QI Macros contain over 80 Fill-in-the-Blanks templates.

To access these templates select Fill-in-the-Blanks templates on the QI Macros menu (Fig. 4-27).

Each template is designed for ease of use. Tools like the flowchart and fish bone diagram make use of Excel's Drawing Toolbar. To view Excel's Drawing

FIGURE 4-27 • QI Macros Fill-in-the-Blanks menu.

Toolbar select View–Toolbars and click on Drawing in Excel 2000–2003 or Insert-Shapes in Excel 2007–2010.

Creating a Control Chart with a Fill-in-the-Blanks Template

The QI Macros contain templates for each kind of control chart. These templates are especially helpful if you have novice personnel (e.g., at nursing stations or on the shop floor) who will be inputting data or you don't have enough data to run a macro (you're just starting to collect the data). To create a chart using a template, click on the QI Macros menu and select the Fill-in-the-Blanks templates (Fig. 4-28). Click on the template you want to use (e.g., g chart).

FIGURE 4-28 • QI Macros templates selector.

The input areas for most of the templates start in column A (Fig. 4-29). Either input your data directly into the yellow cells on the template or cut and paste it from another Excel spreadsheet. As you input data, the chart will populate to the right. The X chart templates also display a histogram, probability plot, and scatter plot.

Running Stability Analysis on a Chart Created by a Template

To check for out-of-control conditions on a chart created using a control chart template, click on the chart (dark boxes will appear at the corners), click on the QI Macros menu (Fig. 4-30), and select Analyze Stability.

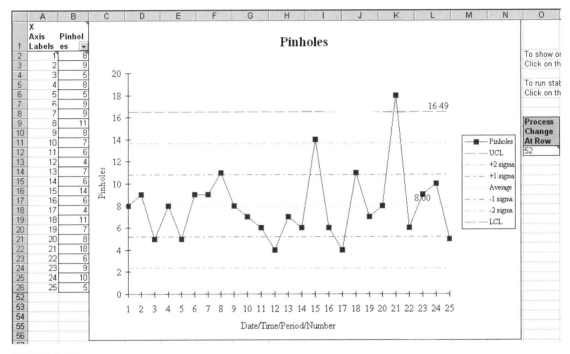

FIGURE 4-29 · QI Macros c chart template.

FIGURE 4-30 · QI Macros analyze stability menu.

Choosing Which Points to Plot

Each template defaults to 50 data points. If you have fewer than 50 points and only want to show the points with data, click on the arrow in cell B1. This will bring up a menu (Fig. 4-31). Select non-blanks to plot only the points with data.

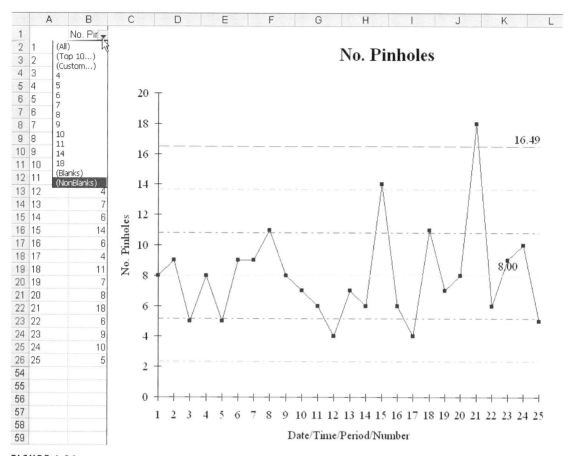

FIGURE 4-31 • Eliminating blanks from QI Macros templates.

In addition to control charts, there are templates for histograms with Cp and Cpk, precontrol charts, probability plots, Pareto charts, and many more.

Templates for Your Quality Improvement Efforts

Examples of other templates you will find in the QI Macros are

- *Focus your improvement efforts* using the Balanced Scorecard, Tree Diagram, Voice of the Customer Matrix, or Cost of Quality template.
- *Reduce defects* using the Pareto, Ishikawa, or fish bone diagram and countermeasures matrix.
- *Reduce delay* using the value stream map, flowchart, value-added flow analysis, time tracking and takt time templates.

- *Reduce variation* using the control charts and histograms.
- *Reduce measurement error* using the Gage R&R template.
- *Design for Lean Six Sigma* using the Failure Modes and Effects Analysis (FMEA), QFD House of Quality, Pugh Concept Selection Matrix, and Design of Experiments.
- *Project management and planning* using the Gantt chart, action plan, and ROI calculator.

Put Your Whole QI Story in One Workbook

Because the QI Macros are an all-in-one toolkit for Lean Six Sigma, you can put your entire improvement story in one workbook by simply adding worksheets. Let's say you've created a control and Pareto chart in one workbook. After you choose Ishikawa/Fish bone from the Fill-in-the-Blanks templates, just go to Edit-Move or Copy Sheet to move the template into the existing workbook. It's a great way to keep all of your information in one place.

Data Transformation

	A	B
1	**Drug**	**Diffrate**
2	Drug 1	8
3	Drug 1	4
4	Drug 1	0
5	Drug 1	14
6	Drug 1	10
7	Drug 1	6
8	Drug 2	10
9	Drug 2	8
10	Drug 2	6
11	Drug 2	4
12	Drug 2	2
13	Drug 2	0
14	Drug 3	8
15	Drug 3	6
16	Drug 3	4
17	Drug 3	15
18	Drug 3	12
19	Drug 3	9

Sheet2 / Drug Tria

FIGURE 4-32 · Single column of data with two samples.

Convert Tables of Data from One Size to Another

What do you do when your gage or database gives you a single column of data, which actually represents several samples (Fig. 4-32). How do you convert it to work with the XbarR or other chart?

1. Select the single column of data.

2. Click on Data Transformation-Stack/Restack to choose various tools, including restack matrix.

3. Enter the number of columns (e.g., 5) and click OK. The macro will reformat your data to 5 columns and however many rows. For example, if you have 18 data points and you input 6 into the prompt, you will get 6 columns and 3 rows of data.

Summarize Your Data with Pivot Tables

The QI Macros will draw graphs, but they won't summarize your data automatically because they cannot read your mind. However, you can use the Pivot Table Wizard to summarize data in almost any conceivable way. For example, what if you have a series of report codes from a computer system or machine? You need to summarize them before you chart them. Just click on 1-to-4 column headings and Data Transformation-Pivot Table Wizard in the QI Macros (or you can select the raw data and go to Excel's menu bar and choose Data–Pivot Table). With a little tinkering, you'll learn how to summarize your data any way you want it.

1. *Select the labels and data to be summarized* (Fig. 4-33), in this case, individual event codes by region. Many processes and gages produce one code or measurement each time an event happens. These often need to be summarized to simplify your analysis.

	A	B
	Region Code	Event Code
1		
2	002	100
3	001	94
4	001	4
5	001	122
6	001	101
7	003	123
8	003	123
9	001	60
10	001	60

FIGURE 4-33 • Pivot table data.

2. *From Excel's menu, choose Data–Pivot Table.* Follow Excel's Pivot Table Wizard until you get a screen like the one in Fig. 4-34.

3. *Click, hold, and drag the data labels* into the appropriate area of the pivot table to get the summarization you want (Fig. 4-35)

   • Page fields: Use this for big categories (e.g., vendor codes, facilities in a company).

   • Left column: Use this to summarize by dates or categories.

FIGURE 4-34 · Pivot table layout window.

	B	C	D	E	F	G	H	I	J	K	L
1 Count of Event Code	Event										
2 Region Code	1	2	3	4	5	6	8	9	10	11	1
3 001	4	376	51	157	34	240	43	87	255	2	1
4 002	1		93	86	17	12	7	9	17	9	
5 003	1	2			2		23				
6 004	2	4	1	1	16		2			3	
7 019	1			2	4			1			
8 020			5			7		1	29	11	
9 029	1				14	13		5			
10 035		9	33	2	24	63	38	116	5	7	1
11 038		2	3		4	1	57	2	1	3	
12 053	1	77	69	20	81	194	49	236	146	7	3
13 Grand Total	11	470	255	268	203	523	220	485	435	31	6

FIGURE 4-35 · Pivot table results.

- Top row: Summarize by subcategories.
- Center: Drop fields to be counted, summed, or averaged into the center.

4. *To change how the data is summarized,* use the Pivot Table Wizard or double-click on the top left-hand cell. For online tutorials, see Google Excel Pivot Table.

5. *Select labels and totals, and draw charts* using your summarized data.

Still Struggling

Sign up for a free QI Macros webinar at www.qimacros.com/webinars/webinar-dates.html.

Using ANOVA and Other Statistical Tools

Most Six Sigma Black Belts get into more detailed analysis of data to determine the variation. ANOVA (or ANalysis Of VAriance) seeks to understand how data is distributed around a mean or average. To use any of the statistical analysis tools of Excel through the QI Macros to perform ANOVA in native Excel, you must have Excel's Data Analysis Toolpak installed. Go to Tools-Addins and check Analysis Toolpak (Fig. 4-36). Excel will either turn these

FIGURE 4-36 • Turning on the analysis ToolPak.

tools on or ask you to install them using your Office or Excel CDs. To check if they have been installed, click on Tools-Data Analysis. If you cannot see Data Analysis in the Tools menu, the statistical analysis tools are not installed.

1. Select the data to analyze. This data must be organized in columns.

2. From the QI Macros menu, select ANOVA and Other Analysis Tools.

3. Click on the appropriate analysis tool (ANOVA, regression, F-test, t-test, etc.).

See sample test data for each tool and test on your computer at c:\qimacros\testdata.

Power Tools for Lean Six Sigma

As you can see from these examples, Excel and the QI Macros are power tools to simplify Lean Six Sigma. By putting your data into Excel, summarizing it with pivot tables, and graphing it with the QI Macros, you can automate and accelerate your journey toward Six Sigma.

1. The QI Macros give you the power to select data and immediately draw all of the key charts and diagrams: line, run, and Pareto charts for problem solving as well as histograms and control charts for reducing variation.

2. The QI Macros templates give you Fill-in-the-Blanks simplicity for control charts, Pareto charts, fish bones, flowcharts, and value stream mapping.

3. The QI Macros Data Transformation tools give you the ability to stack and restack your data and use pivot tables.

4. The QI Macros ANOVA and Analysis tools give you simplified access to Excel's statistical tools and much more.

Start using Excel and the QI Macros to organize, analyze, and graph your data to illuminate the opportunities for improvement.

Analyzing Customer Service Data Hidden in Trouble-Reporting Systems

In service industries, much of the information you need to make break-through improvements is buried in trouble-reporting systems. Help and repair personnel routinely attempt to capture customer complaints, categorize them, and include remarks about the customer's dilemma. Unfortunately, the categories in most information systems are predefined, inflexible, and rarely speak to the true nature of the customer's complaint. And often the customer, who has waited in a call queue for several minutes, has had time to think up several questions they need answered, not just one.

In these situations, the information needed to analyze these customer interactions is in the freeform remarks, not in the convenient categories. The information captured in the remarks invariably will be more accurate than the predefined categories. How do we analyze this wild potpourri of short phrases and abbreviations? The answer lies in Microsoft Excel.

Importing Text with Microsoft Excel

To analyze text with Excel, you must first import the data into Excel. To do this, you will need to export the customer account and remarks information from the trouble-reporting system into your PC or local area network.

To simplify deeper analysis, it will be useful to have something about the customer's account included with the remark. In a phone company, for example, having the customer's phone number will enable further analysis by digging into the customer's records.

Then go to Excel and choose File–Open, select Files of Type-All Files, and open the text file. Excel's import wizard will then guide you through importing the data. Text data can either be *delimited*, which means it contains tab, comma, or other characters that separate fields, or *fixed width*, which means the data is of a consistent length.

The maximum number of characters Excel will store in a cell is 255, so longer text fields should be edited to fit. More than one cell can be used to store an entire remark or comment. Excel will allow up to about 65,000 rows to be imported per Excel worksheet.

Analyzing Text with Excel

Searching the imported text file couldn't be easier. In the QI Macros, select the cells filled with text and choose Data Transformation-Word Count, and the QI Macros will parse the sentences into one and two word phrases, then pivot them to create a list of the most common words or phrases. This often identifies the most common issue even when service representatives are using different words, phrases, or acronyms. For sample data, look in the QI Macros Test Data for crosstab.xls and click on the Word Count sheet.

Native Excel has a function called COUNTIF, which tallies cells if they match certain criteria. The formula for the COUNTIF function is

=COUNTIF(CellRange, "criteria")

The CellRange specifies the range of cells to be counted. If there is only a single column of imported text, this might be $A$3:$A$2154. Or it could include multiple columns if the text fields are longer than 255: $A$3:$C$2154.

Once you've specified the range, the trick is to create criteria consisting of keywords and phrases that match the cells. To do this, you'll need to use Excel's *wildcard* character, the asterisk (*). To match a cell that contains a keyword, the criteria portion of the COUNTIF statement will need to look for any leading stream of characters (*), the keyword, and any trailing stream of characters (*). The simple way of expressing this in the COUNTIF statement would be

=COUNTIF(CellRange, "=*_keyword_*")

To make this easy to change, we might consider putting the keyword in one cell by itself and including it into the *formula*. The formula would be

=COUNTIF($A$1:$A$2154, "=*"&B1&"*")

This would take the keyword from the cell above it, making it easier to change and test various keywords. Getting the keyword right can make the resulting data more accurate.

Consider the following example. Repair and help personnel are busy, so they develop abbreviations for many common words and phrases. In phone companies, *LD* means "long distance." Credit can be abbreviated *crdt*. You may need to scan some of the remarks to understand the most common abbreviations used.

Note in this example, that *ld* is also embedded in words like *would* or *cold*. Simply counting *ld* would lead to inaccurate counts; so we can resolve this by putting a leading space or blank in front of the abbreviation *ld*.

Similarly, notice that some words may be spelled out and some words may be abbreviated like the word credit (cr*d*t). We can use the wildcard character to handle these kinds of keywords, since the wildcard will match zero or more characters.

To test your keyword, use Excel's Find feature to look for the keyword. If it finds words that are incorrect, then tailor the keyword until it gives a more accurate representation of the embedded data.

Graphing the Data

Once you've mined all the data out of the comments, you can then use bar, pie, or Pareto charts to examine the frequency of certain types of customer complaints. Additional digging into specific customer records may be required to determine the root cause of why these calls are being generated and how to mistake-proof the process to prevent them.

Troubleshooting Problems

Users have three types of questions when using the QI Macros.

1. *Statistical Process Control questions.* What chart should I use? If you use the Control Chart Wizard in the QI Macros, the software will choose the chart for you. Otherwise, most of these SPC questions are answered on our website at *www.qimacros.com/spcfaq.html.*

2. *Excel questions.* How do I enter my data? Why don't I get the right number of decimal places? And so on. Most of these are answered at *www.qimacros. com/excelfaq.html.*

3. *QI Macros/Excel/Windows Support questions.* Most of these are answered at *www.qimacros.com/techsupport.html.*

Chartjunk

I recently stumbled on a book called *Visual Explanations* by Edward R. Tufte (Graphics Press, Cheshire, CT, 1997). *The New York Times* calls Tufte the Leonardo da Vinci of data. Tufte says there are right ways and wrong ways to show data; there are displays that reveal the truth and displays that do not. He uses the space shuttle *Challenger* as an example of what not to do.

Space Shuttle *Challenger*

Tufte tackles the data and presentation used by Morton Thiokol to show O-ring damage on previous shuttle flights. The graphs use cute little rockets to show O-ring damage over time (Fig. 4 37).

FIGURE 4-37 • Thiokol rockets example.

The temperature at the time of launch is shown on rocket A, and the O-ring damage on the recovered boosters is shown as gray or hatched areas. As you can imagine, put 50 of these in a row and it's hard to tell what's really going on, because you can't detect the pattern with your naked eye.

If, however, you use the O-ring data to draw a scatter plot (Fig. 4-38), you can use the trend line to back into the potentially catastrophic problems awaiting the space shuttle *Challenger*.

FIGURE 4-38 • O-ring scatter showing projected problems.

If you use a c chart to plot the damage index, you get a chart that tells you that the one 53-degree launch is a special cause variation, but also that the entire launch sequence is unstable (Fig. 4-39).

If the process was this unstable, maybe it needed some serious root cause analysis before liftoff.

The Right Picture Is Worth a Thousand Words

Information displays should serve the analytic purpose at hand. That's why I use the QI Macros to draw as many different charts as possible to explore which one tells the best story. Here are some of Tufte's insights.

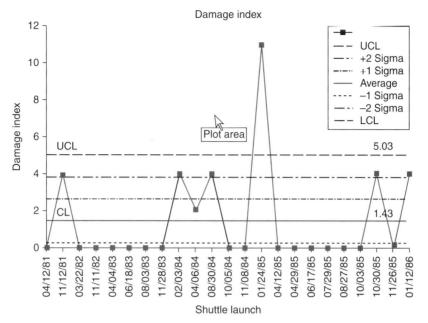

FIGURE 4-39 • O-ring c-chart.

- *Numbers become evidence by being in relation to something.* The numbers indicating the temperature on the rockets aren't really in relationship to anything. Similarly, numbers on a spreadsheet can be hard to read.
- *The disappearing legend.* When the legend on a chart is lost (in this case the meaning of the gray areas on the rockets), the insights can be lost as well.
- *Chartjunk.* Good design brings absolute attention to data. Bad design loses the insights in the clutter.
- *Lack of clarity in depicting cause and effect.* In the rocket charts, no matter how cute, the cause and effect of temperature versus O-ring damage is lost.
- *Wrong order.* A fatal flaw can be in ordering the data. A time series (i.e., a control chart) may not reveal what a bar chart (i.e., a histogram) may reveal. In this case, a scatter diagram reveals all you need to know.

I usually draw as many different charts from the same data as I can to see which one tells the best story. You should too. Every picture tells a story, but some pictures are better than others at telling the story. The QI Macros make it easy to draw one chart after another so that you can quickly discard some of them and select others that engage the eye on the real issues.

As Tufte would say, "Don't let your charts become *disinformation*. There's enough of that in the world already."

Chartjunk and Disinformation

Tufte reminds me about the need for clarity in all of the charts and graphs we create, and their power to misinform. Lurking behind chartjunk is contempt both for information and for the audience. Chartjunk promoters imagine that numbers and details are boring, dull, and tedious, requiring ornament to enliven. If the numbers are boring, then you've got the wrong numbers.

Worse is contempt for our audience, designing as if readers were obtuse and uncaring. In fact, consumers of graphics are often more intelligent about the information at hand than those who fabricate the data decoration. Our readers may be busy, but they are not stupid. Clarity and simplicity are completely opposite to simple-mindedness.

Tufte argues that to make your information more usable, you will want to

- Document the source and characteristics of the data
- Insistently enforce appropriate comparisons
- Demonstrate the mechanisms of cause and effect
- Demonstrate cause and effect quantitatively
- Evaluate alternative explanations

Tufte argues for clarity and content over cuteness. Hence his term for anything that violates these principles is *chartjunk*.

Dark Grid Lines Are Chartjunk

You can use Excel's formatting capabilities to put boxes around cells, but they may not reveal the structure of the data you want to highlight (Fig. 4-40). Instead, you could choose to highlight the four trials (Fig. 4-41), or the three temperatures (Fig. 4-42).

Chartjunk on Graphs

The same is true of Excel. If you draw a plain bar chart using Excel's Chart Wizard, you get a chart cluttered with unnecessary information: grid lines, legends, background colors, and so on (Fig. 4-43).

	A	B	C	D
1	Temperature	1-15	2-15	3 15
2	15	130	150	138
3	15	74	159	168
4	15	155	188	110
5	15	180	126	160
6	70	34	136	174
7	70	80	106	150
8	70	40	122	120
9	70	75	115	139
10	125	20	25	96
11	125	82	58	82
12	125	70	70	104
13	125	58	45	60

FIGURE 4-40 • Grid lines on worksheets can be chartjunk.

	A	B	C	D
1	Temperature	1-15	2-15	3-15
2	15	130	150	138
3	15	74	159	168
4	15	155	188	110
5	15	180	126	160
6	70	34	136	174
7	70	80	106	150
8	70	40	122	120
9	70	75	115	139
10	125	20	25	96
11	125	82	58	82
12	125	70	70	104
13	125	58	45	60

FIGURE 4-41 • Use color to highlight rows of data.

	A	B	C	D
1	Temperature	1-15	2-15	3-15
2	15	130	150	138
3	15	74	159	168
4	15	155	188	110
5	15	180	126	160
6	70	34	136	174
7	70	80	106	150
8	70	40	122	120
9	70	75	115	139
10	125	20	25	96
11	125	82	58	82
12	125	70	70	104
13	125	58	45	60

FIGURE 4-42 • Use color to highlight columns of data.

To fix some of these problems, right-click on the chart and select Chart Options. Click on the grid lines and uncheck Major grid lines (Fig. 4-44). Then click on the legend and uncheck Show Legend.

To clear the background color, double-click on it and select Area: None (Fig. 4-45). The resulting graph becomes easier to read (Fig. 4-46), but the bars are so tall that you can barely tell how much variation there is from month to month. I consider this to be a form of disinformation. The height and weight of the bars makes it look like there isn't really much of a problem.

FIGURE 4-43 · Grid lines on charts are chartjunk.

FIGURE 4-44 · Uncheck major grid lines.

After all, we're over 80% most of the time, aren't we? I can't tell from this graph. It's too hard to read.

To change the scale, double-click on the Y (i.e., vertical) axis (Fig. 4-47) and change the scale (in this case from 60% to 100%). Now you can start to see the amount of variation from month to month (Fig. 4-48).

FIGURE 4-45 · Remove background area.

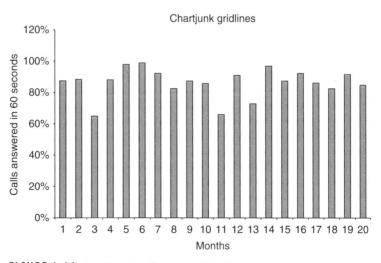

FIGURE 4-46 · Bar chart of calls answered in 60 seconds.

FIGURE 4-47 • Change Y-axis scale to show variation.

FIGURE 4-48 • Bar chart showing variation.

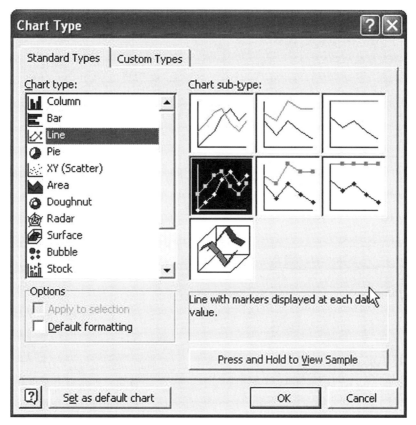

FIGURE 4-49 · Change chart type window.

But bar charts are best for showing differences between two types of data: the height of men versus the height of women. Bar charts are not the right choice for showing how processes perform over time; use control charts instead. To change the chart type, right click on it and select Chart Type (Fig. 4-49) and change the chart to one of the line graphs shown.

As you can see from the Fig. 4-50, with the heavy bars gone, the only thing left to notice is the variation. What caused those big dips? What allowed us to answer the phone in 60 seconds 98% of the time in other months?

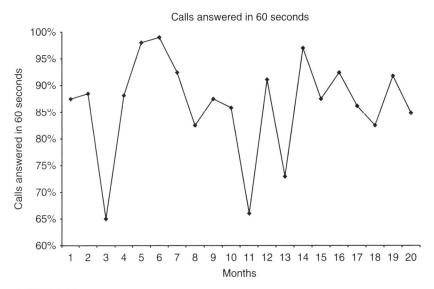

FIGURE 4-50 • Line graph of calls answered in 60 seconds.

Get the Idea?

Chartjunk is a form of disinformation. It confuses the reader. Clean up your charts. Get rid of unnecessary clutter. Choose the right kind of chart for your data, and you'll go a long way toward motivating the readers to understand and align with the business case presented.

Still Struggling

Look at charts in USA Today and other magazines and periodicals. Which ones are easy to read and which ones are hard? Compare these to the PowerPoint presentations you see in your company. Wouldn't junk-free charts communicate everything more clearly?

QUIZ

1. **The QI Macros provide**

   A. charts via the ribbon menu.
   B. templates of charts and diagrams using the Fill-in-the-Blanks menu.
   C. access to statistical tools using the ANOVA and Analysis menu.
   D. data transformation tools.
   E. all of the above

2. **The ideal chart to show performance over time is a**

   A. control chart.
   B. Pareto chart.
   C. histogram.

3. **The ideal chart for narrowing your focus is a**

   A. pie chart.
   B. Pareto chart.
   C. bar chart.
   D. control chart.
   E. histogram.

4. **The optimal way to orient your time-series data in Excel is**

   A. horizontally across the columns.
   B. vertically down the rows.

5. **The ideal way to summarize text and other data is to use**

   A. QI Macros.
   B. Excel Pivot Tables and the QI Macros Pivot Table Wizard.
   C. a check sheet.

6. **After drawing a control chart, you can use the QI Macros menu to**

   A. add data to the chart.
   B. show process changes.
   C. analyze stability.
   D. delete a point.
   E. remove a point from the calculations.
   F. all of the above

7. **The goal of all charts and data is to**

   A. eliminate chartjunk.
   B. present a clear and compelling business case for improvement.
   C. provide a common language for discussing improvement stories.
   D. all of the above

8. **Mistake-proof data collection by using**
   A. employee training.
   B. data transformation.
   C. data validation.

9. **In the QI Macros you can create a control chart using**
   A. menu.
   B. Fill-in-the-Blanks templates.
   C. control chart dashboards.
   D. all of the above

10. **QI Macros can help**
    A. transform data.
    B. draw charts.
    C. analyze statistics.
    D. design work flows.
    E. all of the above

EXERCISES

1. **Install the QI Macros.**

2. **Practice running all of the charts using data in c:\qimacros\testdata.**
   - data.xls—bar, pie, line, or run chart
   - pareto.xls—Pareto chart
   - scatter.xls—scatter diagram
   - matrixplot.xls–matrix plot
   - histogram.xls—histogram (use the specification limits provided).
   - c, np, p, or, u chart.xls—attribute control charts (c, np, p, u)
   - XmR chart, XbarR, XbarS.xls—variable control charts
   - AIAG SPC.xls—attribute and variable control charts for the automotive industry
   - Healthcare SPC.xls—attribute and variable control charts for health care

3. **Control chart templates**
   - Click on Fill-in-the-Blanks templates and choose c, np, p, u, XmR, XbarR, or XbarS.
   - Copy data from the test-data files and paste it into these templates.
   - XmR or c, p, u dashboards for tracking multiple measures.

4. **Drawing templates**
   - Click on Fill-in-the-Blanks templates and choose flowchart, value stream map, or value-added flow analysis.
   - Practice using the drawing toolbar to move objects around (View–Toolbars–Drawing).

chapter **5**

Reducing Defects with Six Sigma

Using simple charts, I've helped teams save over $20 million in just 1 year. The concept is over 100 years old. It's often referenced in every management book ever written. And it all began with an Italian economist who noticed a simple disparity in incomes. But few people know how to leverage its power in business.

CHAPTER OBJECTIVES

In this chapter, you will

- Learn the Six Sigma problem-solving method (DMAIC)

- Learn the universal problem-solving process (FISH)

- Apply key problem-solving tools: control and Pareto charts and fishbone diagrams

- Learn how to avoid the Six Sigma tar pits

151

In 1995, I was struggling with the complexities and inherent problems in a huge telecommunications company. Sitting at my desk, I was staring at a vast spreadsheet of facts and figures about postage costs for the company's bills. With a cranky VP sitting upstairs, I decided to do a simple analysis. There had to be a pattern to the steady increases in postage costs. It wasn't the postal service or ride-along coupons, so it had to be something else.

More and more of the company's bills were being mailed at the 2-ounce (oz) rate instead of the 1-oz rate. So either the postage meters were wrong, or the bills were getting heavier.

On top of this, every month thousands of bills were returned due to bad addresses. I went through the bins of returned bills looking for any bill over the 1-oz rate. One by one I opened them up looking for the secret to unlock the root cause of increased postage costs.

It only took a few dozen bills to discover the culprit. The company had begun billing for smaller telecommunications companies. Each company got their own page in an already thick envelope. Page by page and company by company, the bill was steadily creeping over the 1-oz limit. Of course, the product manager who sold the billing service hadn't priced it to cover the increases in postage costs.

On the basis of my research, a team redesigned the bill to be smaller, lighter, and more readable. In the year after its implementation, postage costs fell by $20 million a year.

What charts did I use to display the problem and garner support for the redesign?

Control Charts, Pareto Charts, and Fishbone Diagrams

I used them again to save $16 million a year in billing adjustments.

And again to save $3 million a year in service order errors. And $5 million a year in denied claims for a hospital system. Isn't it time you discovered the power of control charts, Pareto charts, and fishbone diagrams to laser focus your improvement efforts?

Fire Alarm Case Study

In 1990, I worked at U.S. West's Advanced Technologies Facility. I'd been struggling with the improvement process because my teams weren't really focused on the right thing. They had been tasked with world hunger, boil-the-ocean

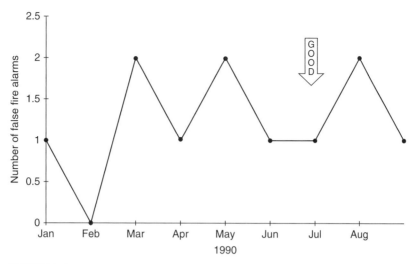

FIGURE 5-1 • Line graph of false fire alarms.

kind of problems. Then I got a chance to apply the methods to the right kind of problem: false fire alarms. This story illustrates the power and simplicity of the problem-solving process.

The president felt there had been too many false fire alarms for a building of our size. In essence, his gut feel told him there was a problem. During that year, there had been 11 false fire alarms that were far higher than the one a year he had expected (Fig. 5-1). So I worked the building manager to analyze the data. It only took us 3 hours to solve the problem! (When you've got the data you need, the Six Sigma improvement process can be done in hours, not days, weeks, or months.)

As usual, there had been a lot of guessing about the cause of the problem. The management had recently added microwave popcorn to the break rooms. Many knee-jerk analysts concluded that particles from the popcorn were causing false alarms. Most of the data that had been collected suggested that faulty detectors were the problem (Fig. 5-2), but that was unlikely, because only one detector a year should fail. So we looked for another reason. Fortunately, recent events had given us a rare insight. As the research facility for U.S. West, at Baby Bell, we were investigating cellular phones. They were relatively new in 1990, and few people had them. So, one of the research groups scheduled a demonstration in the auditorium. They punched in the number and hit send and beep-beep-beep, the fire alarms went off. Everyone exited the building. After 20 minutes everyone came back in, and they resumed the demonstration. They punched in the numbers and hit send and beep-beep-beep, the fire alarms went off again!

FIGURE 5-2 · Pareto chart of causes of false fire alarms.

Could cell phones cause false fire alarms? We checked with the engineers, and they said yes, if the detectors weren't properly shielded from the radio frequency interference (RFI) generated by cell phones. Now all detectors are supposed to be shielded to meet the Underwriters Laboratory (UL) code, so we guessed that some of our detectors might be unshielded and that unshielded detectors were the *root cause* of the false fire alarms (Fig. 5-3).

We had technicians verify that the different kinds of detectors in our building—photoelectric and particulate—were below UL code and had in fact caused the false fire alarms. (You have to verify that you've identified the root cause. You can't just proclaim victory; you have to prove it.)

There were 1,100 detectors in the building and we estimated it would cost $100 to $200 to replace each one ($110,000 to $220,000). The building was rented, and we were planning to move out the following year, so we informed the owner of the problem and devised a simple sign to discourage people from using cell phones inside the building. These were our countermeasures (Fig. 5-4). Since we knew that there were 600 people in the building at any time and that the loaded cost of interrupting their work to exit the building was $50 per alarm, we estimated that we saved $300,000 in lost productivity by eliminating 10 false fire alarms a year. (Six Sigma is about measuring money saved.)

Ishikawa fishbone Diagram
cause effect analysis

FIGURE 5-3 • Ishikawa fishbone diagram of root causes of false fire alarms.

	A	B	C	D	E	F	G	H	I
1	Problem Statement:	During 1990, Faulty Detectors accounted for 64% of false fire alarms which was 7X higher than expected and caused lost productivity and delay.							
2	Root Cause	Countermeasure/Proposed Solutions	Feasibility	Specific Actions	Effectiveness	Overall	Action (Who?)	Value ($/period)	
3	Fire Detectors below UL Code	Make building "cellular free"	5	Post Signs	4	20	DC	$300,000	600 people @ $50 per alarm X 10 alarms
4		Replace Detectors	2	Replace 1,100 detectors @ $100 each	5	10			
5				*US West did not own the building.					
6	http://www.qimacros.com/qiwizard/solution.html		Feasibility: 1-low, 5-high		Effectiveness: 1-low, 5-high				
7			1-Expensive & Difficult to implement		1-Not very effective				
8			5-Inexpensive and easy to implement		5-Very Effective				

Fire Alarm Data / False Alarm Graph / Pivot Data / Pareto of Causes / ISHIKAWA \ **Countermeasures** / Results Pareto / Results Control Chart

FIGURE 5-4 • False fire alarm countermeasures.

As you can see from our graphs of the following year (Figs. 5-5 and 5-6), we did eliminate the root cause of our problem (cell phones). We solved the problem and also initiated national standards efforts around cell phones and fire detection equipment. When we presented this information to our local fire department, they expressed their thanks for gaining an insight into the sharp increase in false fire alarms they'd experienced over the last year.

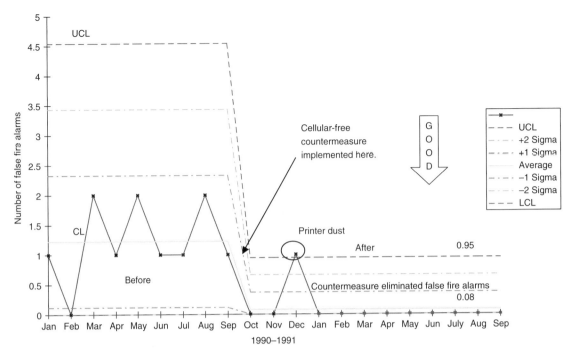

FIGURE 5-5 · Control chart of reduction in false fire alarms.

FIGURE 5-6 · Comparison Pareto charts showing improvement.

156

In 2006, over 15 years later, a *Rocky Mountain News* article reported that some of the downtown hotels experience 100 to 300 false fire alarms a year. Could cell phones be the culprits? Faulty detectors? I informed the article's author.

Six Sigma's Problem-Solving Process

As you can see from this case study, measures, counts, and data about defects and their origins drive Six Sigma's defect reduction process. Without data about defects or variation, Six Sigma just won't work. The standard Six Sigma improvement method is called DMAIC—Define, Measure, Analyze, Improve, and Control. I'm going to suggest that for your first few projects you skip over the Define and Measure steps and start with some data you have already collected about defects in some aspect of your business. Most teams get stuck in this Define and Measure stages and never get on to Analyze and Improve stages. Start with a real problem about which you have some real data and you're half of the way to success. Then you can leap in to Analyze, Improve, and Control stages.

The Six Sigma Problem-Solving Process

While I still think of improvement as following the FISH process: Focus, Improve, Sustain, and Honor, the Six Sigma problem-solving process, DMAIC (duh-maic), which stands for

1. *Define* the problem
2. *Measure* the problem (defects or variations)
3. *Analyze* the root causes of the problem
4. *Improve* the process (i.e., implement some countermeasures and analyze the results)
5. *Control* the process (i.e., measure and monitor to sustain the new level of improvement)

I lump Six Sigma's Define and Measure steps into Focus. If you don't laser focus your improvement efforts using real data about defects or deviation, you aren't doing Six Sigma; you're just doing some version of gut-feel, trial-and-error, knee-jerk problem solving. Or you're trying to retrofit your old way of doing things to look like you're doing Six Sigma. Far too many people start with their pet solution to a problem and try to work their way back to the data that will prove their solution. Too few people start from the data and see where it leads.

The Repair Reduction Fiasco

I learned this lesson the hard way. While I was in the phone company, the honchos started a big project to solve the delays involved in repairing phone service. Over 50% of the calls to the company were for repair. If you called on Monday, our repair service representatives would tell you that we could have it repaired by 5 PM on *Thursday*. Three- and 4-day waits were not uncommon. The old guard repair guys thought that they needed more staff-fixing stuff. So they wanted the quality improvement department *to prove that they needed more people (pet solution)*. By the time I got assigned to the project, they were well down the path toward this "solution." We even had an external quality-consulting group helping them do it at exorbitant fees. This is one of the most common mistakes people make when faced with defects. They think they need more people or they need to be able to fix things faster. Wrong!

You don't need more staff; you need less repair. If there weren't so many problems, you wouldn't need to fix them!

But I couldn't get anyone to listen to me because I was a quality guy; what did I know about telephone repair? Didn't I know that the conditions were different in Seattle with all the rain than they were in Arizona with all the heat? Of course I did; I knew that different regions would need different solutions, but many would be the same. Sadly, I spent 2 months living away from home trying to make that project fly. They brought in technicians from all over the company to bring staffing up to a level they thought was needed. In the end, it failed. Why? Because the management was trying to use Six Sigma to get the answer they wanted rather than the answer the data were trying to tell them.

TIP *Follow your data, not your hunches (or your honchos).*

Too many companies get caught up in trying to *fix it fast*, when what they really need is less stuff to fix. I don't care how good you are at repairing your product or service, because all of that time, money, and effort is non-value-added. It has nothing to do with getting it done right the first time.

The Repair Appointments Success Story

Just to show that everyone in the telephone company wasn't a complete idiot, I'd like to tell you another improvement story. One of the states was getting a lot of customer complaints about unnecessary repair appointments. The customer would take a day off work to wait for the repair technician, but no one would show up. The customer's telephone, however, would magically start working again.

When we looked at the data, we found that the state averaged 11,000 repairs a month (Fig. 5-7). Repair Service Attendants (RSAs) scheduled repair appointments for *every repair*. On the basis of customer complaints and feedback from the repair department, we guessed that about 90% of these were unnecessary.

As we analyzed the data, we discovered that the RSAs also did what's called a *loop test*. They could test the circuit from the company's switching system out to the customer's phone and back while the customer was on the phone with them. Invariably, if the circuit from the switching system was good, then the problem had to be inside the walls of the central office (CO). Better still, most of these problems could be fixed quickly because we always had staff in the central office. When we looked at the data, we found that 92% of the time (Fig. 5-8) the loop tests were okay, but we were still scheduling an appointment.

Why? Why? Why? Why? Why? My guess? Some repair foreperson got tired of sending repair personnel to customers' houses and finding no one home. So, rather than figure out what kind of repairs actually needed an appointment, the

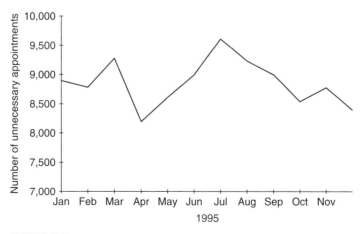

FIGURE 5-7 • Line graph of unnecessary repair appointments.

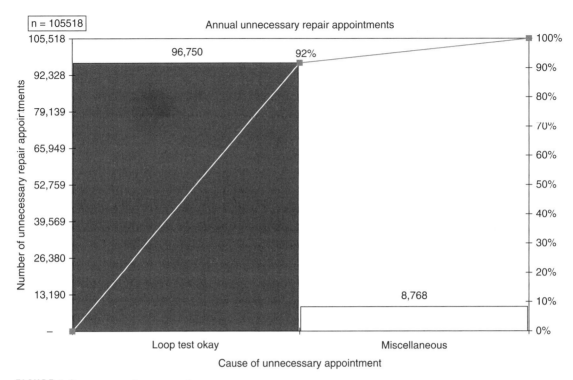

FIGURE 5-8 · Loop test okay Pareto chart.

knee-jerk reaction was to demand that every repair have an appointment. (In Lean, this is classic overproduction.) To be polite, we attributed the problem to not using the loop test to determine the need for an appointment (Fig. 5-9).

We diagnosed this problem on a Thursday, and by the following Monday the RSA managers had implemented the change (Fig. 5-10). Unnecessary appointments fell from 9,000 per month to 50 a week almost overnight (Fig. 5-11). (Some problems, like junction boxes and transmission lines, were still outside of the home.) I can tell you that the repair managers were sweating bullets over this change. They figured that their repair staff would waste a lot of time going to houses where no one was home, but fortunately we also measured the number of times that customer's weren't home for the repair. This measurement didn't move a hair. In a few days time we had collapsed the unnecessary appointments by over 8,000 a month, reduced customer complaints, reduced the amount of time an RSA had to spend on the phone (because they didn't need to schedule so many appointments), and proven that the change didn't affect repair service levels one bit.

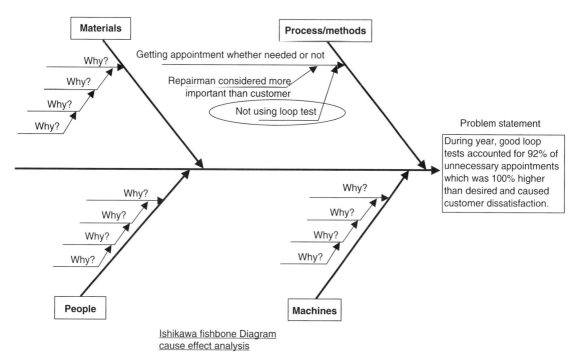

FIGURE 5-9 · Root cause diagram of unnecessary repair appointments.

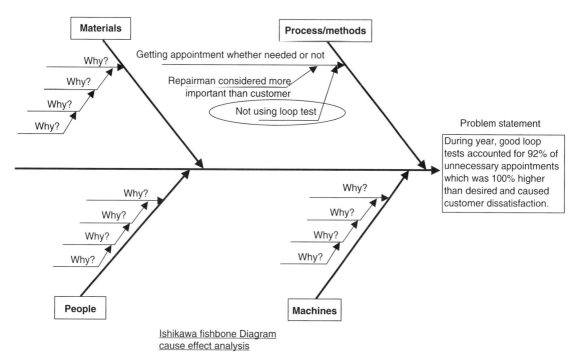

FIGURE 5-10 · Countermeasures for unnecessary appointments.

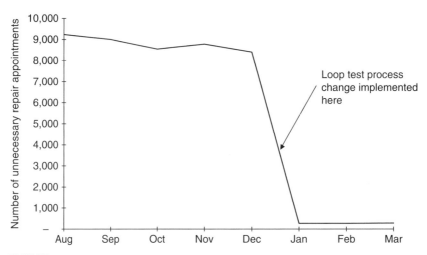

FIGURE 5-11 · Results of implementing countermeasures.

With a few months of data under their belt to prove their solution worked, the team took their improvement story to the other states and replicated the savings across the entire company.

Are you scheduling appointments you don't need? Are you great at fixing things, but not so good at getting it right the first time? How can these case studies be adapted to your business?

Getting to Lean Six Sigma

Most successful companies that have been around for more than 5 years get down to about a 1% defect rate. Most start-up companies, because of the ad hoc nature of their processes, are at 15% to 20% defects. I have found from experience that you don't need a lot of exotic tools to move rapidly up from these levels. Companies I've worked with have used these tools to go from 15% defects to 3% or less in about 6 months and 3% to 0.03% in about 2 years. Once you get to this level, you'll be ready to use more exotic tools to design your work processes for Lean Six Sigma. But until you get there, you may not have the discipline, desire, or rigor needed to use the more advanced tools.

Case Study: Mail Order Fulfillment

In my business, I ship software and training materials; this sometimes results in errors, which can produce a variety of possible fulfillment errors (Fig. 5-12).

	B	C	D	E	F	G
1	Date	Fulfillment Trouble Report				
2	Date	Error	Invoice	Description	Reason	Source
3	2000-10	Duplicate Order	11196	Duplicate of 10422	PO# not checked	Invoicing
4	2000-10	Not Received	10588	1		Unknown
5	2000-10	Payment not applied	10247	Check processed, not applied	Jay typed $10, not $105	Payments
6	2000-11	Not Received	11186	Anglo American (no US addr)	Records not transferred from Jay's system	Transfer from Jay
7	2000-11	Not Received	10434		unk	Unknown
8	2000-11	Not Received	11349	Giffin, Deb	FedEx Saturday not on order	Alphapage
9	2000-11	No PO number	11257	No PO# 27242-00		Unknown
10	2000-11	Wrong Zipcode	11309	Returned Wrong Zipcode 326\9	Order error	Unknown
11	2000-11	Missed orders		B&N PO# 420979 not in system	Ordered 10/15	Unknown
12	2000-11	Missing Credit	10508	$185 applied to 10509, then reversed	Credit not forwarded	Payments
13	2000-11	Not Received	11300	Increase to 5 copies faxed	Unk	Unknown
14	2000-11	Payment not applied	10826	Amex account wrong, revised	payment not applied when account corrected	Payments
15	2000-11	Bad CD, disk, tape	11328	Disk not formatted	Unk	Production
16	2000-11	Duplicate Order	9262	Duplicate of 9290		Order
17	2000-11	Duplicate Order	11200	Duplicate of 11193	No PO on first order	Customer
18	2000-11	Not Received		Faxed 2 weeks ago, no record	Unk	Unknown
19	2000-11	Wrong Product	11349	Sent 230 not 15-100s as ordered		Fulfillment
20	2000-11	Double payment	11022	Shipped 4, then 5 more	Applied payment second time	Fulfillment
21	2000-11	No Street Address	9718	No street address on card, but on invoice		Order
22	2000-11	Forgot to update MYOB	11186	Anglo American invoice not updated		Payments
23	2000-11	Returned Insufficient Addre:	11418	Missing Company Name		Order
24	2000-11	Returned Airmail	11408	No Circular Post Office Stamp	Shipping Rules changed	USPS

RunChart 3 / RunChartData3 / Sheet1 \ **Fulfillment Errors** / Sheet18 / Pareto Chart 19 / Pareto Chart 20

FIGURE 5-12 • Fulfillment errors by type of error.

Define the Problem

On average, we were having 10 errors per month—about a 3% error rate. By analyzing each error, we were able to identify the most common types of errors (Fig. 5-13).

To analyze the problem that shipments were not being received, we then looked at the source of these errors by examining the invoices and any returned packages (Fig. 5-14).

Target: I set a goal of reducing these errors by 50%. As you can see from this chart, invoicing and fulfillment (packaging) contributed over 50% of the problem!

Analyze the Problem

Part of our problem involved the retyping of orders, resulting in address and order errors. Another involved tracking the shipped products (Fig. 5-15).

Prevent the Problem

To prevent these problems, we chose to

1. Capture all orders electronically and import them into the billing software.

2. Capture all phone orders electronically using the Internet.

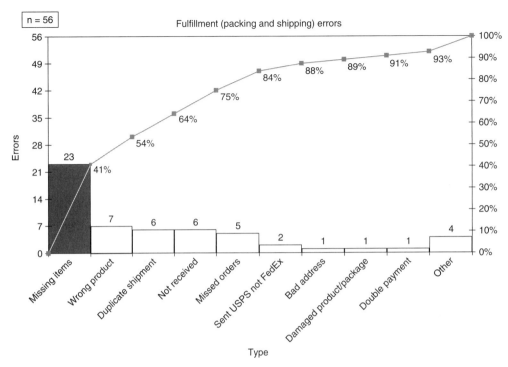

FIGURE 5-13 • Types of fulfillment errors.

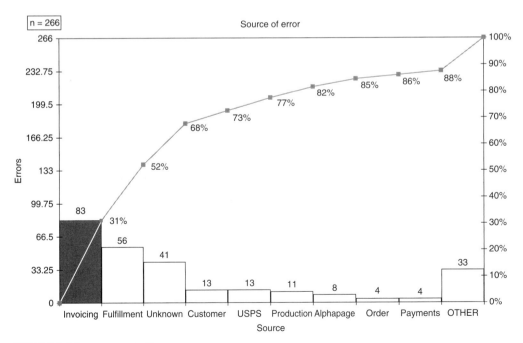

FIGURE 5-14 • Source of fulfillment errors.

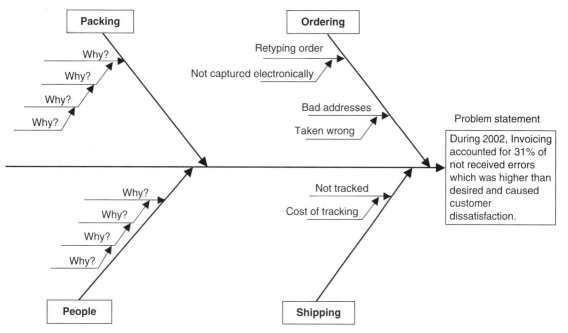

FIGURE 5-15 • Root causes of invoicing errors.

3. Use *Stamps.com* to create the shipping labels, because *Stamps.com* validates the ship-to address and provides free delivery confirmation ($0.45/order savings).

Check Results

It took about 2 months to implement all of these improvements. As a result, *total errors* have dropped from 10 per month to 2.4 per month, a 75% reduction.

Using this data, we are now charting the errors per month using a c chart (Fig. 5-16).

Problem Solving

Our problems are man-made, therefore they may be solved by man. No problem of human destiny is beyond human beings.

—John F. Kennedy

Although many people are willing to say that problems are a force of nature or due to the human factor, I am not. Most problems can be solved with a little effort and ingenuity.

FIGURE 5-16 · Fulfillment errors stair-step control chart.

Key Tools for Defect Reduction

There are three key tools in solving problems with defects.

- Control chart—to measure customer's critical to quality (CTQ) requirements
- Pareto chart—to focus the root cause analysis
- Fishbone (Ishikawa) diagram—to analyze the root causes of the problem or symptom

With these three tools you can solve 80% to 90% of all problems associated with defects or cost.

Problem-Solving Process

The Six Sigma Problem-Solving Process (Fig. 5-17) also follows the FISH model—Focus, Improve, Sustain, and Honor. It focuses on identifying problems, determining their root causes, and implementing countermeasures that will reduce or eliminate the waste, rework, and delay caused by these problems.

So let's look at how to apply the problem-solving process to achieve Lean Six Sigma improvements in quality and cost. The steps include

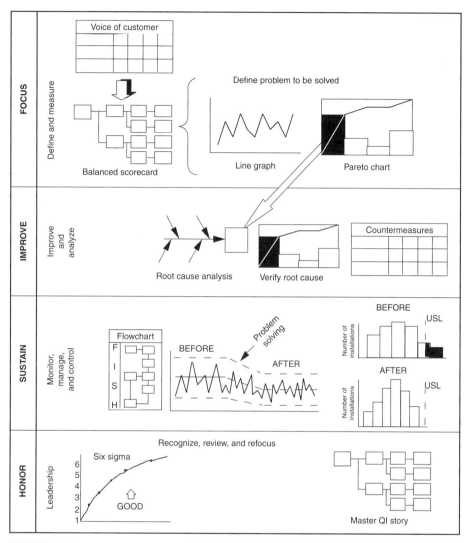

FIGURE 5-17 · Six Sigma problem-solving process.

1. *Define a problem for improvement* using measurements shown as a control chart and Pareto charts or histograms to select elements for improvement.

2. *Use the cause-and-effect diagram* to analyze root causes. Then verify and validate the root causes.

3. *Select countermeasures* to prevent the root causes and evaluate results from implementing the countermeasures.

4. *Sustain the improvement* using control charts.

5. *Replicate the improvement.*

Critical to Quality (CTQ) Measures

There are only two types of defect-related problems: not enough of a good thing or too much of a bad thing, either of which should be measurable and easily depicted with a control chart. Since an increase in the "good" is often a result of decreasing the "bad," measures of the unwanted symptom make the best starting place for improvement.

Since reducing the unwanted results of a process is often the best place to begin, the area of improvement can usually be stated as reduce defects, mistakes, errors, rework, scrap, or cost in a product or service. These are often two sides of the same coin:

An Increase in . . .	Is Equal to a Decrease in . . .
Quality	Number defective
	Percent defective
	DPMO—defects per million opportunities
Profitability	Cost of waste, scrap, and rework

Solving problems is usually easiest when you focus on decreasing the "bad" rather than increasing the "good." What are some of the current problems in your work area? Are these problems due to delay, defects, or cost? Some examples include

- Complaints are defects.
- Outages or missed commitments are both defects and time problems.
- Waste of media, floor space, computers, networks, or people are cost problems.
- Rework to fix problems.

How could these be measured and depicted in a control chart to form the basis of an improvement story?

Still Struggling

Every process is error-prone. What kind of mistakes, errors or defects plagues your process? What work products have to be reworked on a frequent basis? Count the number of times things have to be reworked. How often do you have to scrap a work product—printed document, out-of-spec part, or other interim product? These are the defects, mistakes, and errors you can track, over time, to show performance.

Pareto Charts to Focus Improvement

Problem *areas* are usually too big and complex to be solved all at once, but when we whittle them down into small enough pieces, we can fix each one easily and effectively. This step uses the Pareto chart (a bar chart and a cumulative line graph) to identify the most important problem to improve first. Often, two or more Pareto charts are needed to get to a problem specific enough to analyze easily.

Having the control chart of current performance, you'll want to analyze the contributors to the problem. A Pareto chart might take any of the following forms based on the original data:

- Defects—types of defects
- Time—steps or delays in a process
- Cost—types of costs–rework or waste

What to Look For in Your Company Data

Most companies have lots of data, but sometimes have a hard time figuring out what to do with it. I've found that I often use a common strategy for analyzing a company's data. I usually slice and dice an Excel table in the same way.

1. I sometimes have to summarize the defect, error, and mistake data using Excel's PivotTable function.

2. I use Pareto charts to analyze the total rows and total columns.

3. Then I use Pareto charts to analyze the biggest contributor in each total row or column.

Let's look at an example. Here's a simplified table (Fig. 5-18) from a garage door installation company that was having trouble making a profit because of service and warranty calls.

Because the company installs doors for builders, they sometimes have multiple service calls to install each door piece by

	A	B	C	D	E	F
1		Install	Replace	Adjust	Lube	Total
2	Door	2	5	1	0	8
3	Motor	2	1	11	6	20
4	Track	1	0	6	4	11
5	Vinyl	11	1	0	0	12
6	T-Lock	9	0	1	0	10
7	Total	25	7	19	10	61

FIGURE 5-18 · Garage door repairs spreadsheet.

piece. They may have to install, replace, adjust, or lubricate some part to get the door working properly. They work with five key parts: door, motor, track, vinyl trim, and T-lock.

I've highlighted my first focus: total parts. I use this to run a Pareto chart (Fig. 5-19). Motors are the big bar at 33%. Then I drill down to look at the motor row by type of service (Figs. 5-20 and 5-21).

FIGURE 5-19 • Total service calls by part type.

	A	B	C	D	E	F
1		Install	Replace	Adjust	Lube	Total
2	Door	2	5	1	0	8
3	Motor	2	1	11	6	20
4	Track	1	0	6	4	11
5	Vinyl	11	1	0	0	12
6	T-Lock	9	0	1	0	10
7	Total	25	7	19	10	61

FIGURE 5-20 • Repair types for motor.

FIGURE 5-21 • Motor service calls by type.

Adjusting the motor is 55% of total motor service and lube is the next 30% (85% total). Now we have something to analyze!

A problem well stated is a problem half solved.
—Charles Franklin Kettering (1876–1958)

Once we have narrowed the problem down to a small enough piece, we can write a problem statement about one or more big bars on the Pareto chart. The big bars in the lower-level Pareto charts can be turned into problem statements to fill the head of your fishbone diagram. These will serve as the basis for identifying root causes. We also need to set a target for improvement.

Problem Statement: During 2004, adjustments accounted for 55% of all motor service calls, which is higher than desired and caused customer dissatisfaction and a loss of $60 per service call.

Now let's pull back and look at the service row (Figs. 5-22 and 5-23).

	A	Install	Replace	Adjust	Lube	Total
1		Install	Replace	Adjust	Lube	Total
2	Door	2	5	1	0	8
3	Motor	2	1	11	6	20
4	Track	1	0	6	4	11
5	Vinyl	11	1	0	0	12
6	T-Lock	9	0	1	0	10
7	Total	25	7	19	10	61

FIGURE 5-22 • Services by type data.

FIGURE 5-23 • Total service calls by type Pareto chart.

As you can see, installation is 41% of the total followed by adjustments. These two are 72% of the total. Next, I'll drill down by looking at the installation column (Figs. 5-24 and 5-25).

	A	Install	Replace	Adjust	Lube	Total
1		Install	Replace	Adjust	Lube	Total
2	Door	2	5	1	0	8
3	Motor	2	1	11	6	20
4	Track	1	0	6	4	11
5	Vinyl	11	1	0	0	12
6	T-Lock	9	0	1	0	10
7	Total	25	7	19	10	61

FIGURE 5-24 • Installation part repairs Pareto chart.

FIGURE 5-25 · Installation service calls by part.

Installations of vinyl followed by T-locks are 80% of the total. Now we've got something to analyze. We could have one team analyze all vinyl installs and another team analyzes the T-lock installs.

Get the idea? Pareto charts are power tools for finding the 4% of your business that's causing over 50% of the waste, rework, and lost profit.

Check Sheets

What do you do if you don't have any data to narrow your focus? I find that the best choice is to use a check sheet (Fig. 5-26). A check sheet can be as simple as

	A	B	C	D	E	F	G	H
1					Week			
2	Defect/ Problem/ Symptom	M	Tu	W	Th	F	Sa	Total
3	Delay							0
4	Missed Commitments	ⵢ⃗ I						6
5	Defects							0
6	Errors							0
7	Repeat Repairs							0
8								0
9								0
10								0
11								0
12							⌖	0
13	Total	6	0	0	0	0	0	6
14	http://www.qimacros.com/qiwizard/checksheet.html							

FIGURE 5-26 · Check sheet for collecting defect data.

a map or diagram with hash marks on it or a matrix of stroke tallies. Have your docrs make a mark every time they encounter a certain type of problem.

In Edward Tufte's book, *Visual Explanations*, he recounts the analysis of London's cholera epidemics in the 1850s as originally described in John Snow's book, *On the Mode of Communication of Cholera*. Snow suspected that water pumps in London were the cause of cholera outbreaks (you had to pump water and carry it to your house).

When cholera broke out in September 1854, Snow took a street diagram of London and started marking where each death occurred. The deaths clustered around the pump on Broad Street. Snow analyzed the water, but couldn't see any obvious impurities. Snow realized that "the absence of evidence was not evidence of absence."

Snow took his death diagram to the city board, and they immediately removed the pump handle on the Broad Street pump. Cholera deaths began to decline immediately. Snow chased down every oddball cholera death and found that people from as far away as Chelsea got their water and their cholera from the Broad Street pump.

If you produce a circuit board, can you imagine having a diagram of the board and putting a mark on each component when you find a failure? In a manufacturing plant, can you imagine a floor plan of the production facility and putting a mark on the chart every time a machine breaks down or a problem occurs? If you're an information system developer, can you imagine making a stroke tally for every trouble report or enhancement request to identify the 4% of your code that requires most of the repair or enhancement work?

Check sheets can be your friend when you don't have enough data.

Root Cause Analysis

For every thousand hacking at the leaves of evil, there is one striking at the root.
—David Thoreau

The Ishikawa, cause-and-effect, or fishbone diagram helps work backward to diagnose root causes. For those unfamiliar with root cause analysis, learning to use the fishbone can be frustrating, but, once learned, it helps prevent knee-jerk, symptom patching. There are two main types of fishbone diagrams. One is a customized version of the generic—people, process, machines, materials, measurement, and environment (Fig. 5-27). The other is a step-by-step, process fishbone that begins with the first step and works backward (Fig. 5-28), because errors early in the process often cause the biggest effects.

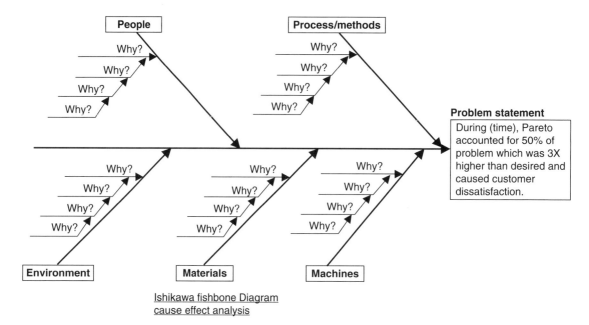

FIGURE 5-27 · Traditional fishbone diagram.

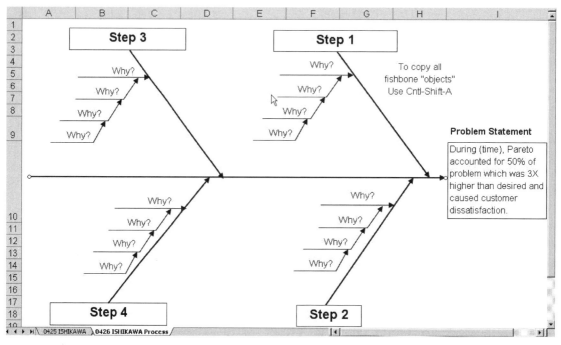

FIGURE 5-28 · Step-by-step fishbone diagram.

FIGURE 5-29 • Cause-and-effect matrix.

Another tool that's sometimes used to identify causes and effects is the cause-effect matrix (Fig. 5-29).

The fishbone is not only useful for identifying the root cause of recurring problems (common cause variation), but it can also be extremely useful when stabilizing a process. Special causes of variation (e.g., power spikes, cable cuts, and so on) result in unstable processes as well.

Suppose there is a computer outage. The problem statement becomes: On January 31, System X went down putting 600 service reps out touch with service systems.

Major contributors to this problem can be identified and root causes determined. When collected over time, these special cause analyses will give you the data to cost-justify the improvements necessary to prevent them.

Still Struggling

Toyota says they don't have a Six Sigma process, they just ask "Why?" five times. Ask: Why does the *process* cause this error? Get an *answer* and ask: Why does this *answer* cause the process to cause this error? Get another answer and repeat until you can go no farther. The answer to the last "why" is usually the cause. Root cause analysis is easy for some people and hard to grasp for others. The only way to understand it is to practice.

Fishbone Tar Pits

There are two main tar pits that teams fall into—whalebone diagrams and circular logic.

- A whalebone diagram (dozens or hundreds of bones) means that the problem wasn't focused enough in step 1. Go back and develop one more pareto at a lower level of detail.

- Circular logic (C causes B causes A causes C again) invariably means the logic wasn't checked as it was developed. Remind participants to ask Why? up to five times as you develop each "bone." Then check your logic each time you add a "bone" by working up the chain saying "B causes A." If the why of A is B but B does not cause A, then the logic is faulty. Cell phones, for example, don't cause false fire alarms. Cell phones cause RFI, which causes unshielded detectors to go into alarm mode which causes false fire alarms. Remind team members to verify their root causes before proceeding.

Identify and Verify the Root Causes

Take away the cause, and the effect ceases.

—Cervantes

Like weeds, all problems have various root causes. Remove the roots, and like magic, the weeds disappear.

Defining Countermeasures

Action should culminate in wisdom.

—The Bhagavad Gita

Purpose: Identify the countermeasures required to reduce or eliminate the root causes

Like good weed prevention, a countermeasure prevents problems from ever taking root in a process. A good countermeasure not only eliminates the root cause but also prevents other weeds from growing.

Verifying Results

Purpose: Verify that the problem and its root causes have been reduced

To ensure that the improvements take hold, we continue to monitor the measurements (CTQs). Both the control chart and Pareto chart will improve if the countermeasures have been successful.

1. Verify that the indicators (CTQs) used in step 1, Focus, have decreased to the target or below.

2. Verify that the major contributor identified in the Pareto chart in step 1 has been reduced by comparing before and after Pareto charts.

To ensure that the improvements take root, we need to develop a flowchart of the improved process and a way to measure its ability to meet customer needs.

There is always a best way of doing everything.

—Emerson

Sustain the Improvement (Control)

Purpose: Prevent the problem and its root causes from coming back

Like crops in a garden, most improvements will require a careful plan to ensure they take root and flourish in other gardens. To transplant these new improvements into other gardens will require a control plan. Sustaining the improvement requires control charts and sometimes histograms to monitor and maintain the new level of improvement.

What? (Changes)	How? (Action)	Who?	When? (Start, Complete)	Measure? (Results)
People	Training			
Process	Define system and measures			
	Implement			
	Monitor			
Machines (computers, vehicles, etc.)				
Materials (forms and supplies)				
Environment				
Replicate	Identify areas for replication			
	Initiate replication			

Multiply the Gains

Purpose: To increase the return on investment from each improvement effort

To maximize your return on investment, you will want to get this improvement into the hands of all the other people who could use it.

Where will this process be useful?	What needs to be done to initiate?	How will the process be replicated?	Who owns the replication?	When? (Start, Complete)
		Adopt process		
		Adapt process		
		Incorporate existing improvements		

A Lean Six Sigma Case Study—Reducing Computer Downtime

One Baby Bell reduced computer downtime by 74% in just 6 months using Lean Six Sigma. How did they do it? By following the defect reduction process.

Define and Measure the Problem

At the beginning, there were 100,000 "seat" minutes of outage per week (Fig. 5-30). Since there were 9,000 service representatives, that means that

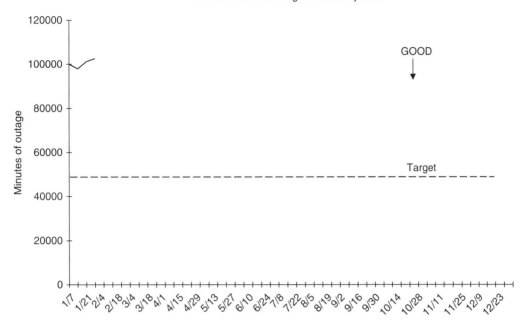

FIGURE 5-30 · Computer system minutes of outage line graph.

each person experienced only 11 minutes of outage per week per person, but all totaled, it meant the loss of 1,667 hours, 208 person days, or five person weeks. In other words, it was the equivalent of having five service reps unavailable. Studies have shown that when a person in interrupted, you don't just lose them for the period of the interruption, because it can take up to 30 minutes to regain full speed.

Target: The VP of Operations set a goal of reducing downtime by 50%, which caused a lot of grumbling, but on analysis, they found that the server software caused 39% of the downtime, 28% was caused by application software, and 27% by server hardware (Fig. 5-31).

Analyze and Improve the Problem

Multiple improvement teams tackled each of these areas. Root cause analysis (Fig. 5-32) and verification determined that password file corruption, faulty hardware boards, processes, and one application accounted for most of the failures.

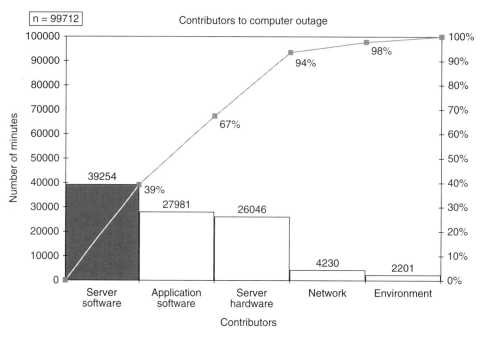

FIGURE 5-31 · Pareto chart of contributors to computer outage.

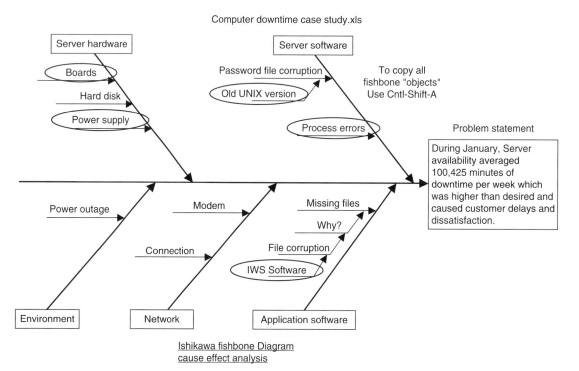

FIGURE 5-32 · Root causes of outages.

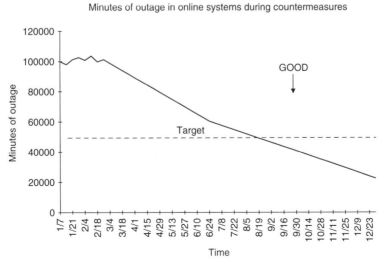

	A	B	C	D	E	F	G	H
1	Problem Statement	During January, Server availability averaged 100,425 minutes of downtime per week which was higher than desired and caused customer delays and dissatisfaction.						
2	Root Cause	Countermeasure/Proposed Solutions	Feasibility	Specific Actions	Effectiveness	Overall	Action (Who?)	Value ($/period)
3	Corrupted Password Files	Upgrade to Latest UNIX Release	5	Develop and implement installation plan acros 633 server environment	5	25	IT	$25,000/wk
4	Multiple other root causes and countermeasures were implemented							
5								
6	http://www.qimacros.com/qiwizard/solution.html			Feasibility: 1-low, 5-high		Effectiveness: 1-low, 5-high		
7				1-Expensive & Difficult to implement		1-Not very effective		
8				5-Inexpensive and easy to implement		5-Very Effective		

0430 Outage Contributors / Pareto Chart 6 / Minutes of Outage / 0431 Root Causes of Outages

FIGURE 5-33 • Countermeasures to outages.

Prevent the Problem

Multiple countermeasures (Fig. 5-33) were implemented including upgrades to the operating system in over 600 servers to prevent password file corruption and other problems.

Check Results

In less than 6 months they had exceeded the goal by achieving a 74% reduction (Figs. 5-34 and 5-35). A system was implemented to monitor and manage outages for both immediate and long-term improvement.

FIGURE 5-34 • Reduction in outages during countermeasures–line graph.

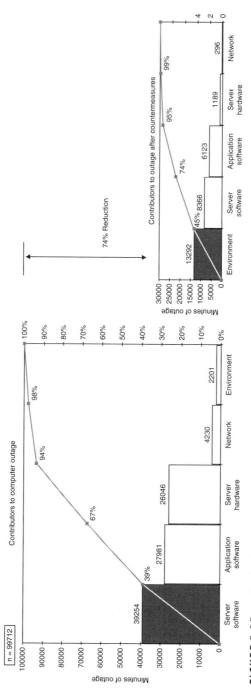

FIGURE 5-35 • Reduction in outages comparison Pareto charts.

The following year they further reduced outages from 22,000 minutes down to 11,000 minutes. This project avoided most of the Six Sigma tar pits.

Hospital Case Study

The Institute for Healthcare Improvement (ihi.org) estimates that preventable physical harm to patients occurs 40,000 times *a day* in U.S. hospitals. The Center for Disease Control and Prevention estimates that 2 million people are affected by surgical site infections, drug reactions, and bedsores. A total of 99,000 people die as a result of hospital-acquired infections.

Dr. Peter Pronovost at Johns Hopkins Hospital came up with a five-item checklist that reduced catheter infections to *zero* in 77 Michigan hospitals. The checklist included simple solutions like washing hands before touching patients, clean patient's skin with antiseptic, wear masks, caps and gowns, and so on.

While infections are a problem, misuse of antibiotics can lead to other problems.

Providence Saint Joseph Medical Center (PSJMC) found that nursing units often failed to discontinue antibiotics within 24 hours of surgery end-time for up to 1,000 patients per year. Failure to stop antibiotics can lead to adverse reactions and increased medical costs.

PSJMC found that average stop time for antibiotics was 39 hours after surgery. Only 25% of cases were compliant with guidelines. And there was no standard process or protocol used in the nursing units. They also found that orthopedic and colon surgeons had the highest noncompliance rates.

Countermeasures

- Revise order sets with support from surgeons.
- Identify applicable cases in the operating room.
- Automate discontinuation of antibiotics by the pharmacy at the 24th hour for applicable cases.
- Add orange stickers to patient charts to visually identify the patients.
- Monitor compliance daily.

In a few months, compliance rose to 90% from 36% which generated $35,000 in savings.

The 4-50 Rule

I keep hammering this point: 4% of any business (1 step out of 25) is causing 50% of the waste, rework, and delay. As you can see from these examples, by slicing and dicing the data horizontally and vertically, we can find two or three key problem areas that could benefit from root cause analysis.

1. Start with the total columns and rows. Draw Pareto charts with the QI Macros.

2. Then use this information to narrow your attention to one key row and column within the table. Draw the lower-level Pareto charts from this data.

3. Use the big bars from the lower-level Pareto charts to create problem statements that serve as the head of your fishbone diagram.

Start using the QI Macros to slice and dice your tables (no matter how large). You'll find it easy to find the 4-50 and start making breakthrough improvements.

Six Sigma Tar Pits

Recently, I facilitated a team that had been in existence for 6 months. All they had to show for their time was a flowchart of a process that was mainly rework. I'd been calling for weeks nagging the team for data about how the process performs. I got part of the data the night before the meeting and the rest of the data by lunch. But after a morning of trying to sort through the issues surrounding the process, the team had fallen into "storming" about the whole process. They were frustrated, and so was I.

Pitfall 1. Brainstorming. Brainstorming is supposed to improve creativity, broaden associations, spark insights, and generate lots of creative ideas. When I first learned TQM, the instructors taught us to brainstorm problems to work on. The difficulty was that we had no idea what a good problem looked like. And it's hard to tell a team to brainstorm a problem to solve and then tell them that their problem is stupid. Lots of teams were started; few succeeded.

This highlights the main problem with brainstorming: if you don't know what you're looking for, you won't get useful ideas.

In the book *Made to Stick*, the Heath brothers reference a study of brainstorming. Groups were supposed to create the marketing ideas for a product.

- One group just started creating ideas.
- The second group was given 2 hours of training in brainstorming methods.
- The third group was given 2 hours of training in the six most successful *templates* for ads.

All ads were evaluated by a marketing director and tested on customers.

- Group one's ads were considered *annoying* by customers.
- Group two's ads were considered less annoying but no more creative.
- Group three's ads were considered 50% more creative and generated a 55% better response from customers.

In other words, brainstorming is useless unless you know what you're looking for or have a template for success.

Solution: When I look for problems to solve with Lean Six Sigma, I'm always looking for something I can solve with the methods and tools.

You can't fix your supplier's or customer's process, which is often the end result of brainstorming; you can see everyone else's faults, but not your own. I can't tell you how many teams I've seen try to fix management or their suppliers or their customers. You can't fix someone else's process, *because you don't own it.*

You can't fix morale with Lean Six Sigma. You can't fix perceptions. You can, however, fix the underlying problems that lower morale and perceptions.

When it comes to Lean Six Sigma, I'm always looking for

Delay

Sluggish processes can always benefit from the application of Lean. Most of the delay is *between* process steps when the product is waiting for the next action.

Defects

Error-prone processes devour profits in waste and rework. If detailed numerical counts of defects and their effects (i.e., costs) exist, then it's easy to use Six Sigma's problem-solving process to find and fix the problem. Where there are no facts and figures about the problem, Six Sigma fails.

Deviation

Variation from the ideal target causes higher costs and lower profit margins. Common types of deviation include

- Too long or too short
- Too big or too small
- Too wide or too narrow
- Too dense or too porous
- Too fast or too slow

Get the idea? It's okay to brainstorm problems about one of these three *templates* for improvement, but it's usually worthless to brainstorm without these focuses.

Worst of all, most teams hesitate to identify the really pressing problems because they don't want to be on the hook for fixing them. In contrast, they should focus on the worst first. Fix those problems, and everything else starts falling into place. We have to stop majoring in minor things.

Recently, I facilitated a team that had been in existence for 6 months. All they had to show for their time was a flowchart of a process that was mainly rework. I'd been calling for weeks nagging the team for data about process performance. I got part of the data the night before the meeting and the rest of the data by lunch. But after a morning of trying to sort through the issues surrounding the process, the team had fallen into "storming" about the whole process. They were frustrated and so was I.

Pitfall 2. Starting a team when you have no data (control chart and Pareto chart minimum) indicates you have a problem that cannot be solved using Six Sigma. Without data to guide you, you don't know who should be on the team, so you end up with different people trying to solve different problems.

Solution: Set the team up for success. (1) Work with data you already have; don't start a team to collect a bunch of new data. (2) Refine your problem *before* you let a group of people get in a room to analyze root causes. You can guarantee a team's success by laser-focusing the problem to be solved. One person can do this analysis in a few days using the QI Macros.

Pitfall 3. Question data. To throw a team off its tracks, some member who doesn't like the implications of the data will state in a congruent voice that the data is clearly wrong. If you let it, this will derail the team into further data analysis. I know from experience that *all* data is imperfect. It has been systematically distorted to make the key players look good and to manipulate the reward system, but it is the systematic distortion that allows you to use the data anyway.

Solution: Recognize that this member is operating on gut feel, not data. Simply ask: "Okay, do you have better data?" (They don't.) Then ask "How do you know the data's invalid? (I just know.) How do you know? (Instinct, gut feel.) Well, unless you have better data that proves this is invalid, we're going to continue using this data. You're welcome to go get your data, but meanwhile, we're moving forward." If the person is unwilling to continue, you should excuse him or her from the team, because he or she will continue to sabotage the progress.

Pitfall 4. Whalebone diagrams. When searching for root causes, if your fishbone diagram turns into a "whalebone" diagram that covers several walls, then your original focus was too broad.

Solution: Go back to your Pareto chart. Take the biggest bar down a level to get more specific. Write a new problem statement. Then go back to root cause analysis.

Pitfall 5. Boiling the ocean. Teams have an unflinching urge to fix big problems or all of the problems at once. If you've done a good job of laser focusing your problem, you'll have a specific type of defect in a specific area to focus on. If you let the team expand its focus, you'll end up whalebone diagramming and have to go back to a specific problem.

Solution: Get the team to agree to solve just this one issue, because its solution will probably improve several other elements of the overall problem. Assure them that you'll come back to the other pieces of the problem, but first you have to nail this one down.

Pitfall 6. Measuring activity, not results. Companies count the number of Six Sigma Black Belts trained and the number of teams started, but fail to measure the results achieved by these teams.

Here's my point. Use data for illumination, not support. Let it be your guide. The answers will surprise you and accelerate your journey to Lean Six Sigma.

Still Struggling

Teams often fail from either a lack of focus or a widening of the focus. The tighter the focus the more successful the team can be. Then pick off problems one by one until they are resolved.

Become a Lean Six Sigma Detective

In the August 2005 issue of *Business Week*, Michael Hopkins explored the best seller *Freakonomics* and it's authors' strategy for using data to explore and explain the world. They wrote: "Morality represents the way that people would like the world to work—whereas economics represents how it actually does work."

The November 2005 issue of *Fast Company* called 2005 the Year of the Economist. Why? Because books like *Freakonomics: A Rogue Economist Explores the Hidden Side of Everything* by Steven Levitt and Stephen Dubner became a best seller. Financial columnist, Tim Harford says: "The idea of the economist as a detective hero suddenly became easy to sell once *Freakonomics* climbed the best seller lists."

Suzanne Gluck, the author's agent, says that people are using *freakonomics* as a code word for unconventional wisdom. What's the secret, *Fast Company* asks? "It's just math," replies coauthor Dubner.

Isn't that the essence of Lean Six Sigma? Using numbers to explore the hidden side of defects, delays, and costs in ways that reveal the hidden gold mine of profits wasted every day in businesses large and small.

What's the "secret sauce" that makes Steven Levitt so successful? Coauthor Dubner says: "He seemed to look at things not so much as an academic but as a very *smart and curious explorer*—a documentary filmmaker, perhaps or a forensic investigator or a bookie whose markets ranged from sports to crime to pop culture." *He is an intuitionist*. He sifts through a pile of data to find a story that no one else has found. The *New York Times* magazine said he's "a kind of intellectual detective trying to figure things out."

Isn't that what Lean Six Sigma is at its core? Sifting through piles of data like an intellectual detective trying to explain the hidden side of defects, delay and cost?

Solution: The Data Strategy

In Hopkins's article, he identifies the key strategies used by Steven Levitt and his coauthor, Steven Lubner. They are

1. *Use your data*. Experts use their informational advantages to serve their own agendas. Hence the numbers can be bent to prove whatever I want to prove. It's amazing how many company managers want to use data to

prove their pet theory or justify their actions. Only after a long struggle do they begin to learn how to use data as a guide to clear thinking and action. I've always liked the quote: "He uses statistics like a drunk uses a light post, for support not illumination." In Lean Six Sigma this holds true far too often.

Knowing what to measure and how to measure it makes a complicated world much less so. If you learn how to look at data in the right way, you can explain riddles that otherwise might have seemed impossible. Companies generate lots of data about orders, sales, purchases, payments, and so on. The bigger the company, the more data they have and the less likely they are to use it. Figure out what data is useful and *use* it. Figure out what data isn't useful and stop collecting it.

2. *Ask quirky questions.* If you're focused on why things go wrong, ask: "What are we doing right? Who is already doing this right?" If you focus on why things are going right, focus on what's wrong and start with the "worst first." In *Freakonomics*, Levit stopped asking why crime rates have fallen since 1990. He started asking what kind of individuals are most likely to commit crimes and then asked, "Why are they disappearing from the population?" His answer to that question is startling, but instructive of his method: "Let the data lead you."

3. *Don't mistake correlation for causality.* The United States spends 2.5 times more on health care than any other country, yet Americans aren't healthier than other countries. Affluent women have a higher incidence of breast cancer than poor women. Does wealth cause breast cancer? Does health care cause illness?

Dramatic effects often have distant, even subtle, causes. Six Sigma looks for direct causes and effects, but systemic effects can amplify subtle causes into dramatic ones.

4. *Question conventional wisdom.* The conventional wisdom is often wrong. If conventional wisdom were correct, then most problems would have already been solved. You can't get new insights from old ways of thinking.

5. *Respect the complexity of incentives.* Incentives are the cornerstone of modern life. In Lean Six Sigma people are rewarded for following systems that cause defects, delays, and cost. Humans will always find ways to beat the system. Rely on it.

The moral of the story: "Make data your friend," says Hopkins. I'd say let it be your guide.

I also like Levitt's confession: "You don't need to know a lot of math. I'm horrible at math." That's why I created the QI Macros SPC software for Excel. The macros do all of the scary math; you just need to know how to interpret the resulting graphs.

Become a Six Sigma detective or treasure hunter superhero. Learn how and what to measure to simplify understanding your business. Let your measurements lead you to find and plug the leaks in your cash flow. Distrust conventional wisdom. Look for subtle causes that amplify themselves into disturbing effects. Share what you learn. Most of all: Get on with it! There's no end to the mysteries to be revealed and problems to be solved.

Still Struggling

Six Sigma only works if you have numbers (i.e., data) about the defects or deviation. When in doubt, start with a problem for which there is already sufficient data. Don't bother trying to collect a new measurement right away. In most companies there's more than enough data about real problems that you can solve now. Later, once you understand more about what makes a good measurement, use a check sheet to gather some new data about a problem that's been hard to diagnose.

Mistakes, Defects, and Errors

At the Institute for Healthcare Improvement conference in Orlando last December, one of the presentations covered the application of the Toyota Production System (TPS) to a hospital. The presenter opened by saying that *health care, in general, was a poor-quality product that cost too much for the value delivered*. I was immediately struck by the guts it took to make that statement. The presenter went on to repeat that thought many times throughout the presentation. I doubt that many people caught it.

The reason for his comments? A 1999 study found that as many as 100,000 people a year die due to *preventable* medical mistakes in U.S. hospitals. That made health care the *eighth leading cause of preventable deaths in the United States.* In 2010, 99,000 people a year die due to preventable hospital-acquired infections. Another 150,000 die due to preventable surgical complications. Better reporting of medical errors has moved health care into the top five leading causes of preventable deaths in the U.S.

One of the biggest challenges to Lean Six Sigma is not the use of the methods or tools, but *creating a mindset that loves to find and fix defects and delays.* Not everyone thinks of these issues under the banner that I call *defects and delays.* So I got into the Synonym Finder to look for other words that mean the same thing. It's amazing how many words exist in the English language to describe mistakes and errors. Here are just a few:

blemish	fallacy	misprint
blooper	false step	misstep
blot stain	fault	mistake
Blotch	faulty	muff
blunder	flaw	off the beam
bobble	flub	omission
boner	foul-up	oversight
boo-boo	fumble	rough spots
botch	goof	scare deformity
breach	human error	scratch
bugs	illogical	screwup
bungle	imperfection	shortage
clinker	imprecise	shortcoming
clunker	inaccuracy	slip up
cockeyed	inadequacy	snafu
crack	incomplete	snags
defect	incorrect	spot
deficiency	inexact	Tear
drawback	kinks	trip
error	leak	Unsound
failing	louse up	weak point
failure	miscue	weakness

If you continue and look at words that describe how people make these mistakes, you'll find another group of words dedicated to describing *the activities that lead to poor-quality products and services.*

misapply	misdoing	Mismanage
misapprehend	misestimation	Mismatch
miscalculation	misguided	Misplace
misconceive	mishap	Misreading
misconception	misidentification	Misreckon
misconstruction	misinterpretation	Misspend
misconstrue	misjudgment	Misstep
miscount	mislay	Mistaken
misdirected	mislead	Misunderstanding
		Misuse

Until you're willing to *stop congratulating yourself for what's working and start looking at the misses, mistakes, errors, omissions, defects, and delay* that are irritating customers, demotivating employees, and devouring your profit margins, all of the Lean Six Sigma methods and tools will not help you. Once you view every mistake as an opportunity to mistake-proof and improve the delivery of your product or service, you'll get hooked on Lean Six Sigma. Until then, the methods and tools will just be another burden in an already crisis-managed world.

Measurement Simplicity

Jack Welch said "Simplicity applies to measurements also. *Too often we measure everything and understand nothing.*" All too often we hear from customers that they are so overwhelmed drawing charts and graphs that they don't have time to analyze and improve anything.

I used to work in the telephone company, and it collected thousands of measurements, most of which were never used. One hospital using the QI Macros was tracking 300 different measures. 300? What's wrong with this picture? I'll tell you what: they can't possibly be using all of these measures. Ten or 12 provide most of the information required to run that hospital. Measurements should help you, not hinder you.

The purpose of measurement is to guide, forewarn, and inform.

1. Guidance provides course corrections "in flight" while you're running the business.

2. Measurement can also forewarn you of potential problems (e.g., trends or instabilities on control charts).

3. And measurement can help keep customers, suppliers, and leaders informed of your progress.

Are you collecting measurements that aren't really useful for any one of these three purposes? Do you really need them? Is some other measurement used in their place? (20% of the measurements cover 80% of your needs.)

First, start systematically suspending measurements that are questionable. Then, if anyone comes out of the woodwork to complain about missing the information, ask, How are they using the information? Would some other measurement serve them better? Second, if a suspended measurement isn't resurrected in two or three months, kill it. Third, start looking for the "vital few" measurements of "failure" that everyone relies on to make improvements and informed decisions. In any business these are invariably defects, delay, and cost. You'll also need measurements of success: profit, ROI, and so forth.

Here are four basic steps to create your own process measures.

1. Define what results are important to you and the business.

2. Map the cross-functional process used to deliver these results.

3. Identify the critical tasks and capabilities required to complete the process successfully.

4. Design measures that track those tasks and capabilities.

What are the most common measurement mistakes?

1. Piles of numbers. Use the balanced scorecard (QI Macros template) to identify the vital few.

2. Inaccurate, late, or unreliable data. If it isn't collected systematically and automatically in real time, it's often suspect.

3. Trying to meet a target instead of trying to understand the process.

4. One size fits all: Trying to use too broad or too specific a measurement.

5. Gauge blindness: Trusting the measurement even when there is evidence to the contrary (e.g., a sticky gas gauge can leave you stranded.).

6. Micrometer versus yardstick. Precisely measuring unimportant things without imprecisely measuring the important ones.

7. Punishing the people instead of fixing the process. Use your data to learn something and make things better.

Simplify and streamline your measurement system to keep the important stuff and to abandon the unimportant stuff. You'll be surprised how much unimportant stuff is sucking up time and resources that could be dedicated to improving your business!

Invisible Low-Hanging Fruit

When I first got into the quality improvement movement in 1990, our Florida Power and Light consultants always spoke about low-hanging fruit just waiting to be plucked. Two years later and tens of thousands of staff hours later, we still hadn't found any low-hanging fruit.

In any company, if there really is low-hanging fruit, it's usually visible from everywhere from the factory floor to the management conference room. When it's *that* visible, anyone can pluck it with a little common sense and a bit of trial and error.

That's why in most companies there is no *visible* low-hanging fruit. Somebody has already plucked it! And this is what stops most leaders from even considering the tools of Six Sigma: they can't see any more fruit to be picked.

But in company after company, my own included, I have found orchards filled with low-hanging, invisible fruit. You just can't see it with the naked eye.

You can, however, discern it through the magnifying lens of control charts and Pareto charts. *They make the seemingly invisible, visible.* They are the microscopes, the MRIs, the EKGs of business diagnosis.

When Louis Pasteur said that there were tiny bugs in air and in the water, everyone thought he was crazy because they weren't visible to the naked eye. Everyone thought it was just an "ill wind" that made people sick.

In today's tough economic times, everyone laments about how hard it is. How an "ill wind" has blown through their business, their industry, and their economy. But have they considered using the modern tools of business medicine to root out the infectious agents in their business? Have they taken the time to look for the invisible low-hanging fruit in their business? I doubt it.

Someone sent me an email today that said that even in the poorest run companies, he'd had no luck finding the low-hanging fruit. But in every company I've ever worked with, I've found millions of dollars just waiting to be retrieved from the caldrons of defects and delay. Are you looking for the obvious? Or investigating the invisible?

The low-hanging fruit is always invisible to the naked eye. Turn the magnifying and illuminating tools of Six Sigma on your most difficult operational problems, and stare into the depths of the unknown, the unfamiliar. You'll invariably find bushels of bucks, just waiting for a vigilant harvester.

Core Score

In Marcus Buckingham's book, *The One Thing You Need to Know*, there's a section on knowing your core score. What's the one thing you need to know about your business?

Core Score for Prisons

Buckingham interviewed General Sir David Ramsbotham who was in charge of Her Majesty's prisons. He says that he knew he couldn't make wardens change. In order to make things happen, he had to change the way they measured success.

- *Old metric.* Number of escapees
- *New metric.* Number of repeat offenders

The old goal was to keep prisoners in, but the General started thinking: Who is a prison designed to serve? Answer: the prisoner! "The main purpose of a prison should be to serve the prisoner. By which I mean that we must do something for the prisoner while he is in prison so that when he is released back into society he is less likely to commit another crime." Armed with this new score, he turned the prison world upside down.

Core Score for Health Care

In the old world of health care, the measure was based on outcomes: Did the patient get better no matter how long it took? I am coming to believe that the new world of health care is measured on speed.

- Door-to-doctor time in the Emergency Room of under 30 minutes
- ED length of stay of less than 2 hours
- ED-to-nursing floor for admitted patients of under 30 minutes
- Length of stay of 2 to 3 days based on diagnosis
- Discharge-to-disposition (patient transferred) of under 60 minutes

Most of these times can run two to four times longer at present. Patients are used to being served in minutes everywhere else; why not in health care? Of course, health care will need a few metrics of patient safety as well.

- ED returns within 7 days
- Hospital returns within 30 days
- Poor outcomes (infection, death, etc.)

Education's Core Score

I recently worked with a school district. The school district gets money on the basis of *attendance*.

Who do school systems serve? The student! So I'm wondering if a school's core score shouldn't be the *dropout rate*. Dropouts are more likely to struggle with finding work and resort to crime. It's an indicator that we've failed to prepare that student for life. Attendance is a *predictor* of dropout rates; it's what I call a *process* indicator. The dropout rate is a *critical to quality* indicator that measures the end result.

What's Your Core Score?

Who do you serve? What do they want? How can you measure that you deliver what they want?

Measurements drive behavior. Bad measures will drive bad behavior. Good measures will drive good behavior. If you aren't getting what you want from your business, adjust what you measure and how you reward it. The system will change!

Still Struggling

Sometimes it's easier to start with someone else's product or service to determine core scores. What might be the core score of a help desk? Percent of issues resolved on the first call. What might be the core score of a credit card company? Accurate, fraud-free bills. Once you start to see the core scores of other industries it builds momentum to figuring out your own.

Customer—Supplier Relationships

Lately I've noticed that too many suppliers are willing to deal with all of their customer's mistakes to get the job which ends up costing them both more money and more time.

Recently, we sent out a mailing to our customers about some new products. Little did we know that our mail house has been cleaning up our file for the last several years. This time, however, a new member of their staff pulled the address file just the way we sent it to them resulting in 1,500 returned mail pieces due to insufficient address. Shouldn't they have caught it just by looking at it? They had in the past. Shouldn't they have caught it during the run? Probably, but they didn't.

When I asked what went wrong, they explained that they had been cleaning up our file, but had failed to do so this time. I asked what they would like from us instead and got some clear requirements about how to provide an address file that would minimize the chance of this happening in the future.

The same thing happened with our printer who finally admitted that he'd have to start charging us for preparation work if we didn't start sending our color artwork as CMYK (four color) instead of RGB. Otherwise he has to convert it all before he prints.

Suppliers Are Customers Too

In both cases, we supply our suppliers with electronic files (addresses and artwork). They become our customers for this part of the transaction. Then they supply us with printed or mailed materials. If I know what suppliers want, I can usually give it to them without much extra effort on my part, but I need to know their requirements. Most don't even have a checklist of criteria for a job.

Clean Up Your Own Act

You know from experience that flawed raw materials will produce a poor quality product. Which of your suppliers rely on you for some sort of input before they can begin? What are the flaws in your "raw materials?" Find out your supplier's requirements. Ask. What will help minimize the cost, time, and chance of error for my job? Change your processes to deliver what they need. This will accelerate the speed with which your job can be completed and minimize the risks.

Train Your Customers

Do you have a checklist of requirements for input from your customers? What would it take to create one? How could you position it as a way for them to save money, reduce risk, and reduce the time required to meet their needs? Learning how to dance well with your customers and suppliers means learning when to lead and when to follow. Ask your suppliers how you can help them do a better job. Train your customers on how to work with you more effectively. It will take some time, but the savings are worth it. And savings translate into more business and greater profits. What have you got to lose?

Bar Codes Bust Medication Errors

Good News: When the VA adopted bar codes for patients and medicines, medication errors plummeted. By bar-coding medications and patients and using handheld scanners, clinicians can ensure that the right patient gets the right dosage of the right medication at the right time.

Bad News: An estimated 7,000 people die in hospitals of medication errors. One out of every 14,000 transfusions get the wrong blood resulting in at least 20 deaths each year. Only about 125 of the nation's 5,000 hospitals use bar codes now.

Good News: The FDA now requires bar codes on all medications.

Bad News: The national average for wristband inaccuracies in hospitals is 3%. (If you get the band wrong, everything else can go wrong too.)

Sadly, safety technology isn't a big diagnostic machine that generates revenue; it's a protective device that reduces the cost of treatment and litigation. The good news is that the technology is out there to make our health care safer than ever before. All we have to do is embrace it.

The High Cost of Bad Data

You may remember when the speed limits were lowered to 55 to "save lives." Yet a study by the Cato Institute found just the opposite: The fatality rate on the nation's roads declined for a 35-year period excluding the period from 1976 to 1980 when the *speed limit was 55*. After the speed limit was raised in 1995, the fatality rate dropped to the lowest in recorded history. There were also 400,000 fewer injuries.

Furthermore, there's no evidence that states with higher speed limits had increased deaths. States with speed limits of 65 to 75 saw a 12% decline in fatalities. States with a 75 mph speed limit saw over a 20% decline in fatality rates.

Wrong Root Cause

What does this data suggest? Higher speed limits weren't the cause of highway fatalities. For those of us who can remember the seventies, you may have owned a Fix or Repair Daily (FoRD) or some other clunker. The main reason that the roads are now safer than ever before is because cars and roads are built better than ever before. Antilock brakes, power steering, and crash protections all help prevent fatalities.

To paraphrase a recent political campaign: It's the car stupid!

The other main cause is bad driving habits: It's the driver stupid!

What did this slow down in delivery of people and goods over the nation's highways cost? Although it's almost impossible to connect all of the dots, the stock market was down and interest rates soared. It did, however, create an overnight market for CB radios and radar detectors.

What's the new rising fatality cause? In 2008, distracted drivers talking or texting on a cell phone killed 5,870 people and injured 515,000. Texting was a factor in 200,000 crashes that year.

Emissions Testing

Similarly in 1995, Denver initiated an emissions-testing program to reduce carbon monoxide and other emissions. The program costs $44 million per year, but has only reduced emissions by 4%, far less than the 33% projected from the initial data. Not surprisingly, 6.7% of the 833,122 cars tested in 2001 failed. This is exactly three sigma.

One of the assumptions was that the owner would have their car fixed after it failed. In reality, about 75% of the owners bring their car back through on another day when the car passed because of variability in the testing process. In other words, the testing process was barely at one sigma level (less than 30% accurate).

But what did it cost to squeeze a few more pounds of emissions out of the air? Were there other ways to spend $44 million per year that might have reaped greater gains? For those of us who waited in line for up to an hour to have our emissions tested, what did that cost—time that could have been spent making money, spending money, being with family and friends?

Not surprisingly, the real difference over the past 10 to 15 years is technology has surpassed the ability of cars to pollute. Cars are running cleaner and staying cleaner longer, and that has made the biggest difference.

It's the car stupid!

Here's my point. Data can provide an excellent rearview mirror into the past. But it can be misused in the same way a drunk uses a lamppost: for support, not illumination.

Forcing your data to support your point of view can lead to more defects, delay, and cost. In the case of the 55 mph speed limit, there were more fatalities, more delay, and more cost. In the case of the emissions-testing program, the 100% inspection process took time and money from taxpayers for a minimal reduction in emissions. And it was too error prone to deliver consistent results.

Identifying the wrong root cause can lead you down a path of waste, rework, and expense that can be avoided.

Let your data guide you; don't force the data to fit your pet hypothesis. Then, once you've implemented your solution, verify that you've actually succeeded at reducing the root cause and its effects. Otherwise, you're not doing Six Sigma; you're just conning your company and customers and hastening the day when the business will be shuttered forever.

Measuring Innovation

In the late '70s, I worked at Bell Labs developing software for the Bell System. Although most software engineers still gag at the thought of measuring software development, we were tracking cycle times, defects, and costs way back then. So I never understood why anyone would think that you can't measure innovation. You just need to tweak the metrics a little bit.

In Christopher Meyer's book, *Relentless Growth–How Silicon Valley Innovation Strategies Can Work in Your Business*, he devotes a whole chapter to measuring innovation! Here's an abstract of his recommendations. He suggests that the five classic measures to watch are

1. *Performance.* How well does the total solution perform relative to requirements and the competition? Sounds like quality function deployment (QFD) and Design for Lean Six Sigma (DFLSS).

2. *Quality.* Defects and delay.

3. *Timing* (i.e., speed to market). Internal development schedule (cycle time) and external market timing.

4. *Financials.* Cost, margins, and revenue expectations.

5. *Development costs.* Specific project costs.

Here are some key measures of innovation used in Silicon Valley.

- Cycle time
- Percent of product or service tests passed
- Turnover (personnel changes)
- Specification or requirement changes (changes)

- Percent reuse (how much tested stuff did you borrow?)
- Percent new parts (how much stuff is untested)
- Percent unique parts (potential integration difficulties)
- Percent new vendors
- Percent staffed to plan (under or over staffed)
- Percent of time lost to other projects

Have you been putting off measuring your innovation processes? What ideas can you reuse from this list to get started now? What ideas do these give you for making immediate improvements in your innovation processes? What measures of innovation are you already using?

Accidents Don't Just Happen

This is the sort of headline that you don't want to read about your company.

Accident kills boy undergoing MRI—A 6-year-old boy was killed when the MRI's powerful magnet pulled a metal oxygen tank through the air fracturing the boy's skull. Westchester Medical Center officials said the tank had been brought into the room accidentally. Officials would not say who brought the oxygen tank into the MRI room.

Forget *who* brought it into the room. Doesn't it seem more desirable that it should be *impossible* to bring metal into an MRI room? I've been through scanners at airports that rant about anything bigger than a quarter. Could such a device be installed in the doorway to the MRI room? Sure. Could an alarm on the metal detector prevent the operation of the MRI? Sure. If it saves the life of one 6-year-old boy, wouldn't it be worth it?

Now ask: Why? Why? Why? Why? Why? Why were oxygen tanks loaded or unloaded anywhere near the MRI? Is the MRI close to the loading dock? Was the boy brought in from surgery with a tank? Why wasn't his tank removed before the MRI?

Using the QI Macros to Analyze Your Data

For some reason, figuring out where to begin seems to be everyone's biggest problem. Over the years, I've developed a simple method for looking at Excel-based data and deciding how to process it.

The Problem-Solving Process

The problem-solving process begins with a *control chart* of current performance. (With the QI Macros, it's so easy to draw a control chart that it's silly to use a line graph. And you'll need the control chart to monitor and sustain the improvement.) You then use the detail behind the performance data to create a *Pareto chart*.

Control Charts

Control charts show performance *over time*. So I'm always looking for some orientation of the data that goes from first to last. This could be production sample numbers, dates, times, or whatever.

The problem-solving process also implies that there is some kind of error, mistake, or defect. So I'm looking for *attribute* data about defects (i.e., mistakes, errors, or out of spec). I'm not looking for *variable* data like money or cycle time or length or weight. Let's look at some sample defect data from the AIAG (Fig. 5-36).

	A	B	C	D	E	F	G	H	I	J	K	L	M	N	O	P	Q	R	S	T	U	V	W	X	Y	Z	AA
1																											Total
2	Undersize	2	4	3	3	2	6	4	0	6	5	4	1	2	2	6	3	8	4	3	4	5	4	2	3	6	92
3	Cold Weld					1													1								2
4	Missing	1		1									1							1						4
5	Off-Location		1					1																1		3
6																											
7	Number	2	5	4	3	3	6	5	0	7	5	4	1	2	3	6	3	8	4	4	4	6	4	2	3	7	
8	Sample	62																									

H ◄ ► H \ GageR&R ⟨ XbarR 2nd ⟨ XmedianR ⟨ XbarR ⟨ XmR ⟨ p chart ⟨ p chart var ⟩ np chart ⟨ c chart ⟨ u chart /

FIGURE 5-36 · Auto assembly defect data.

This example shows defects, over time, by sample. There were 62 samples taken and the number of defects counted. The natural inclination of most people is to subtract the defects from the sample size and show how many were produced correctly (e.g., 62 – 2 = 60 good in the first sample), but this inclination draws your attention away from the problem. To solve a problem, you need to understand the problem.

The np chart of defects can be drawn easy with the QI Macros (Fig. 5-37). Select the data and click on QI Macros—np chart and enter 62 as the sample size.

FIGURE 5-37 · np chart of assembly errors.

Pareto Chart

Since there are no red points or lines, the process is stable. The next step is to look for detail about the types of defects. If you look at the data, you'll want to look for totals by type of defect: undersize, cold weld, missing, or off-location (Fig. 5-38).

FIGURE 5-38 · Total defects by type data.

Just select the titles in column A and then hold down the Control key on your keyboard and select the totals in column AA as shown. Then you can use the QI Macros to draw the Pareto chart (Fig. 5-39).

FIGURE 5-39 • Total assembly errors by type.

As you can see, *undersize* contributes most of the problem. This is clearly a Pareto pattern: One defect accounts for 91% of the defects. Because the part is undersized, it probably isn't possible to rework the part, so it may have to be scrapped.

If we had more detailed data about the undersize error, we might be able to draw another more detailed Pareto chart of the data *inside* this one bar, but we don't. So we continue by creating an Ishikawa or fishbone diagram.

Ishikawa Fishbone Cause-and-Effect Diagram

Just click on the QI Macros and choose *Fill in the Blank templates*. Select *Ishikawa diagram* (Fig. 5-40) and then change the problem statement to match the Pareto pattern.

Your improvement story is now ready for root cause analysis. Knowing that the problem is *undersized,* you can more easily choose the right team members to help analyze the problem.

Move the Fishbone

If you want, you can move the Ishikawa template into the data workbook to continue developing your improvement story in *one* Excel Workbook.

Just click on Edit–Move or Copy sheet to get this dialog box (Fig. 5-41). Then change the "To Book" to the main data workbook (in this case AIAG SPC.xls) and click OK.

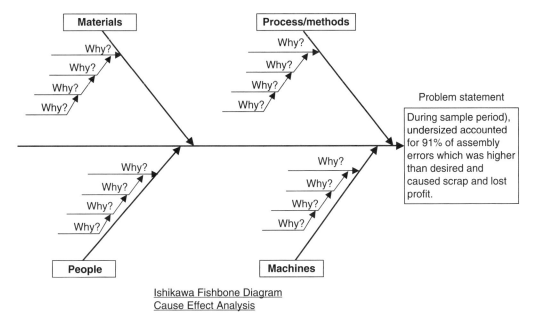

Ishikawa Fishbone Diagram
Cause Effect Analysis

FIGURE 5-40 • Problem statement in fishbone diagram.

FIGURE 5-41 • Move or copy sheets in Excel.

This will move the template into the workbook along with the original data, np chart, and Pareto chart (Fig. 5-42).

Barriers to Success

If you don't have the data to draw the Pareto chart, can you use a check sheet (Fig. 5-26) to collect a week's worth of data about the type of defects? (Click

FIGURE 5-42 • Fishbone in improvement story workbook.

on QI Macros–Fill in the Blanks templates and select *check sheet* to get a template.) A week's worth of data will be more than enough to analyze a stable process.

Analysis Is Easy . . . If You Know What to Look For

The process is simple.

1. *Look for data of defects or deviation over time.* Draw a control chart of performance over time.

2. *Draw a Pareto chart of the types of defects found or histogram of deviation.*

3. *Use the biggest bar of the Pareto chart to create a fishbone diagram* for root cause analysis. The problem statement should reflect the problem identified in the Pareto chart. You now have enough insight into the problem to choose the right root cause analysis team.

4. *Analyze the root causes and verify* that you have found the true root causes *using data.*

5. Show performance before and after implementing the improvement using a control chart.

6. Continue to monitor and improve the process.

I don't know why, but most people try to make it a lot harder than this. You don't have to. You can let your data lead you to dramatic improvements.

QUIZ

1. **What do the following acronyms stand for?**
   - DMAIC
   - FISH
   - PDCA

2. **The Six Sigma problem-solving process works best when you are focused on**
   A. increasing *profits.*
   B. decreasing *defects and deviation.*

3. **What is the correct order for these steps in the problem-solving process?**
   ___ Write a problem statement
   ___ Verify the root causes
   ___ Draw a Pareto chart of types of problems
   ___ Draw a histogram of variation
   ___ Select countermeasures
   ___ Verify the results
   ___ Draw a control chart of current performance
   ___ Do a cause-and-effect analysis using the fishbone diagram

4. **Root cause analysis asks**
   A. what?
   B. where?
   C. when?
   D. why?
   E. how?

5. **What are the tar pits of Six Sigma?**
   A. "Boiling the ocean" scope creep
   B. Brainstorming problems to solve
   C. No data
   D. Doubting the data
   E. Whalebone diagramming
   F. Measuring teams and training, not results
   G. All of the above

6. **When you don't have any data to analyze,**
   A. set up a measurement system.
   B. give up.
   C. use a check sheet to gather a representative sample.

7. Name three of the most common measurement mistakes.

    A. _____

    B. _____

    C. _____

8. Order the following tools in the sequence necessary to create a Six Sigma improvement story.

    ____ Ishikawa or fishbone diagram

    ____ Control chart

    ____ Countermeasures matrix

    ____ Pareto chart or histogram

EXERCISES

1. Over the next week, read your local newspaper and clip all of the articles involving product or service failure and the high costs of poor quality.

2. Develop a control chart of the problem area.
   - In small groups, have participants select one indicator for defects, time, or cost. Using real or best-guess data, have participants graph the current performance of the indicator.

3. Develop Pareto charts of the problem area to laser: focus the analysis.

   Two or more Pareto charts are often necessary to find a specific problem to solve. If the team doesn't narrow the focus here, they will end up with a whale-bone diagram in step 2. Reinforce the link between the control chart and the Pareto charts.
   - In small groups, have participants identify the main contributors to the problem indicator of defects, time, or cost. Using real or best-guess data, have participants identify the biggest contributor to the problem (big bar on the Pareto chart).
   - If possible, have participants further stratify the biggest contributor or have them identify how they would further focus the problem.
   - Have participants use the Pareto chart to write a problem statement.

4. *Purpose:* Develop cause-and-effect diagram.
   - In small groups, have participants select the type of diagram and the most likely main contributor (big bone).
   - Have participants ask 'why?' up to five times to identify at least one root cause of the problem.
   - Have participants discuss how they would verify this root cause using data.

5. Develop countermeasures. During the analysis of the problem, obvious countermeasures will often appear. The first three steps of the process tend to overlap. In the first few minutes of the first meeting, members will often offer unvalidated countermeasures and root causes. These should be captured and stored in the appropriate place in the improvement story.

   Once the root causes have been validated with data to ensure that the team is tackling the true origin of the problem, various alternative countermeasures can be evaluated. There are two key questions.
   - How effective is the countermeasure at preventing the root cause?
   - How feasible (i.e., cost beneficial) is the countermeasure in terms of resources, time, and cost to implement?
     Which countermeasures are the most effective and feasible? Avoid implementing too many at one time; one may cancel out another.

6. **Graph the results. In small groups, have participants use real or best-guess data to anticipate the future performance of the indicators developed in step 1.**

7. **To complete Six Sigma Story,**
   - Identify how the indicators will change if countermeasures reduce or eliminate the root causes. (Since participants can't usually implement the countermeasures during training, we can ask them what to expect from this step. Assuming that the countermeasures where successful, what effect would the participants expect to see in the graphs from steps 1 and 2?)
   - Identify ways to standardize and stabilize the resulting improvement. (Assuming that the countermeasures where successful, what steps would the participants expect to take in order to stabilize the process and lock in the improvements? What changes are necessary in people, process, machines, materials, or the environment? This can be handled as a discussion in class.)
   - Assuming that the countermeasures were successful, ask the participants: "Who else could benefit from what you've learned? How can this improvement be either adapted or adopted by other members of your organization to maximize the resulting benefit?"
   - What next steps would the team recommend? Why?

chapter **6**

Transactional Six Sigma

For the last few decades (and the foreseeable future), the race for productivity and profitability has been led by technology: software, hardware, and network solutions. More and more processes are being integrated into a company's application systems. This both speeds things up and slows them down. Programmers etch process errors into the stone of code, so the software produces the same errors as the manual process, only faster and more of them. Changes to software applications often take months if not years to implement depending on how much clout you have in the endless meetings that prioritize changes to existing systems. Almost any process improvement now involves some sort of application software change, so it's becoming essential to understand how to make dramatic improvements in software systems.

CHAPTER OBJECTIVES

In this chapter, you will

- Learn how to apply Six Sigma for software and Information Technology
- Learn the Dirty 30 process for Six Sigma software

Process or Technology

I was on a plane from Denver to Knoxville to train a hospital on control charts when I opened up the *American Way* magazine and found an interview with Larry Ellison, CEO of Oracle, the second-largest software company. The article tried to show that using its own software helped Oracle save $1 billion dollars, but Ellison said something even more important: "The way you get quality is to define a set of processes and procedures and make sure they are implemented everywhere."

I was stunned! Here's a tech-CEO saying the key was consistent processes. And what he said next resonated with my two decades of software development and maintenance experience: "Before we could automate anything, we had to standardize the new processes we would need. It meant simplifying and modernizing every procedure."

"People ask the wrong question when they automate a company or process: Will this bunch of software allow us to [do] things the way we [do] them today? The right question is Will this bunch of software allow us to [do] things the way we should do them?

After I graduated from the University of Arizona with a B.S. in Systems Engineering (the high art of optimizing systems), I got hired as a COBOL programmer for a telephone company. There I was tasked with writing programs to automate existing manual processes that were so cumbersome and error prone that I often wondered what we hoped to gain by automating them. Here's what I learned: When you automate a poor process, you make it difficult and time-consuming to change. Things you might have changed on the fly now had to go through screening, prioritization, requirements, design, code, and test. Most changes took months, even years.

Years later, it seemed we were still doing the same things, but even dumber stuff. If an existing system caused too many errors, we'd write a mechanized system to fix the errors caused by the first system because the first one was deemed too complex to fix! There were systems that fixed addresses on outgoing bills (150,000 per month were undeliverable). Why didn't we go back into the service order system and prevent the input of incorrect addresses? It might slow down our service reps. Silly huh?

So, if you want to maximize the benefit of your new information systems, use Ellison's and my advice.

1. Simplify, streamline, or reengineer your processes first.

2. Then choose or build a system that reflects the streamlined flow, not the old flow.

3. Expect each new application release to be error-prone. Use systematic problem solving to identify and remedy all of the requirements, design, and coding errors. Resolve problems at their source, not necessarily where they show up.

4. As your new system evolves, simplify and streamline the software to prevent the creeping complexity that will render it inflexible and unchangeable.

Having worked with software for over 30 years, I've noticed some patterns of behavior that in hindsight seem obvious, but, in foresight, are largely ignored.

First, most new application systems arrive at around 2.5 sigma—over a 15% error rate. This is not because the IT department did a crappy job of testing, but because it's almost impossible to specify every condition that you'll encounter when developing a new application for a large company. After their cataclysmic maiden voyage, these systems achieve equilibrium around three sigma—3% to 6% error—while still encountering the enormous costs of human error correction on the remaining fallout (autonomation).

Second, all application systems have some method for detecting errors—input that doesn't match expected parameters—and someplace to store these errors until they can be examined and resolved by a living, breathing person. When you're doing 10,000 transactions a day like most large companies, 15% errors translates into 1,500 errors a day to be corrected. Most company CIOs expect their shiny new systems to be infallible, so this error rate comes as a shock. Squads of error correctors are rounded up to fix the growing backlog of errors that are delaying order fulfillment, billing, and payment. Customer service call centers are pushed to their limits by customers trying to find out what happened to their orders, bills, and payments. After much blood letting, the error rate falls to 3% to 6%, which seems tolerable compared to the previous level. Most large companies, whether they admit it or not, have staffs of 50 to 60 people fixing these ongoing errors created every day on each of their key information systems. Because this error correction is done by people who are inadequately trained and powered by the same technology that created the original errors, as much as 15% of the errors are corrected incorrectly and have to be fixed again, and again, and again.

Information systems usually involve ordering, production, delivery, billing, and collection systems. Like salmon in a stream, most companies try to swim up river from the polluted end of the process rather than correcting the problem at its source. Start with the ordering system and downstream improvements will be substantial. Then move downstream, system by system, eliminating defects and fallout. Mistake-proof the user interfaces to ensure the correct decisions are made automatically at each step of the process.

Although most software developers rely on testing and debugging to exterminate the bugs, delivered systems invariably reject transactions they should accept. The cost of fixing these rejects is often hidden and ridiculously expensive. Most people think these bugs infest the entire system, but they're actually clustered just in a few hives.

Here's the good news. I've discovered a simple, yet highly effective and economical way to solve these problems, but it requires measurement, improvement, and process—three things that software engineers loathe.

Transactional Six Sigma

Although most traditional improvement methods focus on manufacturing, the value in the marketplace has shifted away from manufacturing to *transactions*. Airline reservation systems are more valuable than the airlines themselves. To maximize the benefit of Transactional Six Sigma, you'll want to find ways to use Six Sigma on your *transaction* processes and errors.

Transaction Costs

Larry Downes and Chunka Mui identified six types of *transaction* costs in their book, *Unleashing the Killer App*, to which I'll add one.

1. *Search costs.* How much does it cost you in time and money to find new suppliers and customers?

2. *Information costs.* Buyers have to learn about your product or service. Sellers have to identify and qualify the customer.

3. *Bargaining costs.* How much does it cost to negotiate the terms of a sale? For a CD, not much; for a fleet of airplanes, probably much more.

4. *Decision costs.* How much does it cost in time and money to make the decision to buy one thing or another? How many sign-offs are required? Meetings? How many alternatives need to be evaluated?

5. *Policing costs.* What does it cost to ensure the terms of sale and service are met?

6. *Enforcement costs.* What does it cost to resolve unmet terms?

7. *IT costs.* And I'll add the Information Technologies' cost of ordering, invoicing, purchasing, and payment processing.

Your Product or Service May Be Different, But . . .

Whenever I talk to business people, they all tell me how their business is *different from every other kind of business*. Your product or service may be different or the way you deliver it may be different, but you still have to take orders, purchase supplies, issue invoices or bills, write checks, apply payments, and handle the same financial *transactions* as any other business. The core of your business may be a product or service, but the key to whether you make a profit lies in how good you are at *transaction* processing.

With financial *transactions*, your cash flow depends on

- *Accuracy.* Right quantities, pricing, taxing, and so on. It doesn't matter if you build the perfect product, if the customer asked for something else.

- *Speed.* How fast the *transaction* is created and processed (and how fast you can fix an incorrect one). It doesn't matter if you make the best product, if it takes too long to get it ordered, delivered, installed, or paid for.

- *Cost.* What does it cost to create and process the *transaction* (and what are the scrap and rework costs when you have an incorrect *transaction*)?

The basic tools of Six Sigma such as Control charts, Pareto charts, and fishbone diagrams can be used to find and fix errors in orders, bills, and so on. A p chart and XmR chart can be used to monitor *transaction* errors and cash flow.

The basic tools of Lean can be used to find and eliminate the delays in *transaction* processing in ways that will accelerate your cash flow. If you're only using Lean Six Sigma on your product or service, you're missing a golden opportunity to plug the leaks in your cash flow.

Software Bugs and Six Sigma

Recently, *CheapTickets.com* made a little error loading rates for flights to Reykjavik, Iceland—round-trip airfare from New York for only $61, a far cry from the $787 it should have been. About 800 people took advantage of the glitch during the 22 hours it was available. It seems there's a website where frequent flyers share this kind of information: *Flyertalk.com*. By the time the listing was posted on *Flyertalk*, it was late evening in Iceland and no one probably caught the glitch until the next morning. Unlike some carriers who do not honor their mistakes, *CheapTickets* and Icelandic did honor the fares. It's cheap marketing, because all of the press services picked up on it and spread the word nationwide.

Software Bugs

There are two main kinds of software bugs.

1. *Programming bugs*. Logic errors, mathematical computation errors, and so forth. These are harder to find and fix because you have to debug the code, fix it, recompile it, release it, and rerun the job.

2. *Data bugs*. Rate table errors. These are easy to find and fix.

Clearly, every company has some kind of ordering and billing system. Rates for products and services are loaded into rate tables that the ordering and billing systems use. Load in the wrong rate and you could lose money because of underpricing like *CheapTickets* or lost sales because of overpricing.

When I worked in the telephone company, there were thousands of rates for telephone service and products that varied by city, county, and state due to regulatory requirements. All of these rates had to be kept up to date. Sometimes they were; sometimes they weren't. We used to rate long-distance calls by time and distance. I've seen programming bugs like 2 minutes 30 seconds rounded down to 2 minutes that cost the company millions of dollars. I've also seen the kind of negative publicity you can generate if you try to collect the revenue you failed to bill correctly. The press came down on the telephone company like a ton of bricks.

Mistake Proofing

How could *CheapTickets* have mistake-proofed their rate tables? Seems obvious that any international fare under $300 should raise a red flag. Conversely, an economy fare within the 48 states should not cost over $400. Could a program be developed to analyze table updates as they happen or to analyze the tables for these kinds of anomalies? Sure. Would it be worth it? Certainly, because machines are more precise than people when it comes to examining data. Of course, a programming bug in the analysis program could raise too many red flags or ignore some obvious problems as well. Have you done everything you can to mistake-proof your rating and billing programs? Have you put similar safeguards in place on the purchasing side of the house?

Internet communities now make it easier than ever for huge numbers of people to take advantage of corporate mistakes in the long minutes before you discover the problem and correct it.

Sure there are ethical arguments about taking advantage of irrationally low fares, but you posted them; therefore, they must be valid. It's never the buyer's mistake, only the company's. Will you honor the mistakes you make? If you want to stay on your customer's good side, you'd better honor them. There's no guarantee that an error like *CheapTickets* will garner the same kind of publicity. You may just have to eat the loss, but it still makes a good story that customers will tell to others. Haven't you waited long enough to find ways to mistake-proof changes to your financial systems?

Still Struggling

Electrical cords have a wide prong and a narrow prong to fit into matching outlets. This is a form of mistake-proofing. Any process, including software, can benefit from mistake-proofing to prevent errors. My wife just went to the post office and used the automated machine to send a package. After she completed the transaction, the system thanked her, returned her credit card and *then asked her if she would like another transaction*. If she'd left without pressing "no" the next person in line could have used her credit card to send their package. A mistake-proof system wouldn't give back her credit card until she was done.

Information Technologies (IT) organizations have resisted process, measurement, and improvement with a passion. A culture obsessed with the newest, most innovative technology has a very difficult time valuing customers, procedures, and consistency. But in many ways, process improvement is the one innovation that most software developers have not yet tried. There are, however, some IT departments trying to move up the improvement ladder of the Capability Maturity Model (CMM), especially companies contracting with the Department of Defense (DOD). The evolution of a CMM IT department consists of five steps.

1. *Chaos.* Totally unpredictable software development and maintenance processes.

2. *Repeatable.* A few gurus have figured out a repeatable method for delivering software. The process is still unstable and not capable of delivering software on time and on budget, but does deliver software. At this level, software doesn't release; it escapes.

3. *Defined.* The wisdom of the gurus is captured and formed into a methodology. Six Sigma also refers to this as the Defined step—the D in DMAIC.

4. *Measured*. Departments start to measure the software process—cycle time and defects. This is the M in DMAIC.

5. *Optimized*. Groups start doing root cause analysis and making improvements in the software process. Then they begin to use the measurements to stabilize and control the delivery process. This is the AIC—Analyze, Improve, and Control—in DMAIC.

Unfortunately, this waterfall model of software process improvement forces groups to define and measure their process before they start making improvements. Without improvement, defining and measuring seems like non-value-added work that takes away from the delivery of software. Software developers resist this bureaucracy with a passion. I believe the trick is to throw them right into problem solving and improvement, producing processes and metrics as a by-product of improvement, instead of as a prerequisite.

All software projects follow some sort of process no matter how unstructured. They all have some sort of metrics even if it's just trouble reports, change requests, and daily fallout or error counts. These are more than sufficient to start making improvements in your core application systems. So the question is how do we hook software developers and maintainers on process, measurement, and improvement? After working with various IT groups, I've found that nothing works as well as the exhilaration they feel when they use the root cause tools of Six Sigma to make an improvement, weave it into the existing process, and experience the benefits of their improvement.

From working with teams in various IT departments, I've developed a simple method for achieving breakthrough improvement and getting IT hooked on Six Sigma. I call it the *Dirty 30 Process for Six Sigma Software*. In 2000, I used this simple technique with one wireless telephone company to reduce service order errors and save $250,000 per month in error correction after just 4 months.

The Dirty 30 Process for Six Sigma Software

Although most software quality efforts focus on the development of software—requirements, design, code, and test—this method focuses on the fine tuning of *delivered* software. Yes, it would be better to prevent the kind of problems we see in software, but applications continue to be written by people using requirements and designs that can be flawed. Software is rarely released; it *escapes*.

IT managers and application users often expect a new software project or enhancement release of an application to be flawless, and then are stunned by the additional staffing required to stem the tide of rejected transactions.

The secret is to

1. Quantify the cost of correcting these rejected transactions

2. Understand the Pareto pattern of rejected transactions

3. Analyze 30 rejected transactions one by one to determine the root cause

4. Revise the requirements and modify the system to prevent the problem.

Service Order Case Study

Information systems invariably fail to capture all of the requirements necessary to facilitate smooth processing of all transactions. So every system is designed with places to capture the fallout and turn it over to people for correction. Unfortunately, little of this information is fed back into improving the information systems. Huge error correction units blossom to handle the errors that can't or won't be corrected until some future release of the information system.

Every system produces a variety of error types and, following 4-50 rule, only a few error types contribute most of the overall fallout. The beauty of applying Six Sigma to information system fallout is that virtually every occurrence of these errors can be eliminated completely.

If you count all of the requirements, design, and code defects found in inspections, unit test, integration test, and system test, most software groups have high error rates—somewhere between two to three sigma. We've learned to expect defects in software, long development times, and high costs. The goal of the Dirty 30 process is to find and fix the worst software problems first. Let's look at how the Dirty 30 process helped in this case study.

Problem: Service order fallout from a telephone company's information systems was running at 17% (at 30,000 errors per month). This caused problems with activation, fulfillment, and billing of wireless phones as well as customer disconnect rate (also called *churn rate*), almost twice the industry average.

Process: Typical root cause analysis simply does not work because of the level of detail required to understand each error. Detailed analysis of 30 errors in each of the top six error "buckets" (i.e., the Dirty 30) led to a breakthrough in understanding of how errors occurred and how to prevent them. Simple check sheets allowed the root cause to pop out from analysis of this small sample. As expected, the errors clustered in three main categories: add, change, and delete of customer accounts.

The Dirty 30 process has four steps.

1. *Focus.* Determine which error/fallout buckets to analyze first for maximum benefit. (This analysis takes 2 to 3 days.)

2. *Improve.* Use the Dirty 30 approach to analyze root causes (4 to 8 hours per error type—facilitator with team) and determine requirements for system enhancements to prevent the problem.

3. *Sustain.* Track the fallout after implementation of the system enhancements.

4. *Honor.* Recognize and reward team members.

Quantify the Costs

The first step in the Dirty 30 process is to identify the number of rejected transactions and the associated costs. In working with one wireless company, we found a 17% (170,000 parts per million) level of rejected service orders (Fig. 6-1).

There were over 30,000 errors per month, which, at an average cost of $12.50 to fix (wage cost only), cost $375,000 per month. Over 50 temporary

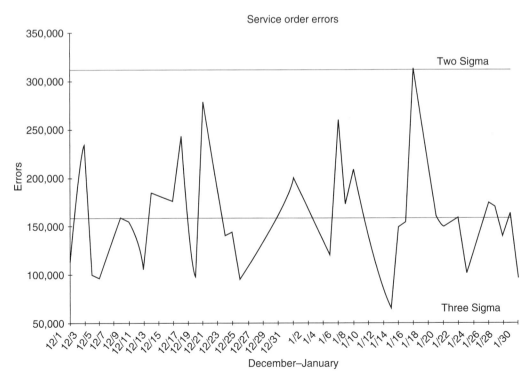

FIGURE 6-1 · Line graph of service order errors.

workers had been hired to deal with the 2-month backlog of unfixed errors. The objective was to cut this level of rejects in half (9%) by the end of the year.

Understand the Pareto Pattern

All systems have routines to accept, modify, or reject incoming transaction data. These are assigned error codes and dumped into error buckets to await correction. In the service order system, the application handled much of the correction, but it still left significant quantities of defects to be corrected manually (Fig. 6-2).

FIGURE 6-2 • Pareto chart of errors by major category.

There were over 200 different transaction error codes, but only six of them (3%) accounted for over 80% of the total rejected transactions. Two affected service directly; four affected the customer's records (Figs. 6-3 and 6-4).

It only took about 3 days to gather the data and isolate these transactions as the keys.

Analyzing the Dirty 30

The next step was to convene root cause teams to investigate 30 rejects of each error type. It took a week or more to get the right people in the room to investigate each type of error. The right people included the IT systems analyst, error

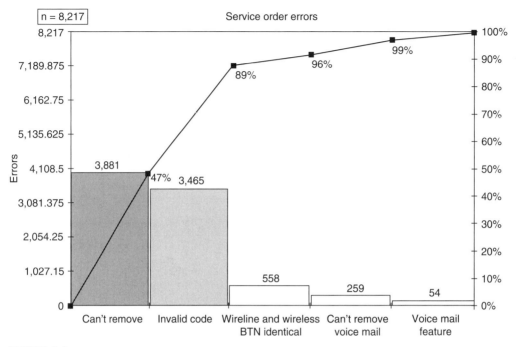

FIGURE 6-3 · Pareto chart of customer-affecting errors.

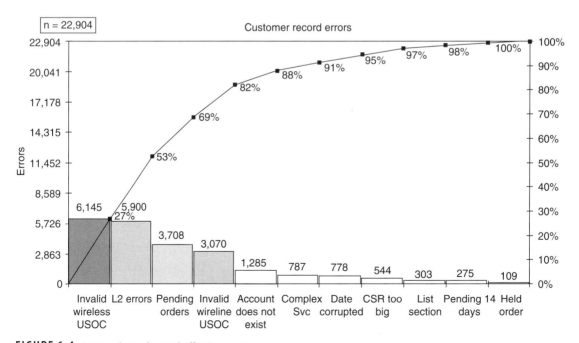

FIGURE 6-4 · Pareto chart of record-affecting errors.

correction people, and service order entry personnel. To attempt to do all six at one time with the same people would have been foolish. The errors required different subject matter experts, and the root causes were too different. By restricting ourselves to just one error type per team, we were able to find the root causes in just one half-day meeting per team.

To prepare for the meeting, we printed out 50 to 100 examples of each error (it helps to have more than 30 when you start, because you'll find some that don't actually belong in the category). Then, we gathered around a computer terminal and investigated each error.

1. Using *all* of the online systems, we investigated the root cause of *each* rejected transaction. Again, we restricted ourselves to analyzing just one transaction at a time. We had one person who really knew how to drive all of the information systems look up the transactions and all related information (e.g., customer records).

2. As the team reviewed all of the information and agreed on the cause of the rejected transaction, I kept a stroke tally for each root cause (Fig. 6-5). Gradually, as we looked at more and more transactions, a pattern would reveal itself. Sometimes it only took 25 transactions, sometimes it took 50, but a pattern would reveal itself clustered around one or more root causes.

	A	B
1	Checksheet of Causes	
2	Defect/ Problem/ Symptom	**Count of Remove Defects**
3	Wireless number mismatch	JHT JHT JHT JHT III
4	Customer Code mismatch	II
5	Billing number mismatch	III
6	**Total**	28
7	http://www.qimacros.com/qiwizard/checksheet.html	

CHECKSHT

FIGURE 6-5 • Check sheet of cause data.

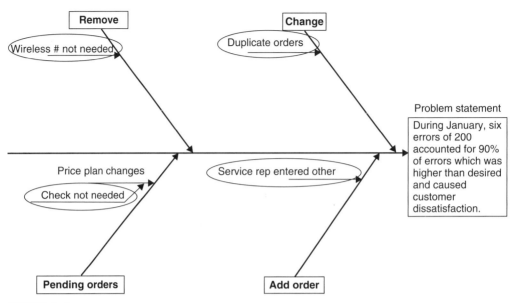

FIGURE 6-6 • Fishbone of root causes.

The great thing about evaluating transactions one at a time is that you verify your root causes as you go.

3. Once the team had identified the root causes (Fig. 6-6), we would stop analyzing and spend an hour defining the new requirements. Most of the time, the original requirements were too tight, too loose, or occasionally nonexistent. The systems analyst would then convey these to the programming staff for implementation.

Analyzing Results

It took 4 months to implement the revisions, but it was worth it. By midyear, the changes *completely eliminated the two top service-affecting errors, and three of the four record-affecting changes*. It cut total errors by 77% (Figs. 6-7, 6-8, and 6-9). This reduction translated to $299,426 per month in savings—over $3 million per year.

Results: This analysis and the resulting changes in the information system resulted in the complete elimination of five error buckets and dramatic reduction in other smaller buckets that benefited from the system changes. This also reduced activation errors (getting the network to recognize the wireless phone)

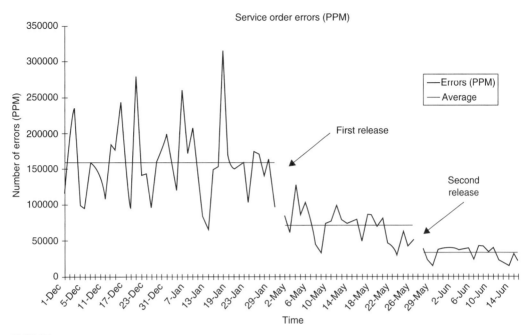

FIGURE 6-7 · Run chart of errors after system release.

FIGURE 6-8 · Customer-affecting Pareto chart after countermeasures.

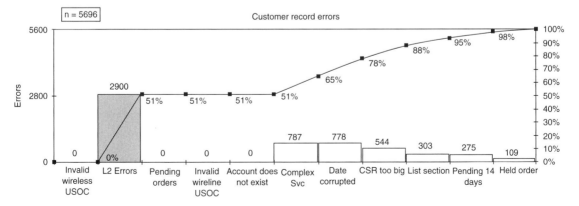

FIGURE 6-9 · Record-affecting Pareto chart after countermeasures.

and trouble calls in to the customer care center. From two sigma, the company moved to three sigma in 3 months.

- From 17% error rate reduced to 3% in just 6 months
- 100% elimination of top five error buckets
- $299,000 per month in savings

Cost

- Three days of planning
- Six half-day team meetings
- Two minor software releases

Common Problems

The core elements of any application involve searching for and then adding, changing, or deleting data. Most applications assume a perfect world, where the data is only created or modified by the system. This is rarely the case. Most systems have a wealth of backdoors used to fix faulty data quickly. Upstream and downstream systems have their own backdoors to fix faulty transactions, so perfect data continues to be a mythological assumption that fosters faulty requirements and designs.

The requirements for adding, changing, and deleting data are often too loose, too tight, or nonexistent; this leads to errors and rejected transactions which must be corrected manually by people hunched over computer terminals for 8 hours a day. The simplest way to fix these IT errors is by using the Dirty 30 process for Six Sigma software.

The Dirty 30 Process Review

1. Pick one top error category.
2. Get 100 to 200 specific errors (e.g., in this case by telephone number).
3. Investigate each error in your online systems to find the root cause of each individual error.
4. Grow a check sheet of causes.
5. By 30 a root cause pattern will *pop out*.

6. Evaluate alternative solutions.

7. Develop business requirements to prevent the problem and an action plan for implementation.

Insights

Using the basic tools of Six Sigma, anyone can learn to use what I call the *Dirty 30 process for Six Sigma software* in a day or less to find the root causes of transaction errors. Once a team has found the root causes of these errors, it's just a matter of changing the code to eliminate these errors *forever*.

Whether it's a wireless billing system or a claims-processing system for an HMO, hundreds of people spend their lives fixing the fallout from these information system errors.

If you're a CIO or IT manager, can you really afford to let your client continue to eat the ongoing costs for fixing these errors? Errors caused by system requirements that are too tight, too loose, or just plain missing? What if you could analyze the cause of these errors in a matter of days? How will this help *leverage your legacy systems to create new value*?

Conclusion

Until you get to where you can prevent errors in requirements, design, code, and test, every system release could benefit from a simple, yet rigorous approach to analyzing and eliminating postimplementation errors. The Dirty 30 process is ideal because the data required to implement it is collected by most systems automatically. Then all it takes is 4 to 8 hours of analysis to identify the root cause of each error. Most of the time, the root cause will reside in the requirements.

One of the positive by-products of this approach is that the systems analysts learn first hand how their requirements and designs most often fail. This allows them to learn how to make their next set of requirements or designs more robust. It also gives the user a closer look at the intricacies of software and the complexities involved. And if you aren't going to start using the Dirty 30 process, what are you going to use to mistake-proof your systems and releases?

Until software engineering finds ways to prevent all of the possible defects inherent in software development, the Dirty 30 process will provide a simple way to tune up a system release and move the application ever closer to Six Sigma performance.

QUIZ

1. **Transactional Six Sigma can be used for IT systems in**
   A. ordering.
   B. invoicing.
   C. billing.
   D. payroll.
   E. purchasing.
   F. all of the above

2. **The state of the IT software development process can be described as**
   A. chaos.
   B. repeatable.
   C. defined.
   D. measured.
   E. optimized.
   F. any of the above depending on the maturity of the IT department.

3. **The process for transactional Six Sigma is called**
   A. the Dirty Dozen.
   B. the Dirty 30.
   C. root cause analysis.

4. **Most software system problems are caused by requirements that are:**
   A. too loose.
   B. too tight.
   C. nonexistent.
   D. all of the above

5. **Transactional Six Sigma can**
   A. reduce transaction errors.
   B. eliminate transaction errors completely.
   C. teach IT how to build more robust systems.
   D. all of the above

6. **To conduct a Dirty 30 improvement project,**
   A. measure rejected transactions over time.
   B. determine the root cause of 30 of the worst transactions.
   C. initiate changes in information systems to eliminate the root causes.
   D. monitor rejected transactions to validate improvement.
   E. all of the above

7. Name three transaction costs.

    A. _____

    B. _____

    C. _____

8. Name two common software bugs.

    A. _____

    B. _____

9. The most common software functions are

    A. search.

    B. add data.

    C. change data.

    D. delete data.

    E. all of the above

EXERCISES

1. Identify one of your computer systems that has too many people fixing errors created by the system.

2. Use Pareto charts to narrow your focus to one or more types of transactions that cause over half of the rework.

3. Do a Dirty 30 analysis on examples of each type of transaction.

4. Write business requirements to prevent these errors forever.

chapter 7

Reducing Variation with Six Sigma

Chapter 5 dealt with reducing defects. Defects are *counted* or *attribute* data (i.e., integers). With defects, the product or service is either bad or good; it either has a scratch or it doesn't. In this chapter we'll look at Six Sigma methods for reducing *deviation* (i.e., variation). Deviation involves *measured* or *variable* data (i.e., decimals). Measured data include time, length, width, height, weight, volume, and money. This means that a part can be too big or too small to fit properly. It means that a service or process can take too long. It means that the wait time in a supermarket, retail outlet, or call center can be too long.

CHAPTER OBJECTIVES

In this chapter, you will

- Learn the Six Sigma improvement process for reducing deviation
- Learn and apply the Six Sigma tools for reducing deviation
- Learn how to conduct a capability study

231

What Is Variation?

Every process varies from its target value: It takes a little more or less time; it makes the product a little bit bigger or smaller, longer or shorter, wider or thinner, taller or shorter, heavier or lighter, or fuller or emptier than its ideal target size, shape, and so on. The variation may be large or almost undetectable, but it's still there. The goal of Six Sigma is to reduce the amount of variation so that your product always fits well inside your customer's specifications for it and hopefully centers on a target value for that product.

Manufacturers get into trouble when they produce products that don't fit the customer's requirements. Services get into trouble when they can't meet the customer's requirements for timeliness.

Imagine for a moment that you're producing piston heads for an engine. The piston heads have to be the right size to fit inside the engine block. If they're too big, they won't fit. If they're too small, they'll leak oil and make noise. And they have to be round so you might want to also measure the roundness of your piston heads. Because you produce these piston heads using machinery, you'll have to factor in the variables: density of the metal, pressure, temperature, and so on. With so many factors, it might take some effort to produce a consistent product that fits the customer's needs.

Now imagine you're producing plastic bottles for a bottler. The product has to be a certain shape and height. It has to hold a certain volume of liquid. It has to seal properly. Using injection-molding machinery, your product will be affected by the temperature of the mold and the plastic. It will be affected by not only the pressure of the injection but also by the atmospheric pressure. The formula of the plastic may affect its ability to accept printing and labeling. The thickness of the plastic will affect its durability. It will take some efforts to ensure that you can produce a consistent product that's easy to bottle but doesn't waste material.

Now imagine that you are a bank. Customers arrive randomly. You have a certain number of tellers scheduled for various times of the day. You know customers don't like to wait for a teller, but how do you adjust your staffing to minimize your cost and minimize your customer's wait time?

Get the idea? Every process has a variety of variables that affect your ability to produce a consistent product or deliver a consistent service. There's going to be variation. Your job, using Six Sigma, is to find ways to reduce the amount of variation to a level that meets or exceeds your customer's expectations. You can affect variation by changing what used to be called the five M's: man, methods, machines, materials, and measurement. I call them a more politically correct people, process, machines, materials, and measurement (P^2M^3).

Still Struggling

Ever try to put a product together only to discover that all of the holes for screws don't line up? That's variation. Ever had to wait at your doctor's office? The wait time varies doesn't it? That's variation.

Goal Posts and Targets

The goal for all solutions to problems associated with variation is to center the distribution over the ideal target value and minimize the amount of variation around that target value. Sounds easy, doesn't it?

For most products, customers have a *target value* and some *tolerance* for products around the target value. Your ability to produce products centered around the target value with a minimum amount of variation will determine the quality of your product.

For parts to fit together properly, the bolt cannot be bigger or smaller than its nut it screws into; the cap cannot be bigger or smaller than its bottle. In many ways, this is like the goal posts in a U.S. football game: There's a left and a right post, and the kicker's job is to kick the ball between the two posts. Anything outside of the posts results in no score (or in Six Sigma terms, a nonconforming part). The left and right post might be considered to be the game's *specification limits*.

Customers specify their requirements for targets and tolerances in one of two ways.

- Target and tolerance (e.g., 74 plus or minus 0.05)
- Upper (USL) and lower (LSL) specification limits (e.g., USL=74.05, LSL=73.95).

TIP *Don't confuse specification limits (i.e., USL and LSL) with control limits (UCL and LCL). Customers set specification limits; control charts use your data to calculate control limits.*

Piston heads, for example, will have specifications for the maximum and minimum height and diameter of the head; roundness of the head, known as cylindricity and concentricity; and a host of other factors like how the shaft connects to the piston and so on. A bottle will have similar specifications. Usually, a manufactured part will have both an upper and lower specification limit.

For most services, customers may have an upper limit, but no lower limit. Teller wait times and call center wait times will usually only have a maximum time (the minimum time is automatically zero). Most customers don't want to wait longer than 5 minutes in a bank and no more than 30 seconds on the phone. These customers have an upper specification limit, but no lower limit other than zero. Go into any fast-food restaurant and you'll see a little digital timer ticking away next to your order. Fast-food restaurants can't afford to be slow, because customers are paying for speed and convenience.

There are rare instances where you will have only a lower specification limit but no upper specification limit.

Causes of Variation

Within these specification limits, there are two causes of variation.

1. *Special causes* (i.e., assignable causes of special events). Special cause variation can be easily detected with control charts, quickly analyzed with the five whys, and corrected by the operator. Special cause variation accounts for only 15% of the problems. Most companies get caught up in firefighting the special causes, but rarely get around to reducing the common causes.

2. *Common causes* are factors affecting the whole system. These will require some deeper root cause analysis. Common causes account for 85% of the total variation. Think about your drive to work. Common causes of variation in your commute time might include time of day, number of red traffic lights, number of cars on the road, and road construction or maintenance. Most weather conditions fall under common cause variation, but in Denver we occasionally get a blizzard and it can take four times as long to get to work. A Denver blizzard is a special cause of variation. Rain in Seattle would be a common cause, because it rains there often. Although I can't change traffic lights or prevent a blizzard, I did find that if I left 15 minutes earlier on normal days and left an hour earlier on snow days, I could shorten my commute by 10 minutes on normal days and 90 minutes on snow days. Why? Because there were fewer cars on the road. Since I

was at work early, I could also leave earlier in the afternoon and beat the evening rush.

HINT *Spend more time reducing common causes than firefighting special causes.*

Similarly, the temperature and humidity in a manufacturing plant can affect the product (Fig. 7-1). Staffing can affect throughput; illness, absenteeism, tardiness, and vacation can all affect lead times.

All kinds of things can cause variation. Lockheed's SR-71 Blackbird spy plane used Burbank city water to rinse the plane's welds. They discovered that rust developed more rapidly on welds at certain times of the year. The manufacturer traced the cause of variation back to the algae that bloom in the city's water supply in the spring and summer. Afterward, they used special filtration to clean the water and prevent rust.

Some sources of variation are short term, such as machine settings, while others are long term such as wear. To reduce variation in your product or service, you will want to focus on the common causes of variation.

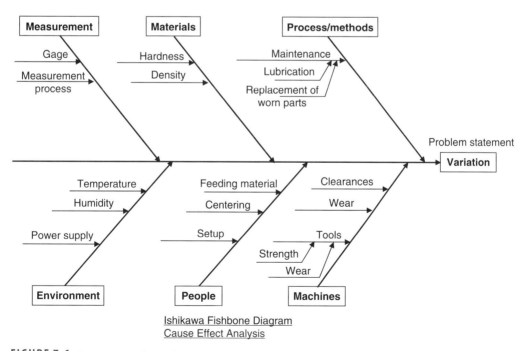

FIGURE 7-1 • Root causes of variation.

Distributions

It doesn't matter if you're measuring height, weight, width, diameter, thickness, volume, time, or money; if you measure the same dimension over time, it will produce a *distribution* that shows the variation. Most people have heard of a bell-shaped curve (Fig. 7-2); this is a *normal* distribution. Distributions have three key characteristics: center, spread, and shape (Fig. 7-3). The *center* is usually the *average* (the *mean*) of all of the data points, although other measures of the center can be used (e.g., *median*—center point or *mode*—most frequent data value). *Spread* is the distance between the minimum and the maximum values. And the *shape* can be bell-shaped, skewed (i.e., leaning) left or right, and so on (Fig. 7-4).

There are two outcomes for your improvement effort.

1. *Center* the distribution over the target value as shown in Fig. 7-5.

2. *Reduce the spread* of the distribution (i.e., reduce variation) as shown in Fig. 7-6.

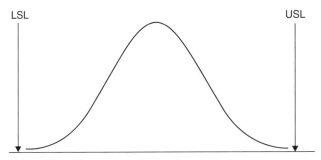

FIGURE 7-2 · Bell-shaped curve.

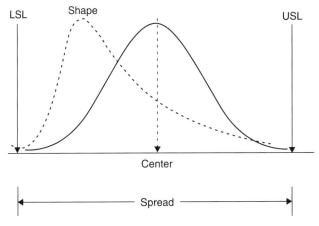

FIGURE 7-3 · Center, spread, and shape of data.

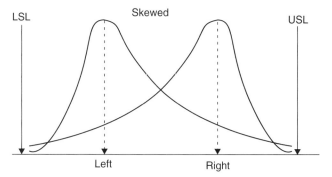

FIGURE 7-4 • Skewed distributions.

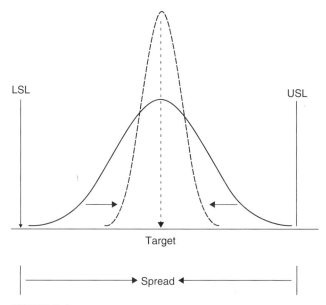

FIGURE 7-5 • Reduce the spread of variation.

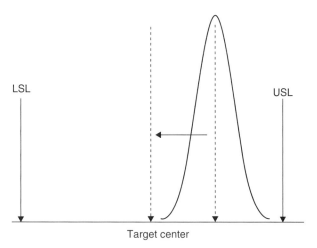

FIGURE 7-6 • Center the distribution.

These two outcomes can be easily monitored using histograms which help you determine the capability of your process.

Histograms and Capability

Perhaps the easiest way to determine the center, spread, and shape of your data's distribution is with a histogram (Fig. 7-7). Histograms are simply bar charts that show the number of times your data points fall into each of the bars on the histogram. When you add the upper and lower specification limits, it's easy to see how your data fits your customer's requirements and what improvements might be necessary.

Capability Indices

Using the specification limits, there are four key indicators of process capability.

FIGURE 7-7 • Histogram of piston head diameters.

1. Cp is the *capability index*. It measures how well your data might fit between the upper and lower specification limits. It doesn't really care if the process is centered within the limits, only if the data would fit if the data were centered.

2. Cpk is the *centering capability index*. It measures how well your data are centered between the upper and lower specification limits. Cp and Cpk use an estimation of the standard deviation to calculate the spread of your data. If the variation between samples is small, Cp and Cpk are better predictors of capability.

3. Pp is the *performance index*. Like Cp, it measures how well your data fit within the USL and LSL. Unlike Cp, Pp uses the actual standard deviation of your data, not the estimate.

4. Ppk is the *performance centering index*. Like Cpk, it measures how well your data are centered between the USL and LSL. Again, Ppk uses the standard deviation to determine the spread of your data.

If you want to dig into the formulas for these indicators, go to my website *www.qimacros.com//formulas/cp-cpk-formula.html* or Google "Cp Cpk."

NOTE *These indicators are only valid when your process is stable (i.e., in statistical process control). We'll look at stability and SPC in Chap. 7.*

Cp and Cpk should be used together to get a sense of process capability. Using Pp and Ppk will help confirm process capability. Ideally, all four indicators should be greater than 1.33 (all data fit within specification limits and are centered and at least four sigma—6,210 PPM). From a Six Sigma perspective, Cp and Cpk directly correlate with Six Sigma targets.

Cp and Cpk and Pp and Ppk	Cr	Sigma Level
1.0	1.0	3
1.33	0.75	4
1.66	0.6	5
2.0	0.5	6

Cr and Z Target or ΔZ

The indicators, Cr and Z Target, provide another way to measure spread and centering (Fig. 7.8).

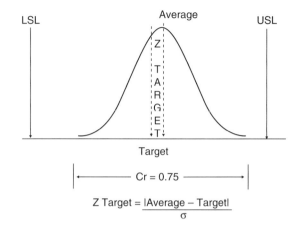

$$Z\ Target = \frac{|Average - Target|}{\sigma}$$

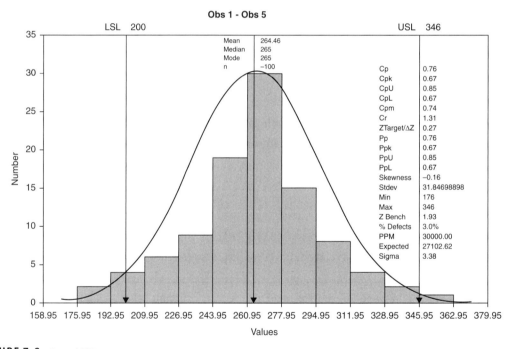

FIGURE 7-8 • Cr and Z Target.

Cr = 1/Cp, so a Cp of 1.33 is equal to a Cr of 0.75. Cr calculates the percent (e.g., 75%) of the tolerance (USL–LSL) taken up by the data. Cr, ideally, should be less than 0.75 (four sigma).

Z Target or ΔZ calculates how far the average varies from the target value (the midpoint between USL and LSL). Ideally, the average should be no more than 0.5 (half a standard deviation) from the target.

Cp and Cpk are more widely used, but some industries prefer Cr and Z Target.

Still Struggling

If you're in manufacturing, most customers use Cp and Cpk to access your product's quality. Using the QI Macros and data from your process combined with customer specification limits, it's easy to check Cp and Cpk.

Defects in Parts per Million

Because we're using a small sample to analyze process capability, it might seem difficult to calculate the estimated defects, but statistics makes it easy. Since we know the standard deviation and the specification limits, through the magic of statistics we can estimate how many parts out of a million will be outside the specification limits. In Fig. 7-9, some of the data points are outside of the specification limits resulting in an actual defect rate in parts per million (PPM) of 30,000 and an estimate (based on standard deviation) of 26,710 (Cp = 0.74, Cpk = 0.66). Figure 7-10 shows a centered distribution of wafer strength and an estimated PPM of only 177 (Cp = 1.19, Cpk = 1.12).

Improvement Objectives

Once you have run a histogram to calculate Cp and Cpk, you can decide how to improve. If the process is off-center, adjust your work so that it becomes centered. If the capability is less than 1.33, adjust your process so that there is less variation. In manufacturing, customers require Cp = Cpk greater than 1.33 (four sigma). If you are producing products for the Asian market, especially Japan, they require Cp = Cpk greater than 1.66 (five sigma).

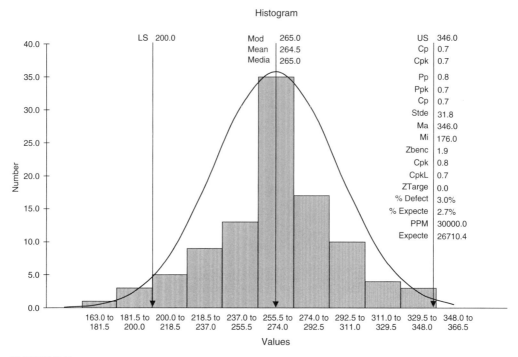

FIGURE 7-9 · Histogram with nonconforming parts.

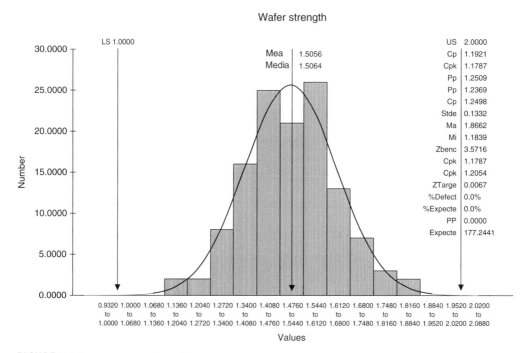

FIGURE 7-10 · Histogram with conforming parts.

Process Capability Indicators	Improvement Objective
If Cp is greater than Cpk Cp > Cpk	Center the process
If Cp is approximately equal to Cpk and both are less than 1.33 Cp = Cpk < 1.33	Reduce variation

Root Cause Analysis

Again, you can use the Ishikawa (fishbone) diagram to analyze the root causes of (1) off-center or (2) excess variation. Remember, common causes of variation may require systemic changes to achieve your capability goals.

Once you've improved the process, you can use the histogram to show the results (Fig. 7-11). The goal is to get Cp = Cpk > 1.33 (four sigma) or 1.66 (five sigma).

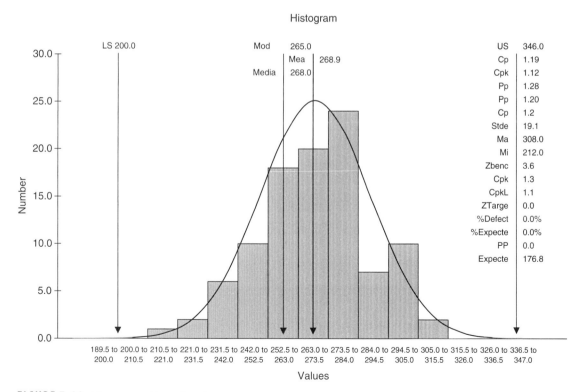

FIGURE 7-11 • Histogram with conforming parts.

Conclusion

Deviation happens, but it is the enemy of excellence. Six Sigma can help measure, analyze, and reduce variation. You may never eliminate all of the variation in your process, but it can be much lower than it is now. Use the histograms and control charts in the QI Macros to start your quest for perfection.

QUIZ

1. Deviation involves what kind of data?
   A. Attribute
   B. Counted
   C. Measured
   D. Variable

2. The key measures of variation are
   A. spread.
   B. shape.
   C. center.
   D. all of the above

3. The capability indexes are
   A. Cp.
   B. Cpk.
   C. Pp.
   D. Ppk.
   E. Cr.
   F. Z Target-Δz.
   G. all of the above

4. The minimum target value for Cp, Cpk, Pp, or Ppk is
   A. 1.0.
   B. 1.33.
   C. 1.66.
   D. 2.0.

5. The minimum target value of Cr is
   A. 1.
   B. 0.75.
   C. 0.6.
   D. 0.5.

6. The minimum target value of Z Target is
   A. 1.
   B. 0.75.
   C. 0.6.
   D. 0.5.

7. **The goals of reducing variation are**
   A. center the process.
   B. reduce spread.
   C. expand to match the specification limits.
   D. meet customer specifications.

8. **What are histograms?**

9. **How are they used?**

10. **What is a capability study?**

11. **What are the two causes of variation?**
   A. _____
   B. _____

EXERCISES

1. Use the QI Macros test data to run histograms of the data in the file histogram. xls using the USL and LSL provided. Which of these data sets are capable of meeting customer requirements?

2. Use the test data in XbarR.xls to run a histogram using the specification limits. Is this process capable?

3. Use XbarR template with the XbarR.xls data to create the same chart.

4. Use time, money, or measured data from your own business to analyze the capability of one of your processes.

5. Use the XmR control chart dashboard with the XbarR Data to create a dashboard.

chapter **8**

Sustaining Improvement

Until the processes that generate the output become the focus of our efforts, the full power of these methods to improve quality, increase productivity, and reduce cost may not be fully realized
— The AIAG Statistical Process Control Manual (second edition)

Once you've made improvements, you'll want to sustain (i.e., control) them to ensure that you stay at the new level of performance. Otherwise, you'll gradually slip back to the old levels of performance. That's why you will want a process control system.

CHAPTER OBJECTIVES

In this chapter, you will

- Learn the control phase of DMAIC
- Learn how to diagram process flows
- Learn how to monitor performance with control charts and histograms
- Learn how to develop a control plan

A process control system of flowcharts, control charts, and/or histograms can help you monitor and maintain your new level of performance. Process control systems consist of

1. The system—suppliers, inputs, process, and outputs

2. Charts of performance—control charts and histograms

3. Corrective actions—changes to the people, process, machines, materials, measurement, and environment—to respond to out of control conditions

4. Rework—to fix defects in finished products

Process Flowchart

Once you've made an improvement, it might be a good time to develop a process flowchart or value stream map of the process. The simplified acronym for a process is RADIO,

1. Repetitive—hourly, daily, weekly, monthly

2. Actions—step-by-step tasks and activities

3. Definable—observable and documentable (flowchart)

4. Inputs—measurable inputs (control charts)

5. Outcomes—measurable outputs (control charts)

Most processes can be diagrammed with four basic symbols.

- Start/End box
- Activity box
- Decision diamond
- Connecting arrow

Additional symbols can be added as required.

Creating a flowchart from scratch is like putting together a puzzle: It's best to get all the pieces out on the table and then try to put them in order. To do so requires flexibility and that flexibility comes from using Post-it notes.

"Swim lanes" flowcharts (Figs. 8-1 and 8-2) extend the flow-charting technique to show "who does what" and the macrosteps of the process.

Guidelines for constructing process flow charts include

- Start with identifying customer needs and end with satisfying them.
- Separate the process into areas of responsibility.

FIGURE 8-1 • Process flowchart.

- Use Post-it notes to layout activities.
- Place activities under the appropriate area of responsibility.

TIPS

- *Use square Post-it notes for activities and decision diamonds.*
- *Draw arrows on any size Post-it note to show the flow, top to bottom, left to right. Post-it notes now come in arrow shapes as well.*
- *Use smaller Post-it notes for process and quality indicators.*

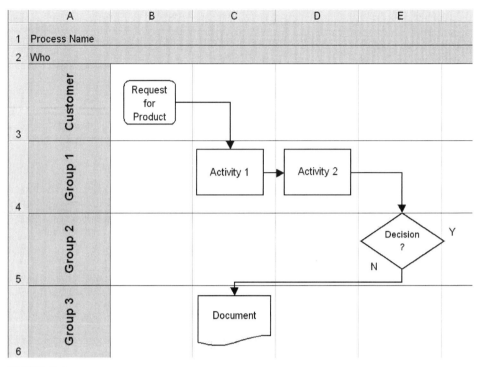

FIGURE 8-2 · Swim lanes flowchart.

- *Participants will often offer activities at different levels of detail. As the higher-level process flow gets more complex, keep moving subprocesses onto micro process diagrams.*

- *Critical-to-Quality indicators (CTQs), which measure how well the process met the customer's requirements, go at the end of the process.*

- *Process indicators, which predict how well the process will meet the requirements, are most often placed at (1) hand-offs between functional groups and (2) decision points to measure the amount work flowing in each direction (this is most often useful for measuring the amount of rework required).*

Flow-Charting Tar Pits

There are a few tar pits for teams to avoid.

- Trying to show too many different kinds of process on one flowchart (e.g., trying to show project management on the same chart as daily operations or trying to show procurement on the same flowchart as operations).

- Trying to show too much detail on any one flowchart. Use macro- and microlevel flowcharts to describe increasing levels of detail.
- Using internal efficiency indicators rather than external effectiveness indicators based on customer requirements.

Control Charts for Sustaining Improvement

Most service businesses will use two main control charts—the individuals and moving range (XmR chart) for cycle times and ratios, and fraction defective chart (p chart). Manufacturing businesses will often use the XbarR, XmR, p, or u charts. Other applications include

- Financial—XmR charts of expenses, revenues, and so on
- Customer satistfaction—XmR chart of percentage satisfied
- Call centers—XmR of wait times, p chart of abandoned calls
- Growth—XmR and p charts

Using the QI Macros Control Chart Wizard, you can just select your data and let the Wizard choose the chart for you.

Still Struggling

Control charts can detect subtle process shifts that can't be detected with the five senses. Once a process improves beyond 3-Sigma, it's almost impossible to detect process shifts without them. Control charts are so easy to draw with the QI Macros that anyone can do it. Then it's just a matter of analyzing the results to detect process problems.

Stability and Capability

In Chap. 6, we looked at how to measure process capability using histograms. To access capability, however, the process must be in statistical process control. If the process is both stable and capable, just keep monitoring. If not, it's time to crank up some improvement efforts:

	Stable—In Control	Unstable—Out of Control
Capable	Good	Analyze and correct special causes
Not capable	Analyze and reduce common cause variation	Correct special causes to get a stable process, then reduce common cause variation

We recently sent out a QI Macros ezine about analyzing manufacturing performance data. Many readers asked an interesting question: If my data fits between the specification limits of the histogram, but the control chart is unstable, is that good or bad?

The Good News

If your data fits between the upper and lower spec limits, then you are meeting your customer's requirements (Fig. 8-3).

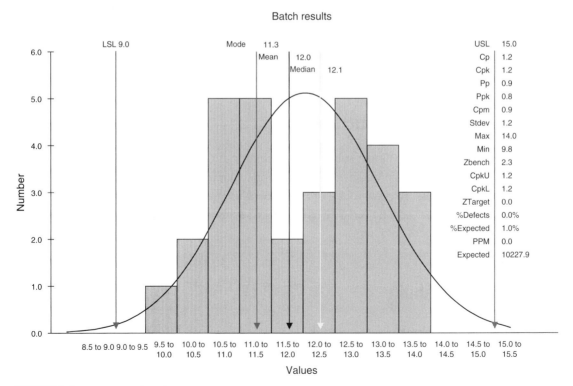

FIGURE 8-3 • Histogram of batch results.

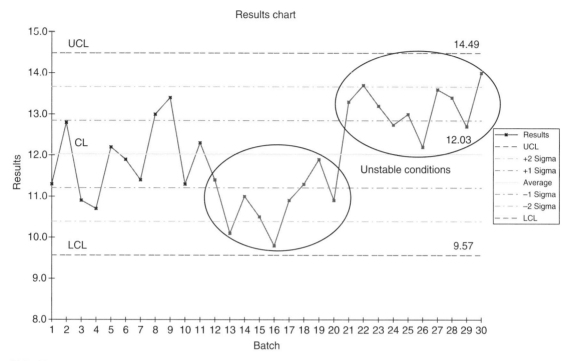

FIGURE 8-4 · Unstable XmR chart of sample variation.

The Bad News

Because the control chart of the data (Fig. 8-4) shows that the process is unstable (shown in red in the QI Macros), you may not be able to meet your customers' requirements consistently and predictably.

In other words, you just got lucky. The process may not deliver on the customers' requirement next time. The question is Does it matter? Taguchi wondered about this as well and did some research.

The Taguchi Loss Function

Taguchi suggests that every process have a *target* value and that as the product moves away from target value, there's a *loss* incurred by society. This loss may involve delay, waste, scrap, or rework. Look at the histogram in Fig. 8-3. Sure, the product fits within the specification limits, but as you can see, the customer might have to reset their production machines several times to accommodate the changes in specifications. *Loss!*

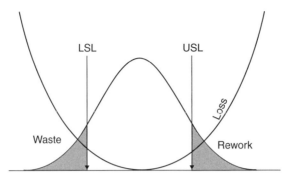

FIGURE 8-5 · Taguchi loss function.

The loss isn't linear. Taguchi theorized that the loss is proportional to the *square* of the distance from the target value (Fig. 8-5).

The parabolic curve describes the cost to society as the product moves away from the target value (center between LSL and USL).

Warranty Example

Many years ago I read about an example from the automotive industry. One company was building transmissions for cars in both Japan and the United States. The U.S. transmissions had five times the warranty issues.

To determine the problem, five transmissions were selected at random from both the Japanese factory and the U.S. factory. Then, they took them apart and measured all of the specifications.

U.S. Transmissions: All of the U.S. transmissions had parts that fell within the USL–LSL. Some measures were a little higher and some a little lower.

Japanese Transmissions: When the inspectors measured the Japanese transmissions, they got worried, because *they got the same value* on each of the parts on each of the five transmissions. They began to suspect that their gages were incorrect.

The Japanese transmissions measured identically on all of the key specifications. There was no variation to speak of. Their graph looked more like Fig. 8-6, with the measures centered closely around the target.

Here's my point. To truly serve your customer, your process has to be both *stable* and *capable*. It can't just be one or the other.

- *Stable.* The control chart is in control (no unstable conditions).
- *Capable.* The histogram fits inside the specification limits (USL–LSL).

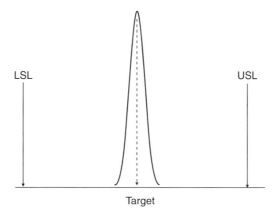

FIGURE 8-6 · Minimal loss from variation.

Stabilize Your Process

When the process moves around like this example, it probably means that someone is changing the settings, without any real need to. Deming called this *tampering*. Let the process run and then adjust the settings to move it onto the target. Then leave it alone unless it starts to drift.

Still Struggling

When you create a control chart with the QI Macros, if there are no "red" points or lines on the chart, then the process is in statistical process control.

Reduce Variation

Once the process is stable, use process improvement to reduce the variation (adjust the process to reduce the variation from the target).

Reduce Loss

Stabilizing your process and reducing the variation will, in turn, reduce the cost of the Taguchi loss function. This will save you and your customers' time and money (rework, waste, and delay). And customers are smart. They can tell the difference between two different transmissions, and they can tell the difference in quality between you and your competitors.

Make sure you're in charge of whom your customers return to year after year. Hitting the goal posts isn't good enough any more. You have to hit the target value most of the time. Your customers will love you for it.

The Hole in Krispy Kreme

My wife and I flew from Kahului, Maui, to Honolulu, Oahu, a few months ago. Almost every Hawaiian who boarded the flight was carrying two to four dozen donuts from Krispy Kreme. It seems that Maui got a Krispy Kreme franchise before Oahu, so everyone who traveled to Maui was picking up the new donuts and muling them back to their families and friends on the other islands.

I thought, "Wow, that's wild word of mouth. Maybe I should buy some stock." Then I did some investigation. As it turns out, the explosive growth was more of a fad than a sustainable business. The stock that went from $21 to $105 in 2000 but has fallen 90% from its 2003 peak.

Changing the Focus

The new CEO and turnaround specialist Steven Cooper says "You can't rely on word of mouth to keep expanding the circuit of loyal customers." Instead, you need to focus on running an efficient operation in an industry with razor-thin margins.

Efficiency and Effectiveness

Having a great product is essential to customer satisfaction, but you also have to deliver it in a cost-effective manner. You can only increase sales so much. There are limits to growth; it doesn't matter if you're McDonald's or Wal-Mart. To maximize profit and sustain success, you also have to trim the delays, defects, and deviation that nibble away at your profit margins.

The QI Macros started out from humble beginnings 15 years ago. Since then, I've added endless enhancements requested by customers from all over the country in everything from health care to automotive industries. At a recent Institute for Healthcare Improvement conference, a number of fans dropped by our trade show booth. It felt great, but I also remember that I have to endlessly improve the QI Macros and streamline their delivery. As Andy Grove of Intel fame once said: "Only the paranoid survive."

Here's my point. It's not enough to have the most innovative new product or the best customer service. If you aren't optimizing and streamlining the delivery of that product or service to reduce the excessive costs of defects, delay, waste, and rework, then your company will be in trouble when the bubble bursts or the fad fades.

It's easy to be seduced by easy success, but it takes clarity of focus to sustain that success. The U.S. economy is recovering, but peaks lead to troughs. Lean Six Sigma methods and tools can help you find the lost profits in your business. Will your company be ready when the tide turns?

Lately I've become concerned about how people learn statistical process control. Most trainers teach participants how to do all of the calculations manually and then show them how to do it using a tool like the *QI Macros for Excel SPC Spftware*.

I don't think people should have to learn how to do things manually. It's like teaching a farmer how to plow a field with a plowshare when there's a brand new tractor that can plow eight rows at a time sitting right on the edge of the field. It's like teaching a person everything there is to know about the generation and distribution of electricity before you let him or her turn on a light bulb. It's a waste of time.

It used to be important to do it manually because you had to if you wanted to get results (which meant that few people ever did it). Many people feel compelled to teach it that way, because that's how they were taught, but it no longer adds value from my point of view. It's just a way to fill up the class time. It's a way to turn a 1-day class into a 5-day class.

I'm biased about this because I spent 5 days in a control chart class doing calculations manually, but only 2 hours discussing what the charts are telling us, *which was the only truly important part of the class.* I came away knowing enough about the calculations to know that they were too complex to do manually and not knowing anything about reading the charts and using them.

Employees are too busy to waste time learning more than they need to know. We no longer have the luxury of learning everything there is to know before we do anything. We only have time for the essence.

The 4-50 rule: 4% of the knowledge about any subject will give you half the benefit. The more you teach beyond this point, the more diffused, esoteric, and seemingly complex the knowledge becomes. If you teach someone everything, he, or she, will have no idea what's important and what isn't. He knows it all, but he knows nothing. He has too many choices to take action effectively.

Let software do the hard work accurately; this will free you up to do the important work of analyzing the charts and making improvements. *Stop majoring in minor things.* Juran said it well: "The vital few versus the trivial many." This applies to knowledge as well as improvements.

Once you've learned the essence, it's easy to add to that body of knowledge. When you've learned the whole body of knowledge in one shot, it's hard to decide which portion to use and when.

Still Struggling

You don't need to know statistics to draw and use control charts. All you need are the QI Macros and Excel.

Choosing a Control Chart

With the recently added I-MR-R chart, there are now 14 control charts in the QI Macros. How do you know which one to use? When I'm working with data in Excel, I follow a simple strategy for selecting the right chart based on the *format* of the data itself. There are three formats I look for.

1. A single row/column

2. Two rows/columns with a numerator and a denominator

3. Two or more rows/columns containing multiple observations from each sample

Single Row/Column

If you only have a single row/column of data, there are only three charts you can use.

1. *c chart* (attribute or counted data). It's always an integer (e.g., 1, 2, 3, 4, 5).

2. *XmR chart* (variable or measured data). It usually has decimal places (e.g., 33.75).

3. *XmR Trend chart.* For variable data that increases (e.g., rising costs due to inflation).

So which one should you choose? If you're counting indivisible things like defects, people, cars, or injuries, then choose the c chart. If you're measuring things like time, length, weight, or volume, choose the XmR chart. Look for these patterns in the data and then select the chart.

Two Rows/Columns

If the data have a numerator and a denominator that vary (e.g., defects/batch, errors/transactions), then you will want to use the

- p chart (one defect maximum per piece)
- u chart (one or more defects per piece)

How can you tell which one to use? I ask myself "Can this widget have more than one defect?" If yes, use the u chart; otherwise use the p chart.

Sometimes, as in this example, you can have more defects than samples. This is another clue. Again, look for these patterns in the data and then select the chart.

Two or More Rows/Columns of Variable Data

Service industries don't use these charts very often. They are mainly used in manufacturing. If you have two or more rows or columns of variable data (time, weight, length, width, diameter, or volume), then you can choose one of four charts.

1. XbarR (average and range, 2 to 10 rows/columns per sample)
2. XMedianR (median and range, 2 to 10 rows/columns per sample)
3. XbarS (average and standard deviation, 5 to 50 rows/columns per sample)
   - I-MR-R (average, moving range between subgroups and range within subgroups, 2 to 50 rows/columns per sample)

Your data should look like Fig. 8-7.

You can run the XbarR, XMedianR, XbarS, or I-MR-R charts on this data. Xbar uses the average as the measure of central tendency. The XMedianR uses the median. If you have more than five samples per period, then the XbarS will probably be the most robust chart for your needs. You can also use the XbarS if your data have a varying number of samples per period. The I-MR-R chart is like a combination of an XbarR and XmR; it measures the variation *within* subgroups with the Range chart and variation *between* subgroups using the Moving Range chart.

FIGURE 8-7 · X chart data.

Again, look for these patterns in your data and then select the chart.

Still Struggling

The QI Macros Control Chart Wizard will automatically do this analysis and select the most likely chart for you. Let the QI Macros do this for you until you learn the pattern.

The np Chart

There's one chart I've left to last because I rarely find situations where it applies. The np chart is like the p chart except that the sample sizes are constant. In business operations, sample sizes are rarely constant. The data look like Fig. 8-8.

Again, look for these patterns in your data and then select the chart.

FIGURE 8-8 • np chart data.

Other Control Charts

There are many other forms of control charts for various applications: Short-Run, ANOM, EWMA, Moving Average, Levey Jennings, and Hotelling Charts.

- Short-Run Charts (DNOM). What if you only make three of this product and five of that one? There's never enough data to do a full control chart. Short-run charts analyze the Deviation from Nominal (target) for each different product (Fig. 8.9).

- ANOM. Analysis of Means control chart shows variation from the mean. It's mainly used for experimental, not production, data (Fig. 8.10).

- CUSUM. Cumulative Sum control chart detects small process shifts by analyzing deviation from a target value (Fig. 8.11).

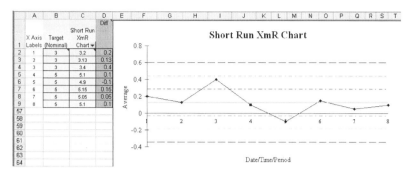

FIGURE 8-9 • Short-Run (DNOM) chart.

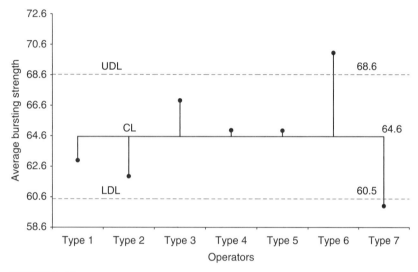

FIGURE 8-10 • ANOM chart

- EWMA. Exponentially Weighted Moving Average (Geometric Moving Average [GMA]) charts are effective at detecting small process shifts, but not as effective as X charts for detecting large process shifts (Fig. 8.12).

- Moving Average charts. Can be more effective at detecting small process shifts than XmR charts. The EWMA chart may be more effective than the Moving Average chart (Fig. 8.13).

- Levey Jennings chart. Average and Standard Deviation chart is used extensively in laboratories (Fig. 8.14).

- Hotelling charts. What do you do if you need to control two things simultaneously like vertical and horizontal placement of a drilled hole? Hotelling charts will assist in controlling these *multivariate* kinds of situations (Fig. 8.15).

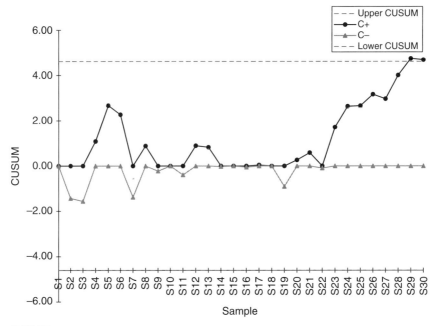

FIGURE 8-11 • CUSUM chart.

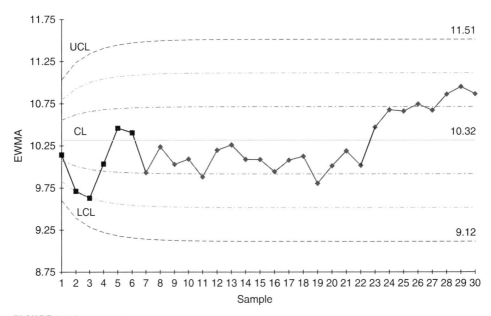

FIGURE 8-12 • EWMA chart.

FIGURE 8-13 • Moving Average chart.

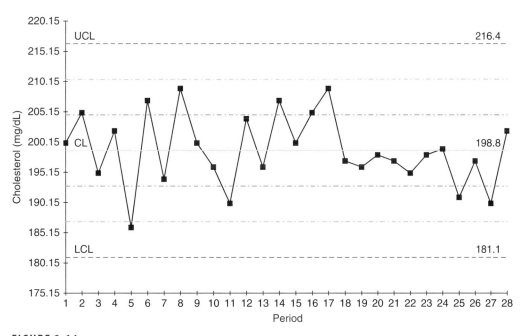

FIGURE 8-14 • Levey Jennings chart.

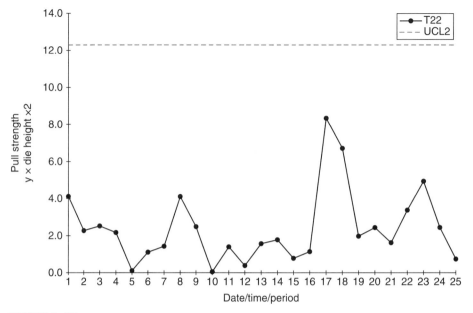

FIGURE 8-15 · Hotelling chart.

FIGURE 8-16 · g charts.

- g and t charts. Geometric Median and Time Between control charts for rare events like wrong site or wrong patient surgeries in a hospital (Fig. 8.16). Hospitals use these charts to track *never events*—things that should never happen, but do.

Still Struggling

I have yet to use any of these charts in standard practice, but obviously some people have advanced applications for them. I recommend getting familiar with the X, c, p, and u charts before turning to these other types of charts.

Summary

So, just recognizing patterns in your data can make it easier to pick the right control chart.

Rows/Columns	Attribute (Integer)	Variable (Decimal)
1	c chart	XmR chart
	np chart	XmR trend
2	p chart	
	u chart	
2 or more		XbarR
		XMedianR
		XbarS
		I–MR–R

If you learn to look for these patterns in your data, it will make it easier to choose the right control chart. And it's so easy to draw these charts with the QI Macros, that you can draw them and throw them away if they aren't quite right.

Stability Analysis

Once you've got a control chart, then what do you do? Processes that are out of control need to be stabilized before they can be improved using the problem-solving process. Special causes require immediate cause-and-effect analysis to eliminate variation.

Any point above UCL — UCL
Two of three points in this area — +2 Sigma
Four of five points in this area — +1 Sigma
Eight points in a row above CL — UCL
Eight points in a row below CL — −1 Sigma
Four of five points in this area — −2 Sigma
Two of three points in this area — LCL
Any point below LCL

FIGURE 8-17 · Stability analysis rules.

The diagram in Fig. 8-17 will help you evaluate stability in any control chart. Unstable conditions can be any of the following:

- Any point above the UCL or below the LCL
- Two of three points between two sigma and the control limits
- Four out of five points between one and two sigma
- Eight points in a row above or below the center line
- Six points in a row ascending or descending (i.e., a trend)
- Nelson Rules that detect statistically unlikely conditions

Any of these conditions suggests an unstable condition may exist. Investigate these special causes of variation with the fishbone diagram. Once you've eliminated the special causes, you can turn your attention to using the problem-solving process to reduce the common causes of variation. You can download my SPC quick reference card from *www.qimacros.com/sustainaid.pdf*.

Still Struggling

Certain patterns of performance are statistically unlikely, not impossible, but unlikely. The QI Macros will identify them for you when you draw a control chart. Then you can investigate them to determine if some "special cause" made performance change.

Understanding Standard Deviation and Control Charts

Many people ask "Why aren't my upper and lower control limits (UCL, LCL) calculated as the mean +/– 3 times the standard deviation?" A simple answer to this question is that the Levey Jennings chart does this exact calculation, but there are other factors to consider. To answer this question, you have to understand some key principles and underlying statistics: variation, standard deviation, sampling, and populations.

> *Variance.* The average of the square of the distance between each point in a total population (N) and the mean (i.e., average). If your data are spread over a wider range, you have a higher variance and standard deviation. If the data are centered around the average, you have a smaller variance and standard deviation.
>
> *Standard deviation* (σ). The square root of the variance.
>
> *Sampling.* Early users of SPC found that it cost too much to evaluate every item in the *total population*. To reduce the cost of measuring everything, they had to find a way to evaluate a *small sample* and make inferences from it about the *total population*.
>
> *Understanding control chart limits.* Ask yourself this question: "If a simple formula using the mean and standard deviation would work, *why are there so many different control charts?*" Short answer: to save money by measuring small samples, not the entire population. Another short answer is to handle different distributions: binomial, normal, and so on.

When using small samples or varying populations the simple formula using the mean and standard deviation just doesn't work, because *you don't know the average or standard deviation of the total population, only your sample.* So why are there so many control charts? Because *you have to estimate the average and standard deviation* using the average and range of your samples. The formulas to do this vary depending on the type of data (variable or attribute) and the sample size. Each control chart's formulas are designed for these varying conditions.

In variable charts, the XmR uses a sample size of 1, XbarR 2 to 5, and XbarS 5 to 50. These small samples may be taken from lots of 1,000 or more. In attribute charts, the c and np charts use small samples and fixed populations; the u and p charts use varying populations. So, you have to adjust the formulas to compensate for the varying samples and populations.

To reduce the cost of inspection at Western Electric in the 1930s, Dr. Walter S. Shewhart developed a set of formulas and constants to compensate for these variations in sample size and population. That's why they are sometimes called Shewhart control charts. You can find these in *any* book on statistical process control. *So stop worrying about the formulas. Start monitoring your process using the charts.*

Control Plan

For those companies that need more rigor in process control, consider implementing a control plan (Fig. 8.18). A control plan is a structured method for identifying, implementing and monitoring process controls. A control plan describes what aspects of the process, from start to finish, will be kept in statistical process control, and it also describes the corrective actions needed to restore control. Process flowcharts and Failure Mode and Effects Analysis (FMEA) documents support the development of the control plan. The QI Macros include fill-in-the-blank templates for flowcharts, FMEAs, and control plans.

The control plan for any part, assembly, or deliverable identifies

- All steps in the manufacturing or service process (e.g., injection molding)
- Any machines used in the manufacture or delivery (e.g., Mold 1)
- Product characteristics to be controlled (e.g., mounting hole burrs and diameters)
- Specifications and tolerances (e.g., 15 mm +/− 1 mm)
- Techniques for measurement and evaluation (e.g., gauges)
- Sample size and frequency of measurement (e.g., five per hour)

	A	B	C	D	E	F	G	H	I	J	K	L	M
1	http://www.aiag.org/							CONTROL PLAN					
2	Prototype		Prelaunch	X	Production	Key Contact/Phone				Date(Orig)		Date (Rev.)	
3	Control Plan Number		12345				Jay A.	Injection Svcs		2/26/2010			
4	Part Number/Latest Change		45678			Core Team				Customer Eng. Approval/Date			
5	Part Name/Description		Dashboard			Organization/Plant Approval/Date				Customer Quality Approval/Date (if Req'd)			
6	Organization/Plant		IS/Plant 1		Organization Code	Other Approval/Date (If Req'd)				Other Approval/Date (If Req'd)			
7					Characteristics				Methods				
8	Part/ Process Number	Process Name/ Operation Description	Machine, Device, Jig, Tools, for Mfg.	No.	Product	Process	Special Char. Class	Product/Process Specification/ Tolerance	Evaluation/ Measurement Technique	Sample Size	Freq.	Control Method	Reaction Plan
9	1	Injection Molding	Mold 1		1 Mounting hole			burrs	Inspection	1	1	Inspection	Adjust/recheck
10								15mm+/- 1mm	Gage	5 pcs	1/hr	XbarR Chart	Adjust/recheck

FIGURE 8-18 · Control plan.

- Control methods (e.g., inspection, XbarR chart, and so on)
- Reaction plan—what to do when the characteristic goes out of control (e.g., adjust, recheck, quarantine)

While control plans are beyond the scope of *Lean Six Sigma Demystified*, it's useful to know that there's more rigor available if needed. There's a checklist for developing control plans, FMEAs, and flowcharts in the QI Macros APQP Checklist template (Fig. 8.19).

	A	B	C	D	E	F	G	H
1						A-8 CONTROL PLAN CHECKLIST		
2		Customer or Internal Part No.				Revision Level		
3		Question	Yes	No	N/A	Comment / Action Required	Person Responsible	Due Date
4	1	Was the control plan developed according to the methodology described in Chapter 6 of the APQP Manual?						
5	2	Have all the controls identified in the PFMEA been included in the control plan?						
6	3	Area all special product/process characteristics included in the control plan?						
7	4	Were DFMEA and PFMEA used to prepare the control Plan?						
8	5	Are Material specifications requiring inspection identified?						
9	6	Does the control plan address incoming (material/components through processing/assembly including packaging?						
10	7	Are engineering performance testing and dimensional requirements identified?						
11	8	Are gages and test equipment available as required by the control plan?						
12	9	If required, has the customer approved the control plan?						
13	10	Are the gage Methodology and compatibility appropriate to meet customer requirements?						
14	11	Have measurement systems analysis been completed in accordance with customer requirements?						
15	12	Are sample sizes based upon industry standards, statistical sampling plan tables, or other statistical process control methods or techniques?						

FIGURE 8-19 • Control plan checklist.

QUIZ

1. What does it mean that a process is *stable* or *in control?*

2. What does it mean that a process is *capable?*

3. In Six Sigma, what is the purpose of SPC?

4. What are control charts?

5. How are control charts used?

6. What is a process *control system?*
   A. Suppliers, inputs, process, and outputs
   B. Control charts of performance
   C. corrective actions
   D. Rework
   E. All of the above

7. How does deviation affect results?
   A. Too big
   B. Too small
   C. Too long
   D. Too short
   E. Any of the above

8. How can stability analysis tell if a problem involves *special* or *common cause* variation?
   A. Special causes are statistically abnormalities.
   B. Special causes are shown in red in the QI Macros.
   C. The rest is common cause variation.
   D. All of the above

9. A process in statistical control is
   A. stable.
   B. predictable.
   C. capable.
   D. A and B.
   E. A and C.

10. **A capable process**
    A. meets customer specifications.
    B. is in control.
    C. produces zero defects.
    D. A and C.
    E. A and B.

11. **Control charts can monitor what kind of data and distributions?**
    A. Variable or measured
    B. Attribute or counted
    C. Normal
    D. Binomial, poisson
    E. Non-normal
    F. All of the above

12. **The benefits of using control charts include**
    A. monitoring existing performance.
    B. detecting potentially unstable conditions.
    C. making the invisible visible.
    D. any of the above

13. **The Taguchi loss function identifies the cost of**
    A. missing the specification limits.
    B. missing the target.
    C. being out of control.

14. **Service industries most commonly use which of the following charts?**
    A. XbarR charts
    B. XmR charts
    C. c charts
    D. np charts
    E. p charts
    F. u charts

EXERCISES

1. **Develop a flowchart of a key business process.**
   - For the participant's group, department, or organization, identify one key business process. Make sure they are focused before they start the exercise.
   - In subgroups, develop a flowchart of the process.
   - Identify the non-value-added rework loops and delays in the process.

2. **Develop process indicators. For improvement efforts to be successful, they must focus on the customer's requirements and ways to measure them—defects, delay, or cost. Earlier, in planning, we developed indicators based on customer requirements. These are usually the quality indicators measured after delivery of the product or service. Now we need to identify the hand-off and decision points where process indicators can be measured to predict the performance of the process.**
   - In small groups, have participants identify one quality indicator on the basis of customer requirements.
   - Using the process flowchart, have participants identify one or two places in the process where a measurement indicator would reliably predict the results (quality indicator). The number errors corrected during the process, for example, will predict the quality of the final product (lots of errors probably mean a poor product).

3. **Graph the process indicators.**
   - In small groups, have participants select one indicator for good, fast, and cheap. Using real or best-guess data, have participants plot the current performance.
   - Which direction is good? (Reduce defects, delay, and cost.)

4. **Evaluate stability.**
   - Review one quality indicator reflecting a customer requirement.
   - On the basis of real or intuitive data, is the process stable? Does it produce consistent results? If not, what would need to be done to improve the consistency of results?

5. **Interpret a control chart. Run control charts on the XmR, XbarR, and XbarS data in c:\qimacros\testdata. Analyze the charts for stability.**

6. **Improve process stability. If a process is not stable, use the Six Sigma problem-solving tools, especially the Ishikawa diagram, to identify the special root causes of the instability, remove them, and make the process stable, repeatable, and predictable.**

   - To identify root causes, use the fishbone, or Ishikawa, diagram. Put a problem statement about the special cause of variation in the head of the fish and the major causes at the end of the major bones. Major causes include
     (1) Processes, machines, materials, measurement, people, and environment
     (2) Steps of a process (step 1, step 2, and so on)
     (3) Whatever makes sense
   - Begin with the most likely main cause.
   - For each cause, ask why? Up to five times.
   - Circle one to five root causes (end of why chain).
   - Verify the root causes with data (Pareto and scatter).

chapter 9

Laser-Focused Process Innovation

So far, we've looked at ways to solve problems with delay, defects, and deviation using the methods and tools of Lean Six Sigma. After Lean Six Sigma teams have sunk their teeth into a few improvement projects, they often begin to wonder if they are working on the right issues and processes. This seems to be a natural progression, from getting success using the improvement tools to wanting to focus the improvement efforts more precisely.

CHAPTER OBJECTIVES

In this chapter, you will

- Learn how to focus the improvement effort with voice of the customer
- Learn how to identify critical to quality measures
- Learn how to use the SIPOC diagram
- Learn how to develop a balanced scorecard

277

Lean Six Sigma has some excellent tools to help refine your improvement focus. Most people aren't ready to use these strategic tools until they've started to understand the basic methods and tools.

I've also noticed that Lean and Six Sigma started out as separate methods and tools, but have been on a collision course for the last few years. There is a trend in the press toward something called *process innovation*. Just as Six Sigma eclipsed TQM, I suspect that *process innovation* will become the new catch phrase that encompasses Lean Six Sigma. Regardless of what you name it, the improvement efforts can benefit from more rigorous focus.

Focusing the Improvement Effort

The focusing process was originally called *hoshin* planning. I call it laser focus. In this chapter, you will learn how to use the key tools required to laser-focus your process innovation.

- Use the Voice of the Customer (VOC) to *define* customer requirements.
- Develop Critical to Quality (CTQ) *measures* to link the VOC to your business processes.
- Create a Balanced Scorecard to focus and align the organization's mission to both the long- and short-term improvement objectives.
- Select and graph indicators to measure your customer's requirements and the progress of the improvement effort.

The planning process feeds directly into problem solving to increase speed, quality, and cost by reducing cycle time, defects, waste, and rework.

Voice of the Customer

If I had asked my customers what they wanted, they'd have asked for a faster horse.
—Henry Ford

The VOC helps the business focus the improvement effort in ways that will achieve breakthrough improvements in speed, quality, and cost that serve the customer. Using the voice of the customer (VOC), business (VOB), and employee (VOE), you can develop a *master improvement story* that links and aligns multiple teams and improvement efforts to achieve quantum leaps in performance improvement.

Michael George speaks of understanding the *heart of the customer,* not just the head. To understand the customers' heart, he suggests that you will want to (1) develop strong links to both the core *and the fringes* of your market, (2) study the behavior of customers to gain insights into how they are using your product or service, and (3) include customers and their knowledge throughout the development process.

The VOC analysis gathers the customers' needs and wants as a basis for establishing objectives. Only customers can create jobs. So customer satisfaction is a central theme of Lean Six Sigma. There are *direct* customers (e.g., actual buyers or retailers) and *indirect* customers (e.g., shareholders, government regulatory agencies). Each customer has unique requirements, which can be related to your business.

All improvements involve moving from a present way of satisfying customers to a more desired method. Before we can set the improvement processes in motion, however, we first have to define our direction of movement. Where most companies and improvement teams fail is in getting properly focused. To succeed, you will want to focus on your customers' needs and follow the data.

Once you've identified your key measurements for each of these goals, set a Big Hairy Audacious Goal (BHAG) for improvement. Forget the 10% improvement. Go for 50% reductions in cycle time, defects, costs, system downtime, and so on. Go for 50% improvements in financial results and customer satisfaction. I have found that when you go for 10% improvements, you only get 10% ideas. When you go for 50% improvements, you get 50% or bigger ideas, and you often get 70% to 80% improvements. Breakthroughs! BHAGs also force you to narrow your focus to the 4% of the business that will produce the biggest return on investment.

Developing the Voice of the Customer

Developing the VOC matrix (Fig. 9-1) is easy, but it forces some rigor into your thinking. This is perhaps the power of Lean Six Sigma; all of the tools force people to go beyond surface-level thinking into a deeper understanding of their business.

FIGURE 9-1 · Voice of the customer matrix.

Step	Activity
1	Identify your direct and indirect customers.
2	Get the direct customer's requirements from surveys, focus groups, interviews, complaints, and correspondence. Review indirect customer requirements (e.g., regulations, laws, codes). Use the affinity diagram to combine the direct and indirect customer requirements into CTQ elements.
3	Enter key customer voice statements on left. Have customers rate the importance from 1 (low) to 5 (high).
4	Identify and enter key business functions for delivering the customers requirements along the top.
5	For each box in the center, rate the contribution of the "how" (top) to the "what" (left). Multiply the importance times the relationship weight to get the total weight.
6	Total the columns. The highest scores show where to focus your improvement efforts.

The VOC uses *the customers'* language to describe what they want from your business. Using a restaurant as an example to elicit the participant's VOC for dining experiences, ask: When you go into a restaurant, what do you want?

Good	Get my order right.
	I want good food.
	I want an accurate bill.
	Give me payment options—cash, check, credit card.
Fast	Greet me and seat me promptly.
	Serve me promptly.
	Serve my food when I want it (fast or slow).
	Have my check ready.
Cheap	Give me good value for money spent.
	Don't waste food.

How do restaurants provide the meals? Greet and seat, take orders, prepare and serve food, bill, collect. What are the most important processes? Figure 9-2 explores how these requirements and processes interrelate. I have found that

FIGURE 9-2 • Restaurant voice of the customer.

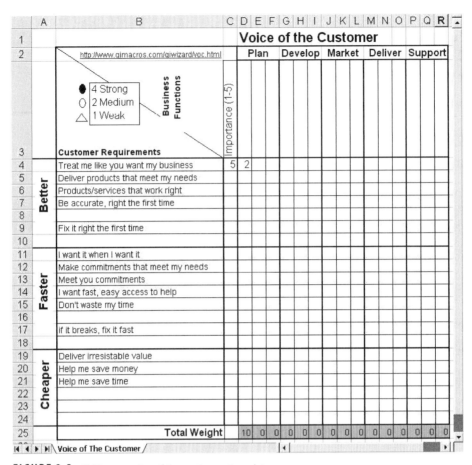

FIGURE 9-3 · QI Macros voice of the customer template.

the VOC has some common requirements no matter what business is involved (Fig. 9-3).

Customers say things like

- Treat me as though you want my business.
- Deliver products that meet my needs.
- Deliver products or services that work right.
- Be accurate, right the first time.
- Fix it right the first time.
- I want it when I want it.
- Make commitments that meet my needs.
- Meet your commitments.

- I want fast, easy access to help.
- Don't waste my time.
- If it breaks, fix it fast.
- Deliver irresistible value.
- Help me save money.
- Help me save time.

These are the most common themes I hear from customers. What are your customers saying?

Still Struggling

Don't get hung up on the format of the VOC Matrix. The goal of Six Sigma tools is to help people discuss needs and issues in a structured way that results in organizational learning and improvement. As you learn the tools you will develop more rigor about how you apply them.

Speak Your Customer's Language

In Denver recently, tragedy struck a family when a 40-ton construction girder fell from an overpass onto their SUV, killing everyone.

I was saddened by the tragedy, but rather than focus on the installation of the girder, my attention focused on the telephone call that occurred earlier in the day that could have saved their lives. A driver with highway construction experience called to report the girder was loose and buckling, apparently unsafe.

After the accident, TV journalists played the call for all to hear. As we listened to the call, the caller kept clearly saying *girder* and the highway call center person kept paraphrasing the man's statement, but used the word *sign*, not *girder:* "There's a loose sign?"

The call center employee reported the problem as a loose sign, which was soon checked by highway maintenance staff. They didn't even notice the girder. Why not? Because they were focused on the sign and not the girder. If the call center person had simply listened and entered what he or she heard, the disaster might have been averted.

HINT *Stop trying to train your customers to speak your language.*

When I worked in a telephone company, I had an opportunity to work in the repair call center and listen to calls. Repair center people had a similar problem listening to what the customer was saying. They tried to teach the customer "phone speak" about central offices, trunk lines, drop boxes, and other in-house terms that meant nothing to the customer. It only infuriated the customer and took up more time than it should have. Stop trying to train your customer to speak your language. It breaks rapport.

HINT   *Be a parrot not a paraphraser.*

In grade school we were all taught to paraphrase what people say, but a sign is not a girder. If you truly want to listen to the VOC, in this case a concerned citizen, you have to actually listen and record what the customers say, not what you want to hear and not what you think you heard. *Parrot what they say*, never paraphrase. It builds rapport.

HINT   *Don't make stuff up.*

Just because you have one picture in your head doesn't mean that the person on the other end of the telephone has the same picture. A picture of a loose girder in one mind doesn't equal the picture of a loose sign in another. If the call center employee had simply written down *exactly* what the caller said, *girder*, the disaster might have been avoided completely.

If you aren't sure what the customer means, don't invent a meaning; just ask: "What do you mean by *girder?*" Then the caller might have said "A gigantic steel beam that spans the highway," which would have changed the picture in the call center employee's head.

When customers call to ask about our QI Macros Lean Six Sigma SPC software, we seek to get clear what the customers are asking before answering their question. Few things are more irritating than getting a great answer to a question that wasn't asked. We use their words, not ours, to describe the solution.

Speak Your Customer's Language

If you want to communicate effectively, you have to use the words the customers give you. Never make the customers translate what you're saying into their language; translate what you're saying into the customers' language so that nothing is lost in translation.

Over a decade ago I became a master practitioner of Neuro-Linguistic Programming (NLP). In NLP, we learned how to develop rapport by matching other people's language.

One of the principles of NLP is "The meaning of your communication is the response you get." If your customers respond in a way that matches what you think you said, it was a good communication. If they respond differently, then your communication was unclear.

The language skills I learned have served me well in everything I've done. It makes me a better husband, because I listen to what my wife says. It makes me a better consultant and supplier, because I listen to what my customers want and then try to deliver it in ways that match their words. I don't always get it right but I keep working on it.

Just because we speak English does not mean that we speak the same language or that we have the same pictures, sounds, or feelings tied to any given word. We have different core values that affect our speech and five very different motivation styles that impact every aspect of our communication.

Train your customer service people to listen and connect with customers on their terms, not yours. It will make your business grow and help you retain customers. One consultant I know worked with a major airline's written complaint department. He taught half of the service people to reply to the customer in language that matched the words in the customer letters. Customers who received matching language letters increased their travel on the airline; customers receiving the usual letters did not.

I wrote a book on how to motivate everyone and a quick reference card that you can download from www.motivateeveryone.com/pdf/mejobaid.pdf. To find out more about your own motivation and communication style, you can also take our free online personality profile at www.motivateeveryone.com/nlpstyle.html. Next, you will want to figure out how to measure your ability to deliver what your customers want.

Still Struggling

Think about a friend or someone you find it easy to talk to. Do they "speak your language?" Now think about someone you have a hard time understanding. You know they are speaking English (or your native tongue), but you just don't seem to understand what they are saying. Do they "speak your language?" Can you learn to speak theirs?

Critical to Quality Indicators

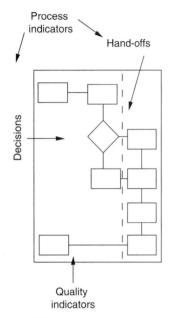

FIGURE 9-4 · CTQ indicators and handoffs.

Goodness is uneventful. It does not flash, it glows.

—David Grayson

CTQs define specific ways to *measure* the customer's requirements and to predict your ability to deliver on those requirements. All business problems invariably stem from failing to meet or exceed a customer's requirement. To begin to define the problem, you need to identify your customer's CTQ needs and a way to measure them *over time*—by hour, day, week, or month.

CTQs measure how well the product or service meets the customer's requirements. Process indicators, strategically positioned at critical hand-off points in the process (Fig. 9-4), provide an early-warning system. For each CTQ there should be one or more process indicators that can predict whether you will deliver what your customers require.

	Indicators	
Requirement	**CTQ or Process**	**Period**
Better	*Number of defects:* Percent defective (number of defects/total)	Minute, hour, day, week, month, shift, batch
Faster	# or % of commitments missed: time in minutes, hours, days	
Cheaper	*Cost:* per–unit cost of waste or rework	

There are usually only a few key customer requirements for any product or service. What do your customers want? How can you measure it over time?

 Still Struggling

You don't need a lot of measurements to manage quality. A few key ones will do. Avoid becoming entangled in too many measurements. They confuse rather than clarify.

FIGURE 9-5 · SIPOC diagram.

SIPOC

Another tool to define your current process is the SIPOC diagram (Fig. 9-5). It shows your suppliers, inputs, main process steps, outputs, and customers (direct and indirect). Identify your main supplier, customer, the product or service used, and the process that creates it. Begin identifying your requirements of the supplier. Then, identify your customers' requirements for the product or service. What do they want in terms of good, fast, and inexpensive? Then, on the basis of your customers' needs, identify how you can measure them with defects, time, or cost. Finally, identify how often you will measure by minute, hour, day, week, or month.

Here are examples from three different environments to demonstrate how to identify the indicators on the basis of requirements. For a restaurant, software developer, or telephone company, who are your main customers, products, services, processes, and customer requirements?

	Restaurant	Software	Telephone Company
Main customers?	Diners	Application users	People
Main products or services?	Food and drink	Software	Connection
Main processes?	Ordering and preparation	Delivery	Billing
Requirements for good?	Right food Right temp Fresh Friendly	Easy to use Bug free Accurate	Good sound quality Worldwide access
Requirements for fast	Prompt • Seating • Service • Check	I want it when I want it, timely updates Fix it fast	Be responsive Available when I want it If it breaks, fix it fast
Requirements for cheap	Value for $ Stop waste	Value for $	Value for $ Help me be effective

HINT *It's often easier, as a customer, to first identify what you want from your suppliers, and then to identify what your customers want from you.*

For improvement efforts to be successful, they must focus on the customers' requirements and ways to measure them in defects, time, or cost (Fig. 9-6) QI Macros Measures.

Type	Requirement	Measurement	Period
Better		Defects per million (outages, inaccuracies, errors) Defective per million (scrap, rework, complaints) Percent defective (number defective/total)	
Faster		Commitments missed Time to design, develop, deliver, repair, or replace Wait or idle time	
Cheaper		Cost of rework or repair Cost of waste or scrap Cost per unit	

	A	B	C	D
1		**Measurements**		
2		Customer/Stakeholder:	Product/Service:	
3		**Customer Requirements**	**Measurement**	**Period**
4	Better	Treat me like you want my business	Customer Complaints	
5		Deliver products that meet my needs		
6		Products/services that work right	% defective	
7		Be accurate, right the first time		
8				
9		Correct/fix it right the first time	Number/% repeat repairs	
10				
11	Faster	I want it when I want it	Cycle time	per product
12		Make commitments that meet my needs	% first choice commitment	
13		Meet your commitments	% commitments missed	Daily
14		I want fast, easy access to help	% calls answered < 60 sec and %calls referred	Daily
15		Don't waste my time		
16				
17		if it breaks, fix it fast	Repair cycle time	per repair
18		If it doesn't work, resolve it fast		
19	Cheaper / Value	Deliver irresistable value		
20		Help me save money		
21		Help me save time		
22				
23				
24				
25				
26				

MEASURES

FIGURE 9-6 · QI Macros measurements matrix.

Balanced Scorecard

A balanced scorecard links all of your efforts to ensure breakthrough improvements, not just incremental ones. The easiest way to depict this is with the tree diagram.

A balanced scorecard begins with a vision of the ideal world. This vision is then linked to long-term customer requirements, short-term objectives, measures, and targets. This is a great place to involve your leadership team.

What's Important about a Balanced Scorecard?

1. If leadership does it, they will commit to achieving it.

2. It links customer needs to the improvement efforts. This clear linkage, which is often missing, helps employees and leaders focus on the customer and align all of their actions to achieve customer outcomes, not internal ones.

3. Measurements based on customer requirements provide an ideal way to evaluate performance.

4. Detailed balanced scorecards can then be developed and linked to this one by individual managers.

5. Results can be measured and monitored easily.

Long-term customer requirements invariably fall into one of three categories (from the VOC matrix).

- Better quality—reliability and dependability
- Faster service—speed and on-time delivery
- Higher perceived value—lower cost

Short-term objectives translate these customer "fluffy" objectives into more concrete ones that can be measured and improved to meet the targets (from indicators).

- Better quality—fewer defects
- Faster service—reduced cycle time
- Higher perceived value

Targets are the BHAGs that challenge our creativity and ability. Fifty percent reductions in cycle time, defects, and costs are both challenging and achievable in a 1-year period. But to do so requires highly focused, not random, improvement work.

Still Struggling

A balanced scorecard helps companies align all of their business activities. When one part gets out of alignment (e.g., when Toyota focused on financial growth instead of quality resulting in extensive recalls), it can cause a company to stumble.

Quality Management Systems

Ultimately, methods and tools like a balanced scorecard, VOC, measurements (e.g., control charts, histograms, Pareto charts, etc.) weave together into a system for producing a quality product. Quality management systems come in many flavors: ISO9000, CMMI, PMI, and a host of other acronyms. They all boil down to a simple series of questions.

1. Do you have a predictable process for delivering your product or service?

2. Do you follow it?

3. Are you improving it?

Look at any mature company that consistently produces a quality product, and it must have some sort of quality management system in place. Although it would be nice to simply install such a system, trying to do it all at once might just kill your business. Consider using a crawl-walk-run approach instead. Start with a few key processes and bring them under control. Add other processes as you gain experience. Continue until you've migrated most, if not all, of the business processes to a quality management system. It won't break the bank. It won't put too big of a strain on the business or employees. And, eventually, it will deliver the desired result.

Regardless of what we call future versions of Lean Six Sigma—quality management or process innovation—business success will continue to depend on the ability to balance innovation and improvement. First, innovate to create new products, then improve to simplify, streamline and optimize delivery of the new products. The methods and tools of Lean Six Sigma must become a part of your business mindset if you are to compete in the global economy. It's that simple.

QUIZ

1. **Process Innovation requires**
   A. laser focus on exceeding the customer's most important needs.
   B. process improvement.
   C. performance improvement.

2. **What are the overarching requirements that every customer requires?**
   A. Faster service
   B. Better products and services
   C. Cheaper products and services
   D. All of the above

3. **Voice of the customer requirements should be stated in**
   A. business rules.
   B. business jargon.
   C. customer language.
   D. techno speak.

4. **The voice of the customer describes**
   A. what customers want.
   B. how to deliver it.
   C. the importance of each process with respect to the customer's needs.
   D. all of the above

5. **The main objectives of the balanced scorecard are**
   A. financial.
   B. customer.
   C. quality.
   D. growth.
   E. all of the above

6. **The balanced scorecard links**
   A. vision.
   B. long-term objectives.
   C. short-term objectives.
   D. measures.
   E. targets.
   F. all of the above

7. **What's a BHAG?**

8. **What are CTQs?**

EXERCISES

1. **Develop a voice of the customer matrix (QI Macros—Fill-in-the-Blank templates—voice of the customer) to explore the interactions between the customer's requirements and your business.**
   - In one large or several small groups, have participants develop the voice of the customer (i.e., their requirements).
   - Have participants identify the processes and steps that participate in the delivery of the product or service.
   - Have participants weight the relationship between the customers' requirements and the processes. Total the weights for each process. Which processes have the most impact on the customers' satisfaction?

2. **Develop a SIPOC matrix (QI Macros—Fill-in-the-Blank templates—SIPOC) to identify your suppliers, inputs, process, outputs, and customers.**

3. **Develop your CTQs.**
   - Identify one key supplier and one key customer.
   - First, for one supplier, identify one requirement for good, fast, and cheap. Identify how you would measure the supplier's quality. (What's your CTQ of them?)
   - Next, select one requirement for good, fast, and cheap from the voice of the customer. Identify a CTQ for this requirement. (What's a CTQ from your customer's perspective?)
     - (a) For the process previously flow charted, identify one quality indicator on the basis of the customer's requirements for good, fast, or value.
     - (b) Identify up to two process indicators at key hand-off or decision points that will predict the process's ability to meet the stated customer requirement.
     - (c) On the basis of the participant's knowledge, is the process stable? Capable?

4. **Develop a balanced scorecard tree diagram (QI Macros—Fill-in-the-Blank templates—Balanced Scorecard) to identify strategic focus. Continue to expand your scorecard by adding the measures and any targets for improvement. If you're at three sigma, can you target four sigma? If you're at four sigma, can you target five sigma?**

chapter **10**

Making Lean Six Sigma Successful

Even though every leader claims to understand the 80-20 rule, they still try to deploy improvement methods everywhere. But Lean Six Sigma is like peanut butter—the wider you spread it, the thinner it gets.

CHAPTER OBJECTIVES

In this chapter, you will

- Learn how to implement Six Sigma successfully
- Learn how to implement Lean Six Sigma
- Learn how to engage the "right" leaders
- Learn how to avoid implementation tar pits

Remember the dark side of the 80-20 rule: If you try to use Lean Six Sigma everywhere, 80% of your effort will only produce 20% of the benefit.

Solution: Use the 4-50 rule to laser-focus improvement efforts for maximum benefit.

Years ago, when I first got started with improvement methods, we used a top-down, CEO-driven, all-or-nothing approach to implementation, just as companies are trying to do today. Following the guidance of our million-dollar consultants, we started and trained hundreds of teams that met for 1 hour a week. Two years later only a handful of teams had successfully solved a key business problem. Most were mired in the early steps of the problem-solving process.

So I decided to try something radical: I applied the improvement method to the improvement method. I looked at

- Each stuck team as a "defect"
- The "delays" built into the process
- The delays between training and application
- The delays between team meetings

I researched and found better methods for doing everything involved in implementation.

1. Using just-in-time (JIT) training, I was able to close the gap between learning and application.

2. Using 1-day root cause teams, I was able to eliminate the delay between team meetings. Solutions that used to take months, now took only hours.

3. Using the power of diffusion, I was able to weave the methods and tools of Lean Six Sigma into the organization with a minimum involvement of key resources.

4. Using root cause analysis, I was able to streamline and simplify the process of focusing the improvement so that we only started teams that *could* succeed. You see, Lean Six Sigma is a data-driven process. If you don't have data—numbers—about the problem, Lean Six Sigma just won't work. You don't have to have perfect data—there's no such thing—but you do have to have data that can narrow your focus.

By systematically applying the improvement process to itself, I found ways to eliminate the failures and accelerate the delivery of results. That's what I call Lean Six Sigma Demystified.

Making Lean Six Sigma Successful

In the 1990s, our CEO committed to quality. Millions of dollars and almost 5 years later, the company abandoned Total Quality Management (TQM). Having the CEO on your side may help, but it's not the holy grail of gaining organization-wide commitment to quality.

If you've read anything about quality improvement, you've heard it repeated endlessly that you want to get top leadership commitment. The emerging science of complexity suggests that this is a mistake. Getting CEO commitment invokes what complexity scientists call the Stalinist Paradox, which lowers your chances of success to 50:50. The emerging science of networks suggests that it's *never* the formal leadership that determines the success or failure of a culture change it's the *informal* leaders—the hubs—in any network that determine success. Informal networks are more like spiderwebs or wagon wheels, not hierarchies.

Formal Network versus Informal Network

In *The Tipping Point*, Malcolm Gladwell argues that any idea tips into the mainstream when sponsored by one of three informal leaders: connectors, mavens, or salespeople.

- *Connectors* connect people with other people they know. Think about your own company. Who is the center of influence who knows everybody and introduces everyone to everyone else?

- *Mavens* connect people with new ideas. Who is the center of influence in your company who gets everyone on board with all the new changes in technology (e.g., Lean Six Sigma, SPC, etc.)? I think of myself as a maven because I'm trying to connect you with the powerful ideas in Lean Six Sigma.

- *Salespeople* do it for money. When you follow the CEO-commitment rule, these folks will show up like vultures to a carcass. Beware.

Seth Godin calls these people *sneezers*, because they *sneeze* the idea virus in ways that gets it into the minds of everyone. Godin separates sneezers into two categories: the powerful and the promiscuous. Powerful sneezers do it because it enhances their status. Promiscuous sneezers (i.e., salespeople) do it for the money.

Still Struggling

Who is the person in your department or company that everyone looks to for advice or guidance? That person is a maven. Who is the person in your department who knows everyone and everything that's going on? That person is a connector.

Don't Confuse the Means with the Ends

To increase results, narrow your focus.

Too many companies are losing sight of the objective when it comes to Lean Six Sigma. The goal is to cut costs, boost profits, and accelerate productivity; it is not the wholesale implementation of an improvement methodology.

At the American Society for Quality's annual conference, many people stopped by our booth drawn by the promise of *Lean Six Sigma Demystified*. They'd been buried in an avalanche of conventional folklore that you have to make a major commitment, spend lots of money training team leaders, and wait years for results. Every one of these disheartened business owners voiced the same question: "Isn't there a better way?"

Of course there is, because all of the conventional wisdom and hype about improvement methods like Lean Six Sigma is *dead wrong!* The goal is bottom-line, profit-enhancing, productivity-boosting results! Lean Six Sigma is merely a means to that end, nothing more. It is not the one-size-fits-all, universal cure to what ails your business. Lean Six Sigma is a power toolkit for solving three key business problems.

1. *Delay.* When the customer's order is idle

2. *Defects.* Errors, mistakes, scratches, imperfections

3. *Deviation.* When the process, machines, or materials vary

Linear versus Circular Causes

Lean Six Sigma works very well on problems with linear causes and effects. If you step on the gas pedal in your car, for example, the car accelerates. This is a linear cause and effect. Lean Six Sigma doesn't work well on problems with *circular*

or systemic causes and effects. In other words, you can't use Lean Six Sigma *directly* to change morale or customer satisfaction. If you engage employees in improving the business, morale may improve. If you improve your products and services, customer satisfaction may improve, but you can't improve morale or customer satisfaction directly. With Lean Six Sigma you can directly engage the power laws of speed and the power laws of quality.

Bell-Shaped Mindset

Because quality principles evolved predominantly in a manufacturing environment, there's a lot of emphasis on variation shown as the *normal* or *bell-shaped* curve, where product measurements are distributed across a range of values. Unfortunately, this emphasis has blinded most leaders to the reality that defects tend to cluster in small parts of the business; they aren't spread all over like butter on bread.

What if you could get over half of the benefit from Lean Six Sigma by investing in just 4% of the business? You can! Pareto's 80-20 rule is a power law. Power laws aren't linear; they grow exponentially. So, if you believe in Pareto's rule, you have to believe that it applies within the 20%. Four percent of the business will cause 64% of the waste and rework. Wherever I go, I find that 4% of transactions cause over 50% of the rework. Four percent of the Americans have over half the wealth.

Better still, the research into the diffusion of innovation shows that true transformational change begins with less than 5% of the workforce (the 4-50 rule). It also suggests that to accelerate results you will want to reduce the number of people involved.

TIP *To increase Lean Six Sigma results, reduce the number of people involved.*

Take the Low Road

Don't confuse activity with results! It doesn't matter how many people you've trained or how many teams you've started. That's just activity, not results. To accelerate Lean Six Sigma, narrow your focus. Traditional implementation wisdom says that you have to take an all-or-nothing, wall-to-wall approach to improvement. This too is dead wrong. It's a myth spread by consultants who directly benefit.

The business world seems to be increasingly divided between the haves and the have-nots, the Lean Six Sigma snobs and the plebeian masses. The reigning wisdom seems to be that to succeed at improvement, you have to embark on a total cultural transformation.

Sadly, I haven't heard anyone talking about the benefits they have achieved from implementing such a transformation. There seems to be this illusion that if you embark on improvement, you'll magically be transported to a place of productivity and profitability. Nothing can be further from the truth. I've heard too many stories of massive investment with little return. One quality auditor expressed concern that if we aren't measuring the ROI of Lean Six Sigma; we're just fooling ourselves. After you pony up an estimated $250,000 (training, salary, projects, and the like) to develop a Lean Six Sigma Black Belt, are you going to get at least $50,000 a project?

So why are all of these big companies trying to do it the all-or-nothing way? Because you can't be criticized for aggressively doing everything possible to implement Lean Six Sigma.

There Has to Be a Better Way

There is a better way that produces better results with minimal risk: I call it the *crawl-walk-run strategy*. First, use the power of diffusion to implement Lean Six Sigma: start small with the first 4% of your business that produces over 50% of the waste and rework, then the next 4%, and so on until you reach a critical mass. Then Lean Six Sigma will sweep through the company, pulled forward by word of mouth. When I explain this crawl-walk-run approach to business owners, each one seems to awaken from his or her fog of despair and envision a path to Lean Six Sigma that is doable.

Set BHAGs

Conventional wisdom suggests that the goal is incremental improvement. But if 4% of the business can produce over half the lost productivity and lost profit, why aren't you shooting for what author Jim Collins (*Built to Last and Good to Great*) calls a Big Hairy Audacious Goal (BHAG).

Set a BHAG to reduce delay, defects, or variation in one of your mission-critical systems by 50% in 6 months. Set a BHAG to reduce cycle time in a customer critical process by 50% in the next 6 months. You'll be surprised how far such a goal will take you.

Use SWAT Teams

Instead of letting teams choose their focus, consider 2-day leadership meetings to define and select key objectives.

Instead of teams that meet indefinitely, consider using data to narrow your focus and having 1-day root cause meetings that bring together the right internal experts to focus on solving a critical business problem that affects customers and therefore profitability. These meetings focus on analyzing and verifying the root causes of problems and then identifying solutions.

There are *instant* solutions that can be implemented immediately by the meeting participants, and there are *managed* solutions that need some leadership and project management to ensure proper implementation.

Instead of widespread training, only train teams that have a real problem to solve.

Right-Size Your Lean Six Sigma Team

The June 12, 2006, issue of *Fortune* magazine focuses on the secrets of greatness: Teamwork. It offers insights into teams past like Apple Computer's Macintosh team and teams of Marines in Iraq. It also argues that "most of what you've read about teamwork is bunk." While you can't just demand teamwork, there are some simple lessons.

- Size matters.
- Stars try to outshine each other.
- It's what you know *and* who you know.
- Location matters.
- Motivation Matters.

The Marine's Recon teams consist of six men. Jeff Bezos at Amazon has a two-pizza rule: If a team cannot be fed by two pizzas, it's too large. A professor at Harvard, J. Richard Hackman, bans student project teams larger than six. Hackman and Neil Vidmar found that the optimum size for a team is 4.6 people (think the Beatles plus their manager Brian Epstein). They also found that the minimum team size is three (two is a partnership). Another model for team size is the number of actors on Gilligan's Island or Friends (six to seven).

With three people, there are three communication paths. With four, there are six paths. With five, there are ten paths. And so on. Too many paths result in delays and errors in communication that lead to delays and defects in the team's solutions.

Dream Teams Can Be Nightmares

Star players often try to outshine each other, leading to conflict, not collaboration. The relatively unknown cast of the movie *My Big Fat Greek Wedding* outperformed *Ocean's Twelve* with a cast of top actors. Sports dream teams sometimes can't play well together. Want to make some progress? Convene a team of knowledgeable, but nonstar performers.

Leverage Your Centers of Influence

As Malcom Gladwell identified in his book, *The Tipping Point*, there are people in your company who are the true centers of influence. They may not have the top job, but they do have the ear of the people. They can make or break your success. There are two types of centers of influence: connectors and mavens. Everyone comes to the maven for his or her encyclopedic knowledge of the business or technology. The connector knows everyone and succeeds by connecting the right resources. It would be a good idea to engage your connectors and mavens in the improvement team.

It's Hard to Think Outside the Box When You're Still in the Same Old Box

Lockheed had the skunkworks. So did Ford with team Taurus and Motorola with team Razr. Sometimes you have to get out of your work environment to disengage the forces shaping your thinking. Get out of the building. Find a park bench or a hotel conference room or someplace that doesn't constantly remind you of the status quo.

Enhance Team Dreams

The best motivator may be impending doom or a fierce competitor. Then team members work together to serve the common good as did Motorola's Razr team. Teams can bond to serve a stellar vision of the future as did Apple's Macintosh or IPOD teams. Whether you're defeating a foe or reaching for the stars, high-performance teams need something to move away from or toward, something that really matters to them and to the company. Otherwise there's little motivation to survive or achieve.

Lean Six Sigma Is Easy; Teamwork Is Hard

For those of us who have been around Lean Six Sigma for a while, we know that the methods and the tools are easy. It's the people and culture stuff that's hard. That's one of the main reasons that I recommend people focus on the 4% of the business that's causing over 50% of the delay, defects, or deviation and only engage the employees involved in that 4%.

I also recommend that the teams be no larger than five to nine people. When focused on the 4%, a handful of people can usually solve any problem in half a day or less, whereas a wider focus and more people often ensure failure.

Teamwork is important to the success of the team, but as they say, it's like getting rich or falling in love; you cannot simply will it to happen. Teamwork is a practice. Teamwork is an outcome. And teamwork leverages the individual skills of every team member. What can you do now to maximize your team's success?

What's Wrong with Most Lean Six Sigma Training?

It's about classroom training, not experiential, on-the-job learning! To put this another way, a way that may be unpalatable for many of you, classrooms are, for the most part, a waste of time.

> *You cannot learn anything in a classroom that is procedural in nature.*
> —Roger Schank

Think about the most useful things you've ever learned. Did you get them in a classroom or through actual practice in the real world? When I look back, it's a little bit of just-in-time learning with some expert coaching and a lot of practice.

In his book, *Lessons in Learning, e-Learning and Training*, Roger Schank examines the limitations of classroom training and the power of experiential learning. Here are some of his insights.

1. *Classroom LIBITI: Learn it because I thought it.* Schank said:

> *Consider Euclidean geometry. You have to agree that Euclidean proofs don't come up much in life. We tend to justify learning such things because we imagine that scholars have determined that the thoughts of great thinkers ought to be learned. The reality is that if we were really concerned with [how this applies to your job] we would teach geometry in the context [of your job], not worrying about proofs so much as worrying about getting the measurements right. The same is true of Lean Six Sigma. You don't need to know how to calculate the statistical formulas for control charts, but you do need to know which chart to choose and how to read the result.*

As absurd as it is in school, LIBITI *is downright crazy in corporate training.*

Principle 1. Just-in-time delivery makes information useful (don't tell people things that they cannot make use of immediately).

Principle 2. Authentic activities motivate learners (don't tell people how to do something they will never have to actually do in real life). Unfortunately, most Lean Six Sigma training isn't connected to the business. One Lean Six Sigma consultant admitted to me that they had 3 days of DOE training in their health care Black Belt curriculum even though health care would rarely need such a skill. This is a form of *overproduction*—teaching things that people won't need.

2. *Things that are true when learning takes place.*

   - There is a goal that learning will help us achieve.
   - The accomplishment of the goal is the reward.
   - After a skill is learned, it's practiced every day for the rest of your life.
   - There is continuous improvement.
   - The skill enables independence.
   - Rewards that accrue from future use are unknown at the time of learning.
   - Failure isn't a problem, because failure occurs with nearly every attempt to learn.
   - The process is not overly fun, but neither is it terribly painful or annoying.

   When I conduct JIT learning, I focus on applying everything I teach to your industry, company, and work environment. Not some mythical pizza joint. You can learn the essential tools and methods in a day. My goal is to help you develop your first improvement stories *during* the class. With improvement teams, we use 1 hour of JIT training to lay the groundwork for what they will experience over the next day or two.

3. *How do learning designers do this? Make sure that*

   - Training is a group process.
   - Training is a problem-solving process.
   - Whatever is learned is merely a prelude to lifelong learning.
   - Make sure independent use of the learning is in sight.

4. How do we do this?

- Ask the experts what goes wrong in their companies.
- Start thinking about training as JIT problem solving.
- Start thinking about learning as *doing*, not memorization.

5. *Use stories in training*, because the unconscious learns from stories. Stories should be about a particular attempt to slay a particular dragon.

- Use real improvement stories.
- Never tell without using a story.
- Make sure the tellers are authentic.
- Tell stories just in time.
- Relive the story; don't just tell it.

Simple truth: People learn by doing.

What's the real problem with most training? Too much training, not enough doing! Ninety percent of what you learn in a Lean Six Sigma class is lost if you don't apply what you've learned within 72 hours. That means that by Thursday of a 5-day Green Belt class, you've forgotten what you learned on Monday. By the following Monday, when you go back to work, you've forgotten most of what you learned the previous week. Overproduction (e.g., training) produces unnecessary inventory (of methods and tools) that confuses the participant.

Why Most Corporate Trainers Fail to Teach by Doing

1. Real life is too hard to replicate in a classroom.

2. It takes too long.

3. No experts are available for one-on-one help.

4. Trainers want to teach general principles.

5. The subject matter doesn't seem doing oriented.

6. The training department has a list of learning objectives that can be learned *without* doing. Learning objectives tend to trivialize complex issues by making them into sound bites that can be told and then tested.

7. The trainers don't know how to do it.

Doing-based learning involves

- Practice
- Feedback
- Reflection

People learn best when they are pursuing goals that they really care about and when what they learn directly helps them attain their goals. The best means of learning has always been experience.

—Roger Schank

People learn best when they

1. Experience a situation

2. Must decide how best to deal with the issues that arise in that situation

3. Are coached by experts

This is the essence of how I teach Lean Six Sigma, through stories, examples, and essentials, not every little detail. Once you understand what I call the *spine*, or the essence, of knowledge you can add to it forever. You can look up the more exotic requirements of Lean Six Sigma when you hit a situation that requires them.

Can you learn *everything* about Lean Six Sigma in a day or less? No.

Can you learn everything you need to know to make dramatic progress from three to five sigma? Yes, you can.

Can you really afford to send your employees to weeks and weeks of training? Maybe if you have deep pockets, but not if you want to get started and make progress.

Still Struggling

Adults learn by doing, not by studying. Get employees right into using the improvement methods and tools to maximize learning and results.

Are You a Lean Six Sigma Salmon?

In 2003, the Benchmarking Exchange conducted a survey of Lean Six Sigma companies. The first question they asked was Within the past 24 months, what business processes have you or your company targeted for improvement?

Top answer? Customer service and help desk–the mouth of the river of defects and delay, not the source!

Most companies make the same mistake. The pain they feel is in their customer service and help-desk areas. Too many calls. One wireless company I worked with received 300,000 calls a month on only 600,000 subscribers. Ouch!

But the root cause is rarely in the customer service center; it's somewhere *upstream:* incorrect orders, fulfillment, service delivery, billing, and so on. The customer service center is a major piece of your company's fix-it factory. It's also a source of excellent data for improvement projects.

In my small SPC software business, I consider every customer service call to represent a defect. Let's face it, if every customer service call costs $8 to $12, how many calls do you want to take? *None,* right?

Me neither. So I ruthlessly try to find ways to make the installation and operation of the software painless and effortless. I try to put all the answers a customer will ever need on my website, so that they can serve themselves when we aren't available. I try to mistake-proof everything in every interaction.

The wireless company I mentioned had set up their entire business to systematically herd customers into the customer service center. They assumed that their customers knew nothing about cell phones and would need to call them to learn how. Every piece of documentation directed customers to call. The monthly bill with roaming charges and extra minutes drove people to call. It was a nightmare.

My business, on the other hand, is more like the Maytag repairman commercials. *I never* want a customer to have to call. What caused most of my calls? When we looked at the data, it was ordering, not the software. So we streamlined and mistake-proofed the ordering process.

Of course, it's possible to go overboard; look at Microsoft. I can't figure out where to call to get help when I need it. There's an enormous knowledge base at *http://support.microsoft.com*, but I can't always find what I need there. Seems like every day I get a new message that there's some new Windows update waiting to be installed. (This makes me think their software is awfully buggy. Does it really need daily updates?)

Get The Order Right!

I must have bad service karma or the quality crisis is growing. In the last couple of weeks, I've been to Chili's and Wendy's and failed to get what I ordered several times.

Chili's

My wife and I went to Chili's and ordered their chicken and shrimp *fajitas* for dinner. We got a plate of chicken and shrimp, but it wasn't fajitas. The manager asked if we wanted to wait for the kitchen to cook up fajitas, but we were going to a movie so I said no. She offered to comp our meal, but later our server said she'd offered to give us a free dessert. Not only couldn't they get the order right; they couldn't get the compensation right either.

A couple of weeks later, after avoiding Chili's, we decided to grab some takeout. I again ordered chicken and shrimp fajitas, but when we got home we only had shrimp; no chicken! Wrong order again.

It costs time and money to correct an inaccurate order. It costs even more money—intangible money—because customers avoid buying from you.

Wendy's

I've driven through Wendy's a couple of times and ordered a #1 which is a hamburger with a side dish and a drink. Wendy's offers side dishes of fries, salad, chili. or a baked potato. Each time I ordered a salad with ranch dressing. Each time when I got to the window, I received a hamburger, fries, and a drink. Most of the time I have to remember to check my order to make sure I get what I ordered. But why should I do Wendy's quality control? It irritates me.

When I remember, they give me the salad, but I end up keeping the fries because they can't take them back. Even a few fries cost money. And I hold up the drive-thru line waiting on my salad.

Wrong order, wrong product, angry customer. Are they so busy trying to remember to supersize me that they can't hear my order?

Lil Ricci's Pizza

Near our house is a New York–Style pizzeria. The servers at Lil Ricci's, no matter what kind of curveball I throw at them—hold the onions, extra mushrooms, or whatever—always get the order right and they do it by memory. Not only is the pizza great, but the service is excellent.

And I tend to overtip them because they do get it right.

And Restaurants Aren't the Only Culprit

Yesterday I spoke with a friend that had a new house built. The builder put in the wrong kind of hardwood for the floors. My friend made them take it out and put in what she ordered. Ouch! There went the profit on that house.

I also worked with my mail-order house yesterday. They have too many tales of woe about not getting an accurate layout of how to print addresses for their clients. Then they have to reprint on labels and manually paste the new address over the old address. And they sometimes duplicate mailings or use the wrong address files. They have checkers, checking the checkers, but errors still slip through.

And I know my printer routinely writes off $100,000 a month in adjustments because they didn't get the print job right.

We Don't Always Get It Right

Even in my business, we don't always get it right. But we do stop to analyze why we didn't get it right and search for ways to mistake proof the order process.

Still Struggling

If you don't get the order right, nothing else will matter. There's rework, waste, and extra cost on your end. There's rework, waste, and extra cost on your customer's end. There's bad feelings that discourage future transactions. And it's not your people's fault. Your systems and procedures let them make mistakes. Change your processes, procedures, and information systems to prevent incorrect orders. Make it impossible to enter one incorrectly!

Wouldn't it be easier to spend a couple of hours figuring out how to prevent order errors than dealing with the seemingly endless rework, waste, and cost they cause? Wouldn't it be easier to spend a couple of extra seconds *listening to your customer* and getting the order right?

It's up to you, but haven't you waited long enough to start shifting how you do business so that you delight customers and earn more trust and more business?

Look Upstream

The customer service center is a great place to *gather data* about the customer's problems, difficulties, and issues. It is a terrible place to try to *solve* those issues. Analyze the data from your customer service center and then initiate root cause teams in the appropriate departments to *solve the upstream problems* that are drowning your customer service help desk.

Don't be a salmon! Start at the source. Clean up the sewage at the headwaters of your business. Keep analyzing why customers call, but use it to fix operations, not the call center. Sure, call centers need improvement too, but if customers don't need to call, do you really need a call center? Maybe, but does it need to be as big as it is?

- Mistake-proof your operations, products, and services.
- Simplify your product or service.
- Make more things self-service.

Spring Forward—Fall Back

This mantra of daylight savings time that I learned as a kid seems to hold true for Lean Six Sigma as well. Back in February, *Quality Digest's* survey found that most large companies were springing forward with Lean Six Sigma and then falling back 2 to 3 years later when time, money, lack of ROI, or a change of CEO cast a shadow over the promise of Lean Six Sigma.

I recently spent some time with a large power company that had actively pursued quality in the 1980s under the leadership of one CEO, only to reverse course during the 1990s under another CEO. Sadly, most of the skilled quality personnel left during that period. And now, in 2003, they're returning to quality under the Lean Six Sigma umbrella, and they are using a version of my crawl-walk-run approach to do it.

Rather than invest in massive training programs, the quality staff is quietly finding operational VPs that want to cut costs and boost profits. Then they use the methods and tools of quality to make those improvements and convince the VP that Lean Six Sigma can help them (1) get ahead personally and (2) move the company forward as well. This develops buy-in to create additional projects and weave quality into the fabric of the department.

Has your company jumped forward? Are you falling back? Are the returns less than expected? Is your leadership changing?

Make It Sticky!

This is the title of Chap. 15 of Jack Welch's new book on winning. He says that Lean Six Sigma "can be one of business's most dreary topics." But he also says

- I am a huge fan of Lean Six Sigma.

- Nothing compares to the effectiveness of Lean Six Sigma when it comes to improving operational efficiency.

- The biggest but most unheralded benefit of Lean Six Sigma is its capacity to develop a cadre of great leaders. It builds critical thinking and discipline.

- Lean Six Sigma is one of the great management innovations of the last quarter century and an extremely powerful way to boost a company's competitiveness.

- You can't afford not to understand it, let alone not practice it.

Yeow! Yet for many people, the concept of Lean Six Sigma feels like a trip to a dentist.

As I've argued since its inception, at its heart, Lean Six Sigma is simple. You only need to know a few key methods and tools to make huge progress in most companies. Eventually you'll need to learn more robust methods, but not right out of the gate.

Creating Stickyness with SUCCESS

Dan and Chip Heath wrote an excellent book on making ideas stick, *Made to Stick*. The found six key principles of sticky ideas (acronym: SUCCES).

1. *Simplicity*. Ideas must be stated simply and also be profound.

2. *Unexpected*. Ideas must be surprising.

3. *Concrete*. Ideas must be stated in concretely in ways you can see, hear, feel, smell, taste, or touch. Sadly, Lean Six Sigma is full of jargon.

4. *Credible*. Ideas must be believable.

5. *Emotional*. Ideas that stick invoke a feeling or emotion that acts like Velcro in the mind.

6. *Stories*. Stories, especially mysteries that reveal the solution at the end, are especially powerful for helping ideas stick in the mind.

This is why I like to tell Lean Six Sigma improvement stories as a way to train team members. A simple, concrete improvement story is the best way to convey the Lean Six Sigma improvement methods and tools. It engages the right brain, not just the left. And the methods and tools leave a lasting impression that sticks.

Think about the things you remember from childhood. Most are jingles or stories. I can't remember a single thing about differential equations, but I can remember an episode of the Lone Ranger. That's the power of simple, concrete stories. They stick.

The Elevator Speech

Most sales and marketing books recommend that you develop an elevator speech (one that can be given in a 30-second elevator ride) about your business. Jack's elevator speech about Lean Six Sigma is "Lean Six Sigma is a quality program that improves your customers' experience, lowers your costs, and builds better leaders." Or more simply, "the elimination of unpleasant surprises and broken promises." Here's mine: "I work with managers who want to plug the leaks in their cash flow." Develop one of your own: Lean Six Sigma lowers costs while boosting profits and productivity.

Get Sticky

Variation in defects, delay, and cost make your business unpredictable, and customers hate unpredictability. Americans love fast-food chains for their predictable menus, quality, and speed. This is part of what Welch calls *stickiness:* creating products and services that make the customer come back time after time.

Still Struggling

How you describe Lean Six Sigma to other people will have a huge impact on its success. Take some time to find the words and phrases that connect with your organization's culture and mindset. It will simplify and streamline the implementation.

Right Tool, Right Application

Lean Six Sigma is not for every corner of a company. Lean Six Sigma is great for streamlining and simplifying repetitive internal processes. Design for Lean Six Sigma (DFLSS) is great for developing complex new product designs. But it's a lousy way to write advertising copy (although I have heard of people using Design of Experiments to test many different versions of a direct-mail piece).

Don't Teflon-Coat It!

Welch offers some insights about how to make it Teflon (how not to do it).

- Hire statisticians to preach the gospel.
- Use complex PowerPoint slides that only an MIT professor would love.
- Present Lean Six Sigma as a cure-all for every nook and cranny.

Welch's advice: "Don't drink the Kool-Aid!"

Fat Cats Don't Hunt

Most companies I've consulted with are making a good living at around three sigma. They have no idea how much profit they could make if they started moving toward four or even five sigma. And you don't need a flock of Black Belts and Green Belts to get going.

But given the choice between developing excuses about why they can't improve or applying the basics of Lean Six Sigma to measure and improve defects, delay, and cost, most people get busy on the excuses.

You can make huge progress in 6 to 12 months. Wait a year and you risk letting your competition get a head start on creating a sticky product or service. And as the U.S. automotive industry discovered, it's hard to catch up once you're behind.

Here's my point: Lean Six Sigma isn't like a trip to the dentist; it's like a trip to the bank to deposit a wad of cash. Use it.

Lean Six Sigma Tar Pits

Over half of all TQM implementations failed. In the language of Lean Six Sigma, that's one sigma: a pathetic track record. And if you study how most companies are implementing Lean Six Sigma, you'll find the same old formula that ruined TQM.

1. Get top leadership to commit to widespread implementation (overproduction).
2. Train internal trainers (Black Belts) to minimize the costs of training everyone.

3. Internal trainers train team leaders (Green Belts).

4. Start a bunch of teams (overproduction).

5. Hope for the best.

Everyone points to GE as a leader in Lean Six Sigma, but if you look more closely, you'll see that Jack Welch had already created a company that managed and even embraced change. So implementing Lean Six Sigma wasn't as hard as it might be in other organizations.

Many people I talk to in various industries say that they tried TQM and it left a bad taste in their mouths. So Lean Six Sigma not only has to overcome resistance to change, but also the bad taste left by failed TQM implementations.

Risk-Free Way to Implement Lean Six Sigma

So how do you implement Lean Six Sigma in a way that's risk free? By using the proven power of diffusion (*The Diffusion of Innovations*, by Everett Rogers). Over 50 years of research into how changes take root and grow in corporations and cultures suggests a much safer route to successful implementation of Lean Six Sigma or any change.

The employee body can make three choices about Lean Six Sigma or any change: adopt, adapt, or reject. In a world of too much to do and too little time, rejection is often the first impulse. People rarely adopt methods completely, so there must be room for adaptation to fit the corporate environment. There are five factors that affect the speed and success of Lean Six Sigma adoption.

1. *Trialability*. How easy is it to *test drive* the change?

2. *Simplicity*. How difficult is it to understand?

3. *Relative benefit*. What does it offer over and above what I'm already doing?

4. *Compatibility*. How well does it match our environment?

5. *Observability*. How easy is it for leaders and opinion makers to see the benefit?

You can also speed up adoption by letting the employees decide for themselves to adopt Lean Six Sigma rather than having the CEO decide for them (although this is how we keep preaching success—get the CEO to commit to widespread change). So, to maximize your chance of success and minimize your initial investment,

1. *Start small.* Forget the 80-20 rule. Less than 4% of any business creates over half the waste and rework. So you don't have to involve more than 4% of your employees or spend a lot of money on widespread training to get results. Get an external Lean Six Sigma consultant to help you find and create solutions using the tools and methods of Lean Six Sigma. Your employees will learn through experience, which is far more valuable than classroom training.

2. *Set BHAGs.* Go for 50% reduction in cycle time, defects, or costs. When you're just starting out, big reductions are often easier to get than you might think, so why not go for them? This also telegraphs the message to your teams that this isn't continuous improvement.

3. *Fly under the radar.* Most companies broadcast their Lean Six Sigma initiative, and employees think "Here comes another one." This usually stirs up the laggards and skeptics—what I call the corporate immune system. You are much better off to make initial teams successful and let the word of mouth spread through informal networks, because this is the fastest way for cultures to adopt change.

4. *Create initial success.* In 1980, the company I worked for brought in a trial of 20 TSO terminals (to replace the punched cards IT used). They selected a small group of programmers to use the terminals. The buzz from this one group caused TSO to be immediately accepted and integrated into the workforce. Do the same thing for Lean Six Sigma. Only start teams that can succeed. Make a small group of early adopters successful, then another, then another.

   When the pioneers (early adopters) become successful, they will tell their friends. The pioneers will convince the early settlers who will eventually convince the late settlers. No one will ever convince the laggards and skeptics; they have to convince themselves.

5. *Fight the urge to widen your focus.* Remember the dark side of the 80-20 rule: 80% of your effort will only produce 20% of the benefit.

6. *Simplify.* Using simple tools like control charts, Pareto charts, and fishbone diagrams, you can easily move from three to five sigma (30,000 parts per million to only 300) in 18 to 24 months. There are lots of complex tools like QFD and DOE in Lean Six Sigma, but you won't be ready to DFLSS until you simplify and streamline your existing processes and lay the groundwork for it.

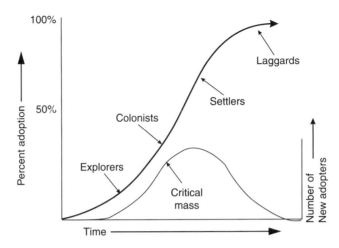

FIGURE 10-1 • Adoption of Lean Six Sigma.

7. *Review and refocus.* Once you solve the initial 4% of your core problems, start on the next 4%, then the next. Diffusion research has shown that somewhere between 16% to 25% involvement will create a critical mass (Fig. 10-1) that cause the change to sweep through the culture.

Good News about Productivity and Profitability

When you focus on the 4% that creates over half the waste and rework, your initial teams get big benefits: 50% reduction in defects, waste, and rework and $250,000-per-project improvement in the bottom line. By the time you've worked your way through the first 16% to 20% of your problems, you will get 80% (the 80-20 rule) of the benefits of Lean Six Sigma. And you'll have minimized your costs of implementation. Now you can grow skilled internal Black Belts from your initial improvement team members. And you can begin to think about DFLSS to design your processes to deliver Lean Six Sigma quality.

Lean Six Sigma payoffs are huge, but you may want to consider using the power of diffusion to ensure that the methods and tools take root in your business and flourish. It's up to you. You can choose the conventional wisdom that gives you only a 50:50 chance at success or choose the power of diffusion that increases your odds substantially. Haven't you waited long enough to start making breakthrough improvements in performance and profitability a permanent part of your business?

Training versus Experience

I just got a request for a proposal from a hospital to train their leaders and staff members. They wanted at least 20 staffers recognized as Green Belts and 20 recognized as Black Belts.

Big contract, lots of training. Sounds seductive, doesn't it? Well, all that training is great for the trainer's pocketbook, but bad for customers. You end up with highly trained and accredited, but unskilled improvement leaders. I suggested that what they really want are experienced professionals that can diagnose, treat, and heal hospital issues concerning speed, quality of care, and costs.

The sad truth is that you lose 90% of what you've learned if you don't use it within 48 to 72 hours. And isn't that what happens? You go to training and come back after a week to a pile of work. By the time you're caught up, you can't remember what you learned just a few days ago.

Looking at this from a value-added flow perspective, the delay between training and application isn't just about the waste of time, but also about the loss of skill. The only way to reengineer this problem is to eliminate the delay: just-in-time training.

In the early 1990s, when I was lured into the in-depth training paradigm, I'd spend a week using a Deming Prize Winning methodology to train 20 team leaders. They, in turn, would start teams that met once a week for an hour. Months went by. Years went by. Nothing got better. Here's what I discovered: You can't learn to swim without getting wet.

So, unbeknownst to my company leadership, I changed the process. I shortened the training down to a couple of introductory hours that I would only teach immediately prior to solving a real problem. Then, in a day or two, I'd guide the team to a solution. They got experience and the good feelings associated with success. Surprisingly, many of these team members could then apply the same tools and process to other problems with equal success. I discovered that I was creating highly skilled, but essentially untrained team leaders in a matter of 1 day. To strengthen their abilities, I'd occasionally conduct a 1-day intensive to review what they'd learned through experience. This helped reinforce what they knew and fill in any gaps.

With 1 day of experience and 1 day of review training, I was accomplishing what the old week of training and endless meetings could not. And, we were getting bottom-line benefits simultaneously.

Sadly enough, by the time I figured this out, the quality department was on its last legs because it had failed to do more than waste time and money defining and measuring cumbersome, error-prone processes that needed major repair. A year later, the department was disbanded and the people laid off.

Don't let this happen to you. Consider using just-in-time training to prep your teams for immediate immersion in problem solving or SPC. Use real data. Use real problems. From the time we are born, we learn by watching other people do things. When you guide a team through the process, they learn an enormous amount just by watching you. Then reinforce what they've learned unconsciously with 1-day review training.

You'll save your company time and money, get immediate results, encourage the adoption of Lean Six Sigma by satisfied employees, generate good buzz, and have more fun.

Prerequisites for Lean Six Sigma

To succeed at any Lean Six Sigma project, you need a few key things.

1. *A project worth doing.* This means that it should be worth at least $250,000 in savings. This applies to any business over $5 million in annual revenue. (Smaller businesses should look for at least $50,000 to $100,000.) If it's not worth doing, find a better project.

2. *A project concerned with operational problems that you can directly control.* You can't directly impact customer perceptions of your business, but you can improve your speed and quality. You can't make customers talk about your product or service, but you can improve it so much that they can't help but brag about it.

3. *Available data about the project.* This means that you need measurements of the problem over time. And you need the underlying measures of various contributors to the problem to be able to laser-focus your analysis. If you don't have the data, you will have to start collecting it. But this takes time. Isn't there a different $250,000 project that has all the data you need to get started right now?

4. *An operational manager or leader who wants to solve the problem.* Without sponsorship, most projects will fail because you won't get the time and resources you need to succeed.

5. *An experienced Lean Six Sigma guide.* Can help you laser-focus the effort, find the root causes, and implement solutions in a matter of days not months.

If you don't have one of these prerequisites, spend the time to change your focus or get what you need to move forward. Otherwise you're just wasting your time and you're doomed to failure.

But when you meet these prerequisites, your chances of success soar. When you have a worthwhile project, the data to support it, committed leaders, and an experienced guide you can get results in days or weeks, not months or years.

Defending Your Data

Another Six Sigma tar pit involves data. Everybody likes to feel good about their job and themselves, and nobody likes to feel bad. This is one of the major challenges of quality improvement. Most people would prefer to focus on what's going well rather than fixing what isn't quite working.

Sadly, when it comes to using facts and figures to improve the business, most people get busy trying to cast a shroud of suspicion over the data to discredit it and avoid doing anything. Almost daily we get calls from QI Macros users who are trying to prepare for the onslaught of criticism they're sure they'll face when presenting their data, charts, and graphs to a "higher power." Nurses tremble when facing doctors. Employees worry when presenting to the boss. Most employees aren't statisticians, just people trying to do a good job for a customer, but they worry that someone will challenge their lack of understanding of math and statistics. Here are some of the common issues we hear. Let us know about yours.

The Data's Not Perfect

And it can happen to anyone. In March 2004, a report by the U.S. Centers for Disease Control (CDC) concluded that poor diet and lack of exercise were responsible for 400,000 deaths in 2000, up 33% from 10 years earlier. In November 2004, the *Wall Street Journal* reported the number may have been overstated by 80,000 because of mathematical errors such as including total deaths from the wrong year.

The CDC acknowledged there may have been statistical miscalculations in the report. The agency plans to submit a correction to the *Journal of the American Medical Association*, which published the original study. Even with the corrections, obesity remains the second leading cause of preventable death.

All data is imperfect. Get over it. You can make a lot of progress using imperfect data.

The Data Is Not Valid

This is the easiest way to throw the hounds off the scent.

Ask: Do you have better data? Show me. (Most of the time they won't.)

Say: Until you bring us better data, we'll have to move forward with what we have.

Why Don't We Measure Our Successes Rather Than Our Failures?

People want to feel good about what's going right, but improvement is about reducing mistakes, defects, and errors. So you have to focus on the failures. Prevent the failures and success will improve automatically.

I Don't Like the Answer

When you start showing people Pareto charts, control charts, and other documents that reveal the extent of a problem, they won't feel good about it. The fastest way out of feeling bad is to discredit the data or the person who brought it up. I've even heard managers say "wrong answer."

When people use our Gage R&R template, they often find that their measurement system needs improvement. Either the gage or the process for measuring has too much variation. And, most often, they don't have enough part variation to conduct a valid study (they need parts that span the tolerance, not ten perfect parts). "There must be something wrong with the analysis," they cry.

When people use a control chart, they find that the process is unstable and needs improvement. "You must be using the wrong chart," they proclaim. Many of these naysayers know how to sound confident and competent enough to make the presenter doubt her or his data. Don't buy it.

Ask: Show me what's wrong with it. What chart would you recommend? Let's draw it now! (And you can use the QI Macros.)

I Don't Get the Same Answer—The Formulas Aren't Right

Some bosses want their people to verify the QI Macros by creating their own formulas and spreadsheets, and then they wonder why their 15-minute effort doesn't correspond with software we've been developing for a decade.

Just because the QI Macros aren't the most expensive piece of SPC software in the world, some people think they're cheap (i.e., poorly constructed, inaccurate). "Wrong answer!" The formulas in the QI Macros have been endlessly tested and come from the most up-to-date statistical references (like *Juran's Quality Control Handbook*) and standards groups (like the AIAG).

More often than not, the user just misinterpreted the formula. I had one customer fiddling with the formulas for Cp and Cpk. He got the formulas (which were correct) off a website, but he missed the little bar over the R for range that means the *average of the ranges*. So he used the maximum minus the minimum to get a range and then choose the wrong value for n to calculate the sigma estimator.

Ask: What formulas are you using? What reference book are you using?

Say: The formulas are fine. If you want to know more about the formulas, buy a copy of a good SPC book. Meanwhile, what is the data telling us?

Why Are There So Many Control Charts?

Why isn't there just one? Why don't you just use standard deviation? Aren't the UCL and LCL supposed to be 3 standard deviations away from the mean? This is another example of people not understanding some basic stuff.

The answer: You could use standard deviation if you have all of the data and it's normally distributed, but when you use samples or have different kinds of distributions (e.g., defects) the formulas vary to account for the differences.

My Statistics Book Doesn't Match Your Statistics Book

One customer asked why Breyfogle's Gage R&R example came up with different results than the QI Macros. On investigation, Breyfogle clearly got his information from the AIAG, Second Edition, 1995, while we're using AIAG Third Edition. Donald Wheeler has a slightly different control chart constant (3.268) for one kind of chart than every other SPC reference book (3.267), but let's face it, 0.001 isn't going to change the control limits by more than a hair.

Another thing I've noticed is that every author has to change the symbols or the layout or something to avoid looking like they copied the stuff from another source. The same customer asked us why the formulas in the GOAL/QPC Gage R&R book weren't in the macros. Would we consider adding them? On further investigation we found that the formulas are there in a format different from the AIAG. No wonder it gets so confusing.

Still Struggling

Given a choice, some people will spend their time trying to make Lean Six Sigma fail. These are just some of the typical attacks you'll face when using Lean Six Sigma. Be prepared. Everyone is not on your side.

One Bad Apple

Many customers have created a histogram and then wondered why they have one big bar on the left side and a small bar way out on the right (or vice versa). A lot of data gets entered manually. We usually find that one data point is entered with the decimal point in the wrong place. For example, we may see data in the form of: 0.01, 0.03, 3.0, 0.02.

Ask: Have you checked your data?

Dummy Data

There's an old saying in information technologies: GIGO (garbage in, garbage out). Several customers have put dummy data into tools like the Gage R&R template, and then been caught off guard because the template tells them their gage system needs improvement. Dummy data can lead to dummy results.

Ask: Where did this data come from?

Preprocessing the Raw Data

Several users have sorted the data before drawing a histogram; this affects how the ranges are calculated and really screws up the Cp and Cpk calculations.

Other customers turn their raw data into ratios or averages, but then try to use the ratio in a chart that needs the raw data. Many health care clients take ratios like falls per 1,000 patient days, but then try to use the ratio in a p chart which needs the raw falls and patient days. Another person tried to use two averages to do a statistical t-test.

Ask: Have you done anything to the raw data?

Not Preprocessing the Raw Data

Several users have tried to get the QI Macros to make a chart out of a bunch of text fields like order error and billing error. We can plot your numbers, but you first have to use Excel's PivotTable function to count the occurrences of these errors.

Focus on the Goal, Not the Methods or Tools or Data

You can make a lot of progress with imperfect data. Stop using your data as a crutch to avoid fixing important problems. Stop using your charts as an excuse to argue about statistics and tools. Instead, ask yourself: "What can we learn from this chart or graph? What's the data telling us? Is there a problem worth solving? Where should we focus our improvement effort?"

Want to feel good again? Improve some mission-critical process by making it far better, faster, and cheaper than ever before. That will make you feel good. Stop haggling about data and formulas. Start making some progress on real business goals.

Can Lean Six Sigma Kill Your Company?

Yes, it can. Peter Keen, in his 1997 book, *The Process Edge*, uses case studies to describe what he calls *the process paradox*.

The process paradox: "Businesses can decline and even fail at the same time that process reform is dramatically improving efficiency by saving the company time and money and improving product quality and customer service."

Continuous improvement is the right idea if you are the world leader in everything you do. It is a terrible idea if you are lagging and disastrous if you are far behind. We need rapid, quantum-leap improvement.

—Paul O'Neil chairman of Alcoa.

Wrong Implementation

Most companies are trying wall-to-wall, floor-to-ceiling implementations of Lean Six Sigma. Sadly, this means that 80% of the people are engaged in trying to get less than 20% of the benefit. Wall-to-wall implementations can siphon valuable resources away from satisfying customers, creating new products, and exploring new markets.

Wrong Process

Invariably, most Lean Six Sigma teams want to start with a pilot project that's not too risky. Unfortunately, they end up majoring in minor things. They don't get the results required to make a case for Lean Six Sigma.

Wrong Team

Invariably, leaders try to form a Lean Six Sigma team before they've analyzed the data to figure out who ought to be on the team. Consequently, the team struggles because they don't have the right people to solve the problem once it's been stratified to an actionable level.

Here's my point: Lean Six Sigma can kill your business just as easily as liberate it. *Ruthless prioritization (laser focus):* Keen suggests that every business tries to boil the ocean or solve world hunger rather than narrowing their attention to a few customer- and profit-critical, value-adding processes where they can make breakthrough improvements.

Use the 4-50 rule to narrow your attention to the 4% of your business that causes over half of the lost profit. Tackle the big hairy audacious problems in your business first.

Assets and Liabilities

Keen suggests that every process is either an asset or a liability. It either adds value or it doesn't. He also suggests that there are five types of processes.

1. *Identity.* Processes that define the company to customers, employees, and investors

2. *Priority.* Processes that are critically important to business performance

3. *Background.* Processes that provide support to other processes

4. *Mandated.* Processes that are required by law (e.g., taxes)

5. *Folklore.* Legacy processes that have no value

Here's Keen's matrix for evaluating your existing business processes. How many fall into the liability and folklore cells?

Far too many departments and individuals think that fixing mistakes is an asset to the business. It's a liability because it eats profit and reduces growth. Isn't it time to narrow your focus to some mission-critical, priority processes?

Process	Asset	Liability
Identity		
Priority		
Background		Repair and rework
Mandated		
Folklore		

- Use data to narrow your focus to the 4-50.
- Stop training everyone. Train 4-50 team members just-in-time, right before they embark on the problem-solving process.
- Aim for a breakthrough (50% reduction in defects or delay).
- Stop majoring in minor things.

Here's what I've observed: *Every company needs two key mindsets: (1) innovation and (2) improvement.* Lean Six Sigma is the best method around for making improvements when you have linear causes and effects. (Other methods are required when you start to investigate circular or systemic causes and effects.)

Breakthrough improvements in speed, quality, and cost often lead to streamlined and simplified products and processes that lead to innovative insights. The innovations need continuous improvements to survive and thrive. And the cycle of innovate-improve starts all over again.

The good news is that *the Lean Six Sigma mindset can benefit any company,* large or small, service or manufacturing, profit or nonprofit. The bad news is that you will need to keep reinforcing it forever so that you keep springing forward and rarely fall back. And the crawl-walk-run approach described in Lean Six Sigma Simplified is the best method I have found to take baby steps with Lean Six Sigma that produce giant leaps in performance.

This is what the science of complexity and the system thinkers call a *vicious reinforcing loop*. Tiny causes have big effects that become self-reinforcing. They lead to more small steps that deliver big results and so on. As you do this, you will systematically weave Lean Six Sigma into the fabric of the business, making it hard to rip out with each successive change of leadership or change in market conditions.

Lean Six Sigma isn't a panacea–a cure for all things, but it is extremely good at what it does well. Get the Lean Six Sigma mindset inside your company so that you can continue to spring forward and stop falling back.

It can, according to Clayton Christensen, author of the *Innovator's Dilemma*. He found that "management practices that allow companies to be leaders in mainstream markets are the same practices that cause them to miss the opportunities offered by 'disruptive' technologies. In other words, well-managed companies fail *because* they are well managed." And he offers many case studies from disk drive manufacturers and other industries that support his findings. What are the hallmarks of good management that cause companies to fail?

1. *Listening to customers.* (Your current customers want more of the same from you. The emerging market doesn't know what it wants in the next big thing. It just wants simpler, cheaper, more convenient products and services.) Think Ipod versus Walkman.

2. *Seeking higher margins and larger markets*, not smaller emergent ones.

3. *Relying on market analysis to find new markets.* (Markets that don't exist can't be analyzed, they can only be explored through trial and error.)

Recently I was asked to consult with a company that had been acquired by a larger company that was obsessed with Lean Six Sigma. The acquired company started training Black Belts and Green Belts and project teams. They required every employee to have their own Lean Six Sigma project. Every project started asking everyone else for data in all kinds of formats and layouts and selection criteria. The company literally became paralyzed doing Lean Six Sigma and forgot to take care of customers and continue their efforts at innovation, which they were known for. Smaller companies were eroding their market share with simpler, more convenient, and cost-effective tools.

As Joel Barker said in his book, Future Edge, *you "manage" within paradigms and you "lead" between paradigms.* Lean Six Sigma is a great methodology and toolkit for managing and improving your product and service. Companies who do this continue to succeed as long as the underlying technology doesn't change dramatically. But when it does change, your company will most likely be incapable of recognizing and taking advantage of it.

Why? Because it means entering smaller markets with products that generate smaller margins until they become mainstream. IBM, for example, ignored minicomputers. DEC, which succeeded in minicomputers, ignored microcomputers. Apple computer started the microcomputer market, but IBM jump-started personal computers by creating a skunk-works to develop the first prototype. And none of these companies succeeded at developing the Palm Pilot.

Intel may be the only company that consistently rides the curve of new technology by using the strategies outlined in Christensen's book.

1. *Set up a separate organization.* It is small enough to get excited by small gains with customers who want the new technology.

2. *Plan for failure.* Make small forays and tailor the product or service as you learn what your emerging customers want. How many companies start down one path only to discover the big market is a derivative of the original idea?

3. *Don't count on breakthroughs.* Many nextgeneration technology markets emerge from recombinations of existing technologies. Smaller disk drives use the same technology as larger disk drives. So why didn't the large disk drive manufacturers spot the need for smaller drives in PCs, and why didn't PC disk drive manufacturers spot the need for still smaller drives for laptops?

Is Lean Six Sigma making you too complacent? Are you ignoring the tug of the emerging markets in your industry? Don't let Lean Six Sigma kill your company. Balance your efforts to improve the existing business and innovate for emerging markets. Stop the insanity. It's not either-or: improve *or* innovate; it's both improve *and* innovate. Otherwise, your future is in jeopardy.

Still Struggling

Using Lean Six Sigma everywhere on everything is a recipe for failure. Remember to narrow your focus and fix mission-critical issues of delay, defects and deviation. Start with the "worst first" and ignore the rest to maximize results.

Innovation Rules

Innovation is clearly a success strategy for businesses in the information economy. Once thought to be the domain of only the creative and gifted, there appear to be some simple rules that encourage innovation.

Google Rules

Marissa Mayer is Google's innovation czar. In the June 2006 issue of *Business-Week's IN-novation* quarterly, she lists her nine notions of innovation.

1. Ideas come from everywhere and everyone. Encourage them.

2. Share everything about innovation projects. Give everyone a chance to add to or comment on the process.

3. If you're brilliant, we're hiring. If your company thrives on innovation, you can't afford to pass up talent.

4. Give employees a license to pursue their dreams. Employees get one free day a week to work on whatever they want to work on. Half of new Google products come from this time.

5. Prototypes versus perfection. Launch early, test small, get feedback, improve until you converge on the best product.

6. Don't BS, use data. Just because someone likes an idea doesn't mean it's any good. As Motorola says: "In God we trust; all others must bring data."

7. Creativity loves restraint. Set boundaries, rules, and deadlines.

8. Worry about users and usage, not money. If you provide something simple to use and easy to love (see Google's home page or our QI Macros SPC Software for Excel), the money will follow.

9. Don't kill projects—morph them. Just like 3M's failed glue that made Post-it notes possible, there's always a kernel of greatness in a failed project.

Types of Innovation

In the *Innovator's Dilemma*, Clayton Christensen identifies two types of innovation: sustaining innovations and disruptive innovations. Sustaining innovations like DSL enables telephone companies to carry more data over the same line that they carry telephone service. Cell phones, however, are a disruptive innovation. Wires cease to be important when you can go wireless. Digital cameras make film cameras obsolete.

Fast Innovation

In Michael George's book, *Fast Innovation*, he suggests that every innovation effort has three imperatives.

1. *Differentiation.* Delivering a product or service that will touch the *heart of the customer.*

2. *Speed to market.* To gain first mover advantage.

3. *Disruptive innovation.* To make your competitors obsolete.

Rapid Prototyping

If a picture is worth a thousand words, we've found that a good prototype is worth a thousand pictures.

—Tom Kelly of IDEO

Speed to market and touching the heart of the customer rely on rapid prototyping of the product or service and testing it with customers in small pilot projects, because people are better at reacting to prototypes than they are at coming up with ideas on their own.

Example: When we develop dashboards of performance measures for companies, we iterate several times to converge on the ideal layout for their measurement data. Then we *reuse* the templates in the QI Macros to create all of their graphs.

Religion of Reuse

Speed to market also depends on what George calls the *religion of reuse.* Toyota reuses 60% to 80% of the designs and parts in new models of cars. This makes it possible to bring new models to the market in half the time of their competitors. You can too. This kind of information led George to formulate the 80-80-80 rule: 80% reuse will cut lead times by 80% at 80% productivity of the innovators which results in

Shorter lead times (50% to 80%)

Higher productivity because you can use smaller teams of highly focused individuals

Reuse can cover not just parts, but documents and ideas as well. Keep a lookout for cool ideas. When Taiichi Ohno saw how U.S. supermarkets stocked their shelves, he immediately saw a way to simplify and streamline inventory in Toyota manufacturing plants.

Simplify for Speed

Brooks's law says that adding people to a late project will only make it later, because the communication costs go up exponentially.

George says that to accelerate the innovation process, *reduce the number of projects*, because you'll free up your critical innovation resources to focus their time on the key projects. One company that did so increased new products by 40% and reduced time to market by 40%.

Innovation isn't about cloning existing products and hanging a new name on them. Between 1996 and 1999 P&G reduced the number of "me too" product stock keeping units (SKUs) by 20%, saving $2 per case or $3 billion annually. They cut the number of Head & Shoulders Shampoo SKUs by 50%, but sales per item doubled.

Measure Your Innovation Rate

As Marissa Mayer suggests, establish measures of innovation.

- Lead time for new products or services
- New products per year
- Revenue from new products per year
- Percent of product from reused components

Innovation is a mindset. It can be learned. There are some simple ideas like prototyping and the religion of reuse that can be learned and applied immediately. What are you waiting for? Go out there and create the next big thing.

Still Struggling?

Lean Six Sigma is about *improvement*. Innovation is about *revolution*. You need both. Apple has always been focused on innovation (e.g., iPad, iPhone). Microsoft has always been about improvement. Both are important.

Conflicting Goals

One of the biggest challenges with Lean Six Sigma is to align goals across the business. Take purchasing for an example. Their goal may be to get the best deal, but in doing so, they may cost the company many more dollars than they save.

One of our customers called and asked if they could still get the discount on 50 copies of the QI Macros, if they bought them 25 at a time. Curious, I explored why they didn't want to buy all 50 at once. The answer was simple: They could put two separate purchases of 25 on their credit card (below their limit), but if they went to 50, it had to go through purchasing, which would take 4 to 6 weeks.

Could I have forced them to pay the extra $10 per copy to avoid going through purchasing? Sure, because it would save them more than $10 in time. Does it cost me twice as much to fill two orders as it does to do one? You bet. Did I give them the deal anyway? I had to, because I despise idiotic bureaucracy.

How Much Are Delays in Purchasing Costing Your Company?

Another state agency wanted to buy an enterprise license that would save them a significant amount over any of our other discounts. All they had to do was get purchasing to issue the order. A purchasing agent called us and asked if we sell our product through resellers. We do, but not our enterprise licenses. He didn't care. He then had to call three resellers and see if he could get a better price through them. So each of the three resellers had to call us to find out about pricing. Of course, they asked about a quantity half the size of the license. So we had to give them a heads up that purchasing was screwing around with all of us. Most of them admitted that the state's purchasing department had given them fits in the past.

Of course, then the purchasing agent fed these quotes back to the buyer, without mentioning that there was a reduction in quantities. So the buyer had to call us, thinking we were trying to finagle something.

How will this all turn out? I don't know because it all started 2 weeks ago when the customer tried to order 100 copies and we tried to do them a favor of upgrading to the lowest enterprise license, which would save them money. Meanwhile, the people who need the software aren't able to do anything. What did all of this churn cost the customer? More than the license is worth, I'm sure of it.

Is a foolish constraint in one department, like purchasing, driving the rest of your company to drink? Is it driving your suppliers to consider firing you as a customer because you cost too much to manage? Is micromanagement in one department killing your ability to perform in the marketplace?

Realign your measures and goals. Purchasing, for example, should be rewarded on speed to issue a purchase order and minimizing total cost. If they only count the pennies saved on each order and not the total cost to the organization of the delays involved, then they will optimize the goal set for them. This is true of any department.

What are the idiotic goals your department lives by that constrain the overall productivity of the company? Does information technologies take too many months to implement a software change? Does billing take too long to issue an invoice? Payments too long to issue payments causing collection calls by suppliers and delays in new shipments?

You're not a silo anymore. Get over it. *Align the goals throughout the company to maximize your speed, quality, and profitability.* Eliminate the ones that slow you down or hold you back.

Honor Your Progress

Clients tell me that it's often hard to sustain the momentum of Lean Six Sigma. When I ask what they've done to recognize and reward teams for success, they often hesitate and then mumble something about money.

We know that you get more of what you reward, and we know from HR studies that lack of money is a demotivator, not a motivator. So what can we do to reinforce Lean Six Sigma behaviors?

To answer this question, I'd like you to think back on the times when you felt most recognized for your contributions. What did your leaders say or do that let you know that they fully understood your accomplishments?

One thing I've noticed, monetary rewards are soon spent and quickly forgotten, but something tangible often remains long afterward to remind employees of their contribution.

My last year at the telephone company, I worked on a project that helped save millions of dollars. All of the team members and I were treated to an off-site retreat, and we were each given a leather jacket from Warner Brothers that had all of the Looney Tunes characters on the back. And our team members were every bit as diverse as those characters, but we'd found a way to work together to achieve outrageous results.

I've also seen teams rewarded with popcorn or pizza parties, votive candles, and just plain time with the executive team to present their story.

I think the key is to find a unique way to recognize the team that reflects their sense of values and their contribution to the success of the business. It's like picking out a gift for a friend or family member: you don't want the same old thing everybody else has; you want something special that they will remember.

What are you doing to recognize and reinforce the spread of Lean Six Sigma in your organization?

The Hard Work Is Soft

Figuring out what to fix can be a slog. In the *Toyota Way*, the author admits that most of the progress occurs through detailed, painstaking problem solving (i.e., a slog).

The biggest challenge is "getting employees to accept that how they've always done things may not be the best way." Another soft challenge is tearing down the walls between divisions to implement some of the changes.

Like any change, the hardest part is getting the people involved to agree to the change. And the best way to do that is to involve them in the analysis of the problem and creation of the solution, because then they own the change.

How can Lean Six Sigma boost your profits?

Six Sigma Roles

I have found that for any improvement team to succeed, they need three things.

1. *A sponsor* in management
2. *A higher-level management sponsor* (or champion)
3. *A change agent* or facilitator

Traditional Six Sigma Roles

Champions actively sponsor and provide leadership for Lean Six Sigma projects.

Master Black Belts (MBB) oversee the Lean Six Sigma projects. If your company is big enough to have more than ten improvement projects running at one time, you probably need a Master Black Belt.

Black Belts (BB) facilitate, lead, and coach improvement teams *full time*. The American Society for Quality (ASQ) has a body of knowledge (BOK) for Black Belts at */www.asq.org/certification/six-sigma/bok.html*.

Green Belts (GB) work on improvement projects part time. For information, see *www.asq.org/certification/six-sigma-green-belt/bok.html*.

Process Owners manage cross-functional, mission-critical business processes. They have the responsibility and authority to change the process.

Get a Faster, Better, Cheaper Business in 5 Days

Using SWAT teams laser-focused on mission-critical improvements, it's possible to get dramatically faster, better, and cheaper in 5 days or less. It doesn't have to take forever, but it does require the right people focused on a well-defined problem.

Would you rather spend 5 days in training or 5 days making dramatic progress on specific business issues? And learn the essential methods and tools of Lean Six Sigma as a byproduct of improvement?

As you can see, there are lots of ways to fail at integrating Lean Six Sigma into your culture. There are many ways for Lean Six Sigma to kill your productivity and profits and even your company if you go overboard on implementation.

Instead, pilot a few projects. Establish a track record of success and expand into increasingly important improvement projects.

QUIZ

1. For Lean Six Sigma to succeed, it needs the commitment of
   A. the CEO.
   B. the leadership team.
   C. informal leaders.

2. According to Gladwell, name the three types of informal leaders.
   A. _____
   B. _____
   C. _____

3. When it comes to Lean Six Sigma, the wider you spread it, the
   A. greater the returns.
   B. thinner it gets.
   C. more major things get fixed.
   D. more you major in minor things.

4. To maximize your results with Lean Six Sigma while minimizing your costs, you need to employ
   A. the 80-20 rule.
   B. the 4-50 rule.
   C. economies of scale.

5. If not applied within 72 hours, you lose what percent of training's effectiveness?
   A. 10%
   B. 25%
   C. 50%
   D. 90%

6. Lean Six Sigma can
   A. kill a business.
   C. heal a business.
   C. grow the business.
   D. delight customers.
   E. all of the above

7. The optimal place to start applying Lean Six Sigma is in
   A. call centers.
   B. fix-it factories.
   C. upstream at the source.

8. **Given a choice, most employees will**
   A. embrace Lean Six Sigma.
   B. find excuses to avoid Lean Six Sigma.
   C. find ways to discredit the data and findings of improvement teams.
   D. wait for this program of the month to go away.

9. **The best way to measure Lean Six Sigma success is**
   A. number of "belts" trained.
   b. number of teams started.
   C. results.

chapter 11

Measurement Systems Analysis

When I first got involved with quality, I learned about the *five M's* that consti-tuted the root causes: man, machine, materials, methods, and *measurement*.

CHAPTER OBJECTIVES

In this chapter, you will

- Learn how to conduct a Gage R&R study
- Learn how to analyze measurement bias
- Learn how to analyze linearity
- Learn how to conduct an attribute Gage R&R study

Because I worked in a predominantly service industry, I couldn't quite grasp how measurement could be a *cause* of variation. But, if you work in manufacturing, you know that *gages* can be used in ways that are inexact and thus a cause of variation. If you're measuring parts to ensure that they meet customer requirements, but your gage or your measurement process vary too much, you might pass parts that should fail, and fail parts that should pass. To ensure that your customers get what they want you will want to make sure that your measurements are accurate.

Measurement Systems Analysis

A measurement system consists of processes, standards, and gages used to measure a specific feature of a product—height, weight, length, volume, and so on. *Measurement systems analysis* (*MSA*) helps determine if the equipment (i.e., the gage) and the measurement process can get the same result consistently.

MSA uses many methods to evaluate consistency:

Type of Measurement System	Methods
Variable data	Average and range, ANOVA, bias, linearity
Attribute data	Signal detection, hypothesis testing
Destructive testing	Control charts

MSA is actually quite simple, but even seasoned SPC veterans don't seem to understand it. So I thought I'd simplify it for you.

First, when you manufacture products, you want to *monitor the output of your machines* to make sure that they are producing products that meet the customer's specifications. This means that you have to measure samples coming off the line to determine if they are meeting your customer's requirements.

Second, *Gage R&R* studies are usually performed on variable data—height, length, width, diameter, weight, viscosity, and so on (Fig. 11-1).

Third, when you measure, there are three sources of variation that come into play:

- *Part variation* (differences between individual pieces)
- *Appraiser variation* (reproducibility). Can two different people get the same measurement using the same *gage?*
- *Equipment variation* (repeatability). Can the same person get the same measurement using the same *gage* on the same part in two or more trials?

FIGURE 11-1 · Measuring variable data.

You want most of the variation to be caused by *variation between the parts*, and less than 10% of the variation to be caused by the appraisers and equipment. Makes sense, doesn't it? If the appraiser can't get the same measurement twice or two appraisers can't get the same measurement, then your measurement system becomes a key source of error.

Conducting a Gage R&R Study

To conduct a Gage R&R study, you will need

- Ten of the same type of parts from one batch or lot, that covers the specification tolerance. For example, if the specification tolerance is ±0.1, then you need parts that start at 0.99 and go to 1.01 (0.99, 0.992, 0.994, 0.996, 0.998, 1.0, 1.002, 1.004, 1.006, 1.008, 1.1).
- Two appraisers (people who measure the parts).
- One measurement tool or *gage*.
- A minimum of two measurement trials, on each part, by each appraiser.
- A Gage R&R tool like the *Gage R&R template* in the QI Macros.

So, pick 10 parts and randomly have each appraiser measure each part at least twice. Plug the results into the Gage R&R template and check to see if the number of distinct categories (NDC) is five or greater. If not; fewer means that you don't have enough part variation to conduct the study.

The most common Gage R&R tar pit is using identical parts, resulting in an NDC less than 5. If there's no part variation, the %R&R will be bad.

Once you've verified that there's enough part variation using the NDC, you can check the results. If the %R&R (total of appraiser and equipment variation) is less than 10%, you're golden. If %R&R is greater than 30%, then your *gage* and your *measurement* method are causing too much error. If your %EV (equipment variation) is higher than your %AV (appraiser variation), then fix your gage. If the reverse is true, improve the measurement process.

Here are samples of the Gage R&R template input sheet and results sections using sample data from the *AIAG Measurement Systems Analysis*, Third Edition (Figs. 11-2 and 11-3).

Gage R&R System Acceptability

- %R&R < 10%. *Gage* system okay (most of this variation is caused by parts, not people or equipment).

FIGURE 11-2 • QI Macros Gage R&R input data sheet.

	A	B	C	D	E	F	G	H	I	J	K	L
44	Acceptability(%)	0.0692		Gage system may be acceptable based on importance of application and cost							
45		% Using	% Using	Operator may need to be better trained or gage is hard to read							
46	AIAG - Automotive Indu	TV	Tolerance								
47	EV (Equipment Variatio	0.2019					Equipment Variation (EV)				
48	%EV	17.6%	27%	# Parts	#Trials	#Ops		% of Total Variation (TV)			
49	AV: (Appraiser Variatio	0.22967		10	3	3	Appraiser Variation(AV)				
50	%AV	20.0%	31%					% of Total Variation (TV)			
51	R&R (Gage Capability)	0.3058					Repeatability and Reproducibility (R&R)				
52	%R&R	26.7%	42%					% of Total Variation (TV)			
53	PV (Part Variation)	1.1046					Part Variation (PV)				
54	%PV	96.4%	150%					% of Total Variation (TV)			
55	TV (Total Variation)	1.1461					Total Variation (TV)				
56	**Calculate GageR&R using Anova**				With Interaction		Without Interaction				
57	**Anova Source**	**df**	**SS**	**MS**	**F**	**P**	**F**	**P**			
58	**Appraiser**	2	3.1673	1.5836	34.44	0.0000	39.617	0.0000			
59	**Parts**	9	88.3619	9.818	213.52	0.0000	245.61	0.0000			
60	**Appraiser x Part**	18	0.3590	0.0199	0.4337	0.9741					
61	**Gage w AP Interactio**	60	2.7589	0.0460							
62	**Gage w/o AP Interact**	78	3.1179	0.0400							
63	**Total**	89	94.647								
64											
65	Without Interaction	Estimate of Variance	Std. Dev		Total Variation	% Contribution	With Interaction	Estimate of Variance	Std. Dev		Total Variation	% Contribution
66	**Repeatability**	0.03997	0.1999	EV	18%	3%	**Repeata**	0.0460	0.2144	EV	20%	4%
67	**Appraiser**	0.0515	0.2268	AV	21%	4%	**Apprais**	0.0521	0.2283	AV	21%	4%
68	**AppraiserxPart**	0	0	INT	0%	0%	**Apprais**	0.0087	0.0932	INT	9%	1%
69	**R&R**	0.09143	0.3024	R&R	28%	8%	**R&R**	0.1068	0.3268	R&R	30%	9%
70	**Part**	1.08645	1.0423	PV	96%	92%	**Part**	1.0887	1.0434	PV	96%	92%
71				TV	5.5893					TV	5.6309	

`|◄ ◄ ► ►|\ GAGER&R / Range Method / Bias / Linearity / Attribute Gage Worksheet / Ana |◄|`

FIGURE 11-3 • Gage R&R results.

- %R&R < 30%. May be acceptable on the basis of the importance of the application and cost of *gage* or repair

- %R&R > 30%. *Gage* system needs improvement (people and equipment cause over 1/3 of variation).

Still Struggling

People often confuse having good parts with having a good Gage R&R. Your ability to measure a part accurately has *nothing to do* with the goodness of your parts. In fact, you need *bad parts* to get a good Gage R&R study. If there's no variation in your parts, all of the variability falls on to either the gage or the appraisers. Either way, the resulting Gage R&R will be poor.

What to Look For

Repeatability. Percent equipment variation (%EV). If you simply look at the measurements, can an appraiser get the same result on the same part consistently or is there too much variation?

Example (looking at measurements from one appraiser only):

No equipment variation (Part 1: 0.65, 0.65; Part 2: 0.66, 0.66)

Equipment variation (Part 1: 0.65, 0.67; Part 2: 0.68, 0.66)

If repeatability (equipment variation) is larger than reproducibility (appraiser variation), reasons include

- *Gage* needs maintenance (*gages* can get corroded).
- *Gage* needs to be redesigned to be used more accurately.
- Clamping of the part or *gage*, or where it's measured needs to be improved. (Imagine measuring a baseball bat at various places along the tapered contour; you'll get different results.)
- Excessive within-part variation. (Imagine a steel rod that's bigger at one end than the other. If you measure different ends each time, you'll get widely varying results.)

Reproducibility. Percent appraiser variation (% AV). Can two appraisers measure the same thing and get the same answer?

Example (looking at *measurements* of the same part by two appraisers):

No appraiser variation (Appraiser 1, Part 1: 0.65, 0.65; Appraiser 2, Part 1: 0.65, 0.65)

Appraiser variation (Appraiser 1, Part 1: 0.65, 0.65; Appraiser 2, Part 1: 0.66, 0.66)

If you look at the line graph of appraiser performance (Fig. 11-4), you'll be able to tell if one person consistently overreads or underreads the measurement.

If reproducibility (appraiser variation) is larger than repeatability (equipment variation), reasons include

- Operators need to be better trained in a consistent method for using and reading the *gage*.
- Calibrations on *gage* are unclear.
- Fixture required to help the operator use *gage* more consistently.

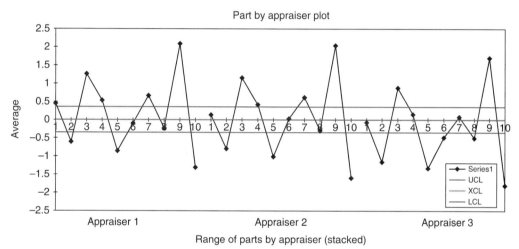

FIGURE 11-4 · Plot of appraiser performance.

Mistakes People Make

Many people call us because they don't like the answer they get while using the Gage R&R template. Most of the time, it's because they didn't follow the instructions for conducting the study. Here are some of the common mistakes I've seen.

- Using only one part. If you only use one part, *there can't be any part variation*, so people and equipment will be the *only* source of variation.
- Using the one part measurement for all 10 parts. There won't be any part variation, so it all falls on the people and equipment.

- Using too many trials. If you use five trials, you have more opportunity for equipment variation.

- Using too many appraisers. If you use all three, you have more opportunity for appraiser variation.

Challenges You Will Face

One customer faced an unusual challenge: they were producing parts so precisely that there was little or no part variation even when measured down to 1/10,000 of an inch. Their existing *gages* had ceased to detect any variation from part to part.

As your process improves and your product approaches the ideal target measurement, you'll have less part variation and more chance for your equipment or people to become the major source of variation. As your product and your process improve, your measurement system will need to improve as well.

Alternatives

Another method of evaluating Gage R&R is to use the specification tolerance method. Simply input the tolerance into the template and read the R&R values from the specification column next to the Average and Range method. The template also provides an ANOVA method of calculating Gage R&R. Any of these methods are valid if the NDC is five or greater.

Bias and Linearity

Two other factors affect the accuracy of your measurement system: bias and linearity.

Bias. Does your *gage* tend to over- or underread the same-size part? (Imagine measuring the length or diameter of a steel rod with known dimensions.)

Linearity. Does your *gage* over- or underread across a range of different sized parts? (Imagine using the *gage* on tin cans of various diameters, from small 6-oz juice cans to 64-oz, family-sized cans.)

If you want to know the *bias* of your *gage*, simply input the *target* or *reference* value for the parts being measured into the Gage R&R template, and the template will calculate the bias of the *gage* (plus or minus). Reference values are determined by using a calibrated gage that is highly accurate.

If you want to know the *bias and linearity* of your *gage*, switch to the linearity worksheet in the QI Macros Gage R&R template and conduct a linearity study.

Linearity Study

To conduct a linearity study, you will need five parts of *different* sizes that have been accurately measured to provide a reference value.

1. Have each of the five parts measured 12 times in random order.
2. Input the data into the Gage R&R template's Linearity worksheet (Fig. 11-5).
3. Input the accurate measurements for each part as a reference.
4. Analyze the linearity using the line graph on the worksheet.

Ideally, there shouldn't be any change in bias from small to large. If you look at the line graph, it should be a horizontal line. More often, however, a *gage* may

FIGURE 11-5 • QI Macros showing nonlinearity.

overread the small and underread the large. If there is too much slope to the line (too much bias), you may want to use the *gage* in its optimal range and find other *gages* to measure where this gage's bias is too large.

Still Struggling

Imagine measuring the diameter of a baseball bat from the narrow handle to the hitting area. Does your gage measure consistently over the range or does it underread or overread one end or the other?

Destructive Testing

What can you do when each piece is destroyed when measured? What if you conduct an impact or other test that makes it impossible to measure repeatedly? Let's look at using an XmR chart.

In this example, there were 10 testers destructively testing 10 samples each from the same production lot. The lower specification limit is 16.7 ft-lb/sq in.

If we put a blank row between each of the 10 testers' data and run the XmR chart, we get an average and range that look like Fig. 11-6.

If all 10 are using the same process to measure samples from a well-known and established process, then we'd expect the averages to be the same and the variations represented by the UCL and LCL to be equal.

If the averages or standard deviations are different from appraiser to appraiser (i.e., technician to technician), then the measurement system needs improvement.

Look at the X chart. Six of the 10 share roughly the same average, and the last three share a different average. If they are all measuring samples from the same lot, then they must be using two different measurement processes. Technician 7 is between the other two groups. Which of the two main groups are measuring correctly? How can you train the others to match? Look at the X chart and the R chart to evaluate the variation (another key factor in Gage R&R).

Technicians 4, 6, and 10 have the least variation. What are they doing that produces more consistent results? How can you train the others to match the consistency? Ideally, all of the appraisers should get close to the same average and standard deviation. Adjust the measurement process until you get the UCL, LCL, and CL to line up more closely.

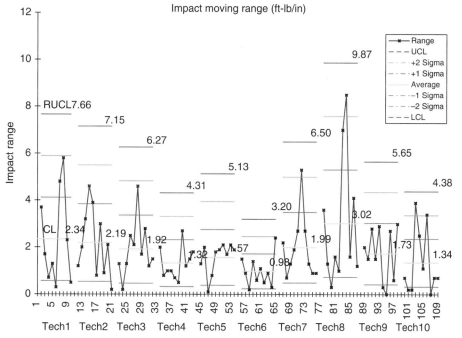

FIGURE 11-6 • Destructive testing X chart.

Conducting a Gage R&R Study

In brief, you should select your parts as follows:

The samples for Part 1 (that will be repeated by a single operator, and those to be reproduced by another operator) should come from *as nearly a homogeneous sample/batch as possible.*

The samples used as Part 2 should be from a different batch or different production run or have sufficient time to allow long-term variation to occur.

Repeat for Parts 3, 4, 5, and so on. (Fig. 11-7).

	A	B	C	D	E	F	G	H	I
1	Gage R&R	http://www.aiag.org/					Part Number		http://ǀ
2	Average & Range Method		1	2	3	4	5	6	7
3	Appraiser 1	Trial 1	2.31	2.12					
4	Enter your data here->	Trial2	2.29	2.15					
5		Trial3	2.34	2.16					
6		Trial4	2.27	2.14					
7		Trial 5	2.3	2.15					
8		Total	11.51	10.72					
9		Average-	2.302	2.144					
10		Range1	0.07	0.04					
11	Appraiser 2	Trial 1	2.29	2.11					
12	Enter your data here->	Trial2	2.31	2.17					
13		Trial3	2.32	2.14					
14		Trial4	2.28	2.13					
15		Trial 5	2.27	2.13					
16		Total	11.47	10.68					
17		Average-	2.294	2.136					
18		Range2	0.05	0.06					

ǀ ◀ ▶ ▶ǀ GAGER&R ⁄ Attribute Gage Worksheet ⁄

FIGURE 11-7 · Destructive testing data in Gage R&R.

The results (Fig. 11-8) will show some variation in equipment because of the variation in destructive tests.

The Gage R&R template will show that 20.7% for the %R&R means that the gage system may be acceptable (given destructive testing has occurred and we can't use the same part twice).

Attribute Gage R&R

Another form of Gage R&R studies is *attribute* Gage R&R. Many gages are designed for operators to quickly assess whether the part passes or fails, not the

	A	B
46	AIAG - Automotive Ind	TV
47	EV (Equipment Variati	0.0236
48	%EV	20.7%
49	AV: (Appraiser Variatic	0.00000
50	%AV	0.0%
51	R&R (Gage Capability)	0.0236
52	%R&R	20.7%
53	PV (Part Variation)	0.1117
54	%PV	97.8%
55	TV (Total Variation)	0.1142

FIGURE 11-8 · Destructive testing results.

actual dimensions of the part. Imagine a hunk of metal with two slots in it: one that will tolerate the part if it's too big and one that will tolerate the part if it's too small. Operators simply take the part and slip it into the slots. If it fits either one, it's out of specifications.

To conduct an attribute gage study, you need at least 10 parts. Measure these accurately with a good gage to determine the reference value. Then have appraisers measure the parts randomly using the pass/fail gage. Using the QI Macros Gage R&R template (Fig. 11-9), insert the upper and lower specification limits and reference value for each part into the template. Then enter a 1 for *pass* or 0 for *fail* based on each appraiser's evaluation.

Do they fail good parts? Do they pass bad ones? (Fig. 11-10) Evaluate the resulting analysis (Fig. 11-11) to find out how your gage and appraisers function. Do you need to upgrade the gage? Do you need some remedial training for the appraisers? Make the changes and repeat the study until you get the level of quality you desire.

	A	B	C	D	E	F	G	H	I	J	K	L	M	N	O	P	Q
1		Appraiser A			Appraiser B			Appraiser C			Reference Results						
2	Part #	Trial 1	Trial 2	Trial 3	Trial 1	Trial 2	Trial 3	Trial 1	Trial 2	Trial 3	Reference	Ref Value	Code	LSL	USL	%R&R	Gray zone
3	1	1	1	1	1	1	1	1	1	1	1	0.476901	+	0.45	0.55	25%	0.02500
4	2	0	0	0	0	0	0	0	0	0	0	0.576459	-	INSTRUCTIONS			
5	3	1	1	0	1	1	0	1	0	0	1	0.544951	X	1. Enter Spec Limits Above			
6	4										0		-	2. Have 3 appraisers accept/reject 10+ pa			
7	5										0		-	3. Enter pass/fail in columns B-J			
8	6										0		-	4. Enter Reference value in column L			
9	7										0		-	5. Evaluate effectiveness columns AJ-AV			

Bias / Linearity \ **Attribute Gage Worksheet** / Analytic Attribute Method /

FIGURE 11-9 · QI Macros attribute Gage R&R worksheet.

FIGURE 11-10 · Measurement system error.

	AJ	AK	AL	AM	AN	AO	AP	AQ	AR	AS	AT	AU	AV
5	**Crosstabulation**					**Crosstabulation**							**Miss**
6			**B**	**Total**				**REF**	**Total**		**Effectiveness**		**Rate**
7	**A**		0	1		**A**		0	1			**A**	89%	11%
8		0	4	0	4		0	3	0	3		**B**	89%	11%
9		1	0	5	5		1	1	5	5		**C**	78%	22%
10	**Total**		4	5	9	**Total**		4	5	9	System	85%	15%
11													85%
12			**C**	**Total**				**REF**	**Total**		**Effectiveness**		
13	**B**		0	1		**B**		0	1		Acceptable	>= 90%	
14		0	4	1	5		0	3	0	3	Marginal	>=80%	
15		1	0	4	4		1	1	5	6	Unacceptable	<80%	
16	**Total**		4	5	9	**Total**		4	5	9			
17													
18			**A**	**Total**				**REF**	**Total**				
19	**C**		0	1		**C**		0	1				
20		0	4	0	4		0	3	0	3			
21		1	1	4	5		1	2	4	6			
22	**Total**		5	4	9	**Total**		5	4	9			

Bias / Linearity \ Attribute Gage Worksheet / Analytic Attribute Method

FIGURE 11-11 · Attribute Gage R&R results.

Still Struggling

Use the Average and Range or ANOVA Gage R&R study when measuring something. Use the Attribute Gage R&R study when the gage is only pass/fail.

Conclusion

So, there, in a nutshell, is Gage repeatability, reproducibility, bias, and linearity. Your goal is to minimize the amount of variation and error introduced by measurement, so that you can focus on part variation. This, of course, leads you back into the other root causes of variation: process, machines, and materials.

If you manufacture anything, MSA can help you improve the quality of your products, get more business from big customers, and baffle your competition. Enjoy.

The QI Macros Gage R&R template is made up of several different templates including average and range method, ANOVA method, bias, linearity, and attribute method.

QUIZ

1. Why is measurement a source of variation?

2. Gage R&R studies evaluate
   A. part variation.
   B. appraiser variation.
   C. equipment variation.
   D. all of the above

3. Gage R&R analysis methods include
   A. average and range.
   B. ANOVA.
   C. bias.
   D. linearity.
   E. attributes.
   F. all of the above

4. Bias evaluates the
   A. appraiser's opinions.
   B. gage's drift.
   C. gage's tendency to over- or underread the same part dimension.

5. Linearity evaluates the gage's ability to measure
   A. the same dimension.
   B. across a range of dimensions.

6. What is the most common Gage R&R tar pit?

7. Acceptable %R&R level is
   A. < 10%
   B. < 30%
   C. > 30%

EXERCISES

1. Use the QI Macros Gage R&R template and data in c:\qimacros\testdata\AIAG SPC to evaluate %R&R.

2. If you use gages in your manufacturing plant, conduct a Gage R&R study on your current measurement system. What do you need to improve?

chapter 12

Design for Lean Six Sigma

So far, we've looked at how to find and solve problems with defects, delay, and deviation. Wouldn't it be great if you could design a new product or service in such a way that you wouldn't have to do all of that problem solving and mistake proofing? You can use the tools of Design for Lean Six Sigma (DFLSS). Unfortunately, most people simply aren't ready for the rigor necessary to do DFLSS until they've got some improvement projects under their belt and they become fed up with fixing processes time after time. But when you're ready, DFLSS is ready to help you create better designs in half the time that will deliver five sigma quality right from the start.

CHAPTER OBJECTIVES

In this chapter, you will

- Learn how to use Quality Function Deployment (QFD)
- Learn how to use Failure Modes and Effects Analysis (FMEA)
- Learn how to use Design of Experiments (DOE)
- Learn how to use TRIZ to innovate and improve

BusinessWeek had an interesting article about how Dow cuts their R&D risk by finding out what customers want. Sounds oddly like DFLSS and Quality Function Deployment (QFD).

Seems the apparel market wanted a new fiber with *soft stretch, cottony feel, and resistance to heat and chemicals.* Until then, Dow had assumed that the big money winner would be a fiber that undercut rivals in price. The result was a fiber called XLA which wil l appear in fabrics this year. Estimated new revenue: $1 billion per year.

Well, instead of developing new products in a vacuum and hoping customers love them, *Dow starts with what the customer actually wants and works backward.*

Step 1: Listen to the customer. Dow gathered 26 industry leaders together and picked their brains for insights into the ideal fiber characteristics. (In QFD, this is the first step: determining the product characteristics.)

Step 2: Identify unique opportunities that are unmet by existing products. (In QFD, this is part of the competitive analysis.)

Step 3: Choose the most lucrative opportunities. (In QFD, the various weights applied to each characteristic lead to selecting the ideal combination.)

Step 4: Develop a prototype and test it with key customers. (Phase two of QFD helps develop the part characteristics.)

Step 5: Commercial production. (The third and fourth phases of QFD develop the process and production requirements to deliver the product at a quality level somewhere around four to five sigma.)

This is the essence of DFLSS; you use the customers' needs to help you design a new product or service that meets their needs and differentiates you from your competitors. If you listen to what your customers are saying when they talk to you in the store or in your call center, you'll soon discover their hidden, unmet needs. If, like Henry Ford, your customers are saying they want a *faster horse,* you have to infer that they really want to get from point *A* to point *B* more quickly. A horse is just one way to do it. Your job is to mash their needs against your capabilities to create a fresh way to answer their needs.

You Can't Make the Dogs Eat the Dog Food

I once worked with a guy who had worked at Purina. He knew that "you can't make the dogs eat the dog food." Yogi Berra used to say about baseball fans "If they don't want to come out to the park, how are you going to stop them?"

They're both saying the same thing: Customers do not have to consume whatever you produce.

There's a risk in starting with a clean sheet of paper and trying to create something totally new. You can minimize your risk by starting from customer requirements that aren't being met in the marketplace and develop from there. Obviously, every business needs to do some of both. You don't want your future riding totally on either long shots or clear shots.

Still Struggling

Consider the Walkman versus the iPod. People want their music with them, but CDs are cumbersome. The unmet need? Portability of the music library. Instead of making better CD cases, what if you could put every track from your personal library onto a device no bigger than a pack of playing cards? Solution: iPod. The same is true of telephones. When I grew up, telephones had to be wired to the network. Unmet need: portability. Cell phones displaced wired phones in record time. Similarly, I'm old enough to remember 45-rpm records that had a best-selling single tune on one side. But they were phased out and replaced by albums. What was the unmet need? People only want the single, not the album. Solution: iTunes.

The goal is simple: Maximize the return while minimizing the risk. DFLSS and QFD can help you do both.

Design Six Sigma Quality into Your Business

Wouldn't it be great to hit the ground running with a Six Sigma capable (3.4 defects per million) process for delivering your product or service? Of course it would, but most three sigma companies don't have the stomach for the kind of rigorous thinking it takes to design and launch a new product or service at these levels, unless, of course, you understand the horrendous costs associated with a typical "seat of the pants" implementation.

DFLSS requires the rigorous application of three key tools: *QFD, FMEA, and DOE.*

Quality Function Deployment (QFD) is a rigorous method for translating customer needs, wants, and wishes into step-by-step procedures for delivering the product or service. While delivering better designs tailored to customer needs, QFD also cuts the normal development cycle by 50%, making you faster to market.

Failure Modes and Effects Analysis (FMEA) is used to analyze and prevent disasters. You can use it to analyze a product, part, or process (PFMEA).

Design of Experiments (DOE) is used to optimize your results by testing various design factors from your QFD House of Quality at the high (+) and low (−) values, not every increment in between, and you can test more than one *factor* at a time.

Quality Function Deployment

QFD uses the *QFD House of Quality* (Fig. 12-1 A Fill-in-the-Blanks template in the QI Macros) to help structure your thinking, making sure nothing is left out. There are four key steps to *QFD*.

1. *Product planning.* Translating *what* the customer wants *in their language* (e.g., portable, convenient telephone service) into a list of prioritized product or service design requirements *in your language* (e.g., cell phones) that describes *how* the product works. It also compares your performance with your competition's performance and sets targets for improvement to differentiate your product or service from your competitor's.

2. *Part planning.* Translating product specifications (design criteria from step 1) into part characteristics (e.g., lightweight, belt clip, battery driven, not hard-wired but radio-frequency based).

3. *Process planning.* Translating part characteristics (from step 2) into optimal process characteristics that maximize your ability to deliver Lean Six Sigma quality (e.g., ability to hand off a cellular call from one antenna to another without interruption).

4. *Production planning.* Translating process characteristics (from step 3) into manufacturing or service delivery methods that will optimize your ability to deliver Six Sigma quality in the most efficient manner (e.g., cellular antennas installed with overlapping coverage to eliminate dropped calls).

Even in my small business, I often use the *QFD* template to evaluate and design a new product or service. It helps me think through every aspect of what

FIGURE 12-1 · Macros QFD House of Quality.

my customers want and how to deliver it. It saves me a lot of cleanup on the backend. It doesn't always mean that I get everything right, but I get more of it right, which translates into greater sales and higher profitability with less rework on my part. That's the power of *QFD*.

Still Struggling

QFD combines the Voice of the Customer (VOC) with competitive analysis. It helps people think through the transition from customer requirements to design requirements to parts requirements to manufacturing requirements. It forces the kind of upfront thinking that makes for better products and services.

Failure Modes and Effects Analysis (FMEA)

FMEA takes your process or product apart step-by-step or piece by piece and asks the questions: What could go wrong? If it does, how will we detect it? What do we do if it happens? How can we design the product to prevent it?

FMEAs (Fig. 12-2) help analyze the design of a part or assembly to (1) identify potential failures, (2) rank these failures, and (3) find ways to eliminate these problems before they occur. FMEAs proactively, rather than reactively, reduce the defects, time, and cost associated with potential errors by preventing crises.

Step	Activity
1	Enter part name and/or block diagram the components
2	List each potential failure mode
3	Describe effects of each type of failure
4	Rank severity of failure
5	Classify any special characteristics
6	List every potential cause or failure mechanism for each failure mode
7	Rank the likelihood of occurrence of each failure/cause
8	List prevention/detection controls
9	Rank detection
10	Identify actions to reduce severity, occurrence, and detection

PFMEAs help analyze a process to (1) identify potential failures, (2) rank these failures, and (3) find ways to eliminate these problems before they occur. FMEAs proactively, rather than reactively, reduce the defects, time, and cost associated with potential errors by preventing crises.

Step	Activity
1	Flow–chart the process
2	Describe process and function
3	List each potential failure mode
4	Describe effects of each type of failure
5	Rank severity of failure
6	Classify any special characteristics
7	List every potential cause or failure mechanism for each failure mode
8	Estimate the likelihood of occurrence of each failure/cause
9	List prevention/detection controls
10	Rank detection
11	Identify actions to reduce severity, occurrence, and detection

http://www.qimacros.com/free-lean-six-sigma-tips/fmea.html **Failure Mode and Effects Analysis** AIAG Third Edition http://www.aiag.org/

System:	Insert System	Design Responsibility:	who		FMEA Number	Insert FMEA#			
Subsystem	system	Key Date:	1/1/2005		Page	1	of	1	
Component	component				Prepared by:	who			
Model:	model				FMEA Date:	1/1/2005			
Core Team:	who								

Item/Part														Action Results				
Function	Potential Failure Mode	Potential Effect(s) of Failure	S e v	C l a s s	Potential Cause(s) / Mechanism(s) of Failure	O c c u r	Current Design Controls Prevention	Current Design Controls Detection	D e t e c t	R. P. N.	Recommended Action(s)	Responsibility & Target Completion Date	Actions Taken	S e v	O c c u r	D e t e c t	R. P. N.
1. Name, Part Number, or Class	Manner in which part could fail: cracked, loosened, deformed, leaking, oxidized, etc.	Consequences on other systems, parts, or people: noice, unstable, inoperative, impaired, etc.			List every potential cause and/or failure mechanism: incorrect material, improper maintenance, fatigue, wear, etc.		List prevention activities to assure design adequacy and prevent or reduce occurrence.	List detection activities to assure design adequacy and prevent or reduce occurrence.		0	Design actions to reduce severity, occurrence and detection ratings. Severity of 9 or 10 requires special attention.	Name of organization or individual and target completion date	Actions and actual completion date				0
										0							0
										0							0
										0							0
										0							0
										0							0
										0							0
										0							0
										0							0
										0							0
										0							0
										0							0
										0							0
										0							0
										0							0
										0							0
										0							0

Severity of Effect:	Occurrence Rating	Detection:	Detection:
1. None	1. Remote -<.01/1000	1. Almost Certain	1. Almost Certain
2. Very Minor	2. Low - 0.1/1000	2. Very High	2. Very High
3. Minor	3. Low - 0.5/1000	3. High	3. High
4. Very Low	4. Moderate - 1/1000	4. Moderate High	4. Moderate High
5. Low	5. Moderate - 2/1000	5. Moderate	5. Moderate
6. Moderate	6. Moderate - 5/1000	6. Low	6. Low
7. High	7. High - 10/1000	7. Very Low	7. Very Low
8. Very High	8. High - 20/1000	8. Remote	8. Remote
9. Hazardous with warning	9. Very High 50/1000	9. Very Remote	9. Very Remote
10. Hazardous w/o warning	10. Very High >100/1000	10. Absolute Unc	10. Absolute Uncertainty

Stakeholder	Effects of Failure	Severity
Consumer (e.g., buyer)	Owner Safety Problem	10
	Major Owner Dissatisfaction	8
	Moderate Owner Dissatisfaction	6
	Minor Owner Dissatisfaction	4
Customer (Manufacturer)	Plant Safety Problem	10
	Possible Recal	9
	Line Stoppage	89
	Warranty Costs	7
AIAG PPAP 4th	Regulatory Penal	7
	Scrap	7
	Moderate Rework (<25%)	5
	Plant Dissatisfaction	4
	Minor Rework (<10%)	3

FIGURE 12-2 · QI Macros Failure Modes and Effects Analysis.

Still Struggling

Consider Toyota's recent recalls. They probably didn't anticipate that an accelerator pedal could get stuck under a floor mat, but I bet it's part of their FMEA process now. What about children's toys? Would an FMEA help prevent accidents? What about medical equipment? Would an FMEA help prevent mistakes, errors, and even deaths? The greater the potential severity, the more an FMEA is an opportunity to avoid the consequences of a failure.

Design of Experiments

Many manufacturing processes and some service processes can benefit from using *DOE* to optimize their results. Without *DOE*, you're stuck with the world's slowest method for success trial and error. With *DOE*, you just have to test at the high (+) and low (–) values for any particular design factor (e.g., pressure, temperature, time) from your QFD House of Quality, not every increment in between. And you can test more than one factor at a time.

You can make *DOE* wildly complex or straightforward and simple. In my first *DOE* class we spent an inordinate amount of time understanding *orthogonal arrays* and all of the other behind-the-scenes mathematics, but you don't need to know all of that to conduct a *DOE* study.

Manufacturing Example

For simplicity, let's assume you are writing a cookbook and want to find the best directions for baking a cake (which is similar to baking paint on a car finish). To do this, you will want to establish the high (+) and low (–) settings for each factor in your study. Let's suppose you have four factors (a *four-factor experiment*).

1. *Pan shape.* Round (–) versus square (+) pan

2. *Ingredients.* 2 (–) versus 3 (+) cups of flour

3. *Oven temperature.* 325 (–) versus 375 (+) degrees

4. *Cooking time.* 30 (–) versus 45 (+) minutes

Let's say that you'll rank each resulting cake on a 1 to 10 scale for overall quality. You then use the ± values in the DOE matrix to guide your testing of every combination (16 total).

- *High.* All high values (+ + + +) = square pan, 3 cups, 375 degrees, 45 minutes
- *Low.* All low values (– – – –) = round pan, 2 cups, 325 degrees, 30 minutes
- *In Between.* Every other combination ("+ + + –", "+ + – –", and so on)

To optimize your results, you might want to run more than one test of each combination. Then you just plug your data into a *four-factor DOE template (Taguchi or Plackett-Burman format)* like the one in the QI Macros and observe the interactions.

Figure 12-3 is a sample QI Macros Plackett Burman DOE template.

In DOE, they talk about *confounding* which simply means that one factor affects another. You'd expect a higher temperature to result in a shorter cooking time, and vice versa, but does a square pan take longer than a round one? Using the results, a DOE program will draw the interactions between each of the *factors* as a line graph.

If the two lines are parallel, there's no interaction. Is one end higher than the other? If so, you can immediately tell which value (high/low) gives you the best result.

If the two lines cross, there is an interaction (confounding). And, by looking at where the two lines intersect on the graph, you can determine the optimum settings (e.g., time and temperature) to get the best cake.

To do this using trial and error would take hundreds, maybe even thousands of trials, not just 16.

Figure 12-4 shows sample charts created by the QI Macros DOE template.

Service Example

People who send direct mail rigorously tally their results from each mailing. They will test one headline against another headline, one sales proposition against another, or one list of prospects against another list, but they usually only do one test at a time. What if you can't wait? Using DOE, you could test all of these factors simultaneously. Design your experiment as follows:

1. *Headline.* Headline 1 (high), Headline 2 (low)
2. *Sales proposition.* Benefit 1 (high), Benefit 2 (low)
3. *List.* List 1 (high), List 2 (low)
4. *Guarantee.* Unconditional (high), 90 days (low)

Design of Experiments		http://www.qimacros.com/free-lean-six-sigma-tips/design-of-experiments.html		
	Factor	Factor Name	Level 1 Low(-)	Level 2 High(+)	
2^2	A	Surface Treatment			Two-factor experiment
	B	Solvent Wash			
	AB	Surface Treatment X Solvent Wash			
2^3	C	Cure Temp			Three-factor experiment
	AC	Surface Treatment X Cure Temp			
	BC	Solvent Wash X Cure Temp			
	ABC	Surface Treatment X Solvent Wash X Cure Temp			
2^4	D	d			four-factor experiment
	AD	Surface Treatment X d			
	BD	Solvent Wash X d			
	CD	Cure Temp X d			
	ABD	Surface Treatment X Solvent Wash X d			
	ACD	Surface Treatment X Cure Temp X d			
	BCD	Solvent Wash X Cure Temp X d			
	ABCD	Surface Treatment X Solvent Wash X Cure Temp X d			

Design	Factors																Responses	
Trial	A	B	AB	C	AC	BC	ABC	D	AD	BD	ABD	AC	ACD	BCD	ABCD	1	2
2^2 1	-	-	+		+	+	+								+	1560	1450
2	+	-	-		-	+	+								-	2625	2490
3	-	+	-		+	-	+								-	1400	1380
4	+	+	+		-	-	+								+	2750	2760
2^3 5	-	-	+	+	-	-	+								+	1910	1850
6	+	-	-	+	+	-	-								+	2230	2150
7	-	+	-	+	-	+	-								+	1865	1810
8	+	+	+	+	+	+	+								-	2920	2860
2^4 9	-	-	+	-	+	+	+	+	+	+	+	+	+	+	-		
10	+	-	-	-	-	+	+	+	-	+	+	+	-	+	+		
11	-	+	-	-	+	-	+	+	+	-	+	+	+	-	+		
12	+	+	+	-	-	-	+	+	-	-	+	-	-	-	-		
13	-	-	+	+	-	-	+	+	+	+	-	-	+	+	+		
14	+	-	-	+	+	-	-	+	-	+	-	+	-	+	-		
15	-	+	-	+	-	+	-	+	+	-	-	-	+	+	-		
16	+	+	+	+	+	+	+	+	-	-	-	+	-	-	+		
	A	B	AB	C	AC	BC	ABC	D	AD	BD	ABD	AC	ACD	BCD	ABCD Average	2158	2094

FIGURE 12-3 · QI Macros Plackett-Burman DOE.

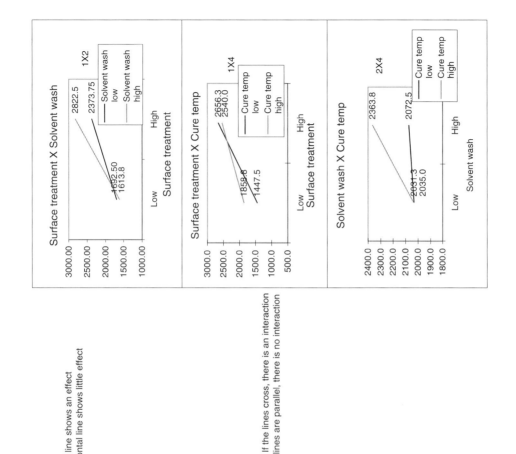

FIGURE 12-4 • Plackett-Burman DOE charts.

This way you might find that Headline 1 works best for List 2 and vice versa. You might find that one headline works best with one benefit.

DOE can help you shorten the time and effort required to discover the optimal conditions to produce Six Sigma quality in your delivered product or service. Don't let the ± (orthogonal) arrays baffle you. Just pick *two, three, or four factors*, pick sensible high/low values, and *design a set of experiments* to determine which factors and settings give the best results.

Start with a two-factor experiment and work your way up. Have fun! It's just not that hard, especially with the right software.

Still Struggling

Rather than use trial and error method of testing various designs, you can use DOE to test many factor *simultaneously* to find the optimal design with a minimal number of tests.

TRIZ

I have always tried to view things upside down.

—Taiichi Ohno

You might hear some buzz in the Lean Six Sigma community about an innovative thinking process called TRIZ. The TRIZ concepts can help you develop better countermeasures to existing problems. TRIZ began in Russia in 1946 with an assumption that there are universal principles of innovation and that these can be learned by anyone. Research on over 2 million patents revealed that (1) problems and solutions are repeated across industries and sciences, (2) patterns of technical evolution are repeated as well, and (3) innovations use insights gleaned from outside of their field.

There are at least 40 principles underlying TRIZ. The six overarching components of TRIZ include

1. Set high goals (voice of the customer).

2. Identify cause and effect (critical functions-CTQs).

3. Eliminate or replace harmful, corrective, enabling, or productive functions or parts (FMEA).

4. Improve function to the extreme (FMEA, DOE).

5. Resolve contradictions (FMEA, QFD, DOE).

6. Expand and consolidate.

Still Struggling

To come up with a solution to a problem TRIZ often asks: What's the opposite? If something is hard, how can we make it soft? If it's rigid, how can we make it flexible? If it's straight, how can we make it curved? We all get stuck in certain mindsets. Asking: "What's the opposite?" will often change the pictures in our mind enough to create a new opportunity.

All of these methods, QFD, FMEA, DOE, and TRIZ are simply means to make you think through your design and implementation of new products and services. Making people think can be a challenge, but that's the power of the Lean Six Sigma toolkit: It makes people think before they act and use data to back up their thinking.

Have fun with Lean Six Sigma and the QI Macros. See how much you can boost productivity and profitability. And remember to have fun doing it.

QUIZ

1. **What is Design for Lean Six Sigma (DFLSS)?**

2. **Quality Function Deployment (QFD) helps translate**
   A customer requirements into design requirements.
   B. design requirements into part requirements.
   C. part requirements in to process requirements.
   D. process requirements into manufacturing requirements.
   E. all of the above

3. **Failure Modes and Effects Analysis helps identify**
   A. what can go wrong.
   B. how failures will be detected.
   C. what to do when a failure occurs.
   D. all of the above

4. **Design of Experiments can**
   A evaluate multiple design factors simultaneously.
   B. identify interactions between design factors.
   C. analyze manufacturing and service designs.
   D. all of the above

EXERCISES

1. Take one of your existing products or services and use the QFD House of Quality (QI Macros Fill-in-the-Blanks templates) to evaluate your existing design and how it compares with your competition.

2. Take the same product or service and conduct a Failure Modes and Effects Analysis on it. Where might it fail? How will you know? What can be done when it happens?

3. Conduct a Design of Experiments on some aspect of your business. What are two factors that you would like to evaluate? What are the high and low values for each? How will you measure or grade the results from each test?

chapter 13

Statistical Tools for Lean Six Sigma

Some tools of Lean Six Sigma aren't graphical; they're analytical. Sometimes you want to be able to compare two processes or products and learn something about their quality using statistics alone. This falls under the category of something known as *hypothesis testing*.

CHAPTER OBJECTIVES

In this chapter, you will

- Learn how to use hypothesis testing
- Learn how to use ANOVA—analysis of variance
- Learn how to analyze data normality
- Learn how to use regression analysis

Hypothesis Testing

I've come to suspect that hypothesis testing is where statistics got the nickname *sadistics*. I found it confusing because it seems to use negative logic to describe everything. But it's really not that hard once you understand how it works.

Let's say that you have two batches of the same product and you want to prove that they are (1) the *same* (i.e., equal) or (2) *different* (i.e., not equal) at a certain level of confidence. Because Lean Six Sigma is obsessed with variation and central tendencies, you might want to prove that the averages or variation are the same or different. Hypothesis testing helps you evaluate these two *hypotheses*.

Whoever dreamed this up decided that the same or equal result would be called the *null hypothesis*. Then, on the basis of the analysis, you want to *accept* the null hypothesis (i.e., the two batches are the same) or *reject* the null hypothesis (i.e., the two batches are different). There are several tools that can help you do this depending on whether you are most interested in the average or the variation.

Hypothesis Testing for Variation

Since variation can affect results, it's useful to determine if variations in two or more samples are the same or different. To evaluate variation statistically, use the *F*-test or Levene's test.

F-Test for Variation

If you have a single factor measured at two levels and you want to know if they have the same or different variability, use the *F*-test. An *F*-test using two samples compares two independent sets of test data. It helps determine if the variances are the same or different from each other. Consider the following example:

F-Test Two-Sample Example
If you're producing rubber made with two different recipes, you might want to know if the variances in tensile strengths are the same or different (Juran's QC *Handbook*, 4th ed., p. 23.74).

	A	B
1	**Recipe1**	**Recipe2**
2	3067	3200
3	2730	2777
4	2840	2623
5	2913	3044
6	2789	2834

FIGURE 13-1 · *F*-test data.

	A	B	C	D	E
1	**Recipe1**	**Recipe2**	F-Test Two-Sample for Variances		
2	3067	3200			
3	2730	2777		*Recipe2*	*Recipe1*
4	2840	2623	Mean	2895.6	2867.8
5	2913	3044	Variance	51713.3	16923.7
6	2789	2834	Observations	5	5
7			df	4	4
8			F	3.055673	
9			P(F<=f) one-tail	0.152407	
10			F Critical one-tail	6.388234	

FIGURE 13-2 · *F*-test results.

- The null hypothesis (H_0), variances are the same.
- The alternative hypothesis (H_a), variances are different.

Now, conduct a test and enter the data into Excel (Fig. 13.1). Use Excel's Data Analysis Toolpak under the Tools menu or the QI Macros to conduct the *F*-test. The QI Macros will prompt for a significance level (default = 0.05). The *F*-test will calculate the results (Fig. 13.2)

Interpreting the F-Test Results

Hypothesis Test	Compare	Result
Classical method	*t*–Test statistic > critical value (i.e., *F* > *F* crit)	Reject the null hypothesis
	Test statistic < critical value (i.e., *F* < *F* crit)	Accept the null hypothesis
p value method	*p* value < α	Reject the null hypothesis
	p value > α	Accept the null hypothesis

Since $F < F$ crit (3.05567 < 6.38823) and *p* value > α (0.15241 > 0.05), we can accept the null hypothesis that the variances are equal.

EXCEL NOTE *Notice that the F-test reversed the order of the recipes. For some unknown reason, Excel requires that the recipe with the largest variance be first to ensure correct calculations. The QI Macros reorganizes your data to ensure that Excel performs the calculations correctly.*

Still Struggling

You are not alone. Some people take to these concepts easily and others struggle with them. Just remember that the goal is to determine if two processes, machines or materials produce the *same* or *different* results. *F*-tests and Levene's tests help analyze variation. ANOVA and *t*-tests help analyze differences in means (i.e., averages). Some of these tests work best with normal data. And some work best with non-normal data. With practice, you will become comfortable with these tools.

Levene's Test for Variation in Non-Normal Data

Levene's test compares two or more independent sets of test data. It helps determine if the variances are the same or different from each other. The Levene's test is like the *F*-test. However, Levene's test is robust enough for non-normal data and handles more than two columns of data. Consider the following example:

Levene's Test Two-Sample Example

Using the *F*-test example data (Fig. 13.1), conduct a Levene's test using the QI Macros (Levene's test is not part of Excel's Data Analysis Toolpak). The Levene's test macro will calculate the results (Fig. 13.3).

	A	B	C	D	E
1	**Recipe1**	**Recipe2**		*Recipe1*	*Recipe2*
2	3067	3200	Median	2840	2834
3	2730	2777	Mean	2867.8	2895.6
4	2840	2623	Variance	16923.7	51713.3
5	2913	3044	n	5	5
6	2789	2834	df	4	4
7				Levene's	
8			Test	1.044	
9			*p*	0.337	

FIGURE 13-3 • Levene's test results.

Interpreting the Levene's Test Results

Since Levene's *p* value $> \alpha$ (0.337 > 0.05), we can accept the null hypothesis that the variances are equal.

	E	F	G	H	I	J	K	L	M	N
1	Batch 1	Batch 2	Batch 3	Batch 4	Batch 5	Batch 6	Batch 7	Batch 8	Batch 9	Batch 10
2	1.006	0.998	0.991	1.005	0.998	1.009	0.990	0.998	1.002	0.991
3	0.996	1.006	0.987	1.002	0.998	1.013	1.004	1.000	0.998	0.995
4	0.998	1.000	0.997	0.994	0.982	1.009	0.996	1.006	0.996	0.984
5	1.000	1.002	0.999	1.000	0.990	0.997	1.001	1.000	0.995	0.994
6	0.992	0.997	0.995	0.995	1.002	0.988	0.998	1.002	0.996	0.997
7	0.993	0.998	0.994	0.994	0.984	1.002	1.000	0.996	1.004	0.997
8	1.002	0.996	1.000	0.998	0.996	0.995	1.018	0.998	1.004	0.991
9	0.999	1.000	0.999	0.996	0.993	0.998	1.010	0.996	0.998	0.998
10	0.994	1.006	0.996	1.002	0.980	0.981	0.996	1.002	0.999	1.004
11	1.000	0.988	0.996	0.996	0.996	0.996	1.002	1.006	0.991	0.997

FIGURE 13-4 • Levene's test data–gear diameters.

Although an F-test works well on two samples of normal data, it isn't robust enough to handle non-normal data or more than two samples. (Notice that Levene's p value differs from F-test's two-tailed value of 0.305; however, both cause acceptance of the null hypothesis.)

	K	L	M
1		Batch 1	Batch 2
2	Median	0.999	0.999
3	Mean	0.998	0.999
4	Variance	0.00002	0.00003
5	n	10	10
6	df	9	9
7		Levene's	
8	Test	1.706	
9	p	0.099	

FIGURE 13-5 • Levene's test results– gear diameters.

Levene's Test Ten-Sample Example

Now, consider the following example of 10 batches of gear diameters (Figs. 13.4 and 13.5). Again the p value is $0.099 > 0.05$, so we accept the null hypothesis that variances are equal from a batch to batch.

Hypothesis Testing for Means

Since the mean (i.e., average) also affects results, it can be useful to evaluate if the means of one or more samples are the same or different. There are a number of ways to do this depending on sample size: t-tests, Tukey test, and ANOVA.

t-Tests for Means

t-Tests evaluate if the means of one or two samples are the same or different. There are several types of t-tests.

- t-test single sample
- t-test two sample assuming *equal* variances
- t-test two sample assuming *unequal* variances
- t-test paired two sample for means

Still Struggling

Use Levene's test instead of the f-test when the data is non-normal or there are more than two subgroups.

t-Test Single Sample

A t-test using one sample compares test data to a specific value. It helps determine if the sample is greater than, less than, or equal to the value. Consider the following example (in QI Macros test data/anova.xls):

Lightbulb Life—t-Test Example

Let's say you want to know if the life of a lightbulb is greater than 2,500 hours. So you develop a null hypothesis (H_0) that lightbulb life is less than or equal to 2,500 hours and the alternative hypothesis (H_a) thatbulb life is greater than 2,500 hours.

- H_0: $\leq$ 2,500 hours
- H_a: > 2,500 hours

Now conduct a test of lightbulb life and enter the data into Excel (column A in Fig. 13-6). Then, select the data with the mouse and click on the QI Macros Menu to select the one-sample t-test (one-sample t-tests are not available in Excel's Data Analysis Toolpak). The QI Macros will prompt for a confidence level (default = 0.95 which is the same as a significance level of

	A	B	C
1	Bulb Life (Hours)	t-Test 1-sample	
2	3150	Test Mean	2500
3	3033	Confidence Level	0.95
4	2862	N	15
5	2827	Average	2836.933
6	3124	Stdev	266.1089
7	2669	SE Mean	68.70901
8	2364	T	4.903772
9	2575	TINV	1.761309
10	3161	p - One sided	0.000116
11	2570	p - two sided	0.000233
12	2860		
13	2423		
14	2843		
15	3134		
16	2959		

FIGURE 13-6 • t-Test single factor–bulb life.

0.05) and test mean/average (in this case 2,500). The t-test one-sample macro will calculate the results (columns B:C in Fig. 13-6).

Note that cell A8 is 2,364 hours, which is less than the target, but the average is 2,837.

Interpreting the t-Test One-Sample Results

Since the null hypothesis is that lightbulb life is less than or equal to 2,500, this is a one-sided test. Therefore, use the one-tail values for your analysis.

NOTE *The two-sided values would apply if our null hypothesis were that H_0: mean = 2,500 hours.*

Since the t statistic $> t$ critical (4.90377 > 1.76131) and p value $< \alpha$ (0.000116 < 0.05), we can reject the null hypothesis that lightbulb life is less than or equal to 2,500.

We can say that we are 95% confident that lightbulb life is greater than 2,500 hours.

Customer Service—t-Test One-Sample Example

Let's say you want to know if wait times in a branch bank are not greater than 3 minutes at a 95% confidence level.

- H_0: ≤ 3 minutes
- H_a: > 3 minutes

Mystery shoppers routinely visit the branch and collect their wait time. This gives us the data we need to test the hypothesis (Fig. 13-7).

	A	B	C
1	Customer	t-Test 1-sample	
2	4	Test Mean	3
3	0	Confidence Level	0.95
4	0	N	43
5	0	Average	4.465116
6	10	Stdev	5.346778
7	1	SE Mean	0.815376
8	3	T	1.79686
9	10	TINV	1.681951
10	4	p - One sided	0.039776
11	2	p - two sided	0.079552

FIGURE 13-7 · *t*-Test single factor–wait times.

The one-sided p value $< \alpha$ [0.039776 is less than 0.05 $(1 - 0.95)$], so we must reject the null hypothesis that bank wait times are less than or equal to 3 minutes.

We can say that we are 95% confident that wait times are greater than 3 minutes.

t-Test—Two Sample Assuming *Equal* Variances

Using the F-test data from Fig. 13-1, you might want to know if the tensile strengths are the same or different.

Define the Null and Alternative Hypotheses

- The null hypothesis H_0 is that the mean difference $(x_1 - x_2) = 0$, or in other words, the means are the same.
- The alternative hypothesis H_a is that the mean difference $<$ or > 0, or in other words, the means are not the same.

Conduct an F-test to Determine If Variances Are Equal

Since the two recipes aren't paired or dependent in any way, the first step is to determine if the variances are equal to identify which t-test to use. Since we've already done this, we know that the variances are considered equal for this data.

Run t-Test Assuming Equal Variances

Now select the data with the mouse and click on the QI Macros Menu to select the two-sample t-test (or Excel's Data Analysis Toolpak: t-test two samples assuming equal variances). The QI Macros will prompt for a significance level (default = 0.05) and hypothesized difference in the means (default = 0). The t-test two sample assuming equal variances will calculate the results (Fig. 13-8).

Interpreting the t-Test Two-Sample Results

Since the null hypothesis is that the mean difference $(x_1 - x_2) = 0$, this is a two-sided test. Therefore, use the two-tail values for your analysis.

Since the t statistic $< t$ critical (0.23727$<$ 2.30601) and the p value $> \alpha$ (0.81841 > 0.05), we can accept the null hypothesis that the means are the same.

	A	B	C	D	E
1	Recipe1	Recipe2	t-Test: Two-Sample Assuming Equal Variances		
2	3067	3200			
3	2730	2777		Recipe2	Recipe1
4	2840	2623	Mean	2895.6	2867.8
5	2913	3044	Variance	51713.3	16923.7
6	2789	2834	Observations	5	5
7			Pooled Variance	34318.5	
8			Hypothesized Mean Difference	0	
9			df	8	
10			t Stat	0.237274	
11			P(T<=t) one-tail	0.409204	
12			t Critical one-tail	1.859548	
13			P(T<=t) two-tail	0.818407	
14			t Critical two-tail	2.306006	

FIGURE 13-8 · *t*-Test two factor assuming equal variances.

Therefore, we can say that the two recipes produce rubber with the same mean tensile strength at a 95% confidence level.

t-Test—Two Sample Assuming *Unequal* Variances

If you want to compare two types of structural steel, you might want to know if the strengths (in 1,000 lb/sq in.) are the same or different.

- The null hypothesis H_0 is that the mean difference $(x_1 - x_2) = 0$, or in other words, the means are the same.

- The alternative hypotheis H_a is that the mean difference $<$ or > 0, or in other words, the means are not the same.

Conduct an F-Test to Determine If the Variances Are Equal

Since the two recipes aren't paired in any way, the first step is to determine if the variances are equal to identify which *t*-test to use. So, select the data (columns A:B, Fig. 13-9) and use the QI Macros or Data Analysis Toolpak to select the *F*-test.

Since $F > F$ crit (3.64394 > 3.1789) and p value $< \alpha$ (0.03376 < 0.05), we can reject the null hypothesis that the variances are equal. Now we can run the *t*-test assuming *unequal* variances.

t-Test Assuming Unequal Variances

Now use the data and the QI Macros or Analysis Toolpak to select the two-sample *t*-test assuming unequal variances. Enter a significance level

	A	B	C	D	E
1	Machine 1	Machine 2	t-Test: Two-Sample Assuming Unequal Variances		
2	25	13			
3	29	25		Machine 1	Machine 2
4	21	16	Mean	23	20.5
5	20	23	Variance	7.333333	26.72222
6	22	21	Observations	10	10
7	20	27	Hypothesized Mean Difference	0	
8	24	16	df	14	
9	24	22	t Stat	1.354709	
10	23	15	P(T<=t) one-tail	0.098485	
11	22	27	t Critical one-tail	1.761309	
12			P(T<=t) two-tail	0.19697	
13			t Critical two-tail	2.144789	

FIGURE 13-9 • *t*-Test two factor assuming unequal variances.

(default = 0.05). The *t*-test two sample for unequal variances will calculate the results (Fig. 13-9).

Interpreting the t-Test Assuming Unequal Variances Results

Since the null hypothesis is that the mean difference $(x_1 - x_2) = 0$, this is a two-sided test. Therefore, use the two-tail values for your analysis.

Since the *t* statistic < *t* critical (1.354709 < 2.144789) and the *p* value > α (0.19697 > 0.05), we can accept the null hypothesis that the means are the same.

The two recipes produce steel with the same mean tensile strength at a 95% confidence level.

t-Test—Paired Two Sample for Means

A paired *t*-test using two *paired* samples compares two *dependent* sets of test data. It helps determine if the means (i.e., averages) are different from each other. An example might include test results before and after training (these are paired because the same student produces two results).

The same would be true of weight loss. If a diet claims to cause more than a 10-lb weight loss over a 6-month period, you could design a test using several individuals' before and after weights. The samples are paired by each individual. You might want to know if the diet truly delivers greater than a 10-lb weight loss. The null hypothesis is less than or equal to 10. The alternative hypothesis is greater than 10.

- H_0: ≤ 10 lb
- H_a: > 10 lb

Since the null hypothesis stated as "less than or equal to," this is a one-sided test. Now conduct a test with several individuals and enter the data into Excel (columns A:B, Fig. 13-10). Then use the QI Macros or Data Analysis Toolpak to select the paired two-sample t-test. At a significance level of 0.05 and hypothesized mean difference of 10 lb, the paired t-test two sample will calculate the results.

	A	B	C	D	E
1	Before Diet	After Diet	t-Test: Paired Two Sample for Means		
2	213.4	200.1			
3	225.0	216.4		Before Diet	After Diet
4	217.0	195.6	Mean	211.65	201.125
5	183.7	175.0	Variance	144.0107	175.1713
6	197.2	201.3	Observations	16	16
7	223.6	214.8	Pearson Correlation	0.583732	
8	224.2	215.7	Hypothesized Mean Difference	10	
9	215.2	200.7	df	15	
10	202.4	211.7	t Stat	0.181578	
11	217.7	216.1	P(T<=t) one-tail	0.429172	
12	221.0	208.5	t Critical one-tail	1.753051	
13	219.9	188.4	P(T<=t) two-tail	0.858345	
14	205.4	206.4	t Critical two-tail	2.131451	
15	195.1	180.9			
16	218.0	184.1			
17	207.6	202.3			

FIGURE 13-10 · t-Test paired two sample.

Interpreting the Paired t-Test Results

Since the null hypothesis is that weight loss is less than or equal to 10 lb, this is a one-sided test. Therefore, use the one-tail values for your analysis. (*Note:* The two-sided values would apply if our null hypothesis were that H_0: mean difference = 10 lb.)

Since the t statistic $< t$ critical ($0.181578 < 1.753051$) and the p value $> \alpha$ ($0.429172 > 0.05$), we can accept the null hypothesis that the weight loss is less than or equal to 10 lb.

Example of t-Test One Sample

We could have cast this as a t-test one sample. If we calculate the difference between the before and after weights, we could test whether the difference is greater than 10 lb (Fig. 13-11).

Again, since the p value of 0.429172 is greater than 0.05, we accept the null hypothesis that weight loss is less than or equal to 10 lb.

	A	B	C
1	Difference	t-Test 1-sample	
2	13.3	Test Mean	10
3	8.6	Confidence Level	0.95
4	21.4	N	16
5	8.7	Average	10.5
6	-4.1	Stdev	11.56526
7	8.8	SE Mean	2.891316
8	8.5	T	0.181578
9	14.5	TINV	1.753051
10	-9.3	p - One sided	0.429172
11	1.6	p - two sided	0.858345
12	12.5		
13	31.5		
14	-1.0		
15	14.2		
16	33.9		
17	5.3		

FIGURE 13-11 • t-Test one sided for diet.

Tukey Quick Test for Means in Non-Normal Data

A *Tukey Quick Test* is like a *t*-test, but it can handle *nonparametric* (i.e., non-normal) data. It helps determine if the means are the same or different from each other. The null hypothesis H_0 is that the means are the same.

Tukey's Quick Test can be used when

- There are two *unpaired* samples of similar size that overlap each other. The ratio of sizes should not exceed 4:3.

- One sample contains the highest value and the other sample contains the lowest value. One sample cannot contain both the highest and the lowest value, nor can both samples have the same high or low value.

By adding the counts of the number of unmatched points on either end, one can determine the 5%, 1%, and 0.1% critical values as roughly 7, 10, and 13 points. Consider the following example:

Tukey Quick Test Example

Using data from Tukey's original paper and the Tukey Quick Test in the QI Macros Nonparametric tools (Fig. 13.12), it's easy to conduct the test.

If the data violate any of the rules, the template will not calculate the Tukey Quick Test.

	A	B	C	D	E
1	Sample 1	Sample 2	Sorted Combined Samples	Tukey Quick Test	
2	15	16.3	15	Total End Count	Confidence %
3	16.5	18.8	15	2	50%
4	17.3	15.8	15	3	63%
5	15.3	17.1	15.1	4	75%
6	15	17.9	15.3	5	84%
7	15.1	17.4	15.8	6	91%
8	15	16.7	16.3	7	95%
9	17.6	17.3	16.5	8	97%
10	17.4	17.5	16.7	9	98%
11	16.7	18.7	16.7	10	99%
12		19.5	17.1	End Count Table	
13			17.3	Top End Count	5.0
14			17.3	Bottom End Count	4.0
15			17.4	Total End Count	9.0
16			17.4	Signficant? (Y/N)	Yes
17			17.5	Confidence? (%)	98%
18			17.6	p	0.018

FIGURE 13-12 • Tukey Quick Test.

Interpreting the Tukey Quick Test Results

If	Then
Total end count ≥ 7	Reject the null hypothesis at 5% confidence level.
Total end count ≥ 10	Reject the null hypothesis at 1% confidence level.
Total end count ≥ 13	Reject the null hypothesis at 0.1% confidence level.
Total end count < 7	Accept the null hypothesis.

The null hypothesis H_0 is that the means are the same. In this example, since the end count = 9, we reject the null hypothesis at a 2% confidence level.

Still Struggling

t-Tests help verify that two samples have the same or a different mean (i.e., average). The resulting p value will tell you if they are the same ($p > \alpha$) or different ($p < \alpha$).

Analysis of Variance

t-Tests can handle only two samples, but analysis of variance (ANOVA) can help you determine if two *or more* samples have the same mean or average. The null hypothesis (H_0) is that $Mean_1 = Mean_2 = Mean_3$. The goal is to disprove this (i.e., show the samples have different means) at a certain confidence level (95% or 99%). Excel and the QI Macros can perform single- and two-factor analysis.

Single-Factor Analysis

From Fig. 13-13 (Montgomery 2005), we want to compare how four different concentrations of hardwood affect paper tensile strength.

FIGURE 13-13 • ANOVA Single Factor hardwood concentrations.

	A	B	C	D	E	F	G
1	Anova: Single Factor						
2							
3	SUMMARY						
4	Groups	Count	Sum	Average	Variance		
5	5%	6	60	10	8		
6	10%	6	94	15.66667	7.866667		
7	15%	6	102	17	3.2		
8	20%	6	127	21.16667	6.966667		
9							
10							
11	ANOVA						
12	Source of Variation	SS	df	MS	F	P-value	F crit
13	Between Groups	382.7917	3	127.5972	19.60521	3.59E-06	3.098393
14	Within Groups	130.1667	20	6.508333			
15							
16	Total	512.9583	23				

1204 Medical Trial Data \ **1202 Anova Results** / Anova 1 / Anova2 / Chi-Squared Tables / Chi-Squared data / F-test /

FIGURE 13-14 · ANOVA Single Factor results.

Using Excel and the QI Macros, select data in columns B2:E8 and click on QI Macros—ANOVA and Analysis Tools—ANOVA Single Factor to run a single-factor ANOVA at the 99% or $\alpha = 0.01$ confidence level (Fig. 13-14).

Since the p value is less than α, the null hypothesis is *not* true (i.e., the means *are* different). You can guess this from looking at the data (averages = 10, 15.7, 17, 21.17), but you wouldn't know *how* confident to be that they are different. In most cases the averages might be much closer to each other, making it difficult to evaluate the sameness or difference.

Just for fun, you might want to run a box and whisker chart on the data to see the variation (Fig. 13-15).

Two-Factor Analysis

To analyze a single column of data with multiple-factor data, Excel requires you to set the data up in a way that can be analyzed. Figure 13-16 shows how to set up the data for two categories of patients treated with three different drugs.

Then, if you're just interested in the single factor *drugs*, select and run a single factor on the three drug columns (Fig. 13-17).

What if you have two populations of patients (male and female) and three different kinds of medications and you want to evaluate the effectiveness of the drugs *and* the type of patient? You might run a study with

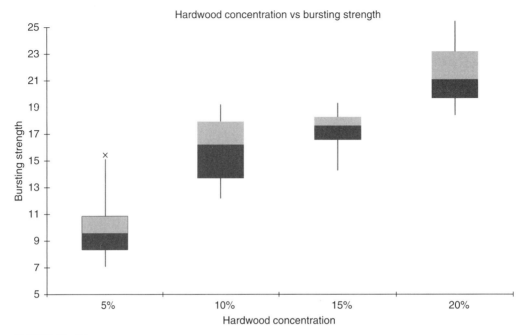

Hardwood concentration vs bursting strength

FIGURE 13-15 • Box and whisker.

Patient	Drug	Diffrate
Male	Drug 1	8
Male	Drug 1	4
Male	Drug 1	0
Male	Drug 2	10
Male	Drug 2	8
Male	Drug 2	6
Male	Drug 3	8
Male	Drug 3	6
Male	Drug 3	4
Female	Drug 1	14
Female	Drug 1	10
Female	Drug 1	6
Female	Drug 2	4
Female	Drug 2	2
Female	Drug 2	0
Female	Drug 3	15
Female	Drug 3	12
Female	Drug 3	9

Patients	Drug 1	Drug 2	Drug 3
Male	8	10	8
	4	8	6
	0	6	4
Female	14	4	15
	10	2	12
	6	0	9

Use CTRL-SHIFT-G on this data using 6 as size
Then COPY and Paste Special-Transpose

FIGURE 13-16 • Drug response data.

ANOVA: Single Factor

SUMMARY

Groups	Count	Sum	Average	Variance
Drug 1	6	42	7	23.6
Drug 2	6	30	5	14
Drug 3	6	54	9	16

ANOVA

Source of Variation	SS	df	MS	F	p-value	F crit
Between Groups	48	2	24	1.343284	0.290642	3.682317
Within Groups	268	15	17.86667			
Total	316	17				

FIGURE 13-17 · ANOVA Single Factor for drug response.

two or more *replications* (more than one patient in the category receives the same drug).

Then, using Excel and the QI Macros, run a two-factor analysis (Fig. 13-18) with replication ($\alpha = 0.05$ for a 95% confidence level).

Here, the p value for male and female is greater than α, so the means are the same. The p value for drugs is greater, so the null hypothesis holds as well (means are the same). The p value for the interaction of the drugs and patients is less than 0.05, so the effectiveness of three drugs is not the same for the two categories of patient.

Is Your Data Normal?

Statistical analysis may rely on your data being *normal* (i.e., bell-shaped), so how can you tell if they are normal? The two tests most commonly used are

- Normal probability plot
- p value, or critical value, method

Normal Probability Plot Method

If you've used any of the QI Macros X Chart templates, you know that the normal probability plot is part of the XmR, XbarR, and XbarS templates (Fig. 13-19).

ANOVA: Two-Factor With Replication

SUMMARY	Drug 1	Drug 2	Drug 3	Total
Male				
Count	3	3	3	9
Sum	12	24	18	54
Average	4	8	6	6
Variance	16	4	4	9
Female				
Count	3	3	3	9
Sum	30	6	36	72
Average	10	2	12	8
Variance	16	4	9	28.25
Total				
Count	6	6	6	
Sum	42	30	54	
Average	7	5	9	
Variance	23.6	14	16	

ANOVA

Source of Variation	SS	df	MS	F	p-value	F crit
Sample	18	1	18	2.037736	0.17894	4.747221
Columns	48	2	24	2.716981	0.106343	3.88529
Interaction	144	2	72	8.150943	0.00581	3.88529
Within	106	12	8.833333			
Total	316	17				

FIGURE 13-18 · ANOVA Two-Factor results for drug response.

FIGURE 13-19 · Normal probability plot.

Just by looking at the histogram (bell-shaped) and probability plot, you can see that these data are fairly normal.

The probability plot transforms the data into a normal distribution and plots it as a scatter diagram.

- Normal data will follow the trend line.

- Non-normal data will have more points farther from the trend line.

p Value and Critical Value Method

The Descriptive Statistics or Normality Test in the QI Macros ANOVA Tools uses the Anderson-Darling method to analyze normality more rigorously. The output includes the Anderson-Darling statistic, *A-squared*, and both a *p* value and critical values for *A*-squared. Using cells A1:A26 from the XbarR.xls in c:\qimacros\testdata, you would get Fig. 13-20.

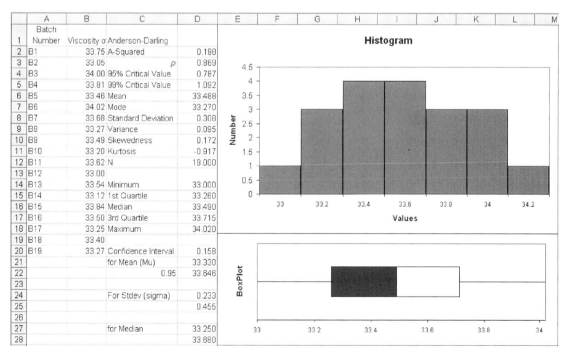

FIGURE 13-20 · *p* value method for normality testing.

The Anderson-Darling values shown are

- A-squared = 0198
- p value = 0.869
- 95% critical value = 0.787
- 99% critical value = 1.092

In this case, the null hypothesis is that the data are normal. The alternative hypothesis is that the data are non-normal.

Reject the null hypothesis (i.e., accept the alternative hypothesis) when $p \leq \alpha$ or A-squared > critical value.

Using the p value = 0.869 which is greater than α (level of significance) of 0.01, we can accept the null hypothesis (i.e., the data are normal).

Using the critical values, you would only reject this null hypothesis (i.e., data are non-normal) if A-squared were greater than either of the two critical values. Since $0.198 < 0.787$ and $0.198 < 1.092$, you can be at least 99% confident that the data are normal.

Another Example

Using cells D1:D41 (after deleting the blank row) from the XbarR.xls in c:\qimacros\testdata, you would get the result in Fig. 13-21. Notice how the normality plot curves at the right so that some of the points are farther from the line. Using Anderson-Darling, we discover that the data are considered normal at one level (99%), but not at another (95%).

Using the p value = 0.028 which is greater than α of 0.01 ($0.01 < 0.028 < 0.05$), we can reject the null hypothesis (i.e., the data are normal) at $\alpha = 0.05$, but not at $\alpha = 0.01$.

Using the critical values, since $0.787 < 0.833 < 1.092$, we can reject the null hypothesis at 95% but not reject it at 99%.

Frankly, the double negatives of not rejecting the null hypothesis make my brain tired. All I really want to know is: Is my data normal? So, in summary,

- If the dots fit the trend line on the normal probability plot, then the data are normal.
- If $p > \alpha$, then the data are normal.
- If A-squared < the critical value, then the data are normal.

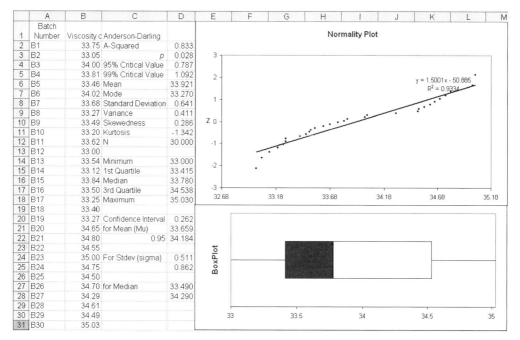

FIGURE 13-21 • Probability plot.

Still Struggling

Normal (bell-shaped) data is more easily analyzed with t-tests and f-tests. Non-normal data like wait times in a bank (skewed left toward zero minutes of wait time) require other types of hypothesis testing like Levene's test. Knowing what kind of data you're using will ensure that you get the best results when analyzing the data.

Tests of Proportion

If a manufacturer claims that their products are less than 3% defective, you can take a sample of products and determine whether the actual percent defective is consistent with his claim. Proportion testing isn't a part of Excel's Analysis Toolpak, but you can use the QI Macros Proportion template.

One-Proportion Test

1. If data aren't summarized, use PivotTables to summarize the trials and successes.

2. Click on the QI Macros pull-down menu and select ANOVA and Analysis Tools, then Proportion tests (Fig. 13-22).

3. Enter test proportion in A3 (e.g., 3% is 0.03).

4. Enter number of trials in B3 (100 products).

5. Enter number of successes in C3 (e.g., defects in 100 products).

6. Enter confidence level in E1 (0.95 = 95%).

7. The null hypothesis is $H_1 = H_0$ (sample proportion = proportion). p values are calculated via direct and normal approximation methods for $H_1 = H_0$, $H_1 > H_0$, and $H_1 < H_0$.

   - If cell H3:H5 (or J3:J5) is green, you can accept the null hypothesis.
   - If cell H3:H5 is red, reject the null hypothesis.

In this example with five defects in 100 samples, you can reject the null hypothesis that $H_1 = H_0$.

	A	B	C	D	E	F	G	H	I	J
1					0.95	Confidence Level				
2	Proportion	Trials	Successes	Sample p	95% Confidence Intervals		p (Direct)		p (Normal)	
3	0.3	100	5	0.050000	0.016432	0.112835	0.000	H1=H0	0.000	H1=H0
4					0.007284	0.092716	1.000	H1>H0	1.000	H1>H0
5							0.000	H1<H0	0.000	H1<H0

FIGURE 13-22 · Proportion tests.

Two-Proportion Testing

If you are sending a direct-mail piece to a group of prospects, you may want to know if the proportion of customers who respond could be increased by offering free shipping. You would offer free shipping on half of your mailings and see if you have more purchases from the group that was offered free shipping than from the group that was not.

Here is how to perform a test of two proportions using the QI Macros Proportion template.

1. If the data aren't summarized, use Pivot Tables to summarize the trials and successes.

	A	B	C	D	E	F	G	H	I
1	First Proportion				Difference		0.95	Confidence Level	
2	Trials	Successes	First p (P1)		0	95% Confidence Intervals		p	
3	50	10	0.2		Est. Diff	-0.086775	0.206775	0.423	P1-P2=0
4					0.06			0.212	P1-P2<0
5	Second Proportion				Z			0.788	P1-P2>0
6	Trials	Successes	Second p (P2)		0.80				
7	50	7	0.14						

FIGURE 13-23 · Two sample proportion test.

2. Click on the QI Macros pull-down menu and select ANOVA and Analysis Tools, then Proportion Tests. A template will open. Click on the tab labeled Two Proportions (Fig. 13-23).

3. Enter Test Difference in E2. The default is 0.

4. Enter number of trials in A3 and A7.

5. Enter number of successes in B3 and B7.

6. Enter confidence level in F1.

7. The null hypothesis is $H_0: P_1 = P_2$; the alternative hypothesis is $H_1: P_1 <$ or $> P_2$. If cell I3:I5 is green, you can accept the null hypothesis. If cell I3:I5 is red, reject the null hypothesis.

Still Struggling

While f-tests, t-tests, and ANOVA are good for measured (i.e., variable) data, proportion tests are good for counted (i.e., attribute) data. Additional attribute methods are chi-square and Fisher's exact test.

Chi-Square Tests in Excel

There are different types of chi-square tests.

- Chi-square Goodness-of-Fit test
- Chi-square test of a contingency table
- Fisher's exact test for 2X2 Tables

Chi-Square Goodness-of-Fit Test

A chi-square Goodness-of-Fit test evaluates the probabilities of multiple outcomes.

Las Vegas Dice Example

Let's say you want to know if a six-sided die is fair or unfair. So you develop a null hypothesis (H_0) that the die is fair (each side will have an equal probability of coming up) and the alternative hypothesis (H_a) that one or more of the sides will come up more often.

- H_0: $p1 = p2 = p3 = p4 = p5 = p6 = 1/6$
- H_a: At least one p is not equal to 1/6.

Now test 120 rolls of the die and enter the data into Excel (Fig. 13-24 cells A23:C29).

Then, in an empty cell, begin typing the formula " = chitest." Excel will prompt for the observed and expected ranges. Use your mouse to select the Observed (B24:B29) and Expected range (C24:C29). Put a comma between the two and a parenthesis at the end and hit return.

The chi-square test will calculate the probability (i.e., p value) of all sides being equal.

Interpreting the Chi-Square Goodness-of-Fit Results

In these results, the p value = 4.55759E – 05 (0.0000456) is dramatically lower than our α value of 0.05, so we can reject the null hypothesis that the die is fair.

D24	▾	*fx* =CHITEST(B24:B29,C24:C29)		
	A	**B**	**C**	**D**
23	Las Vegas Dice	Observed	Expected	
24	1	10	20	4.55759E-05
25	2	25	20	
26	3	30	20	
27	4	20	20	
28	5	30	20	
29	6	5	20	

FIGURE 13-24 · Las Vegas dice.

Chi-Square Test of a Contingency Table

A chi-square test can evaluate if two variables are independent of each other. We've all taken surveys and probably wondered what happened. A chi-square test of a contingency table helps identify if there are differences between two or more demographics. Consider the following example:

Men versus Women—Chi-Square Test Example

Imagine asking men and women if they agree, disagree, or are neutral about a given topic. How will we know if they have the same or differing opinions? We can develop a null hypothesis (H_0) that men and women share the same views and an alternative hypothesis (H_a) that they are different.

- H_0 men < or > women
- H_a men = women

Now conduct the survey and enter the number of responses into Excel (Fig. 13.25, cells A1:C4). As you can see, men seem to agree more than the women do, but is it statistically different?

	A	B	C	D	E	F
1		Men	Women	Total	Chi-Sq	16.16403
2	Agree	58	35	93	p	0.000309
3	Neutral	11	25	36		
4	Disagree	10	23	33		
5	Total	79	83	162		

FIGURE 13-25 • Men versus women.

Select the data and use the QI Macros to select the chi-square test (this is not part of Excel's Analysis Toolpak). The chi-square test macro will calculate the results.

Note that we don't need the same number of responses from each group to get a result.

Interpreting the Chi-Square Results

In the above results the p value is 0.00031.

If the p value (0.000309) is less than the significance (e.g., $\alpha < 0.05$), we can reject the null hypothesis that men and women have the same views on the subject.

Fisher's Exact Test of a 2 × 2 Table

A Fisher's exact test evaluates small, 2 × 2 tables better than because it calculates the *exact* probability. A Fisher's exact test of a 2 × 2 table helps identify if there are differences between two or more demographics. Consider the following example:

Men versus Women Dieting—Fisher's Exact Test Example

Imagine asking men and women if they are dieting. How will we know if one sex diets more than the other? We can develop a null hypothesis (H_0) that men and women diet equally and an alternative hypothesis (H_a) that they are different.

- H_0: men = women
- H_a: men < or > women

Now conduct the survey and enter the number of responses into Excel (Fig. 13-25, cells A1:C3). As you can see, men seem to diet less than the women do, but is it statistically significant?

Use the QI Macros Menu to select the Fisher's exact test (not in Excel's Data Analysis Toolpak). The Fisher's exact test macro will calculate the exact test statistic and the chi-square statistic (Fig. 13-26).

	A	B	C	D	E	F
1		Men	Women	Total	**Fishers**	
2	Dieting	1	9	10	*p 2-Tail*	0.00275946
3	Not Dieting	11	3	14	Chi-Sq	10.9710254
4	Total	12	12	24	*p*	0.00092527

FIGURE 13-26 · Fisher's exact test.

Interpreting the Fisher's Exact Test Results

In the results above, the Fisher's exact test p value is 0.00276. We can reject the null hypothesis at the 0.05 and 0.01 levels, but not the 0.001 level of α.

Notice that the Fisher's exact test p value is higher than the chi-square p value of 0.00093. Chi-square would let us reject the null hypothesis at the 0.001 level.

Determining Sample Sizes

In manufacturing applications, you often need to Figure out how many samples to take to ensure that you get a valid sample size of a larger lot. From the QI Macros pull-down menu, select ANOVA and Analysis Tools.

Click on Sample Size to get Fig. 13-27.

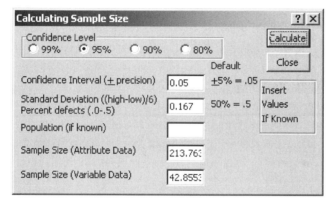

FIGURE 13-27 · Sample size calculator.

Input the confidence interval and level and any other information you have to calculate the sample size required to meet your confidence needs.

To calculate a *sample size*, you need to know

1. The confidence level required (90%, 95%, 99%)

2. The desired width of the confidence interval ($\pm$5%)

3. The variability of the characteristic (e.g., mean)

The QI Macros *Sample Size Calculator* is designed to work with both variable (measured) and attribute (counted) data.

The defaults are set to standard parameters.

- 95% confidence level

- $\pm$5% (0.05) confidence interval

- Variable data with standard deviation of 0.167. (Change this value to 0.5 for attribute data.)

Confidence Level

In sampling, you want to know how well a sample reflects the total population. The 95% confidence level means you can be 95% certain that the sample reflects the population *within* the confidence interval.

Step 1: Select a confidence level (typically 95%).

Confidence Interval

The confidence interval represents the range of values which includes the true value of the population parameter being measured.

Step 2: Set the confidence interval (typically $\pm$ 5% or 0.05).

Attribute (Counted) Sampling

If 95 out of 100 are good and only 5 are bad, then you wouldn't need a very large sample to estimate the population. If 50 are bad and 50 are good, you'd need a much larger sample to achieve the desired confidence level. Since you don't know beforehand how many are good or bad, you have to set the attribute field to 50%, or 0.5.

Step 3: Attribute data—Set percent defects to 0.5.

Variable (Measured) Data

If you know the standard deviation of your data (from past studies), then you can use the standard deviation.

If you know the specification tolerance, then you can use (maximum value – minimum value)/6 as your standard deviation. (The default is $1/6 = 0.167$.)

Step 4: Variable Data—Enter the standard deviation.

Use the Percent Defects/Standard Deviation field for either attribute or variable samples.

Step 5: Enter the total population (if known).

Step 6: Press Calculate to read the sample size.

Use the sample size calculated for your type of data: attribute or variable. In this case, we're using variable data so the sample size would be 43.

Regression Analysis

If you think two different measurements are interrelated (i.e., there's a cause and effect, you can use regression analysis to confirm or deny that they are related. Use the scatter diagram or regression analysis tool under the QI Macros ANOVA menu to validate your suspicions.

To Run Regression Analysis Using Excel or the QI Macros

1. Select the labels and data.

2. In Excel, select Tools-Data Analysis-Regression or in QI Macros select ANOVA and Analysis Tools and then Regression Analysis.

3. Input the confidence level (e.g., 0.95).

4. Evaluate the R-squared (> 0.80 is a good fit).

5. Evaluate the F and p values.

6. Get the equation for the fitted data.

7. Use the equation to predict other values.

Salt versus Paved Roadway Example

Imagine, for example, that we want to know for a system of roads if the salt concentration in runoff is related to the percent of paved roadway area (Fig. 13-28). We could use Excel or the QI Macros to run a regression analysis at confidence level of 0.95 (Fig. 13-29).

Analysis: If R-square (0.951) is greater than 0.80, as it is in this case, there is a good fit to the data. Some statistics references recommend using the adjusted R-square value.

	E	F
	% Paved Roadway Area	Salt concentration (mg/l)
1		
2	0.19	3.8
3	0.15	5.9
4	0.57	14.1
5	0.40	10.4
6	0.70	14.6

FIGURE 13-28 · Salt versus paved roadway data.

FIGURE 13-29 · Salt versus paved roadway regression analysis.

Interpretation: R-square of 0.951 means that 95.1% of the variation in salt concentration can be explained by roadway area. The adjusted R-square of 0.949 means 94.9%.

Now, evaluate the p value. In this case, the p value for % paved roadway is $2.86E - 13 < 0.05$, so we can reject the null hypothesis that salt and paved roadway are unrelated.

To get the equation for the relationshiop, click on the line fit plot and right click on one of the % paved roadway points. Select Add Trendline. Then choose linear trendline and click on Options to show the equation ($y = 17.547x + 2.6765$).

Using the equation salt concentration = 17.547(% roadway area) + 2.6765, you could predict the salt concentration if the percent of roadway was 1% as

$$\text{Salt concentration} = 17.547(1) + 2.6765 = 20.2235 \text{ mg/l.}$$

Still Struggling

Regression analysis, like a two-sample paired t-test, helps determine if one thing causes another. While regression cannot prove that the amount of paved roadway causes salt concentration, it can point your analysis in the right direction. In hospitals, for example, nurses want to prove that having more nursing staff results in better patient outcomes. Having looked at a lot of this type of data, there is no correlation, no cause-effect. Instead, the problem may be one of nursing unit design that causes unnecessary movement or one of monitoring key vital signs in patients.

Multiple Regression Analysis

The purpose of multiple regression analysis is to evaluate the effects of two or more independent variables on a single dependent variable.

Select 2 to 16 columns with the dependent variable in the first (or last) column. Imagine, for example, we want to know if customer perception of quality varies with various aspects of geography and shampoo characteristics: Foam, Scent, Color, or Residue. Use Excel's Data Analysis Toolpak or QI Macros to do multiple regression analysis on this data at the 95% level (Fig. 13-30, matrix-plot.xls).

	A	B	C	D	E	F	G	H	I	J	K
1	Region	Foam	Scent	Color	Residue	Quality	SUMMARY OUTPUT				
2	1	6.3	5.3	4.8	3.1	91					
3	1	4.4	4.9	3.5	3.9	87	*Regression Statistics*				
4	1	3.9	5.3	4.8	4.7	82	Multiple R	0.8944731			
5	1	5.1	4.2	3.1	3.6	83	R Square	0.800082			
6	1	5.6	5.1	5.5	5.1	83	Adjusted R Square	0.7445493			
7	1	4.6	4.7	5.1	4.1	84	Standard Error	2.2055997			
8	1	4.8	4.8	4.8	3.3	90	Observations	24			
9	1	6.5	4.5	4.3	5.2	84					
10	1	8.7	4.3	3.9	2.9	97	ANOVA				
11	1	8.3	3.9	4.7	3.9	93		*df*	*SS*	*MS*	*F*
12	1	5.1	4.3	4.5	3.6	82	Regression	5	350.4359369	70.087	14.4074
13	1	3.3	5.4	4.3	3.6	84	Residual	18	87.56406307	4.8647	
14	2	5.9	5.7	7.2	4.1	87	Total	23	438		
15	2	7.7	6.6	6.7	5.6	80					
16	2	7.1	4.4	5.8	4.1	84		*Coefficients*	*Standard Error*	*t Stat*	*P-value*
17	2	5.5	5.6	5.6	4.4	84	Intercept	90.192183	4.046988933	22.286	1.5E-14
18	2	6.3	5.4	4.8	4.6	82	Region	-3.8591171	1.042809786	-3.7007	0.00164
19	2	4.3	5.5	5.5	4.1	79	Foam	1.8168936	0.35820658	5.0722	7.9E-05
20	2	4.6	4.1	4.3	3.1	81	Scent	1.0346846	0.922490779	1.1216	0.27676
21	2	3.4	5	3.4	3.4	83	Color	0.2326722	0.708123097	0.3286	0.74627
22	2	6.4	5.4	6.6	4.8	81	Residue	-4.0014884	0.811858697	-4.9288	0.00011

FIGURE 13-30 · Multiple regression.

Evaluate the *R*-Square Value (0.800) and the *F* and *p* Values

Analysis: If *R*-square is greater than 0.80, as it is in this case, there is a good fit to the data. Then check *p* values.

The null hypothesis is that there is no correlation. (H_0 = no correlation.) Looking at the *p* values for each independent variable, Region, Foam, and Residue are less than α (0.05), so we reject the null hypothesis and can say that these variables impact quality. Scent and color *p* values are greater than 0.05, so we accept the null hypothesis that there is no correlation.

Conclusion

While these tools are extremely useful for deeper analysis of your data, most Lean Six Sigma practitioners aren't ready to dive into them until they have a firm grasp of the basic measurement and improvement processes. If you want to learn more about these tools, consider *Advanced Statistics Demystified* (Stephens 2004).

QUIZ

1. **Hypothesis testing confirms that**
   A. two batches are same.
   B. two batches are different.
   C. batches are the same or different at a certain level of confidence.

2. **Hypothesis tests can confirm that the**
   A. averages are the same or different.
   B. variation is the same or different.
   C. averages and/or the variation is the same or different.

3. **Excel can assist in hypothesis testing by doing**
   A. ANOVA.
   B. correlation.
   C. descriptive statistics.
   D. F-test.
   E. t-test.
   F. z-test.
   G. regression analysis.
   H. all of the above

4. **What is a null hypothesis?**

5. **Accept the null hypothesis when**
   A. $p > \alpha$.
   B. $p < \alpha$.

6. **Reject the null hypothesis when**
   A. $p > \alpha$.
   B. $p < \alpha$.

EXERCISES

1. Use the test data in c:\qimacros\testdata\anova.xls to practice using these tools.

chapter **14**

Implementing Lean Six Sigma

The essential methods and tools of Lean Six Sigma described in this book are easy to learn and use, but implementing Lean Six Sigma can be difficult. Over half of all implementations fail within 3 years. That's a one sigma failure rate. If all you needed to do is teach everyone the methods and tools, implementation would be easy. Getting people to adopt the methods and tools is often the hardest part. There are ways, however, to ensure that the methods and tools take root and grow. Unfortunately, implementing Lean Six Sigma successfully requires an approach that runs counter to all of the so-called advice available in the literature.

CHAPTER OBJECTIVES

In this chapter, you will

- Learn why people say: It won't work for me
- Learn how to use decisive force in Lean Six Sigma
- Discover the Lean Six Sigma mindset
- Use deliberate practice to learn Lean Six Sigma
- Learn how reward systems affect Lean Six Sigma
- Learn why Lean Six Sigma teams fail

You've probably heard the acronym *WIIFM*—What's in it for me? It's the question everyone asks him- or her-self when faced with any decision. Marketers constantly focus on defining the benefits of their product or service to answer that question.

I recently discovered there's a much more insidious attitude I've labeled *IWWFM*—It won't work for me. Ask any teenager to try something new, and the answer will invariably be "It won't work for me." But it's not just teens; it's people in business, *any kind of business*. Ask people to learn Lean Six Sigma (or anything else for that matter), and the answer is often "It won't work for me."

Excuses, Excuses, Excuses

Sadly, the easiest way to avoid any kind of change is to simply proclaim "It won't work for me," thereby avoiding having to learn or grow. To save time, maybe we should just shorten this phrase to "IWWFM," or phonetically, "I dub-dub FM," so that it will sound as silly as it is.

The mere pronouncement of IWWFM cranks up the excuse machine: It won't work for me *because* (insert lame reason here). One of the things we've learned from research into motivation is that the mere use of the word *because* makes us all think "Oh, he or she has got a reason it won't work." In Cialdini's book, *Influence*, he sights a study where people standing in line for a copier were asked if someone could cut in front of them. One group was asked something like "Can I cut in front of you?" and another group was asked "Can I cut in front of you *because* I need to get this copied?" The first group was usually refused; the second group usually was allowed to cut in.

IWWFM is invariably followed with the word *because* and some lame excuse: "Lean Six Sigma won't work for me *because* we don't manufacture anything." "Lean Six Sigma won't work for me *because* we use an agile software development methodology." It sounds so reasoned and well thought out, but it's pure poppycock.

The Blame Game

The great thing about using IWWFM is that once you've got people to buy the excuse, then you can ruthlessly blame others for your own failure to change: The competition is killing my profit margins. What do these crazy customers expect, perfection? My suppliers give me bad materials. My boss has unrealistic expectations of performance.

Nonsense! If you haven't tried it, you just don't know if it will work for you. Yes, you're probably overwhelmed; isn't everyone? But you have to make time to try new things.

Peak-Performing People

Peak performers never invoke IWWFM. I read stories in the newspapers about handicapped skiers and blind golfers. People who want to do something usually can find a way to do it. Instead of mindlessly chanting IWWFM, they ask

- How will this work for me?
- What's the easiest way to try it?
- Who can help me?
- If it didn't work in the past, how can I adjust it to get the result I want?

It's so easy to blame others for our lot in life, but true courage comes from deciding that the only person holding you back is you. And the only way to stop holding yourself back is to start learning, embrace new ideas and start making progress toward your outcomes.

If you find yourself, your family, or your coworkers muttering IWWFM, then start asking those motivating questions: How could we adapt it to make it work for us? Who could help us figure out how to make it work? What's the easiest way to apply it? Questions like these overcome the mental traps of IWWFM *because* . . . It's up to you; all you have to do is switch from IWWFM and to direction setting questions. Too easy!

Now I know exactly what some of you are thinking: *It won't work for me because* . . .

Still Struggling

People don't like having to change the way they've done things. It requires effort. It's easier to resist Lean Six Sigma than it is to learn it and start doing something new.

Decisive Force

While reading *Words That Work* by Dr. Frank Luntz, I was intrigued by his discussion of Colin Powell's doctrine of military success. Powell called the strategy of military success *decisive force* that "ends wars quickly and in the long run save lives." What Powell meant was force applied that was *precise, clean, and surgical*. The media misquoted him as saying *overwhelming force*. While *overwhelming force* sounds more exciting than *decisive force, overwhelming force* is about *people and process; decisive force* is about a **result**.

Decisive Force in Lean Six Sigma

What does Colin Powell's doctrine of military success have to do with Lean Six Sigma? Everything.

This weekend I played a round of golf with a guy from Honeywell who admitted that he'd been trained as a Green Belt a few years ago as part of Honeywell's *train everyone in Lean Six Sigma* program. He admitted that he still hadn't done a single improvement project. I'm stunned by the number of companies that track how many belts they've trained, as if that matters. It's like measuring the success of a war by keeping a body count.

Success with Lean Six Sigma is not how many troops you put in the field (i.e., Black Belts, Green Belts, etc.). It's about how many profit-enhancing, delay-reducing, defect-reducing, deviation-eliminating, customer-delighting improvements you put in place and keep in place.

Another downside of this universal training program is that it takes time away from customers.

Success with Lean Six Sigma is not about how many platoons are in the field (i.e., Lean Six Sigma projects). *It's about how many capture meaningful objectives.* Too many teams end up majoring in minor things. They move water coolers, not mountains. Too much of the emphasis of Lean Six Sigma involves brainstorming. Letting teams choose their own projects is like turning troops loose in a country and saying Capture whatever you want.

Let's revisit Powell's strategy: *precise, clean, and surgical.* Using data about operational problems, you should be able to narrow your focus down to precise, clean problems that can be dealt with surgically by a small team of experts.

Remember the 4-50 rule.

- 4% of the steps cause 50% of the defects and deviation.
- 4% of the gaps between steps cause 50% of the delay.

Remember the dark side of the 4-50 rule. Fifty percent of the effort will only achieve 4% of the benefit.

Overwhelming force (wall-to-wall, floor-to-ceiling Lean Six Sigma) makes it *seem* like we're doing everything possible to implement Lean Six Sigma. If it's not going well, then we get the urge to *put more troops in the field*. Training more people and starting more teams to brainstorm more problems is an invitation to disaster.

Decisive force focuses your Lean Six Sigma effort on mission-critical problems that can dramatically reduce delay, defects, and deviation while delighting customers and boosting profits.

It's up to you, but I'd like you to consider that Colin Powell's doctrine of *decisive force* will make a dramatic difference in the effectiveness of your Lean Six Sigma efforts. Isn't it time to start minoring in *major* things?

Crisis Junkies

In most companies, it is so much easier to fight fires and fix problems. It's so immediate and gives such a sense of accomplishment when you fix something that's a problem right now.

But it's an addiction not a benefit. As in most addictions, an addict will do anything to get his or her next fix. In companies this means resisting improvement methods like Lean Six Sigma that eliminate the need for fire fighting.

My wife works in software development. In a recent system release, her software worked flawlessly. Most other groups had to work around the clock for days to correct their software bugs and failures.

Guess which groups got rewards for going the extra mile? You guessed it: the groups with the buggy, software failures.

More often than not, reward systems fuel the failure-and-fix addiction cycle.

Rewarding crisis is a mistake. Majoring in minor things like daily problems is a mistake. But you can't just stop doing them. You will have to wean yourself off the addiction.

Minor in Major Things

As I continue to train people in the simple, essential methods of Lean Six Sigma, one thing is painfully clear: Most people are too busy fighting fires to spend much time on fire prevention. They are majoring in minor things, not minoring in major things.

Here's my New Year's challenge to you: Make time to minor in major things.

If you set aside 2 hours a week to work on prevention, mistake proofing, and improvement, you'll make dramatic progress. Put it on your schedule and refuse to leave the office until it's done.

As you reduce the daily fire fighting, you'll have more time to spend on improvement. And more benefits will accrue. Productivity and profits will climb out of their rut and head for new territory.

It's not particularly hard to start making improvements. You just need a little focus.

Week 1. Find or collect the data about a particularly nasty problem. Graph it over time as a control chart.

Week 2. Use Pareto charts to narrow the cause of the problem to specific processes, machines, materials, locations, or whatever.

Week 3. Gather the subject matter experts about the specific aspect of the problem and analyze the root causes of the problem. Verify them with facts and figures. Develop countermeasures to address the specific problem.

Week 4. Start implementing the countermeasures. Process changes take less time. Technology changes take longer.

Week 5. Start on the next problem while monitoring the existing one.

Tools

1. *Control chart* of defects (per million opportunities).
2. *Pareto charts* of main contributors to the problem. Usually two or more levels of Pareto will be necessary to find a specific problem to solve.
3. *Ishikawa diagram* of root causes.
4. *Countermeasures matrix* of potential solutions.
5. *Results graphs* (line, Pareto) of improvements.

Nothing will get better until we carve out time to find and prevent the root causes of mistakes, errors, defects, delay, and deviation. How we choose to spend our time will determine our progress at the end of the year.

Do you want the end of this year to feel the same way last year did? Or would you rather spend a little time on mission-critical improvement projects?

Are you going to major in minor things this year or minor in major ones? The choice is up to you.

Still Struggling

It doesn't take 14 weeks to do a Lean Six Sigma project. With the right data and the right people, teams can solve big problems quickly, usually in a matter of hours not days. Implementing the improvements may take some time, but the actual analysis happens quickly.

Getting the Right People Involved with Lean Six Sigma

Have you ever noticed that some people just seem to be mentally *wired* for improvement work whereas others just can't seem to get it? Is there a mindset that's fertile ground for Lean Six Sigma and others that are not? Is there a way to determine this in advance?

Based on my 17-year research into the science of mindsets and motivation, I believe the answer to these questions is yes. There is a mindset that is fully prepared to embrace the methods and tools of Lean Six Sigma, and there are ways to detect it.

The Improvement Mindset

In 1990 I started learning the science of Neuro-Linguistic Programming (NLP). I think of NLP as software for your mind. With NLP you can discover how people think and what makes them successful and also what makes them fail. One of the most interesting discoveries from NLP involves intrinsic motivation.

In my book *How to Motivate Everyone*, I explore the five core motivation traits and two or more conflicting points of view. A few of them are key to understanding the improvement mindset.

The Improver Mindset

Ask yourself this question: *What's the relationship between your job or work this year and last year?*

There are three answers to this question that reveal a lot about whether you have the right mindset for improvement.

1. It's pretty much the *same*.

2. It's *improved*, enhanced, expanded, and enriched.

3. What do you mean *relationship?* There is no relationship. Are you asking me what's *different* about my job?

People who answer "It's pretty much the same" want things to stay the same. *You can't stay the same and improve.* (These *Traditionalists* represent 5% of the population. They'd rather kill Lean Six Sigma than try it.)

People who answer "What do you mean relationship?" want everything to be *different*. You can't do things differently all of the time and improve. Given a foolproof method of making a million dollars, these people have to fiddle with the formula *before* they try it. (These *Revolutionaries* represent 30% of the population. They'd rather invent their own improvement method than try Lean Six Sigma.)

As in Goldilocks and the Three Bears, the middle answer is just right: *It's improved*. Improvement-oriented *Evolutionaries* represent 65% of the population, but they have to spend a lot of time wrestling the Traditionalists and the Revolutionaries.

If you're interviewing employees for black belt or green belt training, ask them *What's the relationship between your job or work this year and last year?* Then listen to their answer. If it isn't *better, improved, expanded, enhanced,* or *something similar*, it might be time to look for someone else.

Process-Oriented Mindset

Lean Six Sigma focuses on processes and systems, so to be good at Lean Six Sigma, you've got to like processes. Ask yourself *Why did I choose my current job or work?* There are two answers to this question.

1. People who answer with a *list* of criteria (e.g., a chance to learn, meet new people, make more money) have an *innovator* mindset.

2. People who feel confused and don't know how to respond feel that they didn't choose their job; their job chose them. They feel compelled to tell a *story* about how their job chose them. These people have a *process* mindset.

Innovators, like Revolutionaries, aren't interested in improving the existing process. They want to create a new one.

Processors, on the other hand, like process. They are wired for process. They live for process.

If you're interviewing employees for black belt or green belt training, ask them *Why did you choose your current job or work?* If the person gives you a list of criteria instead of a story, continue the search.

Problem-Solver Mindset

Lean Six Sigma is a problem-solving process. Do you like to solve problems? Ask yourself two questions.

1. *What's important about my job or work?* (You often get answers that correspond to one of these categories: people relating, places being, activities doing, knowledge learning, or things getting/having.)

2. Pick one of the answers (e.g., learning) and ask yourself *Why is that (e.g., learning) important?*

Again, there are two answers to this question.

1. If your answer describes what you'll accomplish or *achieve*, then you're an *Achiever*: "I want to get a Black Belt Certification to advance my career and increase my earnings."

2. If your answer describes the pain and suffering you'll *avoid*, then you're a *Problem Solver*: "I can avoid the mistakes most people make because they aren't prepared." Problem Solvers often speak in *not language*: "Using Lean Six Sigma means that our customers *won't* have to put up with all of the problems normally associated with our product launches."

Lean Six Sigma is inherently a problem-solving process; it is not a goal-achievement process. If you want to be good at Lean Six Sigma, you'll want to be a Problem Solver.

If you're interviewing employees for black belt or green belt training, ask them: *What's important about your work?* and *Why is that important?* Then listen for *not language* and the avoidance of consequences, not achievement. You want people who love to solve and avoid problems.

Leader Mindset

Implementing Lean Six Sigma requires leadership on multiple levels. Are you a leader? Ask yourself this question: *How do I know I've done a good job?*

Again, there are two answers to this question.

1. "People tell me."

2. "I just know." (Often these people will touch the middle of their chest when they say this.)

The first answer comes from a *Follower*. They can follow, but they need leadership.

The second answer comes from a *Leader*, who can take in information and decide for her- or him-self.

Lean Six Sigma Black Belts and Green Belts need to be Leaders.

If you're interviewing employees for black and green belt positions, ask them *How do you know you've done a good job?* If they only say "People tell me," keep looking. If they say "I just know," you're on the right track.

The Lean Six Sigma Mindset

There you have it. There is a mindset that is ready for Lean Six Sigma. And two out of every three people have some of it (Evolutionaries). Out of those two, you'll have to ask some questions to find the rest of the recipe for success.

The people that are wired for improvement have the motivation traits of Leaders, Problem Solvers, Processors, and Evolutionaries.

People that are wired for innovation have the motivation traits of Achievers, Innovators, and Revolutionaries.

Every business needs innovators and improvers. You just want to get them into the right jobs. Innovators help create the future. Improvers ensure that you'll maximize your profits and minimize your risks.

Still Struggling

Some people just aren't cut out to be problem solvers. Don't force them to learn how. It's a waste of time. Instead, find people who are natural problem solvers and give them the tools of Lean Six Sigma.

The Motivation Profile

If you're still uncertain about how to ask these questions and evaluate the answers, you can take our online Lean Six Sigma Profile at *www.qimacros.com/profile/six-sigma-mindset.pl* or the complete personality inventory at *www.qimacros.com/nlpstyle.html*.

Once you've got the right mindset, learning Lean Six Sigma requires the right kind of practice.

Talent versus Process

Once you've learned the methods and tools of Lean Six Sigma, you'll need to practice the skills to make them part of your mindset and toolkit. In his book, *Talent is Overrated*, Geoff Colvin argues that talent, IQ, or smarts isn't what makes people successful; it's what he calls *deliberate practice*. In *Outliers*, Malcolm Gladwell argues that it can take 10,000 hours of practice (Colvin says 10 years) to achieve mastery in your chosen field. And I'd like you to consider that companies are no different.

If you go to a golf driving range, you'll see lots of people hitting golf balls, but very few are practicing *deliberately* in ways designed to improve performance. Tiger Woods will step on a ball in a sand trap to practice getting the ball out of a plugged lie. And he'll keep doing it until he's mastered the shot. That's deliberate practice.

What Is Deliberate Practice?

Deliberate practice

- Is designed to improve performance
- Can be repeated *a lot*
- Provides continuous feedback on results
- Is highly demanding mentally
- Isn't much fun

Frankly, most people would rather come to work and mindlessly do the same old thing, and that's what a lot of people do. They do the same thing over and over again without questioning the whys and hows of doing it.

Deliberate Practice and Lean Six Sigma

Colvin says, "Opportunities to practice business skills directly are far more available than we usually realize."

Lean and Six Sigma are precise forms of deliberate practice. Colvin found that an average tennis player and a pro or a good worker and a great worker have many differences.

> *Great players understand the significance of indicators that average performers don't even notice.* Using control charts, histograms and Pareto charts, great companies can detect tiny shifts in process performance that are *invisible to the naked eye.*
>
> *They look farther ahead.* Using the voice of the customer, QFD, FMEAs, and so on, great companies look into the future of what customers really want and how to deliver those wants with a minimum number of mistakes, errors, or problems.
>
> *They make finer discriminations than average performers.* While most companies react to defect rates higher than 1% (10,000 parts per million), great companies react to defect rates greater than 3 parts per million.

Applying Deliberate Practice

When a problem occurs, good companies fix the product or service, but great companies go back and *fix the process that created the problem.*

When creating a new product or service, good companies bootstrap the product, but great companies *Design for Six Sigma.*

Good employees like to fight fires; great employees like to prevent fires.

Here's my point: Are you going to spend part of every day in deliberate practice, getting better, faster, and cheaper? Are you committed to going from good to great? Or are you comfortable being average? It's up to you.

New CEOs Can Kill Lean Six Sigma

I just got an email from a Master Black Belt who I greatly respect.

> After months of waiting on a decision from our new CEO we were informed that our last day is near, but we have opportunity to apply for other jobs internally. The new CEO is not a supporter of Lean Six Sigma. We have saved over $20M in hard dollar savings, trained hundreds who have advanced their careers and made major improvements. It is very disappointing, but after multiple CEOs in a few years it

was going to happen. The former CEOs have all been great supporters, so the new guy is going to do things differently. He uses "what works." No one knows what that is yet.

This shows one of the great fallacies of the "get top-level commitment for Lean Six Sigma." When there's a change in leadership, Lean Six Sigma can go bye-bye, even if you have real savings.

According to the executive recruiting firm Spenser Stuart, in 1980, CEOs served an average of 8 years. By 2005, that number was 7 and dropped to 5 years for the *Fortune* 500. It's closer to 3 years now.

Still Struggling

CEO support of Lean Six Sigma isn't the "silver bullet" for success. A new CEO can kill Six Sigma just as easily as support it.

Be a Money Belt

Keep a record of your projects and the savings associated with them. If you can't measure the dollar savings, you're on the chopping block. If you measure them, then you have leverage with the new leadership and a great résumé even if the new leader doesn't care.

With the economy in trouble, every business leader is going to be looking at the bottom line: what contributes and what doesn't. The quality department has always been an easy target.

It would be great if we could convert every business to a quality management system, but a new CEO isn't brought in to keep things the same; he or she is brought in to shake things up. And many times the good is thrown out with the bad.

Lean Six Sigma is one of the things that new CEOs kill in favor of innovation. When innovation fails, the next CEO will bring in some form of improvement methodology, maybe the next iteration of Lean Six Sigma.

I believe the best we can hope for is to create some Money Belts who can find and fix problems that contribute to lost profits. CEOs may come and go, but Money Belts are invaluable and can work their magic in any climate or culture.

If the corporate culture matures to the point that it embraces a quality management system or some customer demands it as a condition of doing business, fantastic. Until then, be a Money Belt! Tell everyone stories of your improvements. Make yourself invaluable to the business. Then, even if the quality department goes away, you and the improvement methods will remain.

Our Reward Systems Are Broken

One of the biggest challenges to Lean Six Sigma is existing reward systems. They are rewarding the wrong things.

A couple of months ago, I sat on a jury in a juvenile sexual assault case involving alcohol. At one level, the case was about two drunk underage teens having sex, which is not that rare of an occurrence. Our laws, however, state that it doesn't matter how intoxicated the perpetrator is when a crime is committed; she or he is still responsible. And it doesn't matter how drunk the victim was when it happened; she or he isn't responsible. On the basis of our laws, the boy was guilty of sexual assault.

The same principles don't seem to apply to business leaders. Drunk on profits created by subprime lending, banking leadership teams demolished companies, shareholders, and employees. And even a world economy. When asked about their culpability in this debacle, the best they seemed to say was "I didn't know," which isn't that different from "I was drunk."

Rewarding the Fix-It Factory

When I was in the telephone company, we had thousands of people fixing incorrect orders, bills, returned mail, and installation and repair errors. Every one of these employees got raises and bonuses based on fixing errors, not preventing them.

According to one *Business Week* article I read, 15 out of every 100 patients are misdiagnosed. Doctors still get paid for the visit. I've been in emergency rooms when patients return after being discharged because they still have undiagnosed symptoms. That's rework!

Salespeople are often rewarded for making the sale, but not for making a "good" sale, just as lenders were rewarded for making loans, but not good loans. If you sell a monthly service, but customers don't stay long enough for you to make a profit, should salespeople be rewarded? Nope. Adding and removing customers costs a lot of money. The sales call was wasted time that could have been spent on a better prospect.

Rewarding Training, Not Results

Too many Six Sigma implementations measure and reward the quality department for the number of people trained, belts certified, and teams started. Let's face it, it doesn't matter how many people you train if they don't generate bottom-line, profit-enhancing results.

Reward Systems Encourage the Status Quo

Existing reward systems encourage managers and employees to maintain and enhance the status quo. Even though Obama was elected on a platform of change, everyone wants someone else to have to change. "It's not me; it's the other guys. If only my suppliers would change; I could do a better job. If only my customers would change; I could do a better job. It's not my fault."

I'd like you to consider that existing reward systems are holding you and your company firmly in the grip of delays, defects, and deviation that cost you customers and profits. Without improvements to the rewards system, no one will be motivated to fix the process problems that plague the company. They'll just keep plodding along, fixing the products and services that are broken. They'll lament over coffee breaks about how screwed up it is.

Everyone is afraid that if they use Lean to be faster that there won't be enough work and someone will get laid off. Fix-It factories worry that if the production line stops making defects that they won't have a job.

Get over it! If a company accelerates the delivery of quality products and services, customers will flock to it. Customers don't have time to deal will slow service or crappy products.

Reward systems are one of the major barriers to implementing the kind of improvements possible with Lean Six Sigma. They are also one of the hardest nuts to crack in any business because everyone is afraid of how it will impact them. But if you want to accelerate the benefits of Lean Six Sigma, you'll have to remove this roadblock and pave the path to endless improvement. Otherwise you're doomed to slide back into sluggish, defective ways of mediocre performance. It's up to you.

Barriers to Lean Six Sigma

At the 2009 ASQ World Conference, Joe Defeo, president of the Juran Institute, gave an interactive session on the future of quality. Like everyone else,

I probably heard only what I wanted to hear, but the message was clear: The future is upon us and it will be different from the past.

While the past was predominantly about reducing manufacturing variation, the present moment shows signs that quality will be about leaner, greener, global real-time information systems. To improve quality now, there will be massive numbers of transactions— "information that has to be decoded."

Transactional Lean Six Sigma

Where transactions used to happen more slowly, they now happen in real time. What are real-time information systems? On Memorial Day, I had two people in Poland order the QI Macros software, pay with a credit card, and download the software. Electronic medical records keep track of a patient's treatment down to the last medication they received. A laptop purchased at a computer store in Denver triggers a supply chain event that initiates a new laptop's construction at a factory in China.

What does this mean? While reducing variation in manufacturing is still important, the service side of the business, especially the information systems that power these customer interactions, has become critical to quality.

Lower the Barriers to Quality

One participant in the ASQ session suggested that we need to "lower the barriers of entry to quality." Joe Defeo offered some key thoughts on how to lower the barriers.

- Low-cost quality management
- Standard work practices
- Real-time analysis
- Scorecards
- Individual process improvements

Although Lean Six Sigma has been focused on high-cost training, software, teams, and variation, the future belongs to low-cost just-in-time training, software, individuals, and information transactions.

For the last several decades, I've sought to lower the barriers to quality with low-cost software like the QI Macros and our Excel-based scorecards and dashboards. I've applied Lean Six Sigma to itself to identify the essential methods and tools of quality; this led to the Lean Six Sigma Simplified and Demystified books. I've used my software background to identify easy ways to analyze the flurry of transactions produced by most information systems (*www.qimacros. com/pdf/dirty30.pdf*). And I've championed the idea of Money Belts—employees who can find and fix the problems of unnecessary delay, defects, and deviation.

Here's My Point: To implement Lean Six Sigma, most companies spend a lot of money developing a hierarchy of Green and Black Belts. Lately I've heard customers complaining that even the best-trained Black Belts don't seem to know how to plug the leaks in cash flow caused by poor quality. I've heard top consultants say that companies would be better off with a few Green Belts who get coached through their initial projects by Money Belts.

By making Lean Six Sigma sound complex and expensive, we've discouraged too many businesses from learning the essential methods and tools of Lean Six Sigma. We've stopped them from making improvements in their mission-critical processes. With our focus on variation, we've discouraged IT departments from considering Lean Six Sigma. The hierarchy of Master Black Belts, Black Belts, and Green Belts has created a problem of the haves versus the have-nots. Isn't it time we got over our arrogance about Lean Six Sigma and start lowering the barriers to entry for everyone?

Here's an example of what I mean. We looked at one of the many books for sale at the ASQ conference. Here's what one author had to say.

> *Sadly, computers and handheld devices have made statistics too easy to do now. Problems that took hours to setup and solve just a few decades ago can now be handled in nanoseconds by people who do not have the slightest idea what they are doing because the computer requires them to do nothing more than enter some data.*
>
> *Here's the kicker: By virtually eliminating human involvement in doing statistics, computer power has done us a disservice.*
> —Jeffrey Bauer, *Statistical Analysis for Decision Makers in Healthcare*
> (CRC Press, 2009)

Frankly, this sounds like scribes with quills complaining that the printing press has done us a disservice. It's time to lower the barriers to quality. There's an old saying the science advances death by death. As the old guard dies out, it makes room for the new discoveries. Let's hope the same isn't true of quality.

Over the years, I've written many articles on this subject, backed by research into how companies adopt, adapt, or reject change. The answers are out there and they are surprisingly simple, but to apply them, we will need to challenge conventional wisdom and act in the face of ridicule.

Still Struggling

Culture change isn't like flipping a light switch. People are slow to adopt changes that they can't perceive as beneficial. Pig-headed persistence is one of the keys to implementing Lean Six Sigma.

Is There a Million Dollar Improvement Project Lurking in Your Data?

If you suspect there's a problem in your business, but aren't quite sure how to analyze your data to focus the improvement, Jay can help. Send Jay your data about the problem, and he'll analyze it for you. If he can't find an improvement story in your data, there's *no charge*. Learn more at *www.qimacros.com/six-sigma-project-excel.html*.

Management by Quality (MBQ)

I just attended the WCBF Six Sigma Summit in Chicago. The overriding theme from the conference from presentations by Forrest Breyfogle, Thomas Pyzdek, and Peter Pande was that U.S. business leaders need Management By Quality to avoid the kinds of economic disasters we've seen lately. Management schools and MBAs were all skewered on the facts of their failure.

Each speaker issued a challenge to the quality community to elevate Lean Six Sigma methods and tools to better manage U.S. business.

Social Responsibility

When asked the primary reason for the existence of business, the audience answer was to "maximize shareholder value." Unfortunately, this alone can lead to all kinds of idiotic economic behavior. This single-minded focus leaves out several major stakeholders.

- Customers
- Employees
- Society

Without satisfied customers, there can be no shareholder value. Without satisfied employees, there can be no satisfied customers. Without satisfied employees, customers, and shareholders, society suffers.

At every conference lately, I've heard the term *social responsibility* bandied about as the solution to our mess. I'd like to suggest that rather than focus on maximizing shareholder value, businesses need a new definition of success.

Optimize customer, employee, shareholder, and societal value.

This implies a balancing of competing requirements. Does Quality Function Deployment (QFD) come to mind? It should.

Changing the Course of the *Titanic*

Although saying leaders should use Management by Quality sounds good, it's about as likely as the moon reversing its orbit. Consider how much *unlearning* would be required to make room for MBQ. Consider all of the leaders and managers that have succeeded by gut feel, trial and error, and common sense. They aren't going to suddenly switch to a completely new management method without a significant reason to do so. An economic crisis isn't going to do it. We have to think of a better way.

LSS Isn't Blameless

The quality community is not without blame. As most speakers noted, Lean Six Sigma has become a project-oriented methodology with little or no focus on the long-term evolution of businesses and management. Peter Pande also pointed out that narrow focus on process can prevent a company from seeing opportunities. We have become too narrowly focused on improvement projects. We need to think bigger.

Stealth Conversion

Let's face it, most quality practitioners aren't in a position to convert leaders to Management by Quality. We aren't part of the C club. But there are a couple of stealth way's to go about it.

1. The July–August 2009 *Harvard Business Review* (pp. 90–91) had an article "Shareholders First? Not So Fast . . ." by Jeffrey Pfeffer which argues against shareholder capitalism in favor of stakeholder capitalism (stakeholders being customers, employees, suppliers' shareholders, and

the culture at large). This is the kind of article quality professionals can highlight and send to their leadership team to start shifting the business toward Management by Quality. The *Harvard Business Review* can tell leaders things that quality professionals cannot.

2. When I worked in the telephone company IT department, we had several legacy information systems that were growing too cumbersome and expensive to maintain. Several attempts were made to rewrite these monoliths at an expense of hundreds of millions of dollars. Unfortunately, systems that have been around for two decades have too much embedded wisdom; it was impossible for any team to get their mind around all of the requirements. And, the business was changing (cell phones, fiber optics, cable, etc.). In the time it would take to rewrite the system, the business would have changed too much for the new system to work. I was responsible for maintaining several smaller legacy systems. I used a different approach. Whenever I went into a program or module to make a change, I would edit or rewrite the code to optimize future maintainability. Little by little, line by line, I bought these dinosaurs more time and saved several from extinction.

I'd like to suggest that we can do the same with quality.

Shortcut to Management by Quality

Anyone who thinks he or she can institute a whole new way of running a business is probably crazy. There are too many forces holding the old one in place. Remember *reengineering?* Far too many efforts crashed and burned, almost taking companies down with them.

I'd like to suggest that every Lean Six Sigma project can achieve its project goals and add a little dose of MBQ. Maybe the control phase initiates a dashboard of management metrics to help managers keep a finger on the pulse of operations. Maybe a dash of systems thinking that links up cross-functional work. Maybe add a pull system with some one-piece flow.

Little by little, project by project, Lean Six Sigma can add MBQ to any business system and straighten out the value stream. With every project LSS can steer a business away from the icebergs in its path and stealthily convert managers and leaders to a new system of management.

Chaos theory says that a butterfly flapping its wings in Brazil can raise a tornado in Texas. I'd like to invite you to be the butterfly's wings.

Teaching Management by Quality

I had an interesting discussion with Forrest Breyfogle who has created his Integrated Enterprise Excellence system for management. Forrest is a statistician to the marrow of his bones. H would like every manager and leader to have his level of understanding of variation. Heck, I'd like to have his understanding of variation, but we disagree on how to get managers to that level of understanding. Imagine an S-curve of statistical thinking (Fig. 14-1).

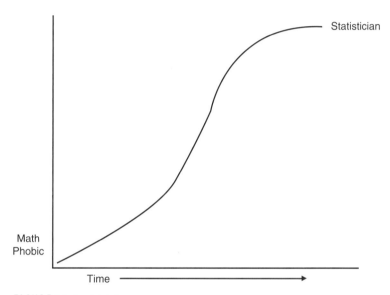

FIGURE 14-1 · Adult learning curve

Although it might be fantastic if every manager or leader (or employee for that matter) could suddenly arrive at *statistician-level understanding*, it's unrealistic to expect it. If, however, we borrow the perspective of marketers who use this curve to invite people to join at whatever level they are comfortable and then lead them up along the curve, I believe we can succeed without alienating anyone.

It's a covert, stealthy approach to shifting the business management system.

Weave the methods and tools of Lean Six Sigma into the fabric of business operations with every project you do. Little by little, employees, managers and leaders will learn the methods and tools of Management by Quality. Little, by little, the business will shift to a more robust way of measuring and delivering quality on time and under budget, which will delight customers which will delight shareholders which will deliver value to society.

I wish we could just flip a switch to change cultures and management systems, but it's just not that likely to succeed. Instead, we should be like the waves that come back again and again, wearing down the rocks that stand in our way.

Why Do Six Sigma Teams Fail?

I worry when I hear about companies shutting down their Six Sigma effort. What's the problem? Six Sigma should be helping, not hurting.

When I first got into quality improvement, we had the best training and started lots of teams, but most of the teams failed to deliver. So, I started applying Lean Six Sigma to itself. I may be the only trainer/consultant to do so.

Root Cause Analysis

I took a step back and started asking Why? Why? Why? Why? Why? Here's what I found.

- *Teams are formed before the data are analyzed.* Why is this a problem? Unfortunately, when you bring a group of people together, but don't have a clear focus driven by data, you end up with what I call "the 100 yard dash for the directionally impaired."
  Solution: Analyze the data first to narrow your focus using line graphs and Pareto diagrams; *then pick a team that has expertise in that area to do the root cause analysis.*

- *Teams choose their own problem to work on.* Why is this a problem? Unfortunately, most of the time, teams want to fix their suppliers or their customers. Union employees want to fix management; management employees want to fix workers.
  Or they choose something trivial to get experience. Remember the dark side of the 80-20 rule: 80% of the effort only produces 20% of the benefit. This is why Six Sigma fails.
  Solution: Let the data lead you to a problem that you can work and that you own. You can't fix someone else's problem. You can give them the data and the analysis, but you cannot solve it for them. They won't implement your solution.

- *DMAIC.* Why is the Six Sigma improvement process a problem? Unfortunately, DMAIC begins with Define and Measure, so most teams get lost in defining the process and implementing new measures.

Solution: Skip Define and Measure; go straight to Analyze, Improve and Control. You already have enough data. Somebody somewhere is keeping a count of the number and type of mistakes, errors, defects, repair, rework, or waste. *Find some data you can analyze to narrow your focus. Then improve and control.*

- *Chartered teams meet one hour a week forever. Why is this a problem?* Because there's 167 hours of delay between meetings. It violates the lean principles of eliminating delay and one-piece flow.
  Solution: SWAT Teams. When the data has been analyzed and the problem solving effort laser-focused, a team of subject matter experts (SMEs) only needs to meet for 2-to-4 hours to identify the root causes, countermeasures and implementation plan.

- *Scope creep.* Teams invariably want to solve world hunger, boil the ocean, and fix everything all at once. When teams scatter their focus, they solve nothing.
  Solution: Use Pareto diagrams to narrow the focus. Then analyze one big bar of the Pareto chart at a time.

- *Whalebone Diagramming.* If a team starts covering the conference room walls with fishbone after fishbone diagram, *the focus is more like a flashlight than a laser.*
  Solution: Go back to the data and narrow the focus.

- *"Just-in-case" training.* Many teams and team leaders (e.g., Green or Black Belts) get lots of training long *before* they apply it. Why is this a problem? Because humans lose 90% of what they learn in 72 hours if they don't apply it immediately.
  Solution: Just-in-time training. Give the SWAT team an hour of training and then throw them right into root cause analysis. They'll learn more working on a real problem than they'll ever learn in training.

If Lean Six Sigma isn't producing immediate, measurable, ongoing benefits, management will kill it. Teams can't afford to waste time. Mistakes in team formation, team meetings, and data analysis can doom a team's chances of success. And team failures can kill Six Sigma.

Bridezilla Meets Lean Six Sigma

Our daughter, Kelly, got married in September. Our oldest grandson, Jake, had his coming of age party in July. One of the themes I've discovered in these ceremonies is the tendency to think that the lavishness of the event determines its quality.

My wife and I, on the other hand, got married in our backyard. It's lasted 21 years and seems to be getting better every year.

What has this got to do with Lean Six Sigma? Everything.

Far too many people judge Lean Six Sigma success by how much money is thrown at it. When Six Sigma becomes an event rather than a process, it is doomed.

Ask yourself

- How long does Lean Six Sigma stick in an organization (3 years is the average tenure of a CEO)?
- What are the costs of Lean Six Sigma?
- What are the bottom-line benefits of Lean Six Sigma?
- Is Lean Six Sigma an event like a wedding or a process like a marriage?

Here's my point: Is your Lean Six Sigma process like a celebrity wedding or a lifelong commitment to excellence? Are you a Black Belt, Green Belt, or Money Belt? Is Lean Six Sigma paying for itself or just a ceremony everyone attends before they return to their real life?

Start using these insights gleaned from two decades of process improvement to make sure. Lean Six Sigma delivers on its promises or start looking for a new job. Once you learn the Lean Six Sigma mindset, methods, and tools, you can use them anywhere. Start now to make your company wildly successful and you will be too.

QUIZ

1. To increase chances of success when implementing Lean Six Sigma,
   A. use a crawl-walk-run approach.
   B. set BHAGs.
   C. use SWAT teams.
   D. all of the above

2. Describe your experiences with IWWFM.

3. What is the Lean Six Sigma mindset?

4. Define deliberate practice and how it affects Lean Six Sigma implementations.

5. How can you use decisive force when implementing Lean Six Sigma.

Final Exam

1. **Lean is a way to**
   A. reduce cycle or turnaround time.
   B. reduce errors.
   C. increase response to customers.
   D. all of the above

2. **Lean Six Sigma requires the use of**
   A. a wide variety of statistical charts and tools.
   B. a handful of methods and tools.
   C. common sense.
   D. all of the above

3. **Lean Six Sigma will help you work faster**
   A. but require more focus.
   B. without working harder.
   C. by cutting corners.
   D. all of the above

4. **Every company has two factories:**
   A. a front room and a back room factory.
   B. a good and a fix-it factory.
   C. design and manufacturing.

431

5. Think about your company. Is its focus
   A. innovation?
   B. customer service?
   C. operational efficiency?

6. To stand out from the crowd in your market every company must
   A. maximize all of these focuses.
   B. optimize all of these focuses.
   C. maximize one of these focuses.
   D. optimize one of these focuses.

7. To support this focus, every company must
   A. maximize the other focuses.
   B. optimize the other focuses.
   C. maximize one of the other focuses.
   D. optimize one of the other focuses.

8. Lean Six Sigma is the key method and tool for achieving
   A. innovation.
   B. customer service.
   C. operational efficiency.

9. Every company has operational demons. They include
   A. delay.
   B. defects.
   C. deviation.
   D. all of the above

10. Lean Six Sigma can be used in
   A. manufacturing.
   B. health care.
   C. service industries.
   D. information technologies.
   E. all of the above

11. **Most large U.S. businesses are currently engaged in**

    A. manufacturing.

    B. services.

12. **Lean Six Sigma works best in**

    A. small companies.

    B. medium-sized companies.

    C. large companies.

    D. all of the above

13. **Lean Six Sigma**

    A. takes a long time to learn.

    B. has a "long tail" of tools used infrequently.

    C. requires an intricate knowledge of statistics.

    D. all of the above

14. **Companies embrace Lean Six Sigma because it helps**

    A. save money.

    B. save time.

    C. boost profits.

    D. all of the above

15. **The cost of not using Lean Six Sigma is what percent of total expenses?**

    A. 5%–10%

    B. 10%–20%

    C. 25%–40%

16. **Lean Six Sigma helps plug the leaks in cash flow caused by**

    A. sales.

    B. customers.

    C. internal processes.

    D. all of the above

17. Most businesses fail to optimize their performance because they try to

    A. make their employees work faster.

    B. buy faster machines.

    C. make inventory in case its needed.

    D. all of the above

18. Even when companies try to improve, they often fail because they are too focused on

    A. the core business or factory floor.

    B. employee training.

    C. operations.

    D. all of the above

19. The secret to Lean Six Sigma is

    A. working on your business.

    B. working in your business.

    C. watching your people.

    D. watching your process.

    E. watching your product.

    F. B and C

    G. A, D, and E

    H. all of the above

20. The Lean Six Sigma improvement method is

    A. DMAIC.

    B. FISH.

    C. PDCA.

    D. all of the above

21. Arthur's extension of the Pareto's 80-20 rule is

    A. the 4-64 rule.

    B. the 4-50 rule.

    C. the 20-80 rule.

22. **The most overlooked and underused step in the DMAIC process is**
    A. define.
    B. measure.
    C. analyze.
    D. improve.
    E. control.

23. **The Power Laws of Speed state that**
    A. haste makes waste.
    B. speed makes profit.
    C. the slow eat the fast.
    D. all of the above

24. **The problem with mass production is that it**
    A. generates an abundance of waste.
    B. causes overproduction.
    C. increases inventory.
    D. all of the above

25. **Inventory is usually**
    A. raw materials.
    B. work in process.
    C. finished goods.
    D. all of the above

26. **One of the keys to Lean is to**
    A. jump the gap.
    B. mind the gap.
    C. shop at the Gap.
    D. all of the above

27. **To analyze a process for delays and waiting, use**
    A. a spaghetti diagram.
    B. a value stream map.
    C. a flowchart.
    D. all of the above

28. **To analyze a process for unnecessary movement, use**

    A. spaghetti diagram.

    B. value stream map.

    C. flowchart.

    D. all of the above

29. **You already understand Lean concepts because you**

    A. have picked a route for weekend shopping.

    B. live in a house with a kitchen.

    C. have eaten at fast food restaurants.

    D. all of the above

30. **Arthur's extension of Stauk and Hout's Lean rule is the**

    A. 3-57 rule.

    B. 15-2-20 rule.

    C. 3×2 rule.

    D. A and B

31. **Lean production was developed by**

    A. Henry Ford.

    B. Toyota.

    C. GM.

    D. all of the above

32. **The Lean mindset is**

    A. if you build it, they will come.

    B. when they come, build it fast.

33. **The most common type of Lean waste is**

    A. overproduction.

    B. excess inventory.

    C. waiting.

    D. unnecessary movement.

    E. unnecessary or incorrect processing.

    F. rework.

34. **The method to use in redesigning for lean production is**

    A. 5S.

    B. value stream mapping.

    C. spaghetti diagramming.

    D. all of the above

35. **The 5S process is**

    A. sort.

    B. straighten.

    C. shine.

    D. standardize.

    E. sustain.

    F. all of the above

36. **The Toyota Production System (TPS) is**

    A. a push system.

    B. a pull system.

    C. a play system.

    D. all of the above

37. **To measure flow, use**

    A. lead or cycle time.

    B. value-added ratio.

    C. travel distance.

    D. productivity.

    E. quality rate or first-pass yield.

    F. all of the above

38. **Work cell design is usually**

    A. square.

    B. V-shape.

    C. U-shape.

    D. all of the above

39. **Value stream mapping and spaghetti diagramming need the advanced technology of**

   A. control charts.

   B. fishbone diagrams.

   C. Post-it notes.

   D. all of the above

40. **Autonomation**

   A. mechanizes production.

   B. stops production when an error is detected.

   C. frees workers.

   D. all of the above

41. **The religion of reuse can help save**

   A. 40% of lead time.

   B. 60% of lead time.

   C. 80% of lead time.

42. **Health care has problems with**

   A. patient flow.

   B. clinical errors.

   C. operational errors.

   D. all of the above

43. **One hospital was able to reduce ED turnaround times from a national average of 4 hours to**

   A. 3 hours.

   B. 2 hours.

   C. 38 minutes for a discharged patient.

44. **Using spaghetti diagramming, one hospital lab was able to reduce staff movement by**

   A. 17%.

   B. 27%.

   C. 54%.

   D. all of the above

45. The key Lean in health care insight is

    A. the patient is idle most of the time.

    B. walking is waste.

    C. speed is critical to patient satisfaction.

    D. all of the above

46. Most of the data needed for Six Sigma can be found in

    A. financial systems.

    B. production systems.

    C. Microsoft Excel.

    D. all of the above

47. In Excel, data are most easily analyzed when organized in

    A. tables.

    B. columns.

    C. rows.

48. Data not readily available in Excel can be collected manually with

    A. a gage.

    B. a checksheet.

    C. a checklist.

    D. all of the above

49. Mistake-proof data collection with

    A. better training.

    B. Excel's data validation.

    C. better gages.

    D. all of the above

50. To succeed at Six Sigma, you need

    A. top-management commitment.

    B. Six Sigma software like the QI Macros.

    C. lots of Black Belts.

    D. all of the above

51. **The QI Macros have**

   A. charts.

   B. Fill-in-the-Blank templates.

   C. statistics.

   D. data transformation tools.

   E. all of the above

52. **When creating an improvement story, prepare the entire presentation in**

   A. Excel workbook.

   B. PowerPoint.

   C. Word.

   D. all of the above

53. **Most improvement stories can be told with**

   A. control charts.

   B. Pareto charts or histograms.

   C. fishbone diagrams.

   D. all of the above

54. **One of the biggest problems with most charts is**

   A. not enough data.

   B. too much data.

   C. chartjunk.

   D. all of the above

55. **Once you've created a control chart with the QI Macros, you can**

   A. add data.

   B. ghost a point.

   C. delete a point.

   D. add text to a point.

   E. reanalyze stability with control chart rules.

   F. all of the above

56. Use Six Sigma to reduce
    A. defects.
    B. deviation.
    C. dissatisfaction.
    D. all of the above

57. One of the most common causes of false fire alarms is
    A. teenage pranksters.
    B. cell phones.
    C. bad wiring.
    D. all of the above

58. The universal problem-solving process is
    A. FISH.
    B. DMAIC.
    C. PDCA.
    D. all of the above

59. Root cause analysis consists of asking what five times?
    A. Who
    B. Where
    C. Why
    D. all of the above

60. Key tools for defect reduction are
    A. control charts.
    B. Pareto charts.
    C. fishbone diagrams.
    D. all of the above

61. CTQs are
    A. certifications.
    B. measurements.
    C. business leaders.
    D. all of the above

62. Use Pareto charts to
   A. sustain the improvement.
   B. honor your progress.
   C. focus the improvement.
   D. all of the above

63. One key tool for summarizing data is
   A. scatter charts.
   B. control charts.
   C. pivot tables.
   D. all of the above

64. The step most commonly overlooked by improvement teams is
   A. focus.
   B. improve.
   C. sustain (i.e., control).
   D. honor.

65. The biggest mistake teams make is a failure to
   A. focus the improvement.
   B. analyze the data.
   C. solve the whole problem.

66. Teams can tell they've failed to focus when they develop
   A. Pareto charts.
   B. fishbone diagrams.
   C. whalebone diagrams.
   D. all of the above

67. Companies can measure Six Sigma success using
   A. number of belts trained.
   B. number of teams started.
   C. bottom-line results.
   D. all of the above

68. A core score measures the most important

    A. defects.

    B. cycle times.

    C. deviations.

    D. all of the above

69. To establish a baseline for improvement, use a

    A. Pareto chart.

    B. control chart.

    C. fishbone diagram.

    D. all of the above

70. To narrow the focus for defect improvement, use

    A. a control chart.

    B. a Pareto chart.

    C. a fishbone diagram.

    D. all of the above

71. To narrow the focus for deviation improvement, use

    A. a control chart.

    B. a histogram.

    C. a fishbone diagram.

    D. all of the above

72. To build better, more reliable information technology systems,

    A. simplify and streamline the existing process first.

    B. use an iterative method to develop the system.

    C. expect each new release to be error prone.

    D. simplify and streamline the software as it ages.

    E. all of the above

73. To improve IT systems, use

    A. Lean.

    B. Six Sigma.

    C. the Dirty 30.

    D. all of the above

74. **Computer systems suffer from**

   A. hardware errors.

   B. programming bugs.

   C. data errors.

   D. all of the above

75. **To find and fix computer system problems,**

   A. get 30 examples of the worst errors.

   B. analyze the root cause of each example.

   C. develop a checksheet of root causes until the Pareto pattern pops out.

   D. all of the above

76. **Deviation is**

   A. variation from a target value.

   B. spread.

   C. shape.

   D. all of the above

77. **The goal of deviation reduction is to**

   A. get measurements to fit between the goal posts (LSL/USL).

   B. reduce the spread.

   C. center the results on the target value.

   D. all of the above

78. **The causes of defects and deviation are**

   A. special causes.

   B. common causes.

   C. A and B

79. **The most common tool to show deviation is**

   A. a control chart.

   B. a Pareto chart.

   C. a histogram.

   D. all of the above

80. The measurements of process capability are
   A. Cp and Cpk.
   B. Pp and Ppk.
   C. Cr and ΔZ.
   D. all of the above

81. In manufacturing the minimum desired level for Cp and Cpk is
   A. 1.0.
   B. 1.33.
   C. 1.66.
   D. 2.0.

82. The key tool for sustaining an improvement (i.e., Control phase of DMAIC) is
   A. a control chart.
   B. a histogram.
   C. a flowchart.
   D. all of the above

83. The most common control chart(s) used in service industries is (are)
   A. XmR.
   B. XbarR.
   C. p chart.
   D. all of the above

84. The most common control chart(s) used in manufacturing is (are)
   A. XmR.
   B. XbarR.
   C. p chart.
   D. all of the above

85. The QI Macros will identify potential out-of-control conditions on a control chart in
   A. red.
   B. yellow.
   C. green.

86. If you have an individual column of decimal (i.e., variable) data, use a
    A. XmR.
    B. XbarR.
    C. p chart.
    D. u chart.

87. If you have two or more columns of decimal (i.e., variable) data, use a
    A. XmR.
    B. XbarR.
    C. p chart.
    D. u chart.

88. If you have an individual column of integer (i.e., attribute) data, use a
    A. c chart.
    B. np chart.
    C. p chart.
    D. u chart.

89. If you have two columns of numerator and denominator data, use a
    A. c chart.
    B. np chart.
    C. p chart or u chart.

90. If you have rare-events data, use a
    A. g or t chart.
    B. XmR or XbarR chart.
    C. p chart or u chart.

91. If you only produce a few of one product and then a few of another, use a
    A. short-run chart.
    B. EWMA chart.
    C. ANOM chart.

92. **To detect small process shifts more quickly, use**
    A. CUSUM chart.
    B. EWMA chart.
    C. moving-average chart.
    D. all of the above

93. **If you have two measurements simultaneously, use a**
    A. CUSUM chart.
    B. EWMA chart.
    C. hotelling chart.

94. **There is more than one kind of control chart because of**
    A. the arying distributions analyzed.
    B. the varying sample sizes.
    C. the number of variables being analyzed.
    D. all of the above

95. **To focus innovations and Design for Six Sigma is to use**
    A. voice of the business.
    B. voice of the customer.
    C. voice of the employee.
    D. all of the above

96. **To link customer requirements to performance, use**
    A. a balanced scorecard.
    B. a CTQ.
    C. a SIPOC diagram.
    D. all of the above

97. **To make Lean Six Sigma take root in an organization, engage**
    A. the CEO.
    B. the employees.
    C. the informal leaders.
    D. all of the above

98. To maximize the effectiveness of Lean Six Sigma,

    A. train everyone.

    B. start lots of teams.

    C. use data to laser-focus the improvement efforts.

    D. all of the above

99. Improvement teams should meet

    A. whenever possible.

    B. once a week for an hour.

    C. once to determine root causes and implementation planning.

    D. all of the above

100. The essential methods and tools of Lean Six Sigma can be learned in a

    A. day.

    B. week.

    C. month.

    D. all of the above

101. The best Lean Six Sigma training is

    A. classroom training.

    B. just-in-time problem solving using the Lean Six Sigma methods and tools.

    C. online training.

    D. all of the above

102. If participants don't apply what they've learned in 72 hours, they lose ___ percent of the knowledge.

    A. 25%

    B. 50%

    C. 90%

    D. all of the above

103. Getting top leadership to commit to widespread implementation is

    A. the secret to success.

    B. a sure way to invoke the dark side of the 80-20 rule.

    C. a way to maximize results.

    D. all of the above

104. A successful Six Sigma project needs

    A. a project worth doing.

    B. an operational problem over which you have control.

    C. available data.

    D. a leadership sponsor who wants to solve the problem.

    E. all of the above

105. Lean Six Sigma can

    A. cut costs.

    B. boost profits.

    C. kill a company.

    D. all of the above

106. The easiest way to get employees to agree to any change is to

    A. mandate it from the top.

    B. get them involved in the analysis and solution.

    C. hire new employees.

    D. all of the above

107. Measurement systems analysis helps make sure

    A. parts and products are good.

    B. processes are good.

    C. measurement systems are good.

    D. all of the above

108. The most common Gage R&R mistake is using

    A. too many parts.

    B. identical parts.

    C. too few parts.

    D. all of the above

109. A measurement system can be acceptable if

    A. %R&R < 30%.

    B. %R&R < 20%.

    C. %R&R < 10%.

    D. A and C

110. **Measurement system variation consists of**

　　A. appraiser variation.

　　B. equipment variation.

　　C. part variation.

　　D. all of the above

111. **Gage R&R studies help determine**

　　A. repeatability.

　　B. reproducibility.

　　C. bias.

　　D. linearity.

　　E. all of the above

112. **The main tool of Design for Lean Six Sigma (DFLSS) is**

　　A. QFD.

　　B. FMEA.

　　C. DOE.

　　D. all of the above

113. **DFLSS can help create production systems that deliver**

　　A. four sigma.

　　B. five sigma.

　　C. Six Sigma.

　　D. all of the above

114. **Hypothesis testing can help determine if two or more samples have the**

　　A. same or different means.

　　B. same or different variations.

　　C. A and B

115. **The most common way of determine whether to reject or accept a hypothesis is using**

　　A. classical method.

　　B. p value method.

　　C. SWAG method.

　　D. all of the above

116. Accept the null hypothesis if
   A. $p < \alpha$.
   B. $p > \alpha$.
   C. $p = \alpha$.

117. Reject the null hypothesis if
   A. $p < \alpha$.
   B. $p > \alpha$.
   C. $p = \alpha$.

118. The main hypothesis test for variation of normal data is
   A. F-test.
   B. Levene's test.
   C. t-test
   D. all of the above

119. The main hypothesis test(s) for means is (are)
   A. ANOVA.
   B. F-test.
   C. t-test.
   D. A and C
   E. all of the above

120. The main hypothesis test(s) for nonnormal data is (are)
   A. ANOVA.
   B. F-test.
   C. Levene's test.
   D. t-test.
   E. Tukey's Quick Test.
   F. A and D
   G. C and E

121. In regression analysis, a good fit exists when
    A. $R^2 > 0.25$.
    B. $R^2 > 0.50$.
    C. $R^2 > 0.80$.
    D. all of the above

122. The main barrier to Lean Six Sigma is
    A. WIIFM.
    B. IWWFM.
    C. WYSIWYG.
    D. all of the above

123. One of the keys to Lean Six Sigma success is
    A. decisive force.
    B. overwhelming force.
    C. Delta force.
    D. all of the above

124. To succeed at Lean Six Sigma, you will need to work at it
    A. 40+ hours per week.
    B. 20 hours per week.
    C. 2–4 hours per week.
    D. all of the above

125. To focus the improvement efforts, use the
    A. 3-57 rule.
    B. 4-50 rule.
    C. A and B

126. The right people to involve in Lean Six Sigma have _____ mindset.
    A. an improvement
    B. a process-oriented
    C. a Problem Solver
    D. a Leader
    E. all of the above

127. The vital few methods and tools presented in this book will solve _____ of operational problems.

   A. 30%

   B. 60%

   C. 90%

   D. all of the above

128. All it takes to initiate a Lean project is

   A. Post-it notes.

   B. employees who do the process.

   C. 2–4 hours to analyze and redesign the process.

   D. all of the above

129. All it takes to initiate a root cause analysis team is

   A. data about the problem.

   B. a control chart of the problem data.

   C. Pareto charts of the problem data.

   D. all of the above

130. Lean Six Sigma can take any company from three to five sigma in

   A. 2 years.

   B. 5 years.

   C. 10 years.

Answers to Quizzes and Final Exam

Chapter 1
  1. G
  2. Good and fix-it
  3. H
  4. A
  5. E
  6. B
  7. C
  8. D
  9. D

Chapter 2
  1. Just in time and autonomation
  2. E
  3. A
  4. Overproduction, excess inventory, waiting, unnecessary movement of work products, unnecessary movement of employees, unnecessary or incorrect processing, defects (rework)
  5. Sort, Straighten, Shine, Standardize, Sustain
  6. F
  7. B
  8. A
  9. B

10. C
11. D

Chapter 3
1. D
2. D
3. B
4. C

Chapter 4
1. E
2. A
3. B
4. B
5. B
6. F
7. D
8. C
9. D
10. E

Chapter 5
1. Design, Measure, Analyze, Improve, Control; Focus, Improve, Sustain, Honor; Plan, Do, Check, Act
2. B
3. 3, 5, 2, 8, 6, 7, 1, 4
4. D
5. G
6. C
7. Piles of numbers; inaccurate, late, or unreliable data; trying to meet a target; one size fits all; Gage blindness; micrometer versus yardstick; punishing people
8. 3, 1, 4, 2

Chapter 6
1. F
2. F
3. B
4. D
5. D

6. E
7. Search, information, bargaining, decision, policing, enforcement
8. Software and data
9. E

Chapter 7
1. C and D
2. D
3. G
4. B
5. B
6. D
7. A and B
8. A snapshot of variation.
9. To determine capability of a process.
10. Analysis of how well the process meets customer requirements.
11. Special and common

Chapter 8
1. Control chart shows no out of control points.
2. Cp and Cpk are at least 1.0.
3. To monitor and improve performance.
4. Time series displays of variation.
5. To monitor and improve performance.
6. E
7. E
8. D
9. D
10. E
11. F
12. D
13. B
14. XmR, p, u charts

Chapter 9
1. A
2. D
3. C
4. D

5. E
6. F
7. Big Hairy Audacious Goal
8. Critical to Quality indicators

Chapter 10
1. C
2. Connectors, mavens, and salespeople
3. B and D
4. B
5. D
6. E
7. B
8. B, C, and D

Chapter 11
1. People measure things differently.
2. D
3. F
4. C
5. B
6. Using identical parts.
7. A and B

Chapter 12
1. DFLSS is a way to design a production system to deliver four sigma or higher.
2. E
3. D
4. D

Chapter 13
1. C
2. C
3. H
4. Compared means or variations are the same.
5. A
6. B

Chapter 14

1. D
2. (personal experience)
3. Processor, problem solver, improver, leader
4. Consistent application of the methods and tools over time.
5. Laser-focus the improvement projects on mission-critical performance problems.

Final Exam

1. D	33. A	66. C	99. C
2. B	34. D	67. C	100. A
3. C	35. F	68. D	101. B
4. B	36. B	69. B	102. C
5. A, B, or C	37. F	70. B	103. B
6. C	38. C	71. B	104. E
7. B	39. C	72. E	105. D
8. C	40. D	73. D	106. B
9. D	41. C	74. D	107. C
10. C	42. D	75. D	108. B
11. B	43. C	76. D	109. D
12. D	44. C	77. C	110. D
13. B	45. A	78. C	111. E
14. D	46. D	79. C	112. D
15. C	47. B	80. D	113. A
16. C	48. B	81. B	114. C
17. D	49. B	82. A	115. B
18. A	50. B	83. A	116. B
19. G	51. E	84. B	117. A
20. A	52. A	85. A	118. A
21. B	53. D	86. A	119. D
22. E	54. C	87. B	120. G
23. B	55. F	88. C	121. C
24. D	56. D	89. C	122. B
25. D	57. B	90. A	123. A
26. B	58. A	91. A	124. C
27. B	59. C	92. D	125. C
28. A	60. D	93. C	126. E
29. D	61. B	94. D	127. C
30. D	62. C	95. B	128. D
31. B	63. C	96. A	129. D
32. B	64. C	97. C	130. A
	65. A	98. C	

Glossary

andon Stop the line system.

autonomation Automation with a human touch.

heijunka Leveling the workload.

hoshin kanri Quality planning.

jidoka Built-in quality.

just-in-time (JIT) Make and deliver the right part, in the right amount, at the right time.

kaizen Continuous improvement.

kanban Card system for visually monitoring flow. Used in a pull system of manufacturing precisely driven by demand, as opposed to the traditional push manufacturing philosophy, in which inventories can pile up. A kanban is a bin or container that can hold only the amount needed by the customer.

muda Waste

nemawashi Decide slowly, implement rapidly.

poka-yoke Mistake-proofing—to avoid inadvertent errors.

takt time Time required to complete one job at the pace of customer demand.

Bibliography

Adrian, Nicole, "A Gold Medal Solution," *Quality Progress*, March 2008, pp. 45–50.

Artis, Spencer E., "Six Sigma Kick-Starts Starwood," *BusinessWeek Online*, 8/31/2007.

Bala, S., "Lean Triage for Hospital ERs," *Quality Digest*, March 2009, pp. 22–24.

Berry, Leonard Eugene, *Management Accounting DeMYSTiFieD*, McGraw-Hill, New York, 2006.

Bohmer, Richard M. J., "Fixing Health Care on the Front Lines," *HBR*, April 2010, pp. 63–69.

Bossidy, Larry, and Ram Charan, *Execution: The Discipline of Getting Things Done*, Crown Business, New York, 2002.

Buckingham, Marcus, *The One Thing You Need to Know*, Free Press, New York, 2005.

Chaudhry, Imran, "Surgical Infection Prevention," *iSixSigma Magazine*, September/October 2008, pp. 49–54.

Christensen, Clayton, *The Innovator's Dilemma*, Harvard Business School Press, Boston, 2000.

Cyr, Jay, et al., "Sustaining and Spreading Reduced Door-to-Balloon Times for ST-Segment Elevation Myocardial Infarction Patients," *Joint Commission Journal on Quality and Patient Safety*, June 2009, pp. 297–306.

Downes, Larry, and Chunka Mui, *Unleashing the Killer App*, Harvard Business School Publishing Corp., Boston, 1998.

Dusharme, Dirk, "Six Sigma Survey," *Quality Digest*, February 2003 and September 2004.

Farzad, Roben, "The Toyota Enigma," *BusinessWeek*, July 10, 2006, p. 30.

Gladwell, Malcolm, *The Tipping Point*, Little Brown, New York, 2002.

Godin, Seth, *Unleashing the Ideavirus*, Hyperion, New York, 2001.

Hall, Kenji, "No One Does Lean Like the Japanese," *BusinessWeek*, July 10, 2006, pp. 40–41.

"Health Care Needs a New Kind of Hero," *HBR*, April 2010, pp. 60–61.

Heath, Dan and Chip Heath, *Made to Stick*, Random House, New York, 2007.

Jones, Dell, "Hospital CEOs Find Ways to Save," *USA Today*, 9/10/2009.

Kaplan, Robert S., and David P. Norton, *The Balanced Scorecard*, Harvard Business School Publishing Corp., Boston, 1996.

Kaplan, Robert S., and David P. Norton, *The Strategy-Focused Organization*, Harvard Business School Publishing Corp., Boston, 2001.

Kauffman, Stuart, *At Home in the Universe*, Oxford University Press, New York, 1995.

Kay, Tan, "Room for Improvement," *Six Sigma Forum Magazine*, November 2009.

Kim, Christopher S., et al., "Implementation of Lean Thinking: One Health System's Journey," *Joint Commission Journal on Quality and Patient Safety*, August 2009, pp. 405–413.

Kohn, Linda T., Janet M. Corrigan, and Molla S. Donaldson, eds., *To Err Is Human*, National Academy Press, Washington, D.C., 2000.

Krasner, Jeffrey, "New Medicine for What Ails Hospitals," *Boston Globe*, January 28, 2008.

Lashinsky, Adam, "The Genius Behind Steve," *Fortune*, November 10, 2008, http://money.cnn.com/2008/11/09/technology/cook_apple.fortune/index.htm.

Lee, Thomas H., "Turning Doctors into Leaders," *Harvard Business Review*, April 2010, pp. 51–58.

Liker, Jeffrey, *The Toyota Way*, McGraw-Hill, New York, 2004.

Measurement Systems Analysis–MSA, 3d ed., AIAG, Detroit, 2005.

Meyer, Christopher, *Relentless Growth—How Silicon Valley Innovation Strategies Can Work in Your Business*, Free Press, New York, 1998.

Moore, Geoffrey, *Crossing the Chasm*, Harper Business, New York, 1999.

Ohno, Taiichi, *Toyota Production System*, Productivity Press, New York, 1988.

Reibling, Nancy B., et al., "CT Scan Throughput," *iSixSigma Magazine*, January/February 2010, pp. 49–54.

Rogers, Everett, *Diffusion of Innovations*, 4th ed., Free Press, New York, 1995.

Schmidt, Elaine, "Crystal Clear," *iSixSigma Magazine*, March/April 2008.

Schmidt, Elaine, "From the Bottom Up," *iSixSigma Magazine*, September/October 2008, pp. 24–32.

Schmidt, Elaine, "RX for Success," *iSixSigma Magazine*, May/June 2008.

Stalk, George, and Thomas M. Hout, *Competing Against Time*, Free Press, New York, 1990.

Statistical Process Control—SPC, 2d ed., AIAG, Detroit, 2005.

Tufte, Edward, *Envisioning Information*, Graphic Press, Cheshire, Conn., 1990.

Tufte, Edward, *Visual Explanations*, Graphic Press, Cheshire, Conn., 1997.

Tukey, J. W., and A. Quick, "Compact, Two-Sample Test to Duckworth's Specifications," *Technometrics*, vol. 1, no. 1, February 1959.

Webber, Rebecca, "Stop Texting Behind the Wheel," *Parade*, June 6, 2010.

Wennecke, Gette, "Kaizen—Lean in a Week," www.mlo-online.com, August 2008.

Widner, Tracy, and Mitch Gallant, "A Launch to Quality," *Quality Progress*, February 2008, pp. 38–43.

Winston, Stephanie, *The Organized Executive*, Warner Books, New York, 2001.

Womack, James P., and Daniel T. Jones, *Lean Thinking*, Simon & Schuster, New York, 1996.

Index

Page numbers followed by *f* denote figures.

A

accidents, 201
agile programming, 72–74
  requirements, 74
  seven speed bumps of Lean and, 73
Analysis of Variance (ANOVA), 124, 133–135, 356, 366
  single-factor, 384–385
  two-factor, 385–389
Anderson-Darling, 389–391
andon, 459
ANOM chart, 262
ANOVA. *See* Analysis of Variance
application systems, error detection with, 213
assets, 324–327

B

balanced scorecard, 25, 129, 193, 278, 289–290
  short-term objectives and, 290
  targets and, 290
batch-and-queue push system, 42
bell-shaped curve, 236, 299
  distribution, 236, 236*f*
benefits
  calculating, 7
  one-piece flow, 51
BHAG. *See* Big Hairy Audacious Goal
bias, MSA, 344–345
Big Hairy Audacious Goal (BHAG), 67
  focusing process and, 279
  setting, 300
Buckingham, Marcus, 195

C

call centers
  customer perception of hold time and, 76
  delays, 74–76
  Lean, 74–76

capability
  access, 192
  Cp and, 239
  Cpk and, 239
  Cr and, 239–243
  histograms and, 238
  Pp and, 239
  Ppk and, 239
  process, 238–243
  stability and, 254–255
capability index (Cp), 238–239. *See also* centering
  capability index (Cpk)
Capability Maturity Model (CMM), 217
cash flow
  external customer, 12–13
  in healthcare, 66–69
  plug leaks in, 16–17
  transaction, financial, 215
cells
  design, 52–54
  Lean layout of, 53, 53*f*
  U-shaped, 53
centering capability index (Cpk), 239
centers of influence, 302
chartjunk, 137–146
  on graphs, 141–146
  gridlines on worksheets as, 141–142, 141*f*
  removing background area and, 142–145, 142*f*
  space shuttle Challenger example of, 138–139, 138*f*
charts. *See also* control charts; flowcharts; Pareto charts
  bar, 126, 141
  chartjunk and bar, 141–143, 142*f*
  pie, 126
  QI Macros creation of, 126–127
  run, 126
  template-created, running stability analysis on, 127–128
CheapTickets, software bugs case study, 216
check sheets, 172–173, 172*f*
chi-square test, 393–395
Christensen, Clayton, 326
  The Innovator's Dilemma, 326–327

467

innovation (*Cont.*):
  process, laser-focused, 277–292
  rate, measure, 330
  rules, 327
  Silicon Valley key measures of, 200–201
  TRIZ and principles of, 366–367
  types of 328
Innovator's Dilemma (Christensen), 326, 328–330
inventory, agile programming and excess, 73
Ishikawa diagram. *See* fishbone diagram

J

jidoka, 459
JIT training. *See* just-in-time
just-in-time (JIT), 41, 459
  training, 296, 304

K

kaizen, 66, 79, 459
kanban, 41, 84, 459
  inventory, 41
Keen, Peter, 323–327

L

large businesses, Lean Six Sigma for, 12
LCL, 233, 268, 269, 321, 346
lead time (Little's law), 77
Lean
  administration, 38
  agile programming, 72–74
  call centers, 74–75
  cell design and, 52–54, 53*f*
  color mistake proofing and, 65–66
  core ideas of, 43–44
  decision making and, 69–72
  Dell and, 74–75
  Demystified, 26–30, 33–85
  do more with less and, 79–80
  doctor's office, 81–83
  downsizing and, 67, 79
  emergency room, 90, 94
  employees and, 21–22, 46, 76
  fast food experience and, 38
  FISH and, 43
  hospital delayed discharge and, 91–92, 101
  hospital housekeeping and, 101
  hospital staffing and, 93
  hospital transfer time and, 93
  hospitals, 89–107
  implementing, 314, 405–429
  kitchen design and, 37–38, 37*f*
  machine size and, 45, 52, 65
  mindset, 44–45
  organization, 84
  piloting, 67
  power of, 33
  process, 43
  reuse and, 76–79
  seven speed bumps of, 46–47
  seven speed bumps of, software and, 73

Lean (*Cont.*):
  Six Sigma and, 68–69
  software, 72–74
  tools, 55–60
  Toyota's use of, 39–68
  TPS and, 39–41
  TRAF and, 38
  transaction processing and, 215
  understanding, 37–38
  value stream and, 37, 48–49
Lean production, mass production versus, 45–46
Lean Six Sigma, 68–69
  adoption, 314–316, 316*f*
  ANOVA for, 338, 344, 364, 364*f*, 365*f*
  application, 312
  application, examples, 72
  barrier to, biggest, 83–85, 419–422
  benefits of, 428
  boosting profits with, 409
  case study, reducing computer downtime, 178–183
  CEO commitment and success of, 297
  challenges, 344
  classroom training and, 303
  corporate trainers, 305–306
  customer satisfaction and, 299
  defects and, 231–234, 241
  delays and, 258
  Demystified, 28–30
    design for, 355–367
  diffusion and, 314–316
  dream teams and, 302
  elevator speech, 312
  employee adoption of, 314, 316*f*, 318
  Excel power tools for, 109–146
  experiential, 303
  failures, 320
  FISH process, 23
  *Freakonomics: A Rogue Economist Explores the Hidden Side
    of Everything* and mindset of, 188–190
  honor progress and, 27, 332–333
  hypothesis testing, 372–383
  implementation, 295–334
  implementation, risk free way to, 314
  improvement focus and tools of, 278
  JIT training and success of, 296, 304
  large businesses and, 12
  learning designers, 304
  manufacturing and, 9
  mindset, 44–45, 85, 325, 411–414
  narrow focus and accelerate, 299
  operational efficiency, 8, 311
  payoffs, 316
  power tools for, 109
  prerequisites, 318–319
  problem solving process, 157
  process, 15, 277
  productivity and, 300
  profitability, 300
  QI Macros and, 320
  regression analysis, 398, 399*f*
  risk-free, 314–315
  root cause and, 426
  service components and, 10
  services and, 5, 9